P9-EEH-454

CRAFTING EQUALITY

For Jim —
For Rhetoric, Humanity'

John

NEW PRACTICES OF INQUIRY

A Series Edited by Donald N. McCloskey and John S. Nelson

Crafting
EQUALITY
America's
Anglo-African
Word

Celeste Michelle Condit
and
John Louis Lucaites

THE UNIVERSITY OF CHICAGO PRESS
Chicago & London

CELESTE M. CONDIT is associate professor of speech communication at the University of Georgia. JOHN L. LUCAITES is assistant professor of speech communication at Indiana University.

The University of Chicago Press, Chicago 60637
The University of Chicago Press, Ltd., London
© 1993 by The University of Chicago
All rights reserved. Published 1993
Printed in the United States of America
02 01 00 99 98 97 96 95 94 93   1 2 3 4 5 6

ISBN (cloth): 0-226-11464-3
ISBN (paper): 0-226-11465-1

Library of Congress Cataloging-in-Publication Data

Condit, Celeste Michelle, 1956–
    Crafting equality : America's Anglo-African word /
    Celeste Michelle Condit and John Louis Lucaites.
        p.   cm.—(New practices of inquiry)
    Includes bibliographical references and index.
    1. Afro-Americans—Civil rights.   2. Equality—
United States—History.   3. Equality before the law—
United States—History.   4. Rhetoric—Political
aspects—United States—History.   5. Rhetoric—Social
aspects—United States—History.   6. United States—
Constitutional history.   I. Lucaites, John
Louis.   II. Title.   III. Series.
    E185.C68   1993
    323.1′196073—dc20   92-30215
                                                                        CIP

⊗The paper used in this publication meets the minimum requirements of the American National Standard for Information Sciences—Permanence of Paper for Printed Library Materials, ANSI Z39.48-1984.

for
Michael Calvin McGee

CONTENTS

Preface: Toward Consideration of the
Rhetorical Culture of Equality   ix
Acknowledgments   xix

I   Introduction: The Story of Equality   1

PART ONE
The Rhetorical Foundations of American Equality

2   The British Rhetoric of Revolt,
    1760–1774   19
3   The Anglo-American Revolutionary
    Rhetoric, 1774–1789   40
4   The African-American Rhetoric of Equal
    Rights, 1774–1860   69

PART TWO
Rhetorical Integrations

5   Separate But Equal, 1865–1896   101
6   Integrated Equality, 1896–1960   147
7   The New Equalities, 1960–1990   188

vii

Afterword   217
Research and Bibliography Essay   233
Appendix: Reference List of Newspapers
and Magazines   249
Notes   251
Index   345

PREFACE

Toward Consideration of the Rhetorical Culture of Equality

This book is a study of the meaning of the word "equality" in American public discourse. Equality is no simple word to understand. It is at once a normative abstraction that resonates with the highest ideals of America's collective being, and a rather narrow and pedestrian, empirical characterization of the sameness or identity of any two objects. As critics and historians our interest is with the tension between these two broad possibilities of meaning and the ways Anglo- and African-Americans have negotiated and managed them over the past 225 years in the public and pragmatic context of crafting a national political identity. The focus we take in this volume is thus *rhetorical*.

Rhetoric is undergoing a major revival in the closing years of the twentieth century. Treated since the seventeenth century as the "harlot of the arts," it has in recent years become the darling of the human sciences.[1] Whereas in the past scholars frequently treated rhetoric and public discourse as simple or "mere" epiphenomena, the contemporary rhetorical turn coincides with the revision of critical theory and a postmodernist shift away from realist epistemologies, including a fairly thorough rejection of rigid objectivism, foundationalism, and essentialism in understanding the human social condition.[2] The result has been a more or less sustained focus on discourse, textuality, and signification as the "material" core of social and political relationships. Some of those writing in this vein have carried the critique of modernity to potentially absurdist ends, devolving dangerously close to nihilistic forms of relativism in the process.[3] Others, however, have come to view discursive interaction as the pragmatic, mediating factor between objectivism and relativism in the world of everyday affairs.

Among this latter group is a wide range of philosophers and sociopolitical theorists who acknowledge one or another form of rhetoric and communication as the dynamic and indeterminate source of social and political community.[4]

Unfortunately, this renewed focus on discourse has not always accompanied a careful consideration of the broad and encompassing role that rhetoric plays in affecting social and political change. In some instances, the treatment of public discourse has been far too situational and instrumental to offer any sense of the impact of rhetoric on the grand sweep of history. In other instances, rhetoric has been cast in the role of "handmaiden," completely subordinated to the inexorable power and presence of a dominant and controlling ideology. The result has been a failure (or refusal) to acknowledge rhetoric as a discursive, ideological practice that is and can be actively affected by both individuals and groups. In either case, the typical contemporary account of the role of public discourse in social and political change has ignored the extent to which the very phenomenon of "change" itself is the function of an active sociorhetorical process.[5]

This problem stems in large measure from the now ancient and long standing debate between rhetoric and philosophy. At issue in this contest of some 2,500 years has been the locus of public, civic morality. Rhetoricians have typically located the roots of moral truth and conduct in opinion (*doxa*), while philosophers have trained their attention on knowledge (*epistēmē*).[6] The real problem, however, derives *not* from what rhetoricians and philosophers have tended to dispute, that is, does rhetoric "create" beliefs or "give effectiveness" to the truth, but from their apparent agreement that rhetoric is an art without substance, a *techne* or "method" of production divorced from any outcome other than the instrumental relationship between intent and effect. *What this consensus ignores, of course, is the sense in which rhetorical interaction is the very foundation of the life of any social or political collectivity.*[7] As an alternative that acknowledges the role of rhetoric as the vital substance of the sociopolitical process, we offer a return to the practical integration of rhetoric and philosophy in the classical writings of Isocrates.

Isocrates was Plato's contemporary and a student of the philosopher Socrates. Both Isocrates and Plato were influenced by Socrates' criticism of the "excesses of Athenian democracy" and the "sham pretences" of sophistic thinkers whose mastery of eristic led them to valorize rhetoric as *techne* to the virtual exclusion of philosophy in the determination of public morality.[8] In each case, however, the effect of that influence bore very different results. For Plato, it led to the attempt to nullify the influences of sophistry on Athenian life by developing an authoritarian social theory that reversed the hierarchy between rhetoric and philosophy, placed severe censures on the practices of rhetoric and poetry, and led to an elitist Republic controlled by Philosopher-Kings. For Isocrates, it led to the attempt to recombine rhetoric and philosophy as the basis for a culturally specific, public discourse that exploited the radical potential of Athenian democracy both to critique itself and adapt to social and political exigencies in an orderly and liberating manner.[10]

Isocrates' perspective was predicated on two important assumptions. The first was that human collectivities are constituted by the *logos*—speech and reason. As he noted in his oration *Nicocles or the Cyprians,* it is the rhetorical impulse motivated by the centrality of the *logos* in collective interaction that distinguishes the moral structure and capacity of human society:

. . . in the other powers which we possess we are in no respect superior to other living creatures; nay, we are inferior to many in swiftness and in strength and in other resources; but, because there has been implanted in us the power to persuade each other and to make clear to each other whatever we desire, not only have we escaped the life of wild beasts, but we have come together and founded cities and made laws and invented arts; and, generally speaking, there is no institution devised by man which the power of speech has not helped us to establish. For this it is which has laid down laws concerning things just and unjust, and things base and honourable; and if it were not for these ordinances we should not be able to live with one another. It is by this also that we confute the bad and extol the good. Through this we educate the ignorant and appraise the wise; for the power to speak well is taken as the surest index of a sound understanding, and discourse which is true and lawful and just is the outward image of a good and faithful soul. With this faculty we both contend against others on matters which are open to dispute and seek light for ourselves on things which are unknown; for the same arguments which we use in persuading others when we speak in public, we employ also when we deliberate in our own thoughts; and, while we call eloquent those who are able to speak before a crowd, we regard as sage those who most skilfully debate their problems in their own minds. And, if there is a need to speak in brief summary of this power, we shall find that none of the things which are done with intelligence take place without the help of speech, but that in all our actions as well as in all our thoughts speech is our guide, and is most employed by those who have the most wisdom.[11]

Isocrates' second assumption was that rhetoric or public discourse functions as a pragmatic, political aesthetic, the artistic object of which is the lived, political world produced by and for a particular human collectivity.[12] Those who participate in this aesthetic are *not* judged on the basis of decontextualized, individual artistic techniques but on the value of the political world that they create.[13] More important, the source of those judgments in a democratic polity is a function of the lived, rhetorical relationship between leaders and people, both as experienced in the context of present circumstances and as located by analogy in the historical or cultural memory of the community.[14] For Isocrates, then, to avoid a public morality guided by either rank sophistry or rigid authoritarianism, it was necessary to integrate rhetoric and philosophy in a critical, social, and political praxis—public argumentation—that drew upon the common rhetorical culture of the social and political collectivity.

There are two key phrases in the previous sentence that require careful consideration: "public argumentation" and "rhetorical culture." By public argumentation we mean the domain of rhetorical interaction through which a community actively negotiates its common needs and interests. Rooted in the classical traditions of forensic and deliberative oratory, the discourse of the law courts and the legislature, public argumentation functions as a contest of competing voices concerned to determine the best course of action in contingent situations.[15] What counts as the "best course of action," of course, is not determined by a rigid set of rules of logic; neither is it simply "discovered" in the sense that one might discover a buried treasure. Rather, it is the result of a consensus represented by the assent that an audience, cast in the role of "public," grants to a rhetor, cast in the role of "leader."[16] To be effective in determining policies that represent the potentially competing needs and interests of diverse individuals and groups, successful leaders must find ways to craft the audiences' understanding of the public good. To that end, they must creatively—in Isocratean terms, artistically—adapt the shared rhetorical culture to the exigencies of the moment. By rhetorical culture we mean to draw attention to the range of linguistic usages available to those who would address a historically particular audience as a public, that is, a group of potentially disparate individuals and subgroups who share a common interest in their collective life. In this rhetorical culture we find the full complement of commonly used allusions, aphorisms, characterizations, ideographs, images, metaphors, myths, narratives, and *topoi* or common argumentative forms that demarcate the symbolic boundaries within which public advocates find themselves constrained to operate.

Although a strong case could be made that all of the components in a rhetorical culture are equally significant in defining and addressing an audience as a public, it is our contention that the central, organizing elements for any rhetorical culture are its "ideographs."[17] An ideograph is a culturally biased, abstract word or phrase, drawn from ordinary language, which serves as a constitutional value for a historically situated collectivity. Ideographs represent in condensed form the normative, collective commitments of the members of a public, and they typically appear in public argumentation as the necessary motivations or justifications for action performed in the name of the public. A survey of American public discourse in the twentieth century would unveil a wide range of substantive or first order ideographs, including "liberty," "property," "privacy," "national security," "freedom of speech," "rule of law," "law and order," "public trust," and so on. Taken in their entirety, the ideographs for a particular rhetorical culture identify the range of acceptable public beliefs and behaviors within any publicly constituted community. To participate in a rhetorical culture one thus must pay allegiance to its ideographs, employing them in ways that audiences can judge to be reasonable. This does not mean, however, that rhetors need *necessarily* pay allegiance to any *particular* usage or interpretation of an ideograph in a particular context.

A key feature of ideographs is their flexibility as cultural signifiers. An ideographic phrase such as "freedom of speech" can take on a wide range of meanings within the practices of a rhetorical culture, depending upon the particular context in which it is employed and the specific phenomenon it is used to praise or blame. Because ideographs are abstractions, and thus lack any rigidly defined meaning, creative rhetors craft their meaning-in-use as they employ them in public discourse to persuade audiences of the public nature of historically specific beliefs and actions. Each such successful usage adds as by precedent to the range of meanings available to a particular ideograph. This is not to say that the meaning of an ideograph is totally arbitrary or absolutely polysemous. There are discernible limits to how an ideograph can be employed in public argumentation, but they are specifically rhetorical limits, that is, a function of the history of it usages in a particular historical community as defined by its diachronic and synchronic structures.[18]

The diachronic structure of an ideograph represents the full range and history of its usages for a particular rhetorical culture. As an American ideograph, the diachronic structure of "freedom of speech" spans the distance from its original and minimalist articulation by the framers of the U.S. Constitution as protection for "political speech," to its most recent usages as the defense for a much more widely defined "freedom of expression" that includes nude photography and dancing. The synchronic structure of an ideograph represents its usage as defined by its relationship in public discourse to other ideographs relevant to the historically specific situation they are collectively employed to modify or mediate. The synchronic structure of "freedom of speech" thus depends on the particular circumstances of its usage. When defined in relationship to "the right to a jury trial" and "national security" in the context of establishing the Alien and Sedition Acts, freedom of speech takes on a very different meaning than when defined in relationship to "liberty" and "privacy" in the context of prohibiting federally funded health clinics from dispensing information about abortions to pregnant women.

Rhetors who employ ideographs in public discourse seek to achieve the assent of a particular audience and thus are constrained to use such terms in ways that are more or less consistent with the rhetorical culture. They must, therefore, be sensitive to the moral tensions between the term's history of usages for the political community being addressed and the range of plausible interpretations of its usage in relationship to other culturally and situationally relevant ideographs. By charting the diachronic and synchronic structures of an ideograph as it is employed in the public discourse of a particular rhetorical culture, we can begin to gain insight into how social and political problems are constituted and negotiated through public discourse. From this perspective the rhetorical process simultaneously reinforces stability while effecting desirable accommodations to competing interests and changing needs.[19]

Other components of a rhetorical culture are undoubtedly important to this endeavor—narratives and metaphors come to mind as being particularly significant—but it is the ideograph that seems to be the most resistant to change. Whereas other components of the public vocabulary tend to disappear from view once their meaning calcifies, ideographs rarely disappear, even though their particular meanings and usages change.[20] Accordingly, ideographs provide an element of the public vocabulary that is central to the definition of the life of a community, and which maintains a discursive constant that allows us to observe the social and political movement of the community across time.

By thinking of the constitution of a public as ideographically constructed, we offer a model of the relationship between rhetoric and ideology that is substantially different from the one commonly employed by those who think in terms of a "dominant ideology." According to the dominant ideology thesis, social and political change is "dictated" from above by a powerful elite—typically and variously reified as capital, the patriarchy, or some presumably purified national or racial difference—who imposes a rigidly defined set of beliefs upon the members of an underclass "duped" into doing its bidding. From this view, rhetoric is simply the handmaiden of ideology, the mechanism of "mental production" whereby the particular interests of the ruling group are seductively imposed upon an otherwise oblivious group of subordinates.[21]

From our perspective, there is no dominant ideology that inexorably governs social and political action. Instead, there is the rhetorical process of public argumentation in which various organized and articulate interest groups negotiate the problems of resource distribution in the collective life of the community, and there is a shared rhetorical culture out of which they all draw as they strive to express their particular interests.[22] The end result of this rhetorical process is generally some form of "the law" that ultimately governs relationships in the community, but that law is not a dominant ideology so much as it is a temporary compromise between competing ideological interests. This is not to say that all of the partici- pants in the public debate influence the law equally, for there is no doubt that some groups have more immediate and complete access to the media of communication and the halls of governance. It is to say, however, that even those who seem to control the law must account for and negotiate with those groups who can make a claim to legitimate ideological interest. Hence, case law might privilege one interpretation of the relationship be- tween various ideographs for a time, but laws are always open to rein- terpretation and change when advocates craft new ideologies or invent new and compelling usages of the components of the rhetorical culture.

In our vocabulary, then, the word "equality" operates in the rhetorical culture of American political discourse as an ideograph. Indeed, it well may be the most important American ideograph; or at least so it would seem from the ways in which some contemporary public advocates tend to employ it as the unique foundation of America's national political identity. From this perspective the Declaration of Independence enshrined "equal- ity" as the nation's credo, and the Emancipation Proclamation consecrated it. Although we too are proud of America's commitment to an egalitarian political society, we find such recent usages of equality troublesome on both methodological and substantive grounds.

Methodologically, the reasoning that identifies current social and polit- ical usages of "equality" with the usages employed by the nation's founders is specious. It presumes that the commitment to equality inscribed by Thomas Jefferson in the Declaration of Independence signified in 1776 in essentially the same way as it signifies today in reference to "equal" jobs, housing, education, worth, and so on. As we will demonstrate, this is simply not the case. The initial commitment to the self-evident truth of equality recognized prior to and during the American revolutionary period referred to an abstract and minimalist state of nature, not a concrete condition of life-in-society, and certainly not our present situations.

This methodological trouble is not unique to the academy; but it is a symptom of how scholars in a variety of fields such as jurisprudence, his- tory, political science, philosophy, and so forth tend to conceive equality in their writings. Generally, those who don't simply treat it as a philosoph- ical ideal acknowledge that its character has changed during the course of American history, but then they focus on its presumed stability as a concept. As a result, they ignore the word's important, if often local and subtle, changes in meaning within public usage. The main reason for this, we believe, is a propensity to treat the development of equality as the result of exceptional political tracts and philosophical treatises. Scholars often ignore, or take for granted, how the usages in tracts and treatises figure within the public discourse of the people who actually carry out the political business of the country: the lawmakers, lobbyists, pamphleteers, public media, and the like. Even when scholars address the pragmatic role of public discourse, they usually treat it as an effect of political philosophy rather than as a distinct contributor or innovative participant in the political dialogue.[23]

This leads to a second and more substantive trouble. To assume an incontrovertible link between original and current usages of equality implies a realist faith that equality as a founding principle or concept has some essential meaning. Though not immediately present to us, the original meaning nonetheless has a moral priority for us. Thus the absence of equality in any current institution or practice becomes a simple failure to live up to the essential meaning inherent in the original idea itself. Such an ideal can be comforting, particularly to people who believe that they live in a condition of equality. People who cannot identify themselves as "equal," however, encounter in that kind of ideal a serious rhetorical obstacle, for it can suggest that achieving equality is merely a matter of cleansing away more-or-less cosmetic conditions to arrive at our essential foundations of equality.

The history of Equality in American public discourse from Jefferson to Malcolm X denies that achieving equality is so simple a task. Worse, such simplistic characterizations point to a deeper trouble with the implication that equality has a determinate, foundational meaning: belief in such a foundational meaning has the potential to erode progressive political action. It intimates that foundational acts in 1776 largely completed the political structure of America, absolving subsequent political generations of responsibility for the nation's moral code. Social and political progress thus becomes an inevitable outgrowth of human evolution, not a contingent achievement of human intelligence, creativity, and action. And consequently our only civic obligation is to insure the proper execution of the fundamental principles undergirding "the law."

To combat these troubles requires that we review our understanding of the meaning of equality as a fundamental principle of American political life. Instead of regarding it as a determinate foundation of life-in-society, we need to appreciate its indeterminate origins in social and political action. And to do that, we need to recognize how the political meanings of equality flow directly from its public rhetorical usages.

[Valuable as it is to acknowledge the family resemblances between the public usages of equality in 1776 and those today, it is just as important to acknowledge the differences.] To fathom their rhetorical and political implications, we must examine how the meaning of equality evolved in the interceding years, taking careful account of all the bloodlines crucial for its existence. We choose the family metaphor advisedly: the character and quality of a family's bloodline change gradually across generations, as a function of their full range of genetic associations; and so, too, does the character and meaning of constitutive political values change across time as a function of the full range of their usages and associations in a rhetorical culture.

Ours is not, therefore, an argument against recognizing any values as "foundations" of American politics. Instead, it is an argument for regarding the word equality as a specifically *rhetorical* and *political* foundation of American life.[24] The rhetorical foundation of equality in America grows from ordinary public conversations far more than extraordinary political tracts and philosophical treatises.[25] And it grows with those conversations, changing meanings with changing times. To understand the meaning of equality as a foundation of American political life thus requires careful attention to its continuing, dynamic genealogy within American public discourse from its inception in the 1760s to the present.

What we offer, then, is a *rhetorical history* of the American ideograph Equality. There was once a time, not so very long ago, when historians commonly wrote totalizing accounts of life in a particular age or epoch and were thus responsible for treating the full range of relevant political, economic, social, and cultural concerns. In the present era, however, the increasing growth of specialized methodologies and disciplines has made us painfully aware of the complexities of human social and political organization, and thus the sheer enormity—if not imprudence—of writing such histories. Just as others might write legal, political, and economic histories of equality, focusing on very specific dimensions of its role in American life, so this is a rhetorical or discursive history. Our concern is to describe and explain the usages of the root word "equality" in the ways in which Americans have talked themselves into a national identity. Some will undoubtedly read our efforts in the following pages as an attempt to suggest that rhetoric is the only or primary *causative* agency in the historical process of social and political change. While we certainly operate from a tradition that maintains that the rhetorical practices of a sociopolitical community provide an interpretive framework in which economic, social, and political concerns come to have meaning, we do not mean to suggest that rhetoric or public discourse, in and by itself, is an isolatable or determinative cause of historical change. Nevertheless, we do believe that it is an element of the historical process that has received far too little attention.

Because we are writing a rhetorical history of the word "equality," we are guided throughout by how it appears in a wide range of public discourse across the breadth of America's history, including speeches, pamphlets, public letters, newspapers, and magazines. We thus do not seek to construct a history of individuals or events, except insofar as they are immediately necessary to a specific understanding of particular usages of equality. And while the book follows a rough chronological development from the period just before the American Revolution to the present, we do not presume to offer a survey of American history.[26] Rather, we are guided by two conceptual questions that serve as an organizational frame for the story we tell: How did the word equality achieve status as a rhetorical foundation of the American national identity? And, once it was established as a formal constitutional value, how was it integrated within the public vocabulary of American rhetorical culture? In Chapter 1 we offer a brief plot outline for that story. Chapters 2, 3, and 4 account for the rhetorical foundations of equality as the relationship between three interacting voices that dominated American public discourse from roughly 1760 to 1860. We describe those voices as characteristically British, Anglo-American, and African-American. Chapters 5, 6, and 7 cover the period from 1865 to the present, accounting for the ways in which the Anglo-American and African-American voices struggled to craft a conception of "American Equality" out of their various interests and experiences, and thus to integrate the word "equality" with the public vocabulary of the prevailing American rhetorical culture. In the Afterword we consider some of the more pressing and complex problems and implications of crafting a pluralistic, egalitarian society in the context of an American rhetorical culture of equality.

ACKNOWLEDGMENTS

The names listed on the title page of this book are in alphabetical order. Each of us contributed equally to the genesis and development of the project from beginning to end. As with most scholarly works, a large cast of players have provided input, feedback, and support at various times and places. To all those who recognize a little bit of themselves in the following pages, we express our deepest gratitude.

The book actually began in 1983 as a rather different project. Both of us were attending a regional research seminar on "Rhetoric and Ideology" sponsored by the University of Alabama–Birmingham and the Speech Communication Association. At this conference, we began to discuss the rhetorical strategies employed by black activists in the 1960s. Condit was interested in Malcolm X and Lucaites was interested in Martin Luther King, Jr. As our discussion progressed, it became increasingly clear that one could neither fully nor adequately explain either advocate in the absence of the other, and so we agreed to collaborate on an essay that would contrast the rhetoric of King and Malcolm X with regard to the word "equality." That essay blossomed into a book proposal. As we tried to write that book, however, we ran into a series of problems. In order to account for how these two advocates employed the word "equality" in the 1960s, we discovered the need for a clearer fix on the rhetorical efforts of black advocates as far back as the early nationalist period. Moreover, we quickly recognized that a comprehensive understanding of how black American discourse on Equality functioned required an equally comprehensive understanding of how white American discourse functioned on the same subject. Our attempt to explain the relationship between Martin Luther King, Jr., and Malcolm X thus drove us deeper, decade by

xix

decade, into the recesses of the history of American public address. Eventually, our frustration and excitement led us to scratch the original project and to start "from the beginning." The book before you was finally sketched out on a snowy January evening in 1986 in Champaign, Illinois.

Along the way we have received financial support from various organizations. Condit received fellowships from both the Institute for Behavioral Research (1990–91) and from the Humanities Center (1991–92) at the University of Georgia, along with research assistance from the University of Iowa. Lucaites received an Indiana University Summer Fellowship (1988), an Indiana University Research Council Grant-in-Aid (1992), and a travel grant from the American Council of Learned Societies (1989). Four excellent public universities have assisted us, not solely by providing direct financial support but also through their outstanding research collections. We give our thanks for these collections and for the helpful research librarians at the University of Iowa, University of Illinois, University of Georgia, and Indiana University. The Lilly Library at Indiana University and the Amistead Research Center at Tulane University also provided valuable assistance at several key stages in our research.

In addition to institutional support, several graduate students have served admirably as research assistants at various stages of the project. Charles Taylor, Robert Frank, Todd Boyd, and Melanie Metcalf all helped in verifying our various discourse samples. John Delicath, Marouf Hasian, John Melvin, and Randy Saisslin all served valiantly at various times in checking footnotes. Earl Croasmun and Julie Thompson performed the final and most extensive check on footnotes, and we are grateful for their painstaking efforts. An early version of the book was taught as S406 Studies in Public Address in the Fall 1989 semester at Indiana University, and the graduate students in that class offered valuable commentary on the development of the argument.

Colleagues in our own field as well as in a variety of other disciplines have also supported our efforts. We wish to thank Fran Teague for her help in using the software program WordCruncher. Sydney James, Charles Nero, and Trevor Parry-Giles all provided valuable assistance in compiling bibliographical materials. Cal Logue and Jean DeHart gave us access to their forthcoming anthology of speeches by Andrew Young. A number of individuals read and commented on various portions of the manuscript in its various stages and guises. We acknowledge in particular the helpful reactions of James R. Andrews, Carolyn Calloway-Thomas, E. Culpepper Clark, Thurman Garner, Robert Hariman, David Henry, J. Michael Hogan, Stephen Karatheodoris, Stephen E. Lucas, Martin J. Medhurst, Michael Osborn, Roxanne Parrott, Martha Solomon, Herbert W. Simons,

David Smith, and Jeffrey D. Wallin. We wish to extend special thanks for the outstanding reviews provided by Raymie E. McKerrow and Robert L. Scott. John Nelson, who enthusiastically supported the project from the very beginning, also provided an extremely valuable reading of the manuscript at several different stages in its development.

We have received excellent help in the form of queries, comments, and suggestions from numerous individuals at the various campuses and academic conferences at which portions of this work have been presented. We thank in particular the conference supporters and the participants at the following: the University of Georgia Culture Studies Workshop; the University of Alabama, Department of Speech Communication Colloquium; the University of Alabama, Language and Social Theory Group; the University of Utah, Department of Communication Seminar; the University of Minnesota, Department of Speech Communication Seminar; the Drake University Humanities Center; the University of Texas, Department of Speech Communication Seminar; "The Power of the Spoken Word: The National Conference on the Oratory of Martin Luther King, Jr.," 1986, sponsored by the Speech Communication Association and the Martin Luther King, Jr. Center for Non-Violent Social Change; the 1989 Biennial Conference of the International Argumentation Association, Amsterdam, The Netherlands; the 1990 Symposium on Rhetorics as Politics: Discourses Civic and Academic, sponsored by the Benjamin F. Shambaugh fund, the National Endowment for the Humanities, and the University of Iowa Project on the Rhetoric of Inquiry; the Speech Communication Association National Conference, 1986, 1988, and 1989; and the Southern States Speech Communication Conference, 1990.

John Tryneski, our editor at the University of Chicago Press, offered invaluable advice at almost every stage in the production of this book, and we gratefully acknowledge his input and support.

We would also like to acknowledge the Central States Communication Association for its permission to reprint a portion of Chapter 3 that originally appeared in our article "The Rhetoric of Equality and the Expatriation of African-Americans, 1776–1826," *Communication Studies* 42 (1991): 1–21.

Finally, each year we find ourselves deeper in debt to our spouses, Loren Bruce Railsback and Virginia Lucaites. They have not only been patient and supportive, but for the past seven years they have been willing to organize our joint vacations around the demands of the book and to tolerate the ways in which the topic of Equality managed somehow to monopolize every conversation. To them goes not only our gratitude but our love.

CHAPTER ONE

Introduction:
The Story of Equality

It might be supposed that the final and necessary result of democratic institutions would be to jumble all the citizens together in private as well as in public life and compel them all to lead a common existence. That would be giving a very coarse and tyrannical interpretation to the nature of the equality produced by democracy.

Alexis de Tocqueville
Democracy in America, 1835

For it is only by reconciling contradictions that power can be retained indefinitely.

George Orwell
1984, 1948

Human beings understand their lives together in large measure through the stories they tell about their past. In the twentieth century, one of the most important stories Americans have told about themselves as a nation has been the tale of equality. The telling of this story usually begins with Thomas Jefferson's declaration that "all men are created equal." It moves next to the Civil War, which it portrays as the inevitable decision by a basically moral, white America to live up to the principle of equality inscribed in the nation's creed, and thus to abolish the "peculiar institution" of slavery. As the plot unfolds in the twentieth century, we find additional rights extended to a variety of minority groups including women and blacks. America's distinction is thus its egalitarian commitment to treat all of its people in the same fashion, "regardless of religion, race, sex, or previous condition of servitude."[1]

While this tale has motivated a great deal of noble action, there are also serious problems with it as a version of events. We wish, in these pages, to tell a different story about AMERICAN EQUALITY.[2] The story we tell is familiar to experts in a variety of historical subfields, and it rests in part on their labors. Our version of the story, however, is a broad and encompassing epic drama, not a comedy of manners tailored to the demands and interests of a narrow, specialized historical epoch. Moreover, we approach the story from a fresh set of documentary resources. Instead of charting

1

American case law, deconstructing political philosophy, surveying political events, or tallying economic records, we focus our attention on the
prevailing usages of the word "equality" in public debates concerning
racial relations. More particularly, we are concerned to explain who employed the word "equality" and its various cognates and the precise ways
in which they did so. Accordingly, we base our account of the history of
American Equality on carefully constructed, representative samples of
public discourse, including speeches, congressional debates and testimony, court decisions, pamphlets and public letters, and newspapers and
magazines.[3] Our interest in examining these documents is neither to identify the etymological origins of particular egalitarian terms nor to trace the
development of minor ideologies and political philosophies backward in
time through the margins of the public realm. Rather, our attention is focused on discovering and describing the main currents of public talk about
Equality in the national political arena.

The story of Equality that we weave is different from the conventional
version in two important ways. First, in our story, the public usage of the
word "equality" is not constant over time. Americans did not simply endorse Equality as a cultural ideal and then gradually learn to live up to its
high moral content. Instead, in the founding period they adopted a very
few, very narrow set of usages of the word, which they employed with
relative infrequence. As the decades passed, the range of usages, their
scope of application, and the frequency with which they were deployed
expanded.

Second, the key characters in our story are not only the great white
American leaders such as Thomas Jefferson, William Lloyd Garrison, and
Abraham Lincoln. In researching the story that unfolds in these pages, we
discovered that among those who have used the term "equality" most fre-
quently and innovatively in our nation's history have been the leaders of
America's black community, people like Absalom Jones, Maria Stewart,
Charles Remond, Frederick Douglass, Mary Church Terrell, Booker
T. Washington, W. E. B. Du Bois, A. Philip Randolph, Martin Luther
King, Jr., Malcolm X, and Barbara Jordan.[4] They, and a whole host of
lesser-known black speakers and writers, play a prominent role in our
story as it develops.

In presenting this story we give the lie to two generally conceded assumptions. First, we deny the claim that America's public values are
"white" and that black Americans have played no role in the intellectual
work of constructing our national heritage. Second, we hope to discredit
the assumption that key value terms possess a fixed meaning, the applications of which are beyond human control. The public usage of Equality,

like the usage of our nation's other key value terms, has always been the continuing responsibility of the nation's citizenry. Consequently, historical exegesis and logical deduction are not by themselves enough to tell us what equality *should* mean for America's future. The only way that we can construct productive and moral usages of our national values is through active public debate among all the interested parties; and that, we conclude, will always be the function of a yet-to-be-told chapter in our nation's story.

The epic narrative through which we convey these morals has two acts, each of which contains three scenes. The tale is extremely complex, containing many twists and turns, and so before we begin the telling proper, we provide here a brief plot summary to guide the reader. The claims we make below are necessarily sketchy, but their purpose is only to provide a broad structure in which to organize the more specific and detailed analysis and evidence that unfolds in Chapters 2 through 7.

ACT I: THE RHETORICAL FOUNDATIONS OF EQUALITY

The first act in our epic explores the rhetorical foundations of American Equality. Unlike philosophical or architectural foundations, rhetorical foundations are not fixed and unchanging structures, nor do they provide definitive and authoritative models for all future behavior. A rhetorical foundation constitutes a starting point for communal life, not an ending point. Nonetheless, it would be a serious mistake to assume that such starting points are totally arbitrary or free-floating. The rhetorical foundations of a public value are constituted of a precise set of relationships among a set of key terms situated in particular historical contexts. Extensive work must be done by a community's leadership, including oppositional leaders, to justify any alteration of this set of relationships. Hence, rhetorical foundations provide substantive constraints on precipitous social change. At the same time, the particularized character of their formation presumes that the public vocabulary must receive at least partial revision when new conditions arise. Such substantive but pliable rhetorical foundations for Equality can be found in three different sources: the British public vocabulary, the unique exigencies of the American Revolution, and the birth of an African-American community in the nineteenth century.

Scene 1: The Revolt from Britain, 1760–1774

As the British colonists became increasingly dissatisfied with the rule of Parliament, they employed the public vocabulary they had inherited from the mother country to characterize their discontent. As "subjects of the

British Constitution" they proclaimed their rights as "freemen" and, more important, their right to Property. They also announced their intention to maintain Liberty. Here, however, they began subtly to revise the British vocabulary. The British used the word "liberty" to refer to a specific, balanced framework of government. The colonists, dissatisfied with what British constitutional government delivered to them, began to treat Liberty as a set of personal rights. They then claimed to hold such liberties equally with their fellow British citizens, adamantly refusing to be cast as "slaves."

Contrary to their modern resonances, none of these statements were understood to be broadly egalitarian. Although radicals in Boston and a few other places would employ fairly extensive usages of Equality that extended these rights to "all men," most colonial leaders were more cautious in how they used these terms.[5] In a manner fully consistent with their broader political philosophy, their public pronouncements limited these rights specifically to British citizens or to freemen. Moreover, although they asserted an equal right to Liberty among freemen, they identified this Liberty primarily as a right to hold property.

This vocabulary could in no sense be said to entail the end of slavery or any other broadly egalitarian proposition. Even when the colonists explicitly proclaimed themselves in favor of liberty and against slavery, they referred to political, not chattel slavery. They said merely that *to be* enslaved was undesirable, not that to enslave others was morally evil. The term "equality" had been introduced into the public vocabulary, however, and it had been employed as a necessary support to Liberty. This provided grounds from which egalitarian usages could be expanded as future circumstances permitted.

Scene 2: The American Revolution, 1774–1789

The revolt against Britain was stirred by the colonists' material interest in protecting their Property from a grasping imperialist fist. But the revolution could not be justified solely by such selfish interests, and many of the colonists were relatively untouched by such concerns, for they neither voted nor obtained enough wealth to be of interest to the British Empire. To gain the support of the full citizenry for independence, as well as to cast their efforts in a light more legitimate than self-interest, a revolutionary rhetoric was needed, and in the story we tell it developed with lightning speed after 1774.

The exigencies of revolution led the colonial leaders increasingly to claim that "all men" had the natural right to Liberty and thus had been created equal. They supported as well the notion of equal representation. The colonial leaders, however, were not broadly egalitarian men. Hence, they limited their assertion that "all men" had certain natural rights by emphasizing that such rights could not all be maintained in social compact. They indicated further that the preservation of rights in social compact was dependent on the vigilance of the "race." The colonists had only to examine the global scene in order to notice that, although human beings might be equally free in nature, most were unable to preserve that freedom in society. Liberty had to be earned and defended by a "people." Therefore, it was of great importance that the American political community encompass only those with the "fixt genious" that allowed them to preserve Liberty and Equality among themselves. Americans were to be, therefore, one homogeneous people. Rather than including African-American slaves, the increased usage of Equality thus arose so as to provide continued support for excluding from the body politic those persons who held an allegiance to African culture. Slavery was also reinforced by the continued allegiance to Property as a national commitment.

Although the extinction of slavery was not a logical entailment of the particular egalitarian commitments of Anglo-Americans, there was, nonetheless, a clear problem generated by the new vocabulary. What should be done with the increasing number of free blacks living in America? How could those committed to a republican form of government live intermingled with a people who were neither their slaves nor members of their community? The answer the nation's framers gave was expatriation. Democrats could not live in such a condition, so they would have to expel the foreign bodies. During the nineteenth century the American Colonization Society arose, offering to solve Anglo-America's dilemma by exporting free Africans back to Africa. The organization initially gained wide support both from slaveholders and white abolitionists. Colonization offered a solution perfectly consistent with the full body of the Anglo-American creed, and it would persist in the dreams of white supremacists for almost two centuries. As the story told below will indicate, however, full-scale colonization turned out to be pragmatically impossible, not only because it lacked economic viability, but because few free Africans wanted to leave their new nation.

With the failure of colonization, America found itself in a moral conundrum. The dilemma did not derive from an inconsistency between slavery and Equality, for the Constitution had been carefully drafted to avoid that problem. Instead, neither Equality nor Slavery were inclusive enough to encompass free blacks. Eventually, as we will see in the next stage of the

A revisionist ~~history~~ does it undersell ~~imp.~~ no other?

story, free blacks themselves would provide the solution by expanding the usages for Equality.

Scene 3: The Rhetorical Formation
of the African-American Nationality, 1774–1860

Free blacks were not generally permitted a voice in the public arena erected by Anglo-Americans. The African-American reaction to this exclusion was to constitute their own public arena, first in the relative safety of local venues such as black churches, and by 1817 on a national basis. Rhetors in the black national arena sponsored an extension of the protection of social rights to "all men," the inclusion of African descendants in citizenship, and a host of new and expansive usages of Equality.

African-American rhetors accomplished the extension of Equal Liberty to "all men" through two simple rhetorical moves. First, they added the word "universal" in front of value terms such as "equality," "liberty," and "rights." Second, they italicized *all men* when quoting the declarations of their white neighbors. Free blacks thereby neatly cut away the exclusions that the British colonists had so carefully crafted to equate them with chattel slaves. Moreover, they accomplished this ploy without white America taking full notice of what they had done.

In addition to these rather straightforward rhetorical methods, African-Americans employed an expanded rationale for human equality. John Locke and his colleagues had based Equality in a "natural right" of creation. Such a natural grant could be taken away by social compact. In the story of American Equality, African-American rhetors altered this account, specifying that Equal Right arose not from a natural, original, and irrevocable grant by a Creator but from existent, persistent, material conditions. Equal Liberty was necessary to all those who could reason and speak because the character of reasoning and speaking required liberty as a material condition and practical consequence. The material condition of being human could not be bartered away in social compact or lost in a "just war," let alone by unjust enslavement, because it persisted regardless of compact, war, or enslavement. It was the condition itself, the living nature of the human individual, that required Liberty.

Black advocates employed a similar argument to attack the exclusion of Africans from American citizenship and to include them as part of the "American people." Instead of defining citizenship based on lineage, they grounded citizenship in territory, emphasizing that all those born in America were by definition Americans. To assist their argument, they promoted the Declaration of Independence to the central status of a constitutional document, over and against the objections of Southern slaveholders who moved directly to repudiate such efforts.

Finally, the African-American people also provided the nation with a new set of usages for the phrase "equal rights." By the 1830s, Jacksonians had added "equal protection," a precursor of "equal opportunity," to the Anglo-American repertoire of political terms. However, Jacksonian "equal protection" simply restrained the government from giving advantage to the rich; it neither mandated nor permitted the government to level the playing field to create equal opportunity. African-Americans offered three alternative usages of Equal Rights. The first offered the phrase "equal laws," which prohibited the government from erecting statutes that discriminated on the basis of race. Second, they supported the phrase "equal opportunity" in an active form that asked the government to redress the inequities generated by history so that all citizens could start the "race of life" in an equal position. Finally, they offered a different usage of Equal Opportunity, suggesting that even if the natural abilities of citizens were so different that they could never have equal opportunities, the government should protect all its citizens so that they might develop whatever native abilities they might have.

These different usages of the phrase "equal rights" were proposed by different rhetors, and each had significant implications for the relationships among Liberty, Property, and Equality. As we shall see, however, none of these usages were cast in opposition to the recognition of criteria of merit, nor did they envision the end of a capitalist economy. More important, they confined themselves largely to the public realm, eschewing demands for Social Equality.

As time wore on, the African-American national arena came increasingly to overlap with the mainstream public arena, largely through the auspices of white abolitionists, including, most prominently, William Lloyd Garrison. As Act I of our story concludes in 1860, it will become clear that some elements of the African-American vocabulary gradually and slowly infiltrated the mainstream public vocabulary. However, it will also be clear that, as the Civil War commenced, a huge canyon remained between the ways of speaking about Equality employed by African-Americans and those preferred by most Anglo-Americans. Anglo-Americans themselves held a wide range of opinions, including a staunch egalitarianism, a grudged abolitionism, and a rabid proslavery sentiment. As the story moves to the second century of American life in Act II, we will see American public discourse focused increasingly on negotiating the concept of Equality between and among these groups.

ACT II: THE INTEGRATION OF EQUALITY

One cannot understand the story of American Equality without recognizing that the outcome of the Civil War elevated Equality to a new place in the American political vocabulary. Not only did Abraham Lincoln dedicate the sacrifices of the war to the "proposition that all men are created equal," but for the first time the Constitution was amended to grant Equality legal status. To enshrine a new value in a national Constitution is only the first step in insuring its integration with a public vocabulary. If the term is to be meaningful to the life of the community, it also must become integrated into the national life at all levels of public discussion, from presidential proclamations to congressional debates, from the statehouses to the nation's factories and inns. Such rhetorical integration represents a complex social and political process by which the range of possible usages of a term are discovered for each of the multitude of contexts in which it might be employed. Different interest groups must negotiate that range of meanings, and they must arrive at compromises if they have any hope of living together under the same constitution. As such rhetorical negotiations unfold, the similarity in the political vocabularies of different groups increases, and as a result the different interest groups themselves begin to integrate. Consequently, in Act II of our story, the reader will see a set of highly fragmented American publics emerge from the Civil War and gradually become knit together across the next century. As we will demonstrate, the product of this rhetorical integration is not uniformity but an increasingly complex rhetorical culture from which heterogeneity might be indulged.

Scene 1: Separate But Equal, 1865–1896

The second half of the nineteenth century brought a series of unsuccessful solutions to the problem of what Equality could mean in America. In each case, the voices of white supremacists, white egalitarians, and African-Americans offered starkly conflicting usages of Equality, but as the chapters that follow will indicate, compromises were forged at the points of overlap in the political vocabularies of the three communities. These compromises never held, however, because the vocabularies of these three different communities migrated in different directions.

During and after the Civil War, African-Americans offered a vision of "complete Equality." This included the right to vote, the right to use all public accommodations, and the right to serve on juries. African-American leaders continued to temporize on the importance of Social Equality, but they insisted that full Political Equality should be the right of all citizens. In seeking to gain proportional patronage within the Republican party, they developed a new usage of Equality that relied on mathematical proportionality to determine when the condition of equality had been achieved.

African-Americans had substantial input into the discussion, but in the years between 1860 and 1870 a minority of egalitarian whites held the upper hand in forming national policy, and they offered a vision of Political Equality with somewhat more nebulous boundaries. They endorsed the end to slavery, the right to vote, and some selected civil rights, but the boundaries of those rights were unclear. It is important to note that their usage of Political Equality was constituted by the belief that the condition of equality could only be achieved "in time" and through political enfranchisement. There was clearly nothing in their view that presumed any kind of substantive equality between America's white citizens and her ex-slaves.

The white egalitarian vision was opposed by white supremacists, who premised their usages of equality on the *permanent* inferiority of blacks. They agreed to the end of slavery, but as ex-slaveholders they offered a political system without any Equality whatsoever. Although white persons would no longer be able to own black people as a form of capital, whites would be complete control of their time and labor. Moreover, ex-slaves would have no voice in the political arena. This stance, given vivid presence by the enactment of the Black Codes, revolted a majority of white Northerners. In so doing, it threatened the political power of white Southerners as federal military governors were sent to enforce egalitarian views upon the South, and the Constitution was amended to grant citizenship and Political Equality to America's black population. The white Southerners rapidly changed their tactics.

The "Negro question" was more important to white Southerners than it was to white Northerners, because the preservation of traditional Southern culture turned on how it was resolved. The allegiance of white Southerners to their culture was so strong that it motivated them to continue a guerrilla war against their ex-slaves after the Civil War had ended. Eventually, control of the race issue in the South passed back into the hands of Southern whites, not only because they had the will and the military might to enforce their preferences but also because Southern patriarchs began to promise Northern republicans that they would preserve equality before the law, at least as far as the rights to life, liberty, and property. White Northerners accepted these assurances, overlooking the fact that the would-be secessionists had *not* promised Political Equality, i.e., the right to vote or to participate in all legal processes. The white North agreed to this compromise in large measure because it held States' Rights to be a more compelling value than Equality, even though the significance of Equality had risen within the value hierarchy of the prevailing rhetorical culture.

The official compromise among these positions entailed a national commitment to equality before the law, but it left the control of rights issues in the hands of the states. Under this compromise the white South had gained control of the race issue within its own borders. In order to avoid violating the informal treaty, however, it could not employ legal measures to subjugate its black citizens. The alternative was to employ violence and brutality as a means of intimidation and repression. White Southerners soon discovered that such practices threatened the stability of the white community itself, and so they sought to effect the legal instantiation of their folkways.

The method employed by white Southerners was to transform the principles of colonization into a policy that would work at home/That policy entailed the political exclusion and social segregation of blacks, and it would eventually be called the "separate but equal" doctrine. White egalitarians were uneasy with such a policy, but they wanted the violence against blacks to end, and so they agreed to it. The new doctrine was finally supported by the national press, which emphasized the differences between the members of the two races. Those differences contravened the underlying commitment of Political Equality, and thus allowed whites, both in the South and in the North, to stall on its practical implementation, even as they held out its possibility as an ultimate goal that might be achieved at some later and unspecified time.

The "separate but equal" doctrine thus placated egalitarian sentiment by promising equality. It also placated white supremacists by legitimizing separation. Even the African-American worldview of the period fit the contours of this proposed usage for American Equality, because the experiences of most blacks had disinclined them to want interracial social contact. Additionally, many blacks agreed with Southern whites that there was a "race instinct" that kept the two races separate and thus prevented Social Equality. Hence, in an ironic twist, the group most likely to suffer the effect of separation supported it in the context of expressing pride for their unique black culture and African roots.

Act II, Scene 1 comes to a close in 1896, when the Supreme Court legitimized the "separate but equal" compromise in *Plessy* v. *Ferguson,* a decision that fit perfectly the overlaps between the public rhetorics of the three major contending groups. However, as Scene 2 demonstrates, even as the "separate but equal" doctrine was formalized, the grounds upon which the compromise leading to it had been erected began to erode.

Scene 2: Integrated Equalities, 1896–1960

Life under the "separate but equal" doctrine polarized the rhetorical efforts of white supremacists and African-Americans. White supremacists became overconfident in the light of what appeared to be their sole right to control the race issue. Consequently, as the century unfolded, their fire-eating, race-hating voice became ever louder in the national public arena, as they arrogantly claimed that blacks were uneducable, justified lynching by insisting that blacks were a criminal race and maintained the necessity of a caste system. They even openly disavowed the goal of Political Equality for blacks. White supremacists thus saw the "separate but equal" compromise as a jumping-off ground for eventually effecting a separate but *unequal* doctrine.

Meanwhile, the experience of blacks under "separate but equal" rapidly taught them that such a system did little more than legitimize the destruction of any and all vestiges of equality for blacks. Under the leadership of Booker T. Washington and others, the Afro-American community began to amass the intellectual and political resources necessary to challenge these conditions. As the nineteenth century gave way to the twentieth, a newly educated generation of African-Americans was ready to repudiate the results of *Plessy* v. *Ferguson*. The Harlem Renaissance reflected the flourishing of the African-American contribution to the nation's culture as blacks once again promoted a vision of America as a "composite" nation, a home for the "rainbow of humanity." They thus insisted on FULL EQUALITY, including SOCIAL EQUALITY, and in doing so they touted their equal achievements in a variety of fields.

The open caste racism now espoused by the white supremacists, placed alongside the increasingly effective organization and political activity of the African-American community, forcefully invited mainstream egalitarians to make a choice. Would they acquiesce to the permanent transformation of "separate but equal" into its malignant other, separate but unequal? Or would they commit themselves to changing the doctrine in a more progressive direction? Most egalitarians started down the path away from segregation and toward greater equality. One can see the shift most clearly in the Northern press, which began to portray America's black population in more positive terms, as well as to characterize the incorporation of black culture as an important component of mainstream American life. Eventually, it even began to portray black citizens as good workers and neighbors.

In the 1930s, the federal government became actively involved in the issue of civil rights, a phenomenon the nation had not experienced since before the turn of the century. President Franklin D. Roosevelt set the wheel in motion by promoting equality of hiring in government contracts, and President Harry S. Truman kept it turning as he began the process of desegregating the federal government itself. Additionally, Truman appointed a Committee on Civil Rights which provided a blueprint for integrating Equality into American life, and Truman himself pushed the issue in his addresses to the American people. The Supreme Court was also active in this period, issuing a cascade of decisions that signaled its commitment to a new vision of Integrated Equality. The most visible and important of these decisions, of course, was *Brown* v. *Board of Education of Topeka, Kansas,* for it was here that the Court legally overturned the "separate but equal" doctrine when it concluded that in matters of education separate was "inherently unequal."

In the face of this assault, white Southerners executed a graduated rhetorical retreat. The public image of the fire-eater was once again replaced by the benign visage of the patriarch promising fair treatment for blacks. By 1950 segregationists all but stopped claiming inherent white superiority, although they continued to denounce black people as "undesirables," frequently disparaging them for their alleged Communist connections. White supremacists even ceased denying that blacks should have Political Equality. Throughout, however, they insisted on segregation, though now they were willing to concede that some semblance of Equality must be granted to protect the doctrine of "separate but equal."

In the 1940s and 1950s, the rhetoric of black Americans expanded. The term "interracial" was widely used, but such usages did not denote effacement of black identity. When most African-American rhetors proclaimed "black is beautiful," they saw interracial interaction as a two-way street designed to strengthen both cultures, not as a one-way avenue to raise blacks to white standards. They also dramatically expanded the proportionality test. The new vision of Equality demanded integration rather than separation, but it assumed that through such integration African-Americans would share proportionally in the goods of the nation. This led to concrete and substantive usages of Equality built around the attainment of specific material goods, e.g., equal housing, equal schools, equal accommodations, equal health, and equal pay for equal work.

By 1960, the public debate over racial equality had shifted, and the story that has developed in its wake is no longer centered on the opposition between accepting or rejecting Equality. Rather, it is a tale concerned with the forms in which Equality ought to be enacted. In noting this, however, it is important to emphasize that America's national white leadership was ahead of much of the white population, and as a result, whatever changes it could effect were arduous and slow to develop. As the 1960s unfolded, African-Americans celebrated the victories they had achieved for the "dream" of Integrated Equality, but as Scene 3 will make clear, they also came increasingly to realize that white resistance meant that legal enactments were not enough to guarantee in practice the Equality they sought.

Scene 3: New Equalities, 1960–1990

During the 1960s, black Americans began the process of enforcing their new civil rights. Their chief tool was mass protest, including marches, sit-ins, boycotts, and freedom rides. In many cases they faced the necessity of using physical force, for where whites refused to concede to the demands of Integrated Equality, only direct confrontation would bring the federal police power to compel compliance with the law. The enforcement process cost America's black people the goodwill of many of the nation's less committed egalitarian white citizens. Had the federal government enacted enforcement on its own, this might not have been necessary. White supremacists, however, were willing to put their bodies on the line to preserve the old order of segregation, as Alabama's Governor George Wallace demonstrated when he defied the federal government by standing in the schoolhouse door. Blacks were forced to do the same, and they did so throughout the South.

This led to a significant ideological shift among African-Americans, for black leaders began to move away from the vision of an Integrated Equality. Frustrated by their failure to achieve progress at a faster pace, they began to argue that a minority group that was actively disliked by the majority could never achieve substantive equality through legal or formal equal opportunity. The new black vision therefore focused on achieving substantial equality or "equality in fact," and thus raised the question of proportional economic benefits for blacks. To support this goal many black rhetors identified all black persons with poverty and all white persons with racism. Ironically, just as the nation's white leadership was finally ready to give up the claim that America was a "white man's country," black leaders adopted the claim. Instead of repudiating racist actions and individuals, black rhetors began to repudiate the "racist system" and "racist America." Gradually, Malcolm X's vision of Equal Power replaced Martin Luther King, Jr.'s dream of Integrated Equality.

These new developments gave congressional conservatives a rhetorical leverage they had not experienced since the beginning of the century. Finally forced to concede the position of Political Equality, segregationists faithfully expressed their commitment to equality before the law, and used it to argue against affirmative action programs that provided special privileges to blacks at the cost of individual whites and the principle of merit. This position achieved substantial mainstream political support. Nonetheless, egalitarians retained political control. While Congress represented a variety of views, most of its egalitarian members saw federal efforts to provide "special preferences" as a short-term measure to make up for past inequities. The function of this special treatment was to insure that someday in the near future the nation could return to Equality Before the Law with good conscience, knowing that each individual would be treated on her or his own terms without regard to race. Few suspected that the treatment of races as permanent groups or castes would evolve from these measures. But that is precisely what the rise of black cultural separatism entailed in the 1980s.

The new rhetoric of Afrocentrism urged America's blacks to repudiate their links to American culture and to return to their authentic African roots. Arguing that European and African values stood in fundamental opposition to one another, Afrocentrists promoted racial culture as more important than the Western values of individual development or merit. This position entailed the reassessment of "special privileges" by mandating that proportional outcomes be transformed from temporary measures into permanent grants to racial castes. The reaction of America's mainstream press against Afrocentrism was vehement. Unfortunately, it conflated Afrocentrism with multiculturalism, the far milder claim that all cultures have something to contribute to the human community, and that Americans should learn about all of these cultures, not solely about the European portion of the nation's heritage. The conflation threatened to cut off an important debate about cultural values.

Public discourse, however, moves on multiple and contradictory tracks. A second major development in this period was the rise of a national black leadership whose constituency cut across racial lines. Leaders like Barbara Jordan, Andrew Young, Shirley Chisholm, and Douglas Wilder drew on their dual histories as black *and* American to provide constructive new leadership for America's mainstream. Significantly, these leaders achieved such success without either repudiating their black heritage or making blacks their only audience. Rather, they marked a path between the increasingly separationist sentiment of black culturalists, and the older, assimilationist sentiment of black integrationists. They offered what might be called a model of interbraided equality. Because it rejected the apparent separatist arguments of Afrocentrists, it was not widely endorsed in the black intellectual community.

Reverend Jesse Jackson offered another kind of mainstream leadership that was very popular with African-Americans, if not with the majority of white Americans. He blended components of black power rhetoric with older black visions of integrated equality to create a "rainbow coalition" that emphasized economic issues common to many groups, but that also allowed for the preservation of cultural identity. His vision contained some problems, not the least of which was that his usages of "economic equality" and "cultural equality" were fundamentally incompatible with one another. At the least, however, Jackson's leadership provided a model for adapting the debate about racial equality to an era in which African-Americans have been joined by other minorities in working on the issue of Equality.

While we provisionally end our story with Jesse Jackson, the effort to envision American Equality continues. Finally, the nation seems to have conceded that the United States of America is not, constitutionally, a "white man's country" but a home for all its citizens. It has done so, however, not because white Americans finally decided to be faithful to "their" foundational principle of Equality. Rather, this outcome derives from two very different causes. First, America's African descendants have managed to sustain a compelling public argument that has virtually required the nation to negotiate the meaning of Equality as a central, constitutional term. Second, the wide range of contributions made by African-Americans in the arts, athletics, politics, and the professions, as well as their presence in the labor market, have established an unalterable fact of American life: to be "American" is not to be European. Rather, to be American is to participate in the uniquely American values and mores that have evolved from the contact between the descendants of African and Europe—and, we hasten to add, increasingly from the contact with Asia and Latin America as well.

America has adopted the value of Equality as a central commitment of its collective life. What the legitimate public usages of Equality shall become remains open to a debate that will continue to include different groups with different interests. The use of the word "equality," however, has grown beyond the abstract proposition that "all persons are created equal" to a sustained effort to insure Political Equality, Public Equality, and Equal Opportunity in some degree and fashion. The various issues of Social Equality have been carefully divided, so that some might be incorporated in Public Equality and Equal Opportunity, and others might be politely bypassed. As the 1990s begin, it appears as if economic and cultural equality will be the chief issues occupying public attention for a number of years, but the course a public argument will take can never be predicted with confidence.

Exploring the path taken by the public argument about Equality is itself

vitally important to that future, but our account of that history also offers a
general model of the rhetorical process of public argumentation. America
cannot accurately be described as founded on a set of inexorably fixed,
basic principles rooted in a primeval past. Instead, it is the complex product of rhetorical foundations that evolve through time to match an ever-
changing environment.

America originally formed as a shared product of citizens with different
heritages, and we are confident that that process will continue. The interbraiding of these heritages is not always easy, for conflict is a necessary and
inherent feature of compromise. The search for commonality, however,
has always been an important component of living together, just as the
persistence of difference has been always a reality of national life. Balancing homogeneity and difference, amalgamation and separation, conflict
and peace are worthy challenges. They are made torturously difficult by
the search for advantage each individual and group undertakes. But to live
in a nation that seeks Liberty, *and* Equality, *and* Property is better than to
live in a nation that seeks only the will of the monarch, or the glory of the
race, or the faith of a religious seer, or the dictatorship of the white
working-class male proletariat, or the triumph of the Internationale, or
even the prospering of the "self-made man." Americans have chosen multiple ends that are worth arguing with one another about. The fact that as a
nation we cannot rest on ancient foundations, but must talk our way together into new possibilities, should not cause us to balk at such an uncertain endeavor but rather to understand its necessity. The chapters that
follow seek to contribute to the quality of that argument.

PART ONE

The Rhetorical Foundations of American Equality

CHAPTER TWO

The British Rhetoric
of Revolt
1760–1774

Resolved: That the present ministry, being instigated by the devil
and led on by their wicked corrupt hearts have a design to take away
our liberties and properties and to enslave us forever.

Proceedings of Farmington, CT
19 May 1774

The conventional story of the American colonists' revolt against Britain holds that the new nation's founders, motivated by a declaration of "the natural rights of man," overthrew the British monarchy to establish a form of government previously undreamed of and unsurpassed in its commitment to human equality. According to this story, there were several mild flaws in the new government, for its leaders neglected their allegiance to the principle of equality, failed to recognize the "common man's" right to vote until the turn of the century, and refused to recognize the Equal Rights of African-Americans. As the story goes, the attempt to correct this latter flaw began in the 1860s as white Americans gradually recognized the need to live in consonance with their commitment to the proposition that "all men are created equal."

There is, of course, a cynical counterstory.[1] It recounts the founders' inherent greed and lust for property and their crass manipulation of the colonial population. It characterizes leaders like Sam Adams, John Adams, Thomas Jefferson, John Hancock, and John Dickinson as having wielded the principles of the Enlightenment merely as deceptive tools, promptly discarded once the Revolution was won. The leaders thus left America, ever after, the home of the landed and elite.

Both of these stories about the values which founded our nation err because they focus exclusively on the words of a supposedly homogenous leadership. They assume further that the voices behind the rebellion were the same as the voices that defined the meaning of the revolution and the new government. In fact, there are important differences between *the rhetoric of revolt* (ca. 1760–74) and *the rhetoric of revolution* (1774–89). Both stories also err in their portrayal of the motivation behind the Revolution as a single, abstract principle. With such a view it is no wonder that we end up choosing between simplistic romance and sheer satire, between a rosy tale of triumphant principles and what Gary B. Nash sadly characterizes as "a failure of ideas in contact with realities."[2]

Public discourse cannot afford the attempt to function on the basis of single, absolute, or transcendental principles. No single principle can ever be enacted effectively into a government, for the successful operation of any government always depends on ordering manifold and competing experiences. Such ambiguity makes political language important, precisely because it allows for the possibility of a multiplicity of political meanings. Individuals and groups use public language to shape and negotiate the common interests of governance, a governance made meaningful through public language. It is therefore important to resist treating the units of public language as if they were timeless philosophical principles. All political principles, all elements of public language, are situated and mutable. In our language they are rhetorical, for their meanings are a function of the full range of *usages in public* available within a particular rhetorical culture. So it is, that to understand the egalitarian roots of American rhetorical culture, we need to begin by examining the specific contexts in which the word "equality" emerged as an element of the new nation's public vocabulary.

The Rhetoric of Liberty and Property

The dominant rhetoric leading the American colonists to rebel against British imperialism featured the words "liberty" and "property," not "equality." Materialist historians have worked hard to document a class basis for the Revolution, toiling away in the wills and tax records of the founders for evidence of economic interests that would justify separating Tories from Whigs, Federalists from Anti-Federalists, and Town from Country.[3] Conservative, mainstream historians have challenged and denigrated such claims.[4] In their turn, mainstream historians have been attacked for neglecting the role of wealth in distinguishing important factors in the constitutional process.[5] The battle of historians has been fascinating and useful, but it is important to notice that the focus on underlying economic factors presumes that an ingenuine egalitarian discourse strove to mask a reality anything but egalitarian. This assumption is false. Even a cursory examination of a representative sample of public discourse from this period makes it clear that what the colonists primarily sought were Property Rights.[6] Equality configured at most a small part of the argument. A careful reexamination of the constitutive values that led to the Revolution is called for.

In prerevolutionary discourse, the words "equal" and "equality" appear in relatively few remarks. In the hotbed of revolt, the Old South Meeting House in Boston, only two of the Boston Massacre Orations delivered before 1776 employed the term at all. The same held for the Election Sermons in Boston and Connecticut. Appeals to Equality were scarce in Northern newspapers like the *Connecticut Courant* and the *Boston Post-Boy,* and they became scarcer still as one moved southward to the *Philadelphia Chronicle,* the *Maryland Gazette,* and the *Georgia Gazette.* Even in radical newspapers like the *Massachusetts Spy* the word "property" appeared three to five times more often than "equality." The pamphlet rhetoric of the period, widely, perhaps disproportionately, emphasized by historians, evidences a similar pattern of word usage. The most radical pamphlet in its usage of Equality, John Wise's *A Vindication of the Government of New England Churches,* printed in 1717, shows "no connection [with] any threads of the Revolution."[7] Moreover, circulation figures tell us something about the reception of these terms. So, for example, the Whig pamphlets of Richard Bland, heavy in their use of Equality, seem to have been far less popular than the comparably whiggish pamphlets of Daniel Dulany, which rarely employed it.[8]

This account clearly departs from our conventional sense of what the American Revolution was about, and there are several important reasons for it. One is that the Revolution portrayed itself in terms significantly different from the prerevolutionary rhetoric that brought about revolt. Prerevolutionary rhetoric roused the radicals, especially in Boston. The revolutionary rhetoric, however, promoted independence and aroused the larger colonial population to defend it. A second reason is that there was a confusion between what the Revolution enabled—a growing political egalitarianism—and what originally motivated it. Hence histories and document collections for this period overemphasize Boston, distort Philadelphia, and focus on a body of public discourse that was more the exception than the norm. A third reason is that Boston's "leadership" of the revolution is taken to imply that the reasons for rebellion announced by Bostonians were shared in every way by other colonists, who, in fact, proved much more reluctant, gradual, and partial in supporting the War for Independence. The radical rationale espoused by Thomas Jefferson and a few others outside of Boston was not widely shared. To characterize the narrow, Northern pamphlet rhetoric as typical or as the philosophy of the Revolution is at best a post hoc construction and at worst an instance of the Whig fallacy.[9] In colonies like Georgia and the Carolinas, the public discourse involved relatively little political discussion beyond concerns about tobacco and slaves.[10] Even in Philadelphia, the discourse of rights was carefully limited to freemen. To understand the dominance of inegalitarian forces in the rhetoric that permeated the prerevolutionary era, and to understand the nonradical motivations that caused actions resulting in a war for independence, we need to explore in detail the usages of the key terms "liberty" and "property."

Liberty as Property

According to newspaper accounts, a favored toast of the Sons of Liberty during the prerevolutionary era was "LIBERTY and PROPERTY."[11] In fact, all colonial newspapers were dominated by a concern for "property." "Where would have been *liberty* and *property* if it had not been for the *resolution* of our ancestors?" asked the *Massachusetts Spy*. The *Maryland Gazette,* concerned that the British "plan" had designed a means to deprive even the British themselves "of their liberty and property," insisted that we are "contending for our just and legal possession of Property and Freedom."[12] Similarly, when *Thomas's Boston Journal* claimed that "the end of government is the preservation of property," the *Maryland Gazette* reprinted the claim directly.[13] The *Connecticut Courant,* a paper reluctant to champion secular political actions or colonial independence, chimed in to support "[t]he Claim that an Individual has upon the Community for the Protection of his Life, Liberties and Properties."[14] Similar sentiments pervaded the *Philadelphia Chronicle* and *Virginia Gazette.*[15]

In most newspapers, relative inattention to political philosophy prevailed. By and large, colonial newspapers reported some foreign news, the comings and goings of ships, tidbits about the weather, and other local curiosities. Most stories featured sales of property or actions of the colonial legislatures on bills to protect property. Occasionally, they emphasized bills to instill religious virtues. The farther south one traveled, the more the colonists' words focused on gathering and protecting their Property. Even in radical Boston, the names of John Hancock and Benjamin Church were as likely to appear in advertisements offering property for sale to the public as they were to appear in the anti-British rhetoric of the Boston Massacre Orations.[16] In fact, even the supposedly radical and anti-British *Boston Gazette* consisted largely of advertisements, even on the front pages, rather than of political rhetoric of any sort.

The major focus of prerevolutionary discourse was clearly property. This was not Tory rhetoric. The taxing of colonists' property ultimately united and moved them to action.[17] The pamphlets of John Dickinson, James Otis, and David Lloyd made this obvious in their almost singular fixation on taxation.[18] The prevalent concern for property in both political and nonpolitical discourse notwithstanding, however, historians and myth-makers alike have tended to deflect attention from the commitment to Property to its discursive pair, Liberty.

Usages of Liberty were widespread. Newspapers often paired liberty explicitly with property, but the most radical orators tended to use it by itself, leaving it largely undefined.[19] Sometimes vague metaphors aug-mented its meaning, as for instance: "Liberty is in this good man's opinion a goddess."[20] Other times its meaning was left ambiguous, as when "A meeting of the Inhabitants of the City of Annapolis" determined to "pre-serve North America and her liberties."[21]

With singular usages generally left undefined, it is significant that when the leaders of the revolt did define "liberties," they made it clear that the *first* liberty was the protection of property.[22] James Otis and Samuel Adams spoke almost identically when they asked, "Now what liberty can there be where property is taken away without consent?"[23] Likewise, when John Hancock railed against the violation of American "rights and liberties," the meaning of those liberties had already been framed by his opening statement to the Boston crowd: "Security to the persons and properties of the governed is so obviously the design and end of civil gov-ernment, that to attempt a logical proof of it would be like burning tapers at noon-day, to assist the sun in enlightening the world."[24] Even the *Con-stitutional Courant* employed the term "liberty" alone and undefined, only to return later to proclaim, "Liberty and property are necessarily con-nected together."[25] Rebellious orators thus agreed that the most important liberty was the freedom to own property, and their fundamental interest in "No Taxation without Representation" indicated as much.[26] In this con-nection, the prerevolutionary rhetoric of Liberty rings in very different tones than when we hear it in later surroundings.

There were other usages of liberty, including rights to a free press and religion, a jury trial, and freedom from unreasonable search and seizure. Especially late in the period, colonists spoke of these and other rights as important liberties.[27] Outside of direct protection of property, however, the most frequently mentioned liberty was the right to representation. The resolutions from Fairfax County Virginia of 18 July 1774 proclaimed Liberty in this fashion:

Resolved, That the most important and valuable part of the *British Constitution,* upon which its very existence depends, is the fundamental principle of the people's being governed by no laws to which they have not given their consent by Repre-sentatives freely chosen by themselves, who are affected by the laws they enact equally with their constituents.[28]

Likewise, a letter from Philadelphia addressed, after the fashion of the Committees of Correspondence, "To All the English Colonies of North America," cited, "the most essential and fundamental principle of the *English* Constitution, viz: *that no ENGLISHMAN shall be bound by any law to which he has not consented.*"[29]

In common usage, however, even the right to representation was firmly linked to Property. The colonists celebrated representation because it enabled them to protect their property: to give up property, they had to consent through their duly constituted representatives. As Stephen Hopkins noted, "British subjects are governed only agreeable to laws to which [they] themselves have some way consented; and are not to be compelled to part with their property, but as it is called for by the authority of such laws."[30] The York County (Virginia) Resolutions declared their association of freeholders to be in agreement: "That it is the first law of legislation, and of the *British* Constitution, that no man shall be taxed but by his own consent."[31] James Lovell even expressed a willingness to give up all other rights but this. "England," he avowed, "has [the] right to exercise every power over us, but that of taking money out of our pockets without our consent."[32]

Liberty was not always linked to Property, but the link was common and important.[33] Therefore, we should take the colonists' repeated insistence on the importance of Liberty as implying, fundamentally, an insistence on the right to Property.

Liberty as English

Another primary limit placed on liberty was its scope of application. Throughout most of the colonies, enumerated liberties were civil rights evolving from the British Constitution, not universal rights applicable to all. Hence the freeholders of Anne-Arundel County proclaimed their "*Essential Inherent Rights, and Constitutional Privileges,* derived to us, as *British Subjects,* from the clear Fountain of the *British Laws*—declared and confirmed to us by our *Charter*—and the *Usages* and *Customs* of our *Province.*"[34] Usually natural rights were mixed too thoroughly with Constitutional rights to tell what part of liberty might be natural and what constitutional. Hence, for example, the *Supplement to Maryland Gazette* reported that "Property and Freedom" is "A Possession that has its Foundation on the Clearest Principles of the Law of Nature, the most evident Declarations of the English Constitution, the plainest Contract made between the Crown and our Forefathers, and all these sealed and sanctified by the Usage of near two Hundred Years."[35] Although many of the colonists had read fragments of the political philosophies which formalized national rights doctrines, such as John Locke, Algernon Sydney, and Samuel Pufendorf, most orators and pamphleteers did not operate from formal and systematic doctrines. Most colonists had no clear concept of natural right, and in point of fact, very few talked as though the rights they sought were traced to any universally available source. By and large the colonists claimed (for themselves and not for all humanity) the historically, geographically, and racially limited "privileges of Englishmen."[36]

The colonists were reasonable to locate the foundation of their liberties in the British Constitution. Vassalage and slavery, not British rights, predominated among the nations of the world. As Andrew Eliot noted in his Election Sermon of 1765, "The presence of our General Assembly, and the business of this day, put us in mind of the liberties we enjoy, while more than nine-tenths of mankind are in the most abject slavery."[37] To claim that "all men are naturally free" in a world where few seemed so, at least by the colonists' definition, had to sound counterfactual. This makes sense of the colonists' inclination to claim liberties for some groups but not for others.

The most frequent claim of the prerevolutionary orators was not, therefore, that all men deserved these liberties. Rather it was that freemen possessed these rights. On this ground Pennsylvanians were usually as cautious as Virginians and Carolinians. The two major sources of leadership outside radical Boston were Philadelphia and Virginia. In Philadelphia, one out of four freemen held property in slaves at some time just as did the articulate classes in Virginia.[38] Consequently, the rhetoric of revolt from both Pennsylvanians and Southerners was cautious to claim only that "the Disposal of their own Property is the inherent Right of Freemen."[39] For the citizens of Maryland, this meant "as we conceive, of our *ancient inherent Rights and Privileges, as Freemen and liege Subject* of the Crown *Great Britain*."[40] Likewise, the Carolinians, surrounded by slave labor, proclaimed only that "the free-born Colonists, who have extended the *British* Empire over this once savage land, will sooner die than surrender the privileges of *Englishmen*."[41] Virginia slavers concurred, declaring as their concern only that the "life, liberty, or property of a freeman should be affected by any law which he did not consent to, or at least which he had not a right to oppose."[42] Consider as well that even James Otis, speaking from relatively slave-free Boston, and seeking to include blacks in American rights, referred this heritage of rights to its British source, arguing, "That the colonists, black and white, born here, are free born British subjects, and entitled to all the essential civil rights of such."[43]

Put simply, the public vocabulary used to justify the American revolt derived from the constitutional liberties of freeborn British subjects. Further, the close ties of Property to Liberty meant that the colonists tended to assign the right to representation to property holders only.[44] In some colonies, this included a substantial majority of free, white males; in others, substantial property holdings were less widely distributed, making property important in determining who had a legitimate voice in the public arena.[45] Though primarily based on property holdings, this prerevolutionary inegalitarianism derived its justification from other sources of hierarchical rank as well. Thus, for example, while colonial rhetoric often opposed the noble classes with furor and sincerity, it still viewed "the ranks of men" as legitimate, basing social and political standing on virtue, education, and ability.[46]

The familiarity of such hierarchical usages naturalized the further ranking of freemen, bound laborers, and slaves. With their ethnicity often denoted as Irish, German, or English, listings for runaway servants frequently outnumbered ads for the sale or return of runaway "Negro men and women." Convicts lost basic liberties by criminal action, and other bound servants had lost liberties through debt and financial difficulties. Such debased whites ranked below the status of freemen and served as models for the Anglo-American tendency to subordinate Africans to even lower ranks. We can find no extensive articulation of the claim that the Africans had lost their rights as captives of war; but Locke, who had direct input into the charter for South Carolina, advanced this reason in his *Second Treatise on Civil Government*.[47] Moreover, antislavery pamphlets took care to refute the claim, strongly implying that it was a major justification for ranking Africans lower than other servants. By contrast, white colonists argued vigorously that their freedom was a birthright that *they* had not forfeited. The "Remonstrance of the Freeholders and Freemen of Anne-Arundel County to their Representatives in Assembly" argued that "By the *unalterable Law of Nature,* we look upon ourselves to be *Freemen,* Providence seemingly averse to the *Miseries of Slavery,* hath placed us in the happy Estate of *Freedom:* And we are conscious to ourselves, that we have in no wise forfeited, or departed with our *natural Right* hereto."[48]

Where Africans were not excluded from the rights of freemen on the grounds that they were legal captives, they were excluded on the basis of racial lineage, for they were not English. The foundation of Liberty in the British Constitution made rights, liberties, and privileges matters of birthright.[49] The excessively heroic poetry of the *Pennsylvania Journal* expressed liberty in typical terms:

> For you, descended from the ancient Race
> of *Britain's* Warlike Sons, great Freedom's Heirs
> Who, When the Iron hand of stern Oppression

>Strove to crush and sink them into Slaves,
>Dar'd, nobly dar'd to stemn the foaming Tide.[50]

The *Massachusetts Spy* expressed the dependence on lineage in prose: "Where would have been *liberty* and *property* if it had not been for the *resolution* of our ancestors?"[51] The *Maryland Gazette* concurred in demanding "the liberty our fathers gave them: Gave them, did I say? They are coheirs of liberty with ourselves."[52]

Africans were neither biological nor cultural heirs to this British heritage. A hundred small reminders recalled this fact to the colonists. Newspaper advertisements frequently noted that slaves spoke little English, emphasizing the fact that until 1770 one-third to one-half of the slave population had come from outside the British colonial empire.[53] Africa was frequently cited as Britain's moral "other," a land of slavery.[54] The cultural assimilation of Africans remained unlikely in a period featuring rapid importation, early mortality, and a relatively low percentage of American-born slaves.[55] Differences between African and English cultures were greater than those that divided the English from other Europeans, such as the Germans (who formed communities of their own) and the Irish (who assimilated into the mainstream of colonial life).

Very little of the rhetoric which roused the colonists to revolt was, therefore, egalitarian. Nor, for that matter, did it even assert minimal universal rights for all humans. Leaders of the revolt could and did justify their actions on principles of property, rank, and limited liberties for select individuals. The public rhetoric that constituted an American people and motivated them to rebel derived predominantly from the need and desire to protect their property from the British home country. The surprise is not that men like John Adams and James Madison formed an inegalitarian constitution but that it was anything less than a total replication of the English aristocracy that had excluded them.

It must be remembered, however, that these ways of speaking did not necessarily represent the majority of colonists. In order to rouse wider popular support, a number of conservative Whigs joined a few eloquent egalitarians in introducing some errant but important equalizing usages into the American public vocabulary. These were the delicate and sparse precursors of a truly revolutionary rhetoric.

EQUALIZING RHETORICS FOR REBELLION

During major social change, leaders arise to articulate, amplify, and coordinate diffuse sentiments of discontent. These are exceptional rather than typical individuals, for they harness unusual rhetorical or organizational skills to provide leadership. In the colonies, a thriving, well-educated, merchant class had access to such skills. They also could make the time needed for sustained leadership. Thus the likes of John Hancock, James Otis, John Adams, and Samuel Adams, although clearly not representative of the average colonist, rose to speak for colonial America. Such elite representation creates important tensions in public rhetoric. It helps to weave the experiences of many classes and groups into a single public discourse. Hence the activist rhetoric of American rebellion represented merchant interests in protecting property, but it also was forced to appeal to the "mob." The combination of these interests constituted a rhetoric effective in moving many colonists to rebel.[56]

Only of late have we begun to study adequately the roles of economically disadvantaged portions of the population and the crowds they formed. Yet we know that the mob violence of the Boston Massacre, the assault on the homes of the British governors, the Boston Tea Party, and other similar incidents agitated the British into overreacting. And we have reason to regard the British overreaction to such events as crucial in consolidating the colonists' indignation and motivating their rebellion. Equally important in this regard were the multiplicity of uprisings throughout the colonies, especially in the western regions, for they demonstrated a widespread dissatisfaction with the status quo often rooted in economic interests.

The shifting divisions in the population had important consequences for the public discourse. Leaders could hardly follow James Otis's postrevolutionary dictum in referring to the masses as "scum" and still hope to move them to action against the British.[57] Instead, colonial leaders asserted the right of their audiences to control their own destinies by participating in government, and they articulated a compelling public concern for British encroachments on such rights.

The private, postrevolutionary statements of some prominent Boston leaders are bound to interest us in this connection, because they betray an antiegalitarian disdain for the common people that is in direct conflict with some of their public statements. However badly the inconsistency between private rhetoric and public rhetoric reflects on revolutionary leaders, though, it should not be read as the essential meaning of the revolution. Public rhetoric, not the private sentiments of elites, persuaded people to revolt. Wherever there was widespread use of popular force against the British, revolutionary leaders augmented concerns for Liberty and Property with more egalitarian appeals.[58] Most rhetorically sensitive leaders created a vocabulary for common ground among various elites and the colonists in general. Developing democratic themes, the leaders of the

Revolution created and legitimated a small but vital field of democratic discourse.

Therefore a minor, though important, portion of prerevolutionary rhetoric was authentically egalitarian. In some ways, this dimension of the discourse appears to be the most effective to twentieth-century readers, for it seems essential in leading a "people" to revolt. Furthermore, it also represents the widest ground for uniting classes and groups of Americans.[59] Thus we have no trouble understanding the tendency of historians to focus on this literature, while disguising the greater frequency of the elite rhetoric of property. Nevertheless we need to acknowledge that its status as a vocabulary of compromise in the prerevolutionary period enforced narrow limits for such egalitarian rhetoric.

Equality

Public usages of "equal," "equality," or "equally" grew less from the political rhetoric of this period than from the counting spirit of the age. The era's commercial discourse featured arithmetic; and arithmetic configures itself through "=," the sign of equality. Consequently, the most frequent usages of the roots of the term "equality" reflected its underlying concern with magnitude. The most conservative speakers, such as those giving the Election Sermons in Connecticut, rarely used "equality" as a noun. But even the most moderate Whigs occasionally used the adjective "equally." In this vein, the *Maryland Gazette* reprinted "A LATE NORTHERN PRINT," saying that "Men cannot be happy, without Freedom; nor free without Security of Property," but also proclaiming Americans "equally intitled to happiness with the Inhabitants of *Great Britain*."[60] Cato likewise asserted that "England is the place in the world where the public is most equally administered."[61] In fact, the form "equally" was the most frequent expression of egalitarianism, and it clearly did not promote equality as a constitutive value.[62]

This foundation of mathematical equivalence in magnitude was not a trivial matter. Moderates and radicals talked most often of equality, where more conservative rhetors used the word "equity."[63] Both terms provided a sense of fairness and were frequently related to justice. Equity defined that fairness in terms of a prior moral code that entailed rankings and necessitated appropriate actions with regards to them. Equality defined justice mathematically, identifying parties as the same in magnitude of some shared quality.[64]

Several usages tied this numerical meaning with the eventual employment of equality as a constitutive value. The second most frequent usage appended the word "equal" to some other key value. A letter from Philadelphia to "All the English Colonies of North America" referred to "equal right and equal authority."[65] Stephen Hopkins spoke many times of "equal laws," "equal freedom," "equal suffrage," and "equal liberty."[66] Samuel Adams talked of "equal and impartial liberty."[67] Probably the most common usage of equality was in the phrase "equal representation."[68]

These transitional usages of Equality asserted equivalence primarily within the narrow community of British citizens. In this manner, the freeholders of Anne-Arundel County proclaimed themselves to be "Equally Free, with our Fellow-Subjects, resident within the Realm of Great Britain."[69] In telling the tale of colonization the British American, No. VI asserted that "with respect to England, they had an equal right, at their own private risk and expense, to acquire . . . a settlement for themselves and their posterity."[70] Likewise the Caroline County (VA) Resolutions referred to the rights "to which they are equally entitled with their fellow-subjects in Great Britain."[71] This scope of usage dominated the public discourse because it bridged the vocabulary and interests of both the elite leaders of the revolution and the larger colonial population, expressing their shared concerns for relating to Britain. As a consequence of this de facto compromise, such usages were conservative. They asserted equality only within a narrow community of British subjects; and they asserted equal British rights rather than universal equality among human beings. The leaders could thus interpret these usages as claims of their equivalence with the British peerage, while the populace could interpret them as implying equivalence among all British subjects.

A few prerevolutionary usages were more radical. These occurred primarily in Boston, where revolutionary discourse occurred well before the revolt. This modest tie between revolutionary rhetoric and a more general egalitarianism stemmed from the rhetorical need to justify revolution against Britain. Until the Declaration of Independence, colonists could easily ground their claim to equal rights in the British Constitution, but independence required a unique and separate rationale. The appeal to natural right provided as much, but it relied on the more radical sense of some original quality of all human beings (or at least of men). Given the link to independence, this radical usage did not appear widely outside of Boston until after the first military engagements had commenced.

One of the earliest usages inside Boston came from Joseph Warren, whose death early in the war was to consecrate the revolutionary slogan "liberty or death."[72] Invoking a natural Equality, Warren explained the rise of British tyranny as a matter of forgetfulness:

In young and new formed communities, the grand design of this institution is most generally understood, and most strictly regarded; the motives which urged to the social compact cannot be at once forgotten, and *that* equality which is remembered to have subsisted so lately among them, prevents those who are cloathed with authority from attempting to invade the freedom of their Brethren.[73]

Benjamin Church echoed the claim forcefully the next year, asserting, "Mankind apprized of their privileges, in being rational and free; in prescribing civil laws to themselves, had surely no intention of being enchained by any of their equals."[74] In Virginia, the *British American, No. VII* referred more gently to the need to "inspire the minds of our lords and masters with some slight sentiments of moderation, some little degree of tenderness and compassion, towards those who were once their equals, are still their brethren, and are not conscious of having merited the base, the abject, the humiliating state, they are reduced to."[75]

This wide-ranging version of equality appealed to commoners, but it had undesirable implications for the elites. Hence it was that a different usage emphasizing the opposition to hereditary nobility became more pronounced, for colonists of most economic stations generally shared a concern to resist both the grasp of a British nobility and the rise of an American aristocracy.[76] Consequently, the most dominant of the radical usages of Equality simply asserted that there were a basic group of rights which transcended the rankings of nobility. The *Massachusetts Spy* expressed the relationship in this manner: "However distinguished by rank or property in the rights of freedom we are all equal. As we are Englishmen, the least considerable man among us has an interest, equal to the proudest nobleman, in the laws and constitution of his country, and is equally called upon to make a generous contribution in support of them."[77] Richard Bland's formulation was similar: "I am speaking of the *Rights* of a People; *Rights* imply *Equality* in the Instances to which they belong, and must be treated without Respect to the Dignity of the Persons concerned in them."[78]

In their positing of rights that transcend rank, such usages highlight how the colonists' initial political commitment to Equality represented a rhetorical compromise. They aligned elite and common interests against the British empire and could be shared widely, even as they could be understood with different intonations by what might otherwise have been two sides. The elite leadership could focus on nobility in the limited sense of a hereditary aristocracy, while others could take equality to deny rankings of any kind. Mediating the artificial property rights created by governments and the "natural," egalitarian condition of human beings, these usages had long-term consequences. They enabled the two sets of interests to coexist by suggesting that while there are rights shared by all Englishmen, regardless of social or economic differences, these rights need not conflict with the granting of privileges to some individuals. Daniel Shutes provided an early example of this balancing act: "The right the supreme ruler of the world has to bestow favours upon some, out of the common course of things, while *others* are left in the enjoyment of their natural privileges, can, in reason, no more be doubted, than his right to create one being superior to another." However, he then went on to claim, "They are to rescue the weak and helpless, the widow and fatherless, from the cruel hands of oppression, and equally secure to all, high and low, their rights."[79] The balancing of fundamental equal rights with property was to become the hallmark of Anglo-America's revolutionary compromise.

Usages, once introduced, however, are no longer under the control of their makers. Often, they broaden into general assertions that stand apart from the carefully compromised discourse which generated them. Thus John Tucker told a Boston audience, "All men are naturally in a state of freedom, and have an equal claim."[80] These broader, more radical usages occurred during the prerevolutionary period, but only occasionally so, and only in a few locales.

On the whole, such usages provoked evermore vigorous attempts to limit their scope than to develop their meaning unencumbered by qualifications.[81] In most cases, broad usages of Equality provoked vigorous, reactionary efforts to limit its application. This was not a particularly difficult rhetorical task, for the public presumption was against a broad conception of Equality, as is evident in Daniel Dulany's popular pamphlet, which averred that "considering the nature of human affections, the inferior is not to be trusted with providing regulations to prevent his rising to an equality with his superior."[82] Often the argument that equality exists as a natural right was recognized only to refute it. Thus Samuel West's Election Sermon of 1776 argued that "a state wherein all are equal" is invalidated by the fact that "the law of nature is a perfect standard and measure of action for beings that persevere in a state of moral rectitude. But the case is far different with us, who are in a fallen and degenerate state."[83] The usual justification for preserving inequalities was that those who were poor and without rights were "undeserving." The *Maryland Gazette* carried articles in which Sarcasticus derided the possibility of a "sausage maker" as a leader and chastised "the blind and credulous people." It also printed the words of Americanus, who argued, "*The mob of Maryland,* like the common people of all countries, are ever ready to receive the first impressions, and being too lazy or ignorant to enquire or examine into causes of complaints, they are ever violent in their proceedings."[84] Such arguments tapped a network of common associations linking wealth with learning and virtue rather than with hereditary title. Power was thus to come through merit rather than heredity.[85]

These arguments were challenged. Some speakers repudiated the characterization of rich men as wise and just, celebrating instead virtues of "the middling sort," while others denounced the claim that leadership is a matter of merit rather than representation.[86] Such recharacterizations were crucial to the claims of equality.[87] Hence Gad Hitchcock argued, "In a state of nature men are equal, exactly on a par in regard to authority. . . . The idea of superior wisdom giving a right to rule, can answer the purpose of power but to one [the Lord]."[88]

The discourse of equality was not a prominent feature of the prerevolutionary period. The term often surfaced only to be repudiated, and usually it was confined within particular groups. Still, the narrow stand for equality as a principle of governance led eventually to the Declaration of Independence. Until then, however, the usage of Equality remained marginal. In its stead, the "rights of man" provided the egalitarian articulation of Liberty and Property as the warrant for the rhetoric of revolt.

The Rights of Humanity

In generating the American rebellion, some radical rebels made claims about "universal rights" and the interests shared by "all men." John Lathrop, in his introduction to his Boston Massacre Oration, cited Cotton and Increase Mather as sources verifying the importance of "that Liberty which the God of nature designed his rational creatures should enjoy."[89] Samuel Adams's *State of the Right of the Colonists* was more formal than most in such proclamations but otherwise typical as he enumerated the claim:

All Men have a Right to remain in a State of Nature as long as they please. . . . When Men enter into Society, it is by voluntary consent; and they have a right to demand and insist upon the performance of such conditions, And previous limitations as form an equitable *original compact*. Every natural Right not expressly given up or from the nature of a Social Compact necessarily ceded remains.[90]

Again, however, hidden qualifiers limited the scope of these apparently radical usages. Most particularly, the speakers limited the list of universal rights to the same narrow ones that dominated the rhetoric of more conservative rebels, including most prominently the rights of property and representation. As Joseph Warren said, "[E]very man has a natural right to personal freedom, consequently a right to enjoy what is acquired by his own labor."[91]

As debates in the Continental Congress show, even this narrowed doctrine of natural rights was not universally shared outside of radical circles.[92] Moreover, as we indicated above, talk of natural rights was often ambiguous, implying that only British subjects "naturally" had such freedom. The radicals, however, had other ways of extending their claims. Even aside from explicit talk of natural rights, the rebels sometimes spoke about all men in ways that could serve, in other contexts, as a rhetorical warrant for extending rights. Thus John Lathrop alternated justifications based on compact with older, religious justifications derived from God's Will to claim that "every individual ha[s] a perfect right to his own person, life, and limbs, and . . . no right is more sacred than that of every innocent man to enjoy his own life."[93] Similarly, a Philadelphia "[D]eclaration . . . of the united colonies of North America" doubted in 1775 "[i]f it was possible for men, who exercise their reason to believe, that the divine author of our existence intended a part of the human race to hold an absolute property in, an unbounded power over others."[94] Both Lathrop and the Philadelphia Committee referred explicitly to relations between Britain and America; but when used later, with the qualifiers omitted, these words could be pulled from their contexts and turned to different purposes. Even a claim about the "privileges of a free people and the natural rights of mankind" could remain altogether vague about the contents of the "natural rights of mankind," but later be construed as support for wide-ranging universal rights.[95]

Egalitarianism in the rhetoric of revolt therefore enjoyed two foundations. The potentially more radical usage asserted human equality, and, though rare, it made an important showing. The more frequently used doctrine of universal human rights was unambiguously inclusive, but it carried very few entailments. Both usages appeared in Boston with some regularity after 1770, although they were directly contested. Outside Boston, however, these usages did not begin to permeate the rhetoric of revolution until 1774–75. Yet a third egalitarian vocabulary appeared widely before then, speaking to later black-white issues by addressing the relationship between Liberty and Slavery.

Liberty and Slavery

In the prerevolutionary period, the single most prevalent, most widely shared discourse of *all* colonists, North and South, radical and moderate, was the absolute refusal to become Slaves. It rang from the likes of Joseph Warren, rousing a Boston crowd over the Massacre: "THE Voice of your Fathers blood cries to you from the ground; MY SONS SCORN TO BE SLAVES!"[96] And it came in more matter-of-fact tones from the "Mem-

bers of the Late House of Burgesses" of Virginia, which followed Boston's
lead in deciding that "a determined system is formed and pressed for reducing the inhabitants of *British America* to slavery, by subjecting them to
the payment of taxes, imposed without the consent of the people on their
Representatives."[97] Whatever the tone, surprisingly few revolutionary
documents omitted the term "slavery."[98]

Many speeches made sharp contrasts between slavery and liberty (or
freedom). Charles Turner declared, "How distressing the thought of
being slaves, how charming that of being free! While liberty is fruitful
. . . slavery clogs every sublimer movement."[99] Even without such em-
phatic juxtapositions, opposing slavery to freedom or liberty was the predominant rhetoric before the revolution.[100] The negative sense of slavery
was as important to prerevolutionary discourse as the positive value of
property. Rhetors painted a dark picture of slavery, declaring it "the worst
of savages," and depicting it as a monster so horrible that "death with tor-
ture [was] far less terrible."[101] Moved by vivid imagery of their necks
crushed under the yoke of slavery, colonists unified around their opposition to slavery as the ultimate reason for independence.

Surely the consequences of such a position are obvious. After all, the
discourse was truly consensual: slavery was abhorrent, and human blood
willingly had been shed to oppose it. As the revolt succeeded, and a new
form of government was enacted by people who considered their nation as
an "asylum of freedom," there could be little question that the chattel slavery of Africans would be eliminated by a simple process of deductive reasoning. So, at least, historical and rhetorical accounts of later events have
suggested. But in fact the situation was very different, for *the colonists
carefully bounded their usage of "slavery" in ways that provided argumentative
grounds to resist such later appropriations*.

As the Continental Congress signaled the shift from revolt to revolution, the colonists argued only against their *own* enslavement, not against
slavery as a system.[102] They consistently argued that *to be enslaved* was bad,
but they hardly ever argued that *to enslave* was necessarily bad. In his Election Sermon, for example, John Tucker warned that Americans were concerned to avoid the "chains of slavery *for ourselves and children.*"[103] The
arguments of many colonists made it clear that it was their own slavery,
not the hierarchy of rank implicit in slavery, with which they were concerned. A letter from Philadelphia "To the Inhabitants of the British Colonies in North America" noted that the colonists were "striving to
maintain *our rank* in the class of freemen [our emphasis]."[104] And instruc-
tions for representatives from the Philadelphia Convention of 15 July 1774
expressed concern only about their own standing when they worried that

"the Colonists will sink from the rank of freemen into the class of slaves."[105]

Equally significant were the reasons given in the Virginia Resolutions for opposing the importation of slaves. Many historians treat these Resolutions as a sign of implicit antislavery sentiment, while others tend to reject this interpretation on the ground that the Virginians were interested only in increasing the value of their property.[106] Both arguments miss important central concerns of these cultures. Some general antislavery sentiment did surface: the resolutions of the county chaired by George Washington (who would free his own slaves in his will) expressed the moral case against slavery.[107] And some slave owners sought economic gain from the increased value of domestic slaves once importations ceased. But most of the resolutions articulated their objections to the foreign slave trade on other economic and cultural grounds. Nansemond County and Caroline County agreed "[t]hat the *African* trade is injurious to this Colony, obstructs the population of it by freemen, prevents manufacturers and other useful emigrants from *Europe* from settling among us, and occasions an annual increase of the balance of trade against this Colony."[108] The Virginians were concerned about creating a homogeneous people with European training, not about the moral evils of slavery or even the direct economic gain of breeding slaves.

As a whole, it was true, the colonists fervently wished to avoid enslavement. They disliked slaves, as well as the influence of slavery, but generally they did not make the leap to the claim that slavery per se was an evil. That argument was to be developed as a nineteenth-century revision of the actual eighteenth-century arguments.

An additional factor might have kept Anglo-Americans from deducing the end of African slavery from their revulsion to their own enslavement. When colonists talked about "slavery," few seem to have referred directly to chattel slavery. Bernard Bailyn cites one inclusive example of direct reference to African slavery, but examination of the public discourse overall suggests it to have been unrepresentative. Generally the colonists cited examples of enslavement from other places around the globe.[109] Thus the *Constitutional Courant* was fairly typical in its focus on Turkey when it noted, "Let us not flatter ourselves, that we shall be happier, or treated with more lenity than our fellow slaves in Turkey." It then went on to remind its audience of the spread of slavery throughout Greece, Rome, and Constantinople.[110] The *Massachusetts Spy* denounced "Slavery, in many hideous forms, I have seen in many parts of the world," and then listed Denmark, Prussia, France, Asia, etc.[111] From Pennsylvania, where African slavery was more common, John Dickinson's "Letters from a Farmer in Pennsylvania to the Inhabitants of the British Colonies" argued, "We are as abject slaves as France and Poland can shew in wooden shoes, and with uncombed hair."[112]

In actual usage, then, the word "slavery" referred to despotic governments usurping popular sovereignty; it had little or nothing to do with African slavery or individual bond labor. In all likelihood, the colonists were incapable of imagining themselves as subject to slavery of the sort experienced by Africans for the same reasons they had originally separated out African slaves from indentured servants during the formation of these practices in the founding period.[113] The colonists said as much, and they did so quite deliberately, but our own interpretation of slavery, now based on the African example and influenced by abolitionist discourse, lead us to misread them.[114] Instead we need to read literally the claim of Benjamin Church that:

By *liberty,* I would be understood, the happiness of living under laws of our own making. . . . That state only is free, where the people are governed by laws which they have a share in making; and that country is totally enslaved, where one single law can be made or repealed, without the interposition or consent of the people.[115]

The only loss of liberty that the white colonists expressed publicly for themselves was not economic or personal but political.

Further clues to the fact that Americans were thinking of slavery in this political and international sense come from public discourse that otherwise would seem counterfactual. If slavery were to mean "individual bond labor" or "African servitude," then the writer of a letter "To the Inhabitants of the Province of South Carolina" would be nonsensical in saying "I never can believe, that in this sacred land slavery shall be so soon permitted to erect her throne on the ruins of freedom."[116] The only way to make sense of the letter from Charleston that urges colonists to "Resolve rather to die the last of *American* freemen, than live the first of *American* slaves," is to exclude Africans from the meaning of "Americans" or to define slavery as political rather than personal bondage. And when the conservative *Connecticut Courant* argued for resistance to the "manifest Tendency to reduce Americans to the most abject Slavery," it referred to a type of slavery quite other than that experienced by the Africans living in servitude in America.[117]

The argument that the colonial revolt against Britain came out of the opposition to all chattel slavery, and that enslavement *therefore* necessarily had to be outlawed in America, did not follow because the premise was false. Instead, abolitionist rhetors would have to transform premises arguing the undesirability of being enslaved into statements denying the desirability of enslaving others. This would require transforming references concerning political liberty into statements about personal liberty.

Rhetorical transformations of this type typically entail two-sided struggles, and their outcome depends on a variety of factors. In the North, as we know, this transformation was highly successful. The newly independent Anglo-Americans succeeded in identifying chattel slavery with political slavery and in generating the moral sympathy necessary to link being enslaved and enslaving as part of a single moral evil. They were successful largely because slaveholders were then a small minority of those influential in forming the government.[118] Thus the North experienced little resistance to this shift in meaning, though it did not move readily to a broader sense of Equality for African-Americans, nor did it easily and generally apply the discourse of the rights of humanity to them.

We thus understand revolutionary and later activities of the white North better if we see talk of equality and universal rights as minor elements of prerevolutionary discourse, and if we recognize antislavery discourse as a major element. The white North's combination of emancipation with hostility toward free blacks came from that rhetorical balance rather than from some skittish inconsistency in pursuing a universal doctrine of egalitarian rights. Northern citizens rapidly accepted the analogy of African slavery to political slavery, and they freed their slaves. They did not, however, act from a public vocabulary that was highly egalitarian, and hence it was that they consigned the former slaves to a new, *but not equal,* class.

In the South, where slaves were valuable property, the situation differed immensely. Only in Virginia, with the exceptional leadership of men such as George Washington and Thomas Jefferson, did revolutionary usages of "equality" and "human rights" have *any* rhetorical presence. Elsewhere in the South, the discourse of equality scarcely existed, and the discourse of the rights of humanity remained rare before the Revolution. Even talk of resistance to enslavement was rarer than in the North. Compared to the powerful and pervasive term "property," concerns about Slavery had very little leverage in the South, and public discourse surrounding the Revolution there foreshadowed the continuation of chattel slavery for African-Americans.

The rhetorics of egalitarianism and human rights inherited by American colonists from Britain have been grossly overstated in scope and effect.[119] The discourse that launched the revolt against British authority was British to a fault, cast in terms of "liberty and property," the conservative public vocabulary of commercial Britain, not the radical Whig vocabulary of Locke and Sidney.

Not only was the usage of Liberty itself interpreted most often simply as the right to own property, but it was applied solely to Englishmen and its use was fully compatible with an extensive social and political hierarchy that assigned dramatically different privileges and limitations among different humans. Although the root word "equal" showed itself in the period, it did so primarily in the adjectival form, "equally." Even when agitators seeking to stir the masses to revolt employed it to modify key values (as in Equal Rights or Equal Representation), such equality was usually presumed to hold only among members of the British lineage. On the whole, the term "equality" was as likely to be explicitly opposed as endorsed, and it specifically sanctioned an end to the system of British nobility rather than the elimination of all distinctions among human beings. Most crucially, the rights of humanity were presumed too fragile to survive the transference from a state of nature to civil society in whole form, and the desire to protect social forms that had preserved maximal rights to Anglo-Americans was taken as the basis for excluding those persons whose experience would produce a different "genious." Even the frequently trumpeted opposition to slavery merely denoted a specific collectivity's refusal to submit to the condition of political disfranchisement rather than a universal condemnation of the practice of chattel slavery.

Eventually, of course, the colonists would reach for the vocabulary and insights of radical British intellectuals, but only once they were forced to deny their ties to Britain's mainstream establishment. And, interestingly, when they did so, they found Locke and Sidney too conservative for their needs. When it became clear that revolution was inevitable, the colonists needed a new and unique political discourse. And subsequent to 1775 this is exactly what they created.

CHAPTER THREE

The Anglo-American Revolutionary Rhetoric 1774–1789

> As we ought with gratitude to admire that decree of Heaven which has numbered us among the free, we ought to lament and deplore the necessity of holding our fellow-men in bondage. But is it practicable, by any human means, to liberate them without producing the most dreadful and ruinous consequences?
>
> Patrick Henry
> 24 January 1788

In order to constitute themselves as a new and independent nation, Anglo-American colonists had to construct a set of shared commitments. The values they adopted in this process were revolutionary in two senses: they justified revolutionary violence, and they consisted of distinctively new ways of speaking about political community. The thirteen states launched new equalities, which destroyed the concept of hereditary nobility, insisted on real rather than virtual representation for citizens, and claimed foundational rights. As revolutionary as these new equalities were, however, they were nonetheless bounded by older conceptions of birthrights, property rights, relations to community, education, and virtue. The end result was a severely constrained vision of popular sovereignty located in a uniform "people." This vision excluded African-Americans as rigidly as had the British rhetoric.

As we have noted, the presence of some moral and religious objections notwithstanding, the majority of British colonists in the new world had no problems with the institution of slavery. Liberty and Property served as their primary public values, and they came to those values as a matter of British birthright. Africans thus were doubly doomed, for not only were they not British citizens but they had become a species of property identified as far back as the Old Testament.

The Declaration of Independence and the ensuing revolutionary war complicated this arrangement but not precisely in the ways our conventional wisdom has held. The popular assumption has been that the egalitarian roots of the American Revolution made it logically and morally impossible for Americans to hold slaves. So, for example, Donald Robinson calls natural rights doctrine and slavery "irreconcilable," David Brion Davis describes them as in "contradiction," and Richard Brun argues that they constituted a "paradox."[1] While scholars have not joined the popular mythology in adopting wholly the perspective of the abolitionists, like Leon F. Litwack they are largely sympathetic to the claim that "the same principles used to justify the American Revolution, particularly John Locke's natural rights philosophy, also condemned and doomed Negro slavery."[2]

Davis points out the pragmatic absurdity of expecting such a contradiction to dissolve the practice of slavery, but even the assumption that such a contradiction existed must be in some measure dissolved.[3] It is neither the case that a single revolutionary ideology existed during and immediately after the war, nor that the dominant worldview adopted by the colonists contradicted slavery. Indeed, Locke himself supported both slavery and natural rights through a rationale of just capture and punishment.[4] Rather, the American version of Equality that would forcefully oppose slavery evolved only gradually and, as we will demonstrate, only through the public rhetorical interaction of blacks and whites.

The most visible principles motivating the American Revolution were developed in the years between 1775 and 1827, and they led not to the emancipation of slaves but to the expatriation of free African-Americans. In this chapter we trace the roots of Anglo-American Equality to the colonists' efforts to establish a more universal foundation for their claim to independence than their British heritage. We then examine how the discursive structure of this commitment to equality led "logically" not to government-mandated emancipation but to the Colonization movement, a movement that advocates on *both* sides of the slavery issue actively supported.

THE DISCURSIVE STRUCTURE OF THE AMERICAN REVOLUTION

In declaring themselves independent of Britain, the American colonists severed their link to Liberty and Property as the privileges of British freemen, and thus forced themselves into the position of identifying a different and preferably more universal rationale for constituting a government. The theory of natural rights had long been imprecisely mixed with claims to British birthrights. So, for example, the Declaration and Resolves of the First Continental Congress in 1774 had located colonial rights in "the immutable laws of nature, the principles of the English constitution, and the

several charters or compacts."[5] As war came, the colonists simply and rapidly erased the British constitution from their vocabulary, creating the appearance of a purer doctrine of natural rights. Thomas Paine's *Common
Sense* announced the new public values, proclaiming that the British government, while appropriate for the "dark and slavish times in which it was
erected," was adequate no more:

> For all men being originally equals, no one by birth could have a right to set up his
> own family in perpetual preference to all others for ever. . . . Where there are no
> distinctions, there can be no superiority; perfect equality affords no tempta-
> tion. . . . Securing freedom and property to all men . . . in America THE LAW IS
> KING. . . . [on] a large and equal representation.[6]

Thomas Jefferson fixed this untidy cluster into an innovation in human
governance in the Declaration of Independence when he announced that

> all men are created equal, that they are endowed by their Creator with certain un-
> alienable Rights, that among these, are Life, Liberty, and the pursuit of Happiness.
> That, to secure these rights, Governments are instituted among Men, deriving
> their just Powers from the consent of the governed.

The importance and impact of these documents meant neither that everyone agreed with Paine and Jefferson nor that such formulations would
be adopted without modification.[7] But they did influence the discursive
boundaries in which the new nation would operate. And in that context
the problem that the founders faced was in large measure a function of the
newness of their public vocabulary: their constitutive values as yet posed
no fixed or clear meanings. Accordingly, in the years between 1775 and
1778, the colonists who would constitute themselves as a nation engaged
complex and heated battles over the foundational meaning of the Revolution. Those debates centered on the relationship between three key terms:
"liberty" as the rights of freemen, "equality," and "property."

The Rights of Freemen

The first modification of Jefferson's declaration of natural rights philosophy concerned the phrase "all men." While many patriots, especially in
Boston, proclaimed "universal Freedom"[8] and the "sacred, unalienable
rights of man,"[9] most white Americans understood natural rights more
narrowly. Like the Maryland convention that ratified the constitution,
they believed only that "no *freeman* ought to be taken, imprisoned, or dis-
seized of his freehold, liberty, privileges or franchises, or outlawed or
exiled, or in any manner destroyed or deprived of his life, liberty or
property, but by the law of the land [our emphasis]."[10] Especially in the

South, but not exclusively there, one was likely to see the phrase "all free-men" rather than "all men." Twentieth-century readers interpret phrases such as "the rights of freemen" as inclusive of human beings. Such an interpretation, however, is anachronistic. When "A Whig" addressed the *Maryland Gazette* about the "defence of the invaluable rights of free citizens," he was not necessarily claiming that all citizens were free.[11] He was defending the rights of those who had already achieved freedom. When Anglo-Americans employed the term "freemen" they were carefully distinguishing between the rights that belonged to themselves and those applicable to the world of "others," including their own slaves.

Those who employed the term "freemen" did not explicitly justify its usage. The rationale underlying the distinction was implicit nonetheless in their public discourse. To begin with, the concept of freemen attached itself to the older notion of freeholders. Accordingly, on the basis of landholdings, it separated those who had rights in the community from those who did not. The colonists here applied the British notion of a "freeman" as one who was independent of others for life's sustenance, and who had thereby earned the right to an independent voice in community governance.[12]

Additionally, the concept of freemen derived from a heritage that portrayed life in community as a constitution of mutual interests. For the American colonists it extended backward in time to the Puritan belief in a covenanted body or to southern proprietary charters, both of which shared the assumption that the community should reflect the interests and concerns of the original body of persons who had staked a claim on the community. Hence, they specified and limited rights according to one's role in the community. Thus, for example, the Pennsylvania Declaration of Rights of 1776 held that "all government ought to be instituted and supported for the security and protection of the community as such, and to enable the individuals who compose it to enjoy their natural rights."[13] Marylanders extended the concept of freemen beyond property holders, but they still limited it to those within the community. Like the Virginians, they declared that "all men having sufficient evidence or permanent common interest with, and attachment to, the community, ought to have the right of suffrage."[14] It was not difficult to deny the Africans' "common interest" in the community, for slaves frequently ran away, and some of those few who had a chance to speak publicly expressed a strong desire to leave America and return to Africa.[15] The colonists further assured themselves that Africans were not part of the American community by augmenting such denials with vivid depictions of slave insurrections motivated by the desire for retaliation and retribution.[16]

The compact theory itself expressed the distinction between freemen and the slaves with whom they shared only an economic and minimal social relationship. It was clear that there had been no compact between Africans and white colonists, for Africans had been brought to North America against their will, and generally they did not participate in the compact forming discourse of the revolutionary and constitutional period.[17] Hence, the Maryland conventioneers could easily exclude blacks from civil rights when they proclaimed that the basis for the civil protection of rights rested in voluntary compact:

That there are certain natural rights of which men when they form a social compact cannot deprive or divest their posterity, among which are the enjoyment of life and liberty, with the means of acquiring, possessing and protecting, property, and pursuing and obtaining happiness and safety.[18]

Once again, to contemporary ears this distinction may seem odd. The colonists admitted the existence of natural rights but refused to guarantee those natural rights after compact. This assumption, however, served as a general principle, and it did not apply exclusively to Africans in America. The colonists did not believe that all natural rights could be transferred to a governed community. The North Carolina ratifying convention, for example, was assured that "[w]hen individuals enter into society, they give up some rights to secure the rest."[19] Repeatedly, those using compact theory as a rationale for revolution emphasized the necessity of sacrificing some rights in order to create a compact.

Moses Hemmenway, in a brilliantly progressive oration tortured by traditionalist concepts, expressed the limitations inherent to compacts, with regards to riches rather than race, in this manner: "Though the *natural rights* of men may, in general, seem much alike, they being, in this respect, 'all FREE and EQUAL'; yet it is in different degrees that they are permitted to use them."[20] In trying to minimize the permissible limitations, Eteocles likewise admitted the necessity of giving up certain natural rights: "In the formation of societies those natural rights alone are given up, or are afterwards subject to be taken from individuals, which in any manner impede, or do destroy the good and well being of the whole."[21] That slavery was necessary for the whole would eventually become a commonplace, but the colonists already used this warrant to limit a wide range of particular rights, including, most prominently, religious liberty. Consider Maryland as an example: a relatively liberal state on the religious issue, it guaranteed freedom of religion only to "all denominations of Christians within this state, whose members conduct themselves in a peaceable and orderly manner."[22] Other states not only discriminated against non-Christians but against Catholics as well. The Natural Rights announced by many colonists were, therefore, not identical to the universal rights that dominate twentieth-century American thought.

Observing the world around them, the colonists concluded that Natural Rights were typically conceded in compact because they were unstable and could not be fully preserved. They therefore assumed that the *securing* of one's natural rights was a function of earning them and passing them along to one's progeny. The public documents of the day consistently attested to the white colonists' belief that their own liberty had been so earned. Jonathan Mason repeated the creed when he proclaimed death "preferable to the yoke of bondage," and that "[a]s a reward for our exertions in the great cause of freedom, we are now in possession of those rights and privileges attendant upon the original state of nature, with the opportunity of establishing a government for ourselves."[23] In the South Rusticus declared any American "who would submit to drink of the bitter cup of slavery, and who would consent to be a father of slaves, is unworthy of manhood."[24] He went on explicitly to associate the willingness to be free to "a people" and "a race." In Boston, Peter Thacher similarly placed liberty on the basis of an earned, "racial" inheritance: "Descended from a race of hardy ancestors, who loved their freedom better than they loved their lives; the Americans are jealous of the least infringment of their rights."[25]

Not all Anglo-Americans truncated their commitment to Natural Rights in these ways. Claims about the rights of "every man" and "all men," in purer forms, were plentiful enough. So, for example, Rev. Isaac Backus was not alone in proclaiming that "the American revolution was built upon the principle that all men are born with an equal right to liberty and property."[26] Moreover, by the time the states ratified the Constitution, many Northerners elided the separation of the state of nature with that of the state of government. The split between the North and South on the scope of the rights of humanity would grow ever broader over time.[27] However, caution is required in interpreting these terms, regardless of the author's home state. Many universal phrases often accompanied more limiting claims elsewhere in the same text. Thus, a Marylander, writing to his representatives, seemed to speak universally when he urged, "In a free government it is the right of every individual in the community, at all times, to declare his sentiments on public affairs."[28] However, he not only limited the application of rights to those "in the community" but he also later specified his understanding of "every individual" by employing the term "freemen" in place of "all men." In like manner, Hemmenway, whose strict limitations on the concept of natural rights we cited above, began his oration by declaring the apparently universal sentiment that "God has called us to liberty. It is his declared will, that mankind should be free. . . . The law and light of nature make it evident that liberty is the right of all mankind."[29] Given the persistence and variety of limitations on such universal claims, we cannot assume that even those claims not explicitly truncated were intended and heard by the auditors in the universal way we hear them today.

Even after the Revolution, therefore, the American usage of Natural Rights held and articulated by large numbers of individuals was not a universally applied concept of universal natural rights. Anglo-Americans understood the state of nature as a jumping-off point from which, in compact, specific peoples would attempt to maintain as many of their natural rights as possible. As we shall see, some Anglo- and African-Americans chose the broadest possible range of rights to be preserved, but they clearly did not represent the consensus of colonial opinion. Indeed, as the new American nation faced the closing decades of the eighteenth century, the scope of natural rights doctrine was still being negotiated in the public discourse; and, at least for the time being, it was the compact-restricted version of natural rights that dominated public opinion.

Equality

Once the war with Britain began, a new and uniquely American term blossomed in Anglo-American public discourse. That term was "equality." It had made tentative appearances prior to the Declaration of Independence, but no sooner did the Revolution commence than it appeared almost everywhere in orations, political tracts, and newspapers throughout both the North and the South. Prior to the battles of Lexington and Concord, Liberty and Property served as the uncontested, constitutive values of the colonial world; subsequent to that event, however, the commitment to Equality edged its way into the public vocabulary.

Like Natural Rights, the word "equality" was not used initially in any broad or universal sense. Indeed, its most frequent usages varied by time and place. In the federal Constitutional Convention, the Equality between states occupied the delegates' attention.[30] In regions ravaged by divisions such as those between farmers and businessmen, rich and poor, and creditors and debtors, local newspapers emphasized Equal Taxes.[31] Such localized usages aside, there were two widespread usages of the word "equal": Equal Liberty and Equal Representation.[32]

Equal Liberty

The usage of the phrase Equal Liberty (or Equal Rights) was the same as that embedded in the Declaration of Independence and thus was understood solely in terms of the "certain unalienable Rights" endowed upon "all men." It was for this reason that the more concise phrase articulated in the Virginia Declaration of Rights, "equally free and independent," appeared more frequently in official documents throughout the states. In employing this usage, the colonists did not assume that all men were equal in all respects. In a society dominated by the talk of "ranks," such a notion would have been inconceivable.[33] For most of the colonists, it probably also did not then mean any kind of minimally shared abilities, either of intellect, morality, or physique. Garry Wills does exceptional work in tracing Jefferson's conception of equality to the Scottish commonsense philosophers, and in describing his belief that blacks were equal in moral ability to whites.[34] It is unlikely, however, that the colonists widely shared this conception for, as we will see, most Anglo-Americans expressed their belief in the moral depravity of Africans. Instead, Equal Liberty pertained to what the public rhetors called "self sovereignty."

According to the compact theory, all men were born equal in a state of nature. That is, outside of a compact, every person could do as they pleased because they had a natural sovereignty over their own actions. Others could act against them through force, but they had no rights over them. Hence, James Wilson claimed in the federal convention: "So each man is naturally a sovereign over himself, and all men are therefore naturally equal. Can he retain this equality when he becomes a member of civil Government? He can not."[35] This concept of self-sovereignty had a compelling persuasive force, for in the nation's founding it was precisely the experience of self-sovereignty that motivated the pioneers to demand equality through representation from the British.

Nonetheless, the usage of Equality to refer to a precompact self-sovereignty was, as Wilson's comments suggest, extremely minimalist in scope. It allowed the colonists to assume that Rights and Equality could be and would be sacrificed in social compact. The selection of those rights which were to survive the compact was inevitably controversial. Ultimately, the colonists employed several formulae. Jefferson's proposal, that the "inalienable rights" consisted of Life, Liberty, and the Pursuit of Happiness (i.e., Property) achieved the most popularity, but it was neither particularly far-reaching in scope nor adequately concrete. The guarantee of a right to Life was almost universally extended. Even slaves enjoyed this right, which distinguished them from mere animals, for even though some owners might occasionally kill their slaves without serious legal consequences, even the most vicious slave states legally extended the right to Life to their slaves.[36]

Although it may have been grounded in a substantial philosophical tradition, Jefferson's concept of "happiness" was inherently vague.[37] The colonists typically sought to protect property rather than happiness as an ultimate value, although having made this substitution they extended the meaning of property quite generally. Technically, even free blacks had legal protection for their property, though their inability to serve on juries or testify against whites made their property less than fully secure.[38] Slaves did not have the legal right to property, since it was not possible for property to own property.

The pivotal phrase was Equal Liberty. To this day, Americans have not yet worked out a full definition of "Ordered Liberty." As John Phillip Reid points out, the founders operated from a British notion of liberty based on the rule of law, not on a derivative list of individual rights.[39] However, after the Revolution, the colonists began to build a conception of Liberty based on individual rights. They clearly agreed on a certain range of liberties, including the right to a jury trial, free press, freedom from unreasonable searches, and freedom from standing armies.[40] They were less unanimous, however, on other Liberties, and it was only over time that they added broadly based Freedom of Speech and Religion to the consensual list of inalienable rights.

As we argue below, the exclusion of slaves from these liberties was determined by the fact that the colonists weighed the value of Property as of equal importance to Liberty. Given that Liberty itself was still entwined with the British notion of property as the first liberty, it is not too surprising that the rhetoric of Equal Liberty did not suffice to eliminate this form of property and to give Equal Liberty to the enslaved. The claim that free blacks should not share equal liberties, however, was more problematic. For reasons we will discuss later, Anglo-Americans excluded the free descendants of Africans from Equal Liberties because they did not perceive them as members of the community. They therefore felt no obligation to protect the Natural Rights of free blacks within the "compacted rights" of the community. This careful and discriminating set of usages became the legal framework of the nation when it was employed in the Bill of Rights, which reserved various rights "to the people," not to "all men."[41] The collective concept of "the people" made it possible to speak *generally* about individual rights without treating them as *universals*. In order to restrict the equal liberty of free blacks, one simply needed to exclude them from the domain of "the people."

Equal Representation

The second widespread usage of Equality was the claim to Equal Representation. If a government of Equal Liberties was the colonists' vision of the ideal society, Equal Representation was the agency for attaining it. After the Revolution, the emphasis on the phrase "no taxation without representation" shifted from a limited concern with taxation to the broader concern with all that representation could mean. As the constitutional ratification debates show, the colonists rested their position on the argument for representation.[42] It was through a representative government that the people would exercise their sovereignty in compact; and it was through representation that government would avoid tyranny. In order for this to occur, however, the colonists had to distinguish their government from the British government, where *virtual* representation existed side-by-side with tyranny. The pivot for this distinction was the concept of *Equal* Representation. According to the implicit doctrine of Equal Representation, legislators had the same interests as the colonists, and they therefore had no incentive to introduce tyrannical and unjust laws that would apply equally to themselves. This argument presumed that the number of representatives from each area would be an equitable portion of the whole, but it also assumed that "no distinctions" would be made between the governed and the governors. James Bowdoin, defending the new Constitution before the Massachusetts ratifying convention in 1788 argued that "Congress could not injure the rights of private citizens without injuring their own, as they must, in their public as well as private character, participate equally with others in the consequence of their own acts."[43]

If such sharing of interests was to be successful, there could be no hereditary distinctions. Hence it was that James Wilson of Pennsylvania answered the charge that the Constitution was aristocratic by describing the nature of an aristocratic government:

What is an aristocratic government? . . . the government of a few over the many—elected by themselves, or possessing a share in the government by inheritance, or in consequence of territorial rights, or some quality independent of the choice of the people. . . . What peculiar rights have been reserved to any class of men, on any occasion? . . . Have they made any particular provisions in favor of themselves, their relations, or their posterity? If they have committed their country to the demon of aristocracy, have they not committed themselves also, with every thing they held near and dear to them?[44]

Likewise, a Maryland "Constituent" sounded ultimately egalitarian when he praised "our constitution, every part of which inculcates the ideas of

equality, and general good" and "[a] constitution established on the principles of freedom and equality." However, the severe limitations on
eighteenth-century equality became clear when he specifically located the
nature of such equality in "[a] general assembly composed of freemen and
equals, not elevated above their constituents."[45] He further narrowed the
scope of Equality as he redeemed the limits on the constitutional rights of
"the people" by claiming that the representatives are "unprivileged by distinct personal rights or rank."

Proclaiming the death of hereditary aristocracy was one of the favorite
topics of those who sought to convince the state conventioneers to ratify
the Constitution.[46] Its importance is easy to underestimate today, given
that we take such a development for granted and know that titled nobility
was in some degree replaced by an aristocracy of wealth and narrowly defined merit.[47] This was, however, the first, clearest, and most immediately
influential usage of Equality presented by revolutionary America. The
concept it provided was applauded by Anglo-Americans and imitated
throughout Western Europe. There can be no doubt that it effected a major
stride in human freedom.

The death of hereditary rule, however, had serious implications for
chattel slavery, because the belief that no one possessed a hereditary right
to rule over others stood independent of social compact. As Thomas Paine
noted, "[T]he exalting [of] one man so greatly above the rest cannot be
justified on the equal rights of nature, so neither can it be defended on the
authority of scripture."[48] Even if the white colonists did not see themselves in a compact with Africans, to the extent that they admitted natural
equality, they invited an obvious comparison between the injustice they
suffered under British rule and the injustice they inflicted as slaveowners.[49]
The comparison of the political rulership of the British aristocracy to the
personal and economic rulership involved in slavery was not, however, a
matter of identical cases but only of potentially analogical ones.[50] Many
would deny the analogy on a variety of grounds, and for them there would
be no contradiction between Equal Representation and Slavery. Others,
however, accepted the analogy. It was only for this group that slavery contradicted the principles of the nation. Among this group, emancipation
was undertaken. Moses Hemmenway, for example, celebrated the end of
slavery in Massachusetts by declaring that "the interests of society require
subordination; but this deprives none of liberty . . . we rejoice to find that
the right of *enslaving* our fellow men is absolutely disclaimed."[51] Similar
sentiments led the delegates of almost every Northern ratifying convention to use slavery and the slave trade as a political weapon against the

South. Consider the measured words of Gouverneur Morris as he declared against the possibility that,

the inhabitant of Georgia and S.C. who goes to the Coast of Africa, and in defiance of the most sacred laws of humanity tears away his fellow creatures from their dearest connections & damns them to the most cruel bondages, shall have more votes in a Govt. instituted for protection of the rights of mankind, than the Citizen of Pa. or N.J. who views with a laudable horror, so nefarious a practice.[52]

This relatively narrow concept of human equality, based in the absence of a hereditary right to rule, led to gradual abolition in all the Northern states, beginning with Vermont in 1777, and then following in Massachusetts, New Hampshire, Pennsylvania, and the others. The process was slow and painful. As a number of historians have pointed out, the determining factor was not a superior morality in those states which enacted emancipation statutes.[53]

Three primary factors influenced the white residents of different states in their acceptance or rejection of the analogy between heritable political rule and heritable chattle slavery. First, the states had long featured different degrees of egalitarianism in their discourse. Those states with the most slaves had been the most careful to avoid employing unqualified usages of terms such as "human rights" and "equality." Therefore, the commitment to universal rights achieved greatest salience in nonslave states. Sadly, then, those states least in need of a countervailing force to slavery were precisely the ones most likely to evidence it. The behavior of the slave states was thus not inconsistent with their adoption of the language of universal rights, for they simply never dedicated themselves to it in the first place. At most they had adopted a "compact rights" doctrine for "freemen," not for "all men."[54] There is an error, therefore, in attributing moral consistency to the Northerners who urged emancipation, and moral inconsistency to the Southern advocates of slavery. In the face of the Revolution, and in large measure because of the local presence or absence of slavery, Northern and Southern states had already adopted different moral codes.

The second factor conditioning the rejection of the analogy between hereditary political rule and hereditary enslavement was the fact that the choice between slavery and emancipation was not a simple domestic matter, especially as it derived from the natural rights doctrine of self-sovereignty. The choice was between serving the country's interests by enslaving foreigners, or violating the interests of one's country in favor of the rights of foreign individuals. This is still a moral choice, to be sure, but it is of an entirely different order than the relatively simple tension between "self-interest" and the admonition to "love thy neighbor." To this day, many national leaders and citizens hold that morality stops at national boundaries. Slaveholders thus would be guilty only of placing national interest over foreign rights. And in this context, John Rutledge's principle, that "Religion & humanity had nothing to do with this question—Interest alone is the governing principle with Nations," is a value proposition that continues to hold sway in our own era.[55]

Finally, even given a combination of the strongest possible formulation of the natural rights doctrine, and an obligation to Equal Liberty and Equal Representation in compact, slaveholding did not conflict with the principles of the Revolution *taken as a whole*. As in the prerevolutionary period, Equality and Liberty were not the only important principles constituting the national community and guiding collective action. The commitment to Property continued as a moral imperative in its own right, and as such it justified the continued holding of slaves. In those states where the property value of slaves was high, the constitutive status of Property had great enough salience to block the analogy between chattel slavery and hereditary political rulership.

Statements proclaiming hereditary rule to be immoral, therefore, had relatively little import for the institution of slavery. They did not entail a logically necessary identification between political rule and chattel slavery. An analogy between the two was possible, but the array of other values was such that it was likely to be persuasive only where the longstanding practice of slavery had not already shaped the values of the rhetorical culture. The legitimacy of slavery was further entailed by other characteristics of the constitutive value of Property.

Property

Although some scholars have duly noted the dominance of the value of Property in the discourse of the American Revolution, it is worth emphasizing again, for it is repeatedly lost in descriptions of America's earliest sociopolitical foundations.[56] Following the Declaration of Independence, the commitment to Equality joined the colonists' prerevolutionary fervor for Liberty and Property, but it never abated that zeal. The delegates at the federal Constitutional Convention exhibited a startling preference for Property over all else. Gouverneur Morris, John Rutledge, Pierce Butler, and Rufus King all proclaimed property as "the primary object of Society," and other delegates at least agreed that it ought to be directly represented in the government, especially through the Senate.[57] The delegates also urged property qualifications for suffrage and for officeholding. In the end, they agreed to apportion representation to the states based on population rather than wealth, but only because the former served as an expedient index of a state's wealth.[58] The claim that property should be directly represented in government reappeared in the *Federalist Papers* in muted form, but it virtually disappeared in the debates held before the various state ratifying conventions.[59] In moving from the federal Constitutional Convention to the state conventions, Property was gradually sublated, but it by no means vanished or lost its force.

The concern for Property had serious implications for the concept of Equal Representation. The delegates who identified Property as the radical foundation of society also maintained that the primary purpose of government was to protect property, not individual liberties. Their experiences with paper money, creditor-debtor conflicts, and armed rebellions led them to fear the threat that equal representation posed to the security of their property, and so they argued against it vociferously.[60] James Madison put the issue most succinctly:

An increase of population will of necessity increase the proportion of those who will labour under all the hardships of life, & secretly sigh for a more equal distribution of its blessings. These may in time outnumber those who are placed above the feelings of indigence. According to the equal laws of suffrage, the power will slide into the hands of the former. No agrarian attempts have yet been made in this Country, but symptoms of a leveling spirit, as we have understood, have sufficiently appeared in a certain quarters [sic] to give notice of the future danger.[61]

The issue of protecting Property aside, the majority of speakers in the federal convention declared a deep suspicion for the judgment and abilities of the common person. Most declared themselves in favor of the upper classes who had access to university training or who had demonstrated their merit through the acquisition of wealth.[62] John Dickinson, for example, wished "the Senate to consist of the most distinguished characters, distinguished for their rank in life and their weight of property, and bearing as strong a likeness to the British House of Lords as possible."[63] George Mason, Edmund Randolph, Pierce Butler, John Rutledge, and Charles Pinckney all joined Elbridge Gerry when he exclaimed that the "evils we experience flow from the excess of democracy," and that the people should not elect their governors because "the representation would not be equally good if the people chose them."[64] He likewise expressed a widely shared opinion among the elite framers when he declared that "the people will be imposed on by corrupt and unworthy men."[65] James Madison, William Paterson, Wilson, and a few others were more moderate, insisting on the importance of government by the people, but on the whole the Constitutional Convention was a Property-loving group that did not trust the common people.[66]

There can be little doubt that the value of Property survived the convention and that the framers successfully wove it into the very fabric of the Constitution. However, it faced a serious contest in the ratification process which limited the scope of its influence. Both the love of property and the opposition to it found vivid expression in the state conventions of New York, Massachusetts, and Pennsylvania as well as in the popular press. Aristocratic protectors of Property spoke in the Northern conventions and dominated the Southern ones. New Yorkers echoed the federal convention when they proclaimed that "the people . . . could not know their own good" because they did not have the "discernment and stability necessary for systematic government."[67] The defense of ordinary people, however, was much stronger at the state level and, unlike the proceedings of the federal convention, we find a clearly articulated class hostility against the rich. John Coffin Jones of Boston defended the commoners from the aspersions cast by the wealthy conventioneers, arguing that "the people of the United States are an enlightened, well-informed people, and are, therefore, not easily imposed on by designing men."[68] The Honorable Amos Singletary, representing the nay-saying spirit of the County of Worcestor (which voted 43–8 against the new Constitution) proclaimed:

These lawyers, and men of learning, and moneyed men, that talk so finely, and gloss over matters so smoothly, to make us poor illiterate people swallow down the pill, expect to get into Congress themselves; they expect to be the managers of this Constitution, and get all the power and all the money into their own hands, and then they will swallow up all us little folks, like the great *Leviathan*, Mr. President; yes, just as the whale swallowed up *Jonah*. This is what I am afraid of; but I won't say any more at present.[69]

M. Smith likewise recognized the class differences in appealing to the New Yorkers for a house large enough to encompass several types of representatives:

The knowledge necessary for the representative of a free people not only comprehends extensive political and commercial information, such as is acquired by men of refined education, who have leisure to attain to high degrees of improvement, but it should also comprehend that kind of acquaintance with the common concerns and occupations of the people, which men of the middling class of life are, in general, more competent to than those of a superior class.[70]

Back and forth, the New Yorkers debated the merits and vices of the rich.[71] In general, the Anti-Federalists expressed hostility to the aristocracy of wealth, but Property was of interest to these middling sorts as well. The question was not so much whether one was for Property or against it, but how *directly* Property was to be represented in the Constitution.[72]

The conflict between those who would make Property more central and those who would make persons supreme resolved itself into a workable form of government through three major compromises. First, at least until the Bill of Rights, no explicit recognition of peculiar powers or rights devolving from individual Property found expression in the Constitution.[73] The principle of representation by persons, not Property, was established. However, in charting the development of arguments in the debates it becomes clear that the elimination of references to Property qualifications occurred only because of the compromise that had to be wrought between the large and small states.[74] In reshaping the discussion to emphasize "which state" should be represented, rather than "who" should be represented, the delegates placed suffrage requirements in the hands of the states. And in the short term, at least, this allowed property interests to influence elections.

The transformation of an aristocracy of wealth into one of "merit" served as the second accommodation to property. It was easy to reject government by the rich, but much harder to oppose government where "personal merit alone could be the ground of political exaltation."[75] It is fascinating to trace the debates in the Constitutional Convention and to see how the delegates who began by talking about government as designed for the protection of Property gradually came around to Madison's and Mason's way of phrasing the desired quality as one of "ability." Madison managed to link the economically "Superior Orders" with those who were most "able." He did this by arguing for a property qualification for the Senate, and then suggesting that "the Senate is to consist in its proceeding with more coolness, with more system, & with more wisdom, than the popular branch."[76] By simple repetition, the phrase "wealth and ability" established and reflected the assumption that wealth led inexorably to ability. Slowly, throughout the colonies, the skills necessary to effect virtuous and successful governance became defined as those the rich could most easily achieve, including a college education, status as a lawyer, elite church membership, and leisure for extensive reading. In political satire directed against popular participation in politics, for example, Aesop lamented to Solon and Lycurgus:

In our days it was thought necessary to prepare oneself by a course of study to go about that kind of business; but there's nothing of that sort there; no, nothing is more necessary than just sufficient instruction to enable them to read a newspaper, and to write their names; they are then qualified to enter the lists as orators, and legislators.[77]

Likewise, Morris urged the exclusion of Westerners from governing rights because of their inherent incapacities. As he noted, "the Busy haunts of men not the remote wilderness, [is] the proper School of political Talents."[78]

The men of Property represented in the Convention thus inserted an aristocratic component into the Constitution without specifically naming it as such.[79] Instead, they employed cultural warrants to specify that the "best men" should rule, and then defined men of Property as "the best men." The concept that legislators should reproduce an accurate "picture of the people," being truly "representative" of that people, was tamed by a view of legislation as a trainable skill.

The third accommodation was the compromise on slavery. Property survived as a central Constitutional value, but not in the direct forms sought by the aristocrats who wrote it. The form was direct enough, however, to provide protection for slavery.[80] In every case where emancipationists appealed to the doctrine of rights as the grounds for abolishing slavery, the slaveholders responded with the equal and opposite national doctrine of Property. The mainstream discourse clearly indicates no doubt that slave owners had acted as purchasers when they took on the position of master, and as such they expected their slave property to be protected. General Charles Coatesworth Pinckney's famous lines went without refutation: "[P]roperty in slaves should not be exposed to danger under a Govt. instituted for the protection of property."[81] Indeed, we find these words echoed and accepted by the delegates at the Northern state ratifying conventions who indicated that "[i]t would not do to abolish slavery, by an act of Congress, in a moment, and so destroy what our southern brethren consider as property."[82]

The belief that slaves were Property found daily expression in newspaper ads: "RAN away from Mr. William Young, of Baltimore-town, an African negro man named Tom, the property of the subscriber."[83] As Robinson points out, this argument served as a significant brake to abolition in the North.[84] Wherever legislators were responsible for abolition, there was also always an insistence on formulating a plan to compensate the owners. And therein lies the ultimate reason why even men like Thomas Jefferson, John Jay, and Patrick Henry could not find their own way out of slavery. Each testified to the value of the economic interest they had in slaves as a value equivalent to that of justice.

This can, however, be made too simple. Southerners and Northerners alike recognized that slaves were people as well as property. Newspaper ads explicitly offered "men, women, and children" for sale to their readers.[85] The fact that slaves were treated as both human persons and Property was formalized in the "three-fifths compromise" explicitly defended by Alexander Hamilton in *Federalist* #54 where he argued that "we must deny the fact, that slaves are considered merely as property, and in no respect whatever as persons. The true state of the case is, that they partake of both of these qualities: being considered by our laws, in some respects, as persons, and in other respects as property."[86] This led James Madison to the infamous passage declaring that the "compromising expedient of the Constitution be mutually adopted, which regards them as inhabitants, but as debased by servitude below the equal level of free inhabitants; which regards the *slave* as divested of two-fifths of the *man*."[87] Madison carefully described how the slaves were "born equal" but deprived by the actions of the slave owners of that which made them fully human.

The true Anglo-American contradiction, therefore, did not rest in an inconsistency between actions and values nor between the terms Liberty and Equality. It rested, instead, in the belief that people could live under both the signs of property and humanity.[88] Locating the contradiction in this fashion explains a great deal. The typical account of the postrevolutionary period suggests that the spirit for human rights initially ran high and thus motivated passionate attitudes in favor of the liberation of the slaves. According to this story line, the Northwest Ordinance, Northern emancipation bills, and Southern antislave trade limitations all emerged in the first flush of revolutionary egalitarianism. In the end, however, it is presumed that this spirit died out as Americans went about their business, including that of tending to their slaves.

The extant records would seem to encourage this narrative. In Northern states almost all of the ratifying conventions contained tirades against the slave trade. Meanwhile, the Southern states went along with the abolition of the slave trade with little protest. More strikingly, they had themselves largely eliminated the foreign trade, and several Southern leaders expressed the hope that slavery would gradually die out.[89] Further, in the 1780s, the number of slaves emancipated by private owners in Virginia was larger than all of the slaves emancipated in all the Northern states in the postrevolutionary years.

Despite such impressive documentation, this tale assumes an original and pure fervor for equality that gradually died out. This account misses too much, precisely because it assumes that the primary motivating force of antislavery sentiment was a simple incompatibility between slavery and human rights. Instead, from the very beginning, the most widespread sentiment in public discourse throughout the nation was for the elimination of slavery *only insofar as it did not violate the rights of property*. Northern states were capable of compensating owners for the small amounts of Property they held in slaves, so they willingly and actively promoted emancipation in their own states. Ironically, however, this practice conceded the status of slaves as property and thereby virtually guaranteed that slavery would never be extinguished. The humanitarian hope that "[s]lavery in time will not be a speck in our Country," because "although slavery is not smitten by an apoplexy, yet it has received a mortal wound, and will die of consumption," was ill-founded.[90] The values that the Anglo-American framers of the Constitution embraced put them on a course that would abolish enslavement only when to do so did not violate Property rights. Once the new nation achieved that accomplishment, the antislavery sentiment motivated by the extremely limited notions of Equality and Natural Rights born of the Revolution had expanded as far as it could.[91]

ENACTING THE ANGLO-AMERICAN CONSTITUTION

In retrospect, it is fairly easy to understand how the development of the Anglo-American Constitution, predicated on the rights of Freemen, Property, and minimal Equality, moved the new nation from revolution to civil war. The story is familiar and often told. Northern and Southern states agreed to participate in a common government by shifting the concern for the Equal Representation of individuals to the Equal Representation of states, and by limiting Equal Liberty to the members of the compacting race.[92] As the economies of the North and the South diverged, greater conflicts arose between them, and, as abolitionists sought to promote the commitment to Equal Representation over the commitment to Property, the secession much prophesied in the ratifying conventions became a reality.[93]

This story is largely correct, but it misses both a major phase of America's history and a major facet of the relationship between the nation's white and black peoples. As abolition in the North and emancipation in the South moved forward at the dawn of the nineteenth century, the Europeans-turned-Americans faced a serious problem. There was an increasing number of free blacks within the nation's boundaries. Even where the limited doctrine of Equal Rights did not conflict with Property rights in slaves, the minimalist commitment to equality could not fully accommodate the presence of free African-Americans. The doctrine that prevented hereditary rule of one person by another did not entail that all peoples be required to protect all of the rights of other peoples, and the Anglo-Americans did not otherwise feel compelled to compact with the descendants of Africans. Anglo-Americans therefore did not know how to live together with free blacks. Legislators in free states such as Ohio and Pennsylvania attempted to prevent or minimize the problem by prohibiting or severely restricting the migration of free blacks into their borders.

Likewise, many Southern states passed laws prohibiting the emancipation of slaves without their exportation beyond the state's border. Where state officials failed to act, many white citizens refused to employ, to trade with, or to rent to free blacks.[94] Additionally, mobs of angry whites resorted to violence, as in city after city they beat free blacks with clubs and burned their homes.[95]

The adherents of Equal Liberty faced a growing challenge for which they were ill prepared: there was rapidly and increasingly no place for the freed Africans in America.

One People

To wish for Equal Rights and Representation for freed Africans and then to drive them from your midst would seem to be contradictory behaviors. Such dissonance, however, was not felt by nineteenth-century Anglo-Americans, who convinced themselves that Africans in America lived outside the social compact and could not be made a part of it, even upon emancipation. To understand the strength and source of this conviction one must remember that, in uniting as a national political unit, white Americans had provisionally overcome many severe conflicts and had been able to reach compromises because they identified themselves as one people. The federal Constitution formally justified the point by proudly proclaiming its authorship as "We the People," but the claim was forcefully and ritualistically repeated throughout the early national period in public speeches and pamphlets that repeatedly praised "the people" at work. As Edmund Pendleton put it in the Virginia ratification debates, "The happiness of the people is the object of this government, and the people are therefore made the fountain of all power."[96]

The colonists believed that the effectiveness of the people relied upon homogeneity and stability. They referred repeatedly to the "fixt genious" of the people, describing an underlying character that demanded certain forms of government.[97] This sentiment derived, in part, from the belief that government should be for a "common good" defined by shared values such as "industry, frugality, humility, piety, honesty, [and] charity."[98] Underneath the minimalist talk of rights, white Northern colonists were tightly knit and heavily interdependent. William Tudor expressed the sentiment in his Boston Massacre Oration in 1779 as he referred to "the origin of civil society, which, founded in reciprocal advantage, and begun in social virtue, on the mutual necessities and mutual assistance of individuals, built the combined happiness of the community."[99]

The colonists saw a great deal at stake here. The comparison of their own lives and government to those in other portions of the globe suggested that the ability to maintain a representative government was rare. As Phillip Payson warned in his election sermon of 1778, civil liberty "admits of different degrees, nearly proportioned to the morals, capacity, and principles of a people, and the mode of government they adopt; for, like the enjoyment of other blessings, it supposes an aptitude or taste in the possessor."[100] The admission of aliens into the community, with their different capacities and principles, threatened the community's ability to insure its own liberty or to preserve its property.

The two key elements of commonality that the colonists perceived as necessary for a fruitful compact were Christianity and European bloodlines. Thomas Paine delimited the community when he declared in *Common Sense* that "we claim brotherhood with every European Christian, and triumph in the generosity of the sentiment."[101] He was probably defining a broader community than any experienced by humankind before, but it was still not broad enough to take into consideration those of African descent.

Religious and moral grounds provided the first line of demarcation. The Maryland House of Delegates resolved "that it is the opinion of this house, that the happiness of the people, and the good order and preservation of civil government, depend upon morality, religion, and piety; and that these cannot be generally diffused through a community but by the *public* worship of Almighty God."[102] Colonel Jones was even more specific, explaining to the Ratification Convention of Massachusetts that "a person could not be a good man without being a good Christian."[103]

As much recent scholarship shows, enslaved African-Americans maintained many of their own religions, and many of the religious customs they practiced diverged dramatically from those of white Christians.[104] Many African religions, for example, were polytheistic, and even where Africans worshipped a single deity, it was often a Muslim God that they sanctified. Additionally, Africans typically worshipped their gods through highly self-expressive dance and music, such as in the ritualistic "ring shout."[105] America's white, European colonists typically thought of dance as sacrilegious and often condemned their slaves for "profaning the Sabbath."[106] Many important social customs also differed. The colonists railed against bigamy because it "disturbs the order which is wisely established in every christian country," but it was nevertheless a legitimate marriage practice for some Africans.[107] The colonists took such religious deviations seriously, going so far in some instances as to prescribe the death penalty for a third offense of blasphemy.[108]

The second line of demarcation was the European bloodline. The public discourse is clear in suggesting that white Americans simply refused to enter a social compact with those they could not identify as blood brethren. In debating the role of Western states in the new government, many of the delegates to the federal convention seemed to view even these white inhabitants as "other" and, therefore, to be put under different rules to insure their subordination to the original states. Only George Mason's ability to represent the future settlers as "brethren," literally the children and grandchildren of the delegates, forestalled this discrimination against white settlers.[109] Mason's appeal to family worked because the colonists had become accustomed to the importance of family ties in holding governments together in their own local communities.[110] They thus could imagine the bloodlines linking them to Western settlers. Such an analogy simply could not work with Africans, for their black skin made it impossible for the colonists to imagine them as blood brethren.

Finally, the colonists were averse to giving citizenship to those with "foreign habits opinions & attachments."[111] Africans in America clearly were foreigners, and they retained their strangeness, in part, because they actively strove to maintain as much of their own culture as possible. Additionally, of course, the continuation of their alienation was forced upon them by virtue of their systematic exclusion from the Anglo-American communities in which they resided.

Anglo-Americans thus conceived the people as a narrow, relatively homogeneous group who shared a common religious orientation as well as values, customs, and language. White European-Americans routinely used the first-person pronoun in talking about their government, directly excluding Africans from their usage: "[W]e do not admit with the writer, that America is as much the country of the blacks, bond or free, as it is ours."[112] Congress debated the issue in 1820. Although some representatives defended blacks as "part of the people,"[113] the voice that gained the greatest adherence claimed "[t]hat the Constitution of the United States was framed by the States respectively, consisting of the European descendants of white men; that it had a view to the liberty and rights of white men."[114] Although the technical outcome of the debate was "compromise," Charles Pinckney solidified the position that was to dominate the public vocabulary and state actions for the next forty years by placing the issue on constitutional grounds when he testified to Congress as the author of the portions of the Constitution on citizenship: "I perfectly knew that there did not exist such a thing as a black or colored citizen, nor could I have conceived it possible such a thing could ever have existed."[115]

The definitive hearing in the Supreme Court did not come until the *Dred Scott* v. *Sandford* decision in 1857, but at that time the Court certified the legislative record, finding that the U.S. Constitution was an exclusively Anglo-American document. Today, with our post–Civil War values, that decision sounds outrageous. At the time, however, Justice Taney's majority opinion merely recounted a pervasive public vocabulary:

The words "people of the United States" and "citizens" are synonymous terms, and mean the same thing. They both describe the political body who, according to our republican institutions, form the sovereignty, and who hold the power and conduct the Government through their representatives. . . . The question is simply this: Can a negro, whose ancestors were imported into this country, and sold as slaves, become a member of the political community formed and brought into existence by the Constitution of the United States, and as such become entitled to all the rights, and privileges, and immunities, guaranteed by that instrument to the citizen? . . . We think they are not, and that they are not included, and were not intended to be included, under the word "citizens" in the Constitution, and can therefore, claim none of the rights and privileges which that instrument provides for and secures to the citizens of the United States.[116]

To transcend this narrow "we," or to change it to a plural "peoples," required a new and broader concept of Equality than the minimalist one with which postrevolutionary society came equipped. Indeed, America's concept of equality was so minimal at this point that it could not even guarantee amity between rich and poor, Catholic and Protestant, Irish and English, or the Western territories and Eastern states.[117]

The Anglo-Americans committed to Equal Rights thus faced a grave problem with regard to free blacks: they were unwilling to enslave them, and equally unwilling to admit them to the "body of the people."[118] The problem of abstract ideals became increasingly serious as Americans lived out their new found creed. As the Northern states made emancipation mandatory, and as substantial numbers of Southerners voluntarily chose Liberty over Property, the population of free blacks in America rapidly became a substantial portion of the inhabitants, increasing from 7.9 percent (59,557) in 1790 to 13.5 percent (186,446) in 1810.[119] Not only did whites refuse to absorb these free blacks into their political community, they also despised them and forced them into poverty by refusing to share land or work with them.[120] The resulting pragmatic burdens intensified the social and political costs. Whites refused to share suffrage with blacks and gradually increased their discrimination against them in a variety of domains, including housing, education, and the use of public facilities. As one contemporary observer commented, it created "the anomaly in a republican government of a class of freemen enjoying none of the privileges and advantages of freedom."[121] To remove the contradiction from their midst, whites turned to colonization.

African Colonization

The move to colonize free blacks in Africa has not received adequate attention in our national histories. When it is treated at all, the African colonization movement is depicted as a minor and temporary aberration, extraneous to the ideas and history of the United States and, therefore, destined to failure. This is understandable given that from our contemporary perspective the very idea of expatriation is a national embarrassment. The colonization movement, however, was not an aberration but rather an inherent and enduring outcome of the principles encoded in the Anglo-American Constitution. Historians usually portray the heyday of colonization as lasting from 1820 to 1830, at which time abolitionism became prominent.[122] This grossly underestimates the influence and popularity of the American Colonization Society and the solution it offered to America's race problem. It is true that after the mid-1830s the fervor for colonization declined among abolitionists, but it is not true that such a decline took place among the general populace, where wide sentiment for colonization was weak only during the 1840s. The colonizationist solution had considerable status in the 1850s, and a number of influential national leaders, including Abraham Lincoln, gave it serious consideration well into the Civil War.[123]

Although abolitionism overshadowed colonization after the 1850s, prior to that time it garnered *national* support in a way the abolition societies never did. Its presence as a public issue dominated the magazines or weeklies of the period, second in frequency only to discussions of the slave trade. Further, the majority of states passed resolutions in support of the Colonization Society's efforts, and some even funded it. Indeed, whether for or against the American Colonization Society, contemporary public documents throughout the pre–Civil War years are consistently clear in their depiction of colonization as a popular and viable alternative to the "extremes" of slavery and unrestrained emancipation.[124]

The idea that African slaves should be returned to Africa upon emancipation occurred most visibly during the eighteenth century in the 1781 writings of Thomas Jefferson on emancipation.[125] But as Early Lee Fox notes, "The idea of colonization of the negro sprung full grown from the brain of no individual. Henry Clay thought it was the product, not of the minds of men, but of the very requirement of the times, because it was 'an obvious remedy'."[126]

The idea was institutionalized on 1 January 1817, when the American Society for Colonizing the Free People of Colour of the United States was formed in Washington City. The Society was immediately active. By January 14, it had presented a memorial to Congress, requesting national support for the their objectives.[127] The House Committee responded favorably in February, asking the president to negotiate with Great Britain to employ Sierra Leone as a colonization site.[128] The Society engaged agencies and local committees all over the country but especially in the middle states. According to Fox, it was never very popular in South Carolina or Georgia, but otherwise it had widespread support.[129] Slave state newspapers gave positive support to the Society,[130] and although it never received direct financial support from the federal government, it did receive a range of support from state governments, including legislative commendations and small amounts of financial aid.[131]

The Society and its supporters expressed the basic dilemma of race relations in the period. They did not want slavery, and they did not want to share Equal Liberty with free blacks. The Society has been and was then castigated for insincerity about its desire to end slavery. Its opponents and deprecators charged that its hidden goal was to make slavery a safer institution by removing those who threatened it and constituting them as a group that was neither a fully oppressed "them" nor a self-interested "us."[132] While it is clear that some segments of the populace supported it for this reason, the Society included large numbers of people whose opposition to slavery was sincere. Officially, the Society declared that "the hope of the gradual and utter abolition of slavery, in a manner consistent with the rights, interests, and happiness of society, ought never to be abandoned."[133] Moreover, the tone of its opposition to slavery conveyed its sincerity. In their memorial to Congress they said, "Your memorialists cannot believe that such an evil, universally acknowledged and deprecated, has been irremoveably fixed upon us."[134] Henry Clay, the most prominent of the Society's spokespersons, referred to slavery as the "deepest stain" and a "foul blot" on the land, even though such language was likely to alienate potential supporters in the South.[135] In fact, as the 1823 annual report of the New York auxiliary indicates, Society members frequently conceived of colonization as a method for emancipation: "To this country it offers the only possible means of gradually ridding ourselves of a mighty evil, and of obliterating the foulest stain upon our nation's honor."[136]

Although they wanted to eliminate slavery and even saw colonization as a means to that end, those who supported the Colonization Society did not want to live with free blacks. Their reactions indicate a great deal about the long-term problems of Anglo- and Afro-Americans outside the limited issue of slavery. The response of Anglo-Americans to the possibility of coexistence with free blacks was gutteral, clearly not grounded in any kind of reason. They claimed both interest in the good of blacks and the knowledge of "experience," but they spoke their real purpose in a dim inarticulate appeal to "necessity" that today we would label as blatant racism.

The claim that took up the greatest part of the Society's argumentation was that colonization represented the best interests of free blacks. The Society first catalogued the evils faced by free blacks in America and did so quite accurately, noting "their anamolous and indefinite relations to the political institutions and social ties of the community" and the "deprivation of most of those independent, political, and social rights so indispensable to the progressive amelioration of our nature."[137] By contrast, they argued that Africa "offers an asylum in the land of their fathers, where they may stand forth in the character of men, and enjoy the rights and privileges of freemen."[138] The Society insisted that in the United States a free black was bound to be a "felon or a pauper."[139] In Henry Clay's words, "[T]hey are [here] in the lowest state of social gradation: aliens—political, moral, social aliens—strangers though natives. There, they would be in the midst of their friends and their kindred, at home."[140] These arguments were joined by the claim that colonization would be good for the continent of Africa itself, as returning blacks would bring with them "the orient star" of civilization, Christianity, and enlightenment.[141]

While advocates touted colonization as good for free blacks, they depicted it as "a necessity" for Anglo-America.[142] The deep emotions arousing this necessity are evident in Robert G. Harper's description of the "mark" of Africans which "make us recoil in horror from the idea of an intimate union with the free blacks, and *precludes the possibility of such a state of equality, between them and us, as alone could make us one people.*"[143] The colonizationists incessantly repeated the insurmountability and irreparability of racial prejudice that "in this country, must ever keep them inferior and degraded members of society."[144]

This was clearly racial prejudice, but it was not the vicious form of white supremacy that would emerge in the postreconstruction era. While some supporters of colonization described blacks as less intelligent than whites and emphasized their alleged inferiority, the Society itself officially characterized blacks as industrious and intelligent. Of course, in order to make colonization seem workable, they had to do so. Instead of basing perceptions of inferiority on race, they ascribed the "degradation" of blacks to those circumstances deliberately engineered by whites. They suggested that,

debased as the blacks are but too generally among ourselves,—their misfortune and not their fault,—the most ignorant and humble of them were capable of becoming, under favorable circumstances, intelligent, industrious and competent, in every point of view, for all the offices of an independent, social and civil community.[145]

An elaborate ideology of inherent racial inferiority was already in the making. This discourse indicates, however, that *the mere fact of difference,* without any explicit hierarchicalization, was adequate as a grounds for separation.

Repeatedly, white colonists emphasized the heterogeneity of blacks and whites as an adequate reason for their prejudice. The General Assembly of the Presbyterian Church put it this way: "In the distinctive and indelible marks of their colour and the prejudices of the people, an insurmountable obstacle has been placed to the execution of any plan for elevating their character and placing them on a footing with their brethren of the same common family."[146] It was toward the same end that Henry Clay emphasized the goal of colonization "to accomplish the desireable objects of domestic tranquillity, and render us one *homogeneous* people."[147]

The prejudice against the existence of "two incongruous portions" of the population was charged by fear.[148] The Society's director cited "[t]he alarming danger of cherishing in our bosom a distinct nation, which can never become incorporated with us, while it rapidly increases in numbers, and improves in intelligence; learning from us the arts of peace and war."[149] Congress itself took up this concern, refusing to provide territory for colonization on the North American continent for fear that, "should the colony so increase to become a nation, it is not difficult to foresee the quarrels and destructive wars which would ensue, especially if the slavery of people of color should continue, and accompany the whites in their migrations."[150] This attitude emerged, in part, as the product of a guilty conscience, but it was also rooted in a long-standing fear of slave insurrections. Ultimately, however, it represented a desire for racial dominance. Clay joined congressional memorialists in leading their reports with numerical accounts of the growth of the Anglo-American population: "What is the true nature of the evil of the existence of a portion of the African race in our population? It is not that there are *some,* but that there are so *many* among us of a different caste, of a different physical, if not moral constitution, who never can amalgamate with the great body of our population."[151] In 1839 he argued, "In the slave States the alternative is, that the white man must govern the black, or the black govern the white."[152] The colonizationists, like most other Anglo-Americans, were not being inauthentic; they simply had no ability to conceive of Africans as anything other than an unalloyable "other." Given their perception, they felt bound by compact to protect the national interest.

As many of the quotations above indicate, this "otherness" was grounded largely in sheer color. However, there was an additional complication. As some colonizationists argued, slavery itself had become part of the cause. Anglo-Americans could not see blacks as equals without imagining the possibility of their own enslavement. In Harper's words:

These persons are condemned to a state of hopeless inferiority and degradation, by their color; which is an indelible mark of their origin and former condition, and establishes an impassable barrier between them and the whites. This barrier is closed forever by our habits and our feelings.[153]

Slavery and racism thus solidified each other into permanence. Slavery could not be eliminated without creating a free African-American population that Anglo-Americans considered intolerable. Anglo-Americans could not revise their estimates of Africans as long as they remained in bondage.

Had colonization succeeded, there is reason to believe that the minimalist interpretation of equality as equal liberty might have survived, and white Americans might yet today be unable to conceive of a community that encompassed racial difference. Yet, as we know, colonization failed. There were several widely agreed upon reasons for that failure. The Society faced problems of corruption, but, beyond that, the very mission itself was impossible, for America's African slaves had already become African-Americans. The tremendous cost of the Atlantic passage had been justified originally because Africans had been brought to North America as profit-producing property, and they had been brought in profitable but inhumane conditions. Anglo-America had already declared its valuation of Property as higher than that of the rights of Africans.[154] Hence, the only thing that could have justified the enormous cost of expatriation would have been an equally profitable commercial end, and that did not exist.[155]

Transportation costs were not the only barrier. The local diseases and hostile tribes of African brought death and destruction to the emigres, as over 50 percent of the colonists died each year. This death rate reasonably paralyzed much support for colonization. Finally, and most important, while the African-American community lacked a consensus concerning the desirability of colonization, it expressed a unified hostility to the efforts of Anglo-Americans to initiate the process of expatriation.

By 1827 the issue of race relations in America had become peculiarly difficult because the existence of slavery added a special intensity to racial prejudice that could only be overcome by the abolition of slavery. However, even beyond the issue of slavery, the U.S. Constitution was ultimately incapable of dealing with the race issue. The extant array of public values left African-Americans and Anglo-Americans no way to live together as "Americans." These essentially Anglo-American values granted rights only to freemen, those persons who, if not landholders, were at least descendants of persons who held common interests and values and who had freely compacted together to share in the life of a community. The continued and pervasive strength of Property prevented Equal Representation from granting rights to slaves because it made unpersuasive any analogy between the repudiation of heritable political rule and the end of heritable enslavement. Even in the North, where the value of Property in slaves was weak enough to allow emancipation on the grounds of such an analogy, the usages of Equal Liberty granted life, liberty, and property to "the people," not to all human beings. Free blacks were excluded from protection for Equal Rights because they were not viewed as sharing the interest of the community and were, therefore, not "of the people." Colonization was promoted as the only available method for avoiding a nation in which citizens received the protection of the state, while their darker, noncitizen, but free neighbors did not.

African-Americans and Anglo-Americans had found no way to live together as "Americans" under the rhetorical and discursive institutionalization of essentially Anglo-American public values. The dominant Anglo-American interpretation of Equality within a government of "one people" could overcome neither the conflict between Liberty and Property, nor the differences between black and white skin. America would achieve its fullest constitution as a unified nation only once African-Americans supplemented the Anglo-American usages of Equality with a discourse of their own.

The African-American Rhetoric of Equal Rights 1774–1860

> They saw that when the siren song of *liberty and equality* was sung through the land, that the groans of the oppressed made the music very discordant.
>
> William Hamilton, 1809

The new nation's postrevolutionary black population faced a momentous task. As a group, their lives and fortunes, not to mention their dignity, depended literally upon their ability to persuade America's European descendants to alter the prevailing Anglo-American interpretation of the Constitution so as to produce an integrated and inclusive definition of what it meant to be an American. To achieve this goal they needed to effect a shift in the national public vocabulary that would join the commitment to Equality to the prevailing constitutive values of Liberty and Property. The first step in this process was to create a unified people out of the thousands of individual, disaffected Africans living in the United States. Once formed, this African-American nationality spoke with a very different voice than its Anglo-American "other." It roundly denied that humans could be a species of property, and in so doing it introduced a range of broad and more concrete public usages for the heretofore abstract and minimalist notion of Equality.

BEYOND THE ABOLITIONISTS

Popular histories of antebellum America typically neglect the role played by free blacks in promoting abolition. The story of the movement that pushed the new nation to civil war typically focuses on the contributions of white men like William Lloyd Garrison, Henry Seward, Henry Ward Beecher, Wendell Phillips, and Gerrit Smith, and white organizations such as the American Anti-Slavery Society, the Quakers' Society of Friends, and the Republican party. There can be no question that these individuals and organizations played a major role in the agitation that sought to undermine the legally sanctioned institution of slavery. And in point of fact, they were far more visible than most black abolitionists, Frederick Douglass perhaps being the sole exception. White abolitionists could address white audiences from within a shared rhetorical culture that employed a familiar repertoire of persuasive conventions derived from Anglo-American beliefs and values. They also had adequate economic resources to support their campaigns. And, perhaps most important, they were in a position to influence the legislative process both as voters and officeholders. The visibility and national public presence of white abolitionists should not, however, be mistaken as *the* primary source of antebellum egalitarian discourse. The generative force of abolitionist discourse was not solely the product of white sympathizers, but emerged in equally large measure from the public rhetorical efforts of African-Americans.

America's dark-skinned population prompted the call for a revolution in the nation's constitutive values in a variety of ways. The first locus of change rested in the actions of those runaway slaves who "acted out the Declaration of Independence."[1] The vital role that fugitive slaves played in the agitation against slavery cannot simply be measured by the number of runaways. Fugitive slave laws were a major source of the escalation and polarization of hostilities between free and slaveholding states. When the citizens of Boston, Syracuse, and Oberlin "rescued" fugitives from the hands of the federal government that would have returned them to their "rightful owners," Southern slave masters perceived the willful disregard of their property. Their sense of outrage was matched by Northerners who maintained that federal court rulings subordinating Northern state laws to the rights of Southern slave owners was an infringement of states' rights. The shouting over fugitive slaves increased throughout the first half of the nineteenth century. Next to the issue of territorial expansion, it was the longest and most incendiary fuse held to the powder keg of North/ South relations. America's blacks were the central locus of this source of agitation, not only through their choice to escape the system of slavery, but also because they were key agents of the Underground Railroad and a variety of other organizations dedicated to protecting free blacks from bounty hunters who would return them to Southern slavery.[2]

The second locus of change derived from the sheer physical presence and potential power of a black population. The role of slave insurrections is underestimated by those who emphasize the improbability of a national slave revolt, for regardless of its likelihood or potential effectiveness the threat of insurrection was grippingly real to the governments of the South.[3] When small-scale and largely ineffective local insurrections occurred, Southern whites typically responded with frenzy, indiscriminately

lynching blacks, passing oppressive slave codes, and condemning Northern interference. Significantly, the major reason Southern leaders gave for
refusing to discuss the issue of slavery was the fear that such talk would
incite their slaves to revolt.[4] By cutting off discussion, however, they insured that the peaceful, persuasive revisions affected by gradual emancipation in the North would not occur in the South.[5] The mere threat of
insurrection thus loomed very large in the South, and it only became more
pronounced as the first half of the century unfolded.

   In addition to these powerful but largely inarticulate influences, America's African descendants also had their own effective rhetoric, the impact
of which was fairly widespread. Contact with black rhetors strongly influenced William Lloyd Garrison, directly inducing his conversion to the
anticolonizationist stance in 1830. In like fashion, Frederick Douglass's famous taunt, "Look at *me*—and judge between *me* and that gentleman's
theory—*am* I not a Man?" evoked a thunderous national affirmation, and
his eloquence led to many conversions from white supremacist foundations of the Anglo-American interpretation of the Constitution.[6] Such advocacy was equally effective on the private level, as many slaves managed
to gain their own freedom by persuading their masters of the immorality
of slaveholding.[7]

   These are fairly crude measures of rhetorical effect, however, and we do
not want to rest the significance of African-American rhetoric on such anecdotal evidence alone. What made this rhetoric important was that it
pushed harder in subtly and significantly different directions than the rhetoric of white abolitionists.[8]

   The fundamental difference between white and black abolitionists evidences itself in the initial responses of each to the American Colonization
Society. Blacks immediately opposed the Society, vigorously refusing it
their support.[9] The majority of whites supported the Society until persuaded otherwise by black abolitionists. The white abolitionists' immediate response to colonization thus was not to challenge the Anglo-American
interpretation of the Constitution but to enact it through a combination of
emancipation and expatriation. African-Americans offered a different and
more egalitarian path that stretched the limits of the meaning of the
Constitution.

   These differences played out at a number of discursive levels. The primary interest of white abolitionists was to end slavery, while their interest
in "the elevation of colored citizens" was clearly secondary. Free African-
Americans, living the horrors of nominal freedom in their daily lives, put
as much emphasis on advancing their own rights as upon the elimination
of slavery. As we will see, Equal Rights became at least as important as

Equal Liberty in their public discourse. Additionally, white abolitionists tended to treat Equality as an ideal abstraction. This led them to dilute their focus on the problems of slavery as their interests branched out to a broad field of social and political causes.[10] The daily, material experiences of black advocates compelled them toward pressing and concrete concerns that undermined the appeal of abstract conceptions of Equality. So, for example, when Garrison's followers occupied themselves with a proposal to divide the Union, Frederick Douglass emphasized the useless idealism inherent in such a position: "Disunion would be a grand dodge of the whole question of slavery on the part of the North. . . . Purity is not attained by running away from duty. . . . The North has the political power necessary to abolish slavery under the constitution."[11]

Finally, white abolitionists employed less active means of agitation than their black counterparts, who were both earlier and proportionately more unanimous in their acceptance of political action *and* violence as legitimate means of solving the problem of inequality.[12] In sum, black and white abolitionists can be found making many of the same arguments, and white abolitionists often made them in more visible public fora, including the halls of Congress. The difference in underlying motivation nevertheless makes it clear that the generative center of egalitarian rhetoric of the nineteenth century rested in the strivings of African–Americans.

For these reasons we wish to refocus the standard narrative of antebellum America. The drama of that age did not rest in the struggle of a few well-meaning, white Christians to liberate the enslaved. Rather, the antebellum era was dominated by the struggle of America's African descendants, assisted by white abolitionists, to bring the nation to a more egalitarian vision of its constitutional foundation.

From Free Colored People to African-Americans

The first task the free colored people faced was to form a collectivity with its own identity and voice. The formation of that identity was problematic. The individuals enslaved in the New World were not technically Africans. Those born in Africa, as well as those later born in the West Indies, did not characterize themselves as a united people.[13] Instead, they were a cluster of tribes and kin groups who, despite their apparent intertribal similarities and kinships, were not a nationally unified collectivity.[14] Once in America, however, whites treated them generically as Africans without any concern for their tribal roots or affiliations. Gradually, the identities of "colored people" and "Africans" merged, and America's darker-skinned inhabitants formed a separate and unified people.[15]

The choice of name for this people was a matter of serious contention, and none of the alternatives were fully satisfactory.[16] "Black" was a popular descriptor, but it offered no particular cultural identity. "Colored people" offered a wider range of inclusion and was not quite as tainted by the English association of black with evil, but it too lacked a cultural context. The "African" designator provided a cultural basis for replying to claims of white racial superiority by creating a genetic link to the mighty empires of Egypt and Ethiopia, but it failed to specify the identity of a people who were now native to America rather than to Africa.[17]

The issue of names was simply the most pointed form in which the larger problem of cultural identity found expression. Ultimately, this problem would be resolved by formulating a new culture, a unique and powerful mix of African and European elements designated by the label "African-American."[18] But this would be a slow and laborious process, and even in the beginning there were serious disagreements about the character of the identity of those who would create this new culture. Some blacks preferred to maintain a separate identity distinct from Anglo-America. At a proemigration convention of blacks in Ohio in 1854, the participants declared that "no people, as such, can ever attain to greatness who lose their identity, as they must rise entirely upon their own native merits," and that "we shall ever cherish our identity of origin and race, as preferable, in our estimation, to any other people."[19] David Ruggles abhorred the possibility of amalgamation, seeing "my race bleached to a pallid sickly hue."[20] H. Ford Douglass went so far as to argue for a "Colored Nationality" produced by emigration, although the convention as a whole approved only indigenous separatism, expressing its desire to "unite us, as one people, on this continent."[21]

Other leaders, arguing that assimilation was already a fact, preferred to adopt the Anglo-American culture and to merge with the white populace, constituting one American people. The California Negro Convention argued that "[m]ost of us were born upon your soil; reared up under the influence of your institutions; become familiar with your manners and customs; acquired most of your habits, and adopted your policies."[22] Henry Highland Garnet offered the most radical version of this argument when he claimed that the biological amalgamation of the races had already occurred: "[O]ur blood is mixed with every tribe from Cape Horn to the Frozen Ocean. Skillful men have set themselves to work at analyzation, and yet in many cases they are perplexed in deciding where to draw the line between the Negro and the Anglo Saxon."[23] Consequently, he continued, "It is too late to make a successful attempt to separate the black and white people in the New World."[24] Samuel Ward, another black activist, agreed, noting that "you cannot tell who is white or black."[25] Black newspapers emphasized the same point in a dozen different ways. With almost peculiar frequency they reported stories of the enslavement of "nearly white" women who had some African ancestry, or of Southerners enslaving their mulatto children.[26]

There were problems, however, with both separatist and assimilationist ideals. Pragmatic concerns, as always, made it impossible to implement fully the extremes that language could portray. The separatist dream of a sovereign Negro Nationality could not be achieved within the United States because of the power and malice of whites. As Frederick Douglass's *The North Star* pointed out, blacks would fare no better in such circumstances than had the continent's indigenous population.[27] A separate Negro Nationality could be achieved abroad, but never in the form of a complete and total out-migration of all African descendants, for some of Africa's sable hue would remain forever on North American soil.

The full assimilationist dream fared no better. While some blacks might seek equal treatment with whites, disregarding "complexional differences," these and other culturally inherited differences were enforced by whites, and that made such a dream unlikely. Consequently, the extremes of separation and assimilation gradually evolved to a compromise that rested on the formation of an African–American people committed to racial nationalism.

Had Anglo-Americans been able peacefully to accommodate free blacks in their social and political life, an African-American people might never have emerged. Anglo-American economic interests, however, prevented such incorporation and contributed to the rhetorical stigmatization and marginalization of the free colored population. The founding of the African Methodist Episcopal Church in the 1790s provides a classic example of this process. Absalom Jones and Richard Allen were reasonably content to participate in the white church. However, once church officials decided to segregate black and white worshippers, and literally dragged Jones and Allen from their knees in the middle of prayer, they decided to form their own churches.[28] This relationship was reenacted in a multitude of contexts as blacks formed their own institutions when whites refused to share a unified American identity with them.

Free blacks banded together, not only because of the stigma attached to racial exclusion from white society but also to protect themselves from physical violence and legal oppression. Free or otherwise, blacks were long held up as social pariahs, even in the North where white parents would threaten their children with the claim that "the old *nigger* will carry you off."[29] It is little wonder that packs of white children taunted black men and women as they went about their business. But the abuse of colored people was not merely a child's game. Free colored people faced maiming (and occasionally death) on an irregular but frequent basis, even in the supposedly progressive cities of Boston, New York, and Philadelphia. Such violence was especially pronounced during white communal celebrations and times of economic depression, but it never receded so far into the background as to be forgotten or minimized in the consciousness of the black community.[30] And for those blacks who considered fighting back, there was the very real threat of being returned to the daily violence of slavery.[31]

Physical violence, however, was not the only threat free blacks faced. They had also to protect themselves against state legislatures and local political bodies that constantly proposed and passed laws seeking to restrict or abuse their rights. Hence, James Forten organized a group of Philadelphia blacks to fight a law designed to require registration of blacks and the emigration of free negroes.[32] Free blacks in South Carolina likewise organized to resist the efforts of the state to employ increased taxation as a means of forcing black emigration.[33] But the problem was not simply state-organized oppression, for most free blacks were not protected by many of the basic freedoms of the Bill of Rights. So, for example, they could not testify in courts of law, or serve on juries. The notion of a legal contract between a black and a white was a virtual absurdity, for any effort to enforce such a contract against a white participant relied entirely on his or her honor. It should come as no surprise, then, that free blacks were defrauded of their hard-earned property with appalling frequency.[34]

The actions of the white community thus forced even those who would be fully assimilationist into a partially separatist position. Hence, the dominant position of African-Americans in the nineteenth century became an amalgam of separatist and assimilationist voices. The *Colored American* wrought the combination in this manner:

While we believe that, being of the *American nation,* we ought to identify ourselves with the American people, and with American interests, yet there are and will be, special interests for us to attend to, so long as American caste exists, and we have not equal rights, in common with the American people. When such shall be our condition, there will then be no longer special interests to be attended to.[35]

Whether perceived as a temporary expedient or as an end in itself, the descendants of Africans in America formed themselves into a unified people. As Robert Alexander Young concluded, "[I]mperious duty exacts the convocation of ourselves in a body politic; that we do, for the promotion and welfare of our order, establish to ourselves a people."[36] America thus had two peoples and two national voices.[37]

Once so conceived and organized, free colored people set their collective mind to the "elevation" of their people. The pages of *Freedom's Journal,* the *Colored American,* the *Weekly Anglo-African,* and Frederick Douglass's various papers constantly exhorted the black community to improve itself. *Freedom's Journal* reprimanded the free black community in this way: "Is it not a fact, that the great body of our people, who are free, remain ignorant, indolent, dishonest and degraded?"[38] This earliest black newspaper thus proclaimed one of its central missions as "urg[ing] upon our brethren the necessity and expediency of training their children, while young, to habits of industry, and thus forming them for becoming useful members of society."[39] Further, it announced that "we trust also, that through the columns of the FREEDOM'S JOURNAL many practical pieces, having for their bases, the improvement of our brethren, will be presented to them."[40] The *Colored American* spoke in similar terms:

[I]t is our imperative duty as well as interest, to use every exertion to elevate the character of the free colored population, which can be done, in my humble opinion, by adhering strictly to the principles of temperance, the promotion of education, and adopting a system of rigid economy in our expenses.[41]

The rhetorical effort to "elevate" the black community has been interpreted by twentieth-century Afrocentrists and Marxists as a cultural imperialism that resulted in the denigration of African values. However, we might also portray it as the cooptation of American opportunities and values by a wily leadership of former slaves. More objective than either of these positions would be to recognize this as the rhetorical process by which a creative and active leadership began to fuse African and American values so as to form a unique African-American cultural identity.[42] It is clear that many elements of African and slave culture persisted in the African-American community.[43] It is also beyond dispute that many former slaves found themselves empowered by the addition of some elements of Euro-American intellectual and moral culture to their own cultural identity.[44]

Early African-American leaders, therefore, should not be dismissed as the tools of cultural imperialism. These men and women sought to construct a unified people from the full range of cultural resources available to them. Some saw the goal as complete assimilation with American society, others saw it as achieving a permanent place for a distinct African-American people, and others still focused only on the short-term, strategic issue of exploiting Euro-American culture to address the immediate social and economic needs of the black community. Whatever their broad vision, however, they all actively engaged in generating a collective entity—a people—to articulate in public the pressing survival needs of its constituents.

The development of a public voice that would speak for the needs of African-Americans occurred in several stages.[45] The first stage extended from the end of the revolutionary war to about 1817. During this period the number of free blacks increased as some slaves earned their freedom by serving in the war, and others by self-purchase, by appeal to the egalitarian spirit of their masters, or by escape.[46] In this phase the formation of a black community was locally oriented. It emphasized petitioning state legislatures and forming mutual protection and improvement societies, literary societies, and churches.[47] Free blacks had much greater freedom of assembly and movement in Northern states than in Southern states, and so the formal records available for study are primarily from northern organizations. Southern states, however, featured both black churches and other informal organizations as early as the 1790s.[48]

The formation of the American Colonization Society in 1817 stimulated the shift from a local to a national audience, and it marks the beginning of the second stage of the development of an African-American public voice. The shift began when local black groups in Philadelphia, Brooklyn, Boston, Richmond, and elsewhere organized a national response to the Society's argument for colonization and thus provided a springboard for a national cultural identity. The road to that identity featured several landmark events over the next several years. In 1827 John B. Russwurm and Samuel E. Cornish launched *Freedom's Journal,* the first black newspaper.[49] *Freedom's Journal* formally announced the arrival of a national black voice, declaring its desire to "plead our own cause" and to "make our Journal a medium of intercourse between our brethren in the different states of this great confederacy."[50] In 1829 David Walker printed and distributed nationally his militant *Appeal to the Coloured Citizens of the World.* The final effective step in moving from a collection of individual Africans and colored people to a unified African-American people occurred in 1830 with the organization of the National Negro Conventions. This resulted in a series of annual national meetings, as well as state conventions, and the publication and distribution of official addresses to both colored people and whites.[51]

RHETORICS OF EQUALITY

The African-American voice generated in these various arenas posed a vigorous challenge to the Anglo-American vocabulary espoused by the Colonization Society. Black orators used the process of public argumentation to focus and amplify the decision of former slaves to become African-Americans.[52] To be successful in this endeavor, however, they required a very different vision of America than the one offered by the Colonization Society. In vehemently opposing the Society, they led the most devoted white abolitionists, such as Garrison, to oppose it as well.[53] The "Report on African Colonization" of the National Convention of 1833 accentuated the terms of that opposition:

That all the people of the States they represent, feel themselves aggrieved by its very existence, and speak their sentiments of disapprobation in language not to be misunderstood. . . . the life-giving principles of the association are totally repugnant to the spirit of true benevolence. . . . That the inevitable, if not the designed tendency of these doctrines is to strengthen the cruel prejudices of our opponents . . . to retard our advancement in morals, literature and science, in short to existinguish the last glimer [sic] of hope.[54]

To replace the colonization perspective, black orators urged Americans to add a more concrete usage of Equality to the primary values of Liberty and Property.[55] Two different usages of Equality dominated this black discourse. Until 1817 the most popular specification of equality as a public value mimicked the Declaration of Independence by claiming that all human beings had been "born equal" or created "equally free." After 1817, the phrase "Equal Rights" joined this earlier language, and from 1848 forward it grew in specificity and presence.

Equally Free

Promoting the claim to Equal Freedom or Equal Liberty was a complicated task. The challenge was to revise Anglo-America's idealist notion of Equality so that it created a substantive contradiction between the commitments to Liberty and Property that would be resolved in favor of Liberty.

As we have noted, Anglo-Americans already employed the concept of Equality. President Polk's inaugural address in 1845 typifies the prevailing, Anglo-American usage in his celebration of America's revolutionary political achievement: "All distinctions of birth or rank have been abolished. All citizens, whether native or adopted, are placed upon terms of precise equality. All are entitled to equal rights and equal protection." This limited equality offered its protection only to American citizens. Hence, like his contemporaries, Polk could also oppose emancipation declaring, without the hint of contradiction,

It is a source of deep regret that in some sections of our country misguided persons have occasionally indulged in schemes and agitations whose object is the destruction of domestic institutions existing in other sections—institutions which existed at the adoption of the Constitution and were recognized and protected by it.[56]

Because equality applied only to citizens, slavery was a logical possibility, and the Anglo-American commitments to Liberty and Property remained wholly consistent with one another. In order to craft a contradiction between Liberty and Property in this context, African-Americans had two choices. They could deny that Equality applied only to citizens, or they could assert the citizenship of Africans living in America. They did both.

Equal Liberty for All

To argue that "all men are created equally free" is a *universal* statement that applies to all human beings seems redundant to twentieth-century ears, for the universalist argument has been so thoroughly internalized by our contemporary rhetorical culture. Such was not the case in the early part of the nineteenth century. Slaveholders frequently disavowed any notion of Equality at all, and even those mainstream politicians who employed it did so only in the strictly limited forms described in Chapter 3.[57] Consequently, a great deal of rhetorical revision was necessary to extend the scope of the term. African-American advocates and white abolitionists accomplished this goal by asserting that these key words applied universally. To the Anglo-American claims to Equality they added "*universal* equality of man" or "*universal* human rights" or *universal liberty.*"[58] They thereby insisted that Equality was not merely a right of "freemen" or for the descendants of British subjects.

The second rhetorical move made by egalitarians was to specify fully the broad range of groups encompassed by universalism. They did not settle for the white abolitionist, idealist, Christian argument that all men were made of "one blood" or that God was "no respecter of persons," for such vaguely general statements had been submerged too easily within external qualifying phrases. Thus, although they employed such maxims, they also made their conception of Equality materially specific by enumerating the various subgroups of people who must be incorporated in the phrase "all men." Such arguments went beyond the mere assertion of Equal Liberty for Africans. James Forten's version went like this:

We hold this truth to be self-evident, that God created all men equal, is one of the most prominent features in the Declaration of Independence, and in that glorious fabric of collected wisdom, our noble Constitution. This idea embraces the Indian and the European, the savage and the Saint, the Peruvian and the Laplander, the white man and the African.[59]

The *Colored American* extended the position beyond nationality when it asserted "the equal political and civil rights of all men, . . . recognizing no legalized prerogatives on account of birth, wealth, learning, or complexion."[60] Others even extended it beyond race, to include women: "[A]ll persons, of every nation and color should be 'deemed, adjudged and holden to be freemen and freewomen.'"[61] Here then was a universalism that did not depend upon the sublation of human difference; indeed, it overtly recognized equality across difference.

The Anglo-American claim that Equality derived from a precompact, abstract state of nature was here converted to the African-American claim that one ought, therefore, to be equally and materially free in society. They insisted that "equal liberty was originally the position, and *is still the* birthright of all men."[62] If a natural right to Equality meant anything as a foundation of society, they pointed out, it had to include a natural right of "appropriating my own body to my use."[63]

In order to make this argument effective, the abolitionists had to reply to the opposition argument that deficiencies in some human beings made them incapable or unworthy of such freedom. At this point, the inexorable link between Equal Liberty and the larger, more abstract notion of Equality becomes evident. "Equality" was a word with mathematical origins; its usage entailed a sense of the identity of worth. The ability of African-American rhetors to apply that sense of worth to persons who were evidently different from one another was vital for all humanity. Their efforts rested on their ability to combine material and ideal sources.

The material ground of African-American human Equality can best be summed up anecdotally. In telling the story of his life as a slave, Frederick Douglass recounted the crucial incident in which he confronted and overcame the slave breaker. At that precise moment in the story Douglass emphasized not the concept of physical superiority but the realization of what he would later call "equality." In so doing, he characterized his transition from a state of existential inferiority—the willingness to accept commands and the unwillingness to use his own strength and talent at his own discretion—to a vital consciousness of equality with his slave master. Douglass put it this way:

This battle with Mr. Covey was the turning-point in my career as a slave. It rekindled the few expiring embers of freedom, and revived within me a sense of my own manhood. It recalled the departed self-confidence, and inspired me again with a determination to be free. The gratification afforded by the triumph was a full compensation for whatever else might follow, even death itself. He only can understand the deep satisfaction which I experienced, who has himself repelled by force the bloody arm of slavery. I felt as I never felt before. It was a glorious resurrection, from the tomb of slavery, to the heaven of freedom.[64]

The ground of this Equality was the material experience of one person, like another, pitting sinew against muscle, blood against bone, mind against spirit. It thus rooted equality in the material fact that when blacks and whites face each other, one on one, they must each rely on similar resources as they respond to each other from within the strikingly similar limitations of being human.

The second component of Equal Freedom was derived from Christian origins. The ideal of Human Equality spawned by the concept of Christian brotherhood has often been treated as the substance of Anglo/African Equality. It was not, for in the abstract it was fully compatible with the concept of earthly slavery. Thus slave owners frequently applauded it, for they could easily turn it to an otherworldliness that urged the slaves to endure the hardships of the here-and-now in view of the egalitarian riches they would receive in heaven. Christian equality was a cultural ideal, not a political principle.

Nonetheless, the Christian ideal had great power, both because of its centrality to Anglo-American culture, and because fugitive slaves recognized in it an expression of their deepest desires for brotherhood and salvation. Many black Americans thus heartily endorsed the Christian religion. However, African-American advocates did not rest content with the abstract conception of equality that they found in the Old and New Testaments. Instead, they combined it with their own experiences and thus forged a concrete political usage.

Frederick Douglass combined the material experience and the ideal into a single potent vision, arguing that there were no gradations of men. One either put man on his "own characteristic pedestal" or threatened the rights and identity of all men, including one's own.[65] Black advocates expanded this argument by maintaining that natural rights either applied to all men or they applied to no men:

We ask you to ponder the danger of circumscribing the great doctrines of human equality, which our fathers promulgated and defended at the cost of so much blood and treasure, to the narrow bounds of races or nations. All men are by nature equal, and have inalienable rights, or none have. We beg you to reflect how insecure your own and the liberties of your posterity would be by the admission of such a rule of construing the rights of men.[66]

By locating this shared vulnerability in the substantive similarities of whites and blacks as living, breathing persons, African-American advocates prevented arbitrary lines from being drawn between the two. As one speaker pointed out at the Ohio Negro Convention in 1856:

That we are men, we will not insult your intelligence by attempting to prove. . . . Statutes and ordinances are not necessary for the regulation and control of animals, but men, reasoning men, who can understand and obey, or plot to overthrow. . . . We ask any who doubt our manhood, Hath not the *negro* eyes? Hath not the *negro* hands, organs, dimensions, senses, affections, passions?—fed with the same food—hurt with the same weapons—subject to the same diseases—healed by the same means—warmed and cooled by the same summer and winter as the *white* man is? If you prick us, do we not bleed? If you tickle us, do we not laugh? If you poison us, do we not die?[67]

Asserting the substantial identity of all persons was important to the development of human consciousness, but it was not enough. For Southerners like John Calhoun the crux of the issue was intelligence, and the dominant political philosophies of the day made intellect a primary requirement for rights.[68] Abolitionists of all colors replied by insisting that the descendants of an African heritage possessed the same intellectual abilities as Anglo-Saxons. Prince Saunders claimed that "we are endowed with intellect, that our natural capacities are good, and that they would be equal to those of Europeans if we had the same advantages."[69] Others asserted that negroes possessed both equal potential and equal accomplishment: "[W]e compare favorably with the white population in intelligence, and morality."[70] For those not convinced, the delegates to the Negro Convention of Ohio pushed the argument further by suggesting that the crucial factor was not the degree of one's intellectual ability but the capacity to reason: "Any being, however low in the scale of civilization, that yet preserves the traits that serve to distinguish humanity from the brutes, is endowed with all rights that can be claimed by the most cultivated races of men."[71]

The argument was clinched by turning the abstract notion of natural right into the material principle that one's rights derive from their nature. Each person's rationality led her or him to demand freedom. The very ability to conceive of and demand equal treatment thus warranted political equality as a necessary commitment of rational societies. African-Americans proved their argument by enacting the premise in exercising their reason and making the demand.[72] The delegates to the New York Convention of 1840 expressed the political philosophy in this manner:

[Rights] are inferrable from the settled and primary sentiments of man's nature. The high dignities and exalted tendencies of our common humanity are the original grounds from which they may be deduced. Wherever a being may be found endowed with the light of reason, and in the exercise of its various exalted attributes, that being is possessed of certain peculiar rights, on the ground of his nature.[73]

By generating an understanding of human rights grounded on lived human nature, rather than based in an abstract "state of nature," the African-Americans constructed a political theory that outdistanced the Lockeian conception of equality.[74] Egalitarians unanimously agreed that, at the minimal level of personal freedom, all persons should be equally free "to use what is respectively theirs."[75] This argument rested on a broad and unique conception of Human Equality that presumably derived human dignity from the material possibilities of human development.[76]

It was through this usage of Equality that African-American advocates demanded Liberty for their people. They reduced the scope of Property and increased the scope of Liberty, thereby creating a contradiction between the prevailing constitutive values of the Anglo-American culture.[77] They then gradually characterized slavery as an aberration, claiming that it was "only slave law that abolishes the distinctions between persons and things."[78] From this base they could then loudly and eloquently castigate "the wild and guilty fantasy that man can hold property in man."[79] They made the argument a constitutional one at the Negro Convention of 1855, concluding their legal analysis by observing:

All human beings who may be born in this land, in whatever condition, and all who may come or may have been brought to this land, under whatever circumstances, are declared by the Constitution to be PERSONS: the idea that such may be property, or may become property, is no where recognized, but every where excluded by the Constitution.[80]

Black rhetors and their allies promoted Equality to the position that it ultimately would come to hold in the twentieth century alongside of Liberty and Property as an uneasy triumvirate of constitutive values. Their contribution, however, should be recognized as an integrative one, neither inherently African nor Anglo-American but specifically African-American. On their own, Africanist rhetors did not use the universalizing word Equality; indeed, black separatist orators, pamphleteers, and newspaper writers were nearly as self-interested, misogynist, and racist as the great mid-stream of Anglo-Americans.[81] Similarly on their own, Anglo-American rhetors emphasized a minimalist conception of Equality as a cultural ideal altogether incapable of influencing broad action in the here and now.[82] By combining the two, however, the African-Americanists crafted a conception of Equality that encompassed tremendously wide varieties of human life, and yet projected concrete ways of treating all human beings with Justice and Freedom.

Equal Citizenship

This was a grand but diffuse vision. In addition to it, African-American rhetors sought vigorously to extend the more pragmatic concept of Equal Liberty by demanding a right to citizenship based on their American birthright. In the words of Theodore Wright, "They lifted up their voice and said, this is my country, where I was born, here I have toiled and suffered, and here will I die."[83] To make the claim to Equal Liberty as Americans, they challenged directly the Anglo-American concept of political birthright, which rested on the principle of patriarchal inheritance. Instead, they argued, political communities are constituted through their physical location. Free blacks thus frequently identified the right of citizenship in terms of the place of birth. The Ohio Convention of 1854 made the argument most eloquently, insisting "[t]hat the right to breathe the Air and *use* the Soil on which the Creator has placed us, is co-inherent with the birth of man, and coeval with his existence."[84] The *Colored American* agreed, concluding that "the strongest claim to citizenship is birth-place," after which it noted that 75 percent of all colored Americans were "*native American born*" and that they were, therefore, *not* Africans. They then expressed the hope that "we shall yet be elevated with the American people here. . . . it is our duty and privilege to claim an equal place among the *American people*."[85] They strengthened this principle by contrasting it with the treatment accorded blood-related, but nonnative, naturalized persons. Peter Williams argued, "We are NATIVES of this country, we ask only to be treated as well as FOREIGNERS. . . . We have toiled to cultivate it, and to raise it to its present prosperous condition; we ask only to share equal privileges with those who come from distant lands, to enjoy the fruits of our labour."[86] African-American rhetors and their allies thus introduced a significant conceptual alteration in the principle of "birthright" by shifting the criteria of its determination from lineage to place of birth.

African-Americans also grounded their resistance to expatriation in the concept of the "consent of the governed" by claiming that geographical location created an inherent bond between a nation and those who lived within its borders.[87] Thus, they argued, "We are native Americans, and since allegiance is due from us, protection and equal rights are due from the Government."[88] This structure of mutual duties was deepened by the past history of the relationship. Black leaders, therefore, emphasized the many ways in which America's people of color had long paid their just share through "blood and tears."[89] After a detailed and eloquent examination of the concept of citizenship, the delegates of the Negro Convention of 1853 noted:

We and you stand upon the same broad national basis. Whether at home or abroad, we and you owe equal allegiance to the same government—have a right to look for protection on the same ground. We have been born and reared on the same soil; we have been animated by, and have displayed the same patriotic impulses; we have acknowledged and performed the same duty; we have fought and bled in the same battles; we have gained and gloried in the same victories; and we are equally entitled to the blessings resulting therefrom.[90]

By redefining key elements of the Anglo-American conception of community such as "merit" and "consent of the governed," while simultaneously rejecting its prevailing assumptions of racial homogeneity and inheritance, African-Americans produced a less fanciful and more pragmatic conception of "the people" than one finds in the compact theory. They grounded governmental authority in the consent of those living and interacting together in the present rather than in some utopian and mythical past. In 1827, a group of Baltimore's free blacks raised their glasses to the toast: "*Emancipation* without *emigration, but equal rights on the spot; this is republicanism.*"[91] And when the National Convention addressed white America's citizens in 1853, it did so with great confidence: "We are Americans, and as Americans, we would speak to Americans. We address you not as aliens nor as exiles, humbly asking to be permitted to dwell among you in peace; but we address you as American citizens asserting their rights on their own native soil."[92]

The claim to citizenship did not stand solely on the merits of this argument. It was entwined with the popular understanding of the nation's traditional Anglo-American commitments, and this led to a dispute over the meaning and status of the Declaration of Independence and its world-historical proclamation: "All men were created equal." As Philip Detweiler points out, neither the Declaration nor its egalitarian sentiments received wide circulation in the mainstream white press and public oratory of the postrevolutionary and early national periods.[93] However, black abolitionist orators and pamphleteers employed both the term and the document with noticeable frequency throughout these periods. The impact of the Declaration on the black community is suggested by the fact that in Massachusetts, a group of "blackes" never once used the word "equality" in petitioning for their rights; immediately after the signing of the Declaration they resubmitted their petition with only a few word changes, the most substantive of which was the addition of the word "equalley."[94] Hundreds of others picked up the refrain.[95]

During and after the War of 1812, the Declaration of Independence enjoyed a general resurgence in the public discourse of the nation's Anglo-American political mainstream. There is little doubt that the general mood of the period worked to the advantage of black abolitionists, as white egalitarians sought to enhance their own position by establishing more equal political privileges and equal protection. However, Southern slaveholders were absolutely resolute in their resistance to promoting the Declaration to constitutive status. Consequently, the role of the Declaration of Independence was essentially contested in this period. The argument of the Southern whites took two forms.

First, they argued that the Declaration of Independence did not apply to "negro slaves." Representative Louis McClane of Delaware argued,

> If the abstract principles contained in this memorable paper could possibly be supposd to have any reference to the condition of the black population in the United States, yet, as it preceded the adoption of the Constitution, their practical effect must depend altogether upon the positive provisions of that charter. But the truth is, sir, that the Declaration of Independence had no reference to those persons who were at that time held in slavery. . . . The Declaration of Independence was the act of open resistance on the part of the white freemen of the colonies, against the pretensions of the mother country to govern them without their consent.[96]

Representative Benjamin Hardin of Kentucky shared this argument when he asked, "What are the efficient parts of the Declaration of Independence?" The answer he gave restricted the scope of the document to its most immediate and original context: "The answer is, those parts only which declare our dependence upon Great Britain to be at an end. . . . The balance of the declaration is nothing but a manifesto to the world, assigning and setting forth the causes which led to and brought about that mighty event."[97]

Some were driven to a second and even more extreme stance, as they mocked the Declaration and the Equality it proclaimed. John Calhoun articulated the political ideology of the white plantation owners of the deep South when he declared himself unafraid to attack the "error" in the principle that "all men are born free and equal." Thus, he insisted: "Taking the proposition literally (it is in that sense it is understood), there is not a word of truth in it." He proceeded to argue that men are not born (infants are), that infants are incapable of freedom, and that they are not all born with equal abilities. Further, he maintained that a state of nature was purely hypothetical and that liberty "instead of being equal in all cases, must necessarily be very unequal among different people, according to their different conditions." Finally, he indicated that Liberty was the reward for "mental and moral development."[98] John Tyler of Virginia, seeking to defend slavery, similarly denounced the values of Liberty and Equality:

" . . . that all men are, by nature, equally free, sovereign and independent." Can this proposition admit of application to a state of society? Does not its fallacy meet you in every walk of life? Distinctions will exist. . . . Liberty and equality are captivating sounds; but they often captivate to destroy. England had her Jack Cades and levellers. Look, I pray you, to revolutionary France. . . . Is this your boasted equality? If it be, sir, "I will have none of it."[99]

Speaking from within the traditional Southern heritage, with its social, political, and economic interests in preserving the institution of slavery, men like Calhoun and Tyler felt compelled to deprecate the concept of Equality as inherently inconsistent with their commitments to the values of Property and merit. Consequently, those advocates of Equality who wished to base their argument on the Declaration of Independence faced two major rhetorical tasks. First, they had to establish its standing, and second they had to defend Equality as its essential, foundational principle.

They did so, first, simply by proclaiming its importance. The delegates at the convention of 1853 noted:

That ALL MEN ARE CREATED EQUAL; that "LIFE, LIBERTY, AND THE PURSUIT OF HAPPINESS" ARE THE RIGHT OF ALL. . . . —are American principles and maxims, and together they form and constitute the constructive elements of the American government.[100]

They also emphasized the pivotal role that the Declaration had played in the nation's founding. In 1837 Theodore S. Wright referred to "the convention of 1776, when the foundations of our government were laid." He then described the Declaration as even more fundamental to the nation than the Constitution, on the grounds that the union preceded the Constitution both logically and in time.[101] The *Weekly Anglo-African* agreed, celebrating "the principles of the Declaration of Independence, which is the foundation of the American Revolution."[102] The most extended treatment was provided by *Frederick Douglass' Paper,* which circulated the argument made in Congress by Gerrit Smith:

The Declaration of Independence is the highest human authority in American politics . . . but for it . . . there would have been no American constitution, and no American nation, and no American liberty . . . it was by this sign—that our fathers conquered. . . . Again: but for this commanding principle, and this mighty inspiration, the aid—the indispensable aid—that came to us from foreign shores, would not have come.[103]

In addition to arguing that the Declaration of Independence was a constituting document, America's colored people also had to argue that its abstract phrases were racially inclusive. This they did by pointing out that the Declaration made no exceptions for color. So, for example, Peter Osborne argued, "The Declaration of Independence has declared to man, without speaking of color, that all men are born free and equal."[104] James Forten offered a more extended claim, concluding that "[a]ctuated by these sentiments they adopted the glorious fabric of our liberties, and declaring 'all men' free, they did not particularize white and black, because they never supposed it would be made a question whether *we were men or not*."[105] The National Negro Convention of 1853 clinched the argument by pointing out that the designator "white" had not been a part of the nation's original founding charter and had only been imputed to it at a later date:

There is in this clause of the Constitution, nothing whatever, of that watchful malignity which has manifested itself lately in the insertion of the word "*white*," before the term "*citizen*." The word "*white*" was unknown to the framers of the Constitution of the United States in such connections—unknown to the signers of the Declaration of Independence. . . . It is a modern word, brought into use by modern legislators, despised in revolutionary times.[106]

The North Star offered the same argument with its usual sarcastic wit: "When 'all men' then are spoken of as being entitled to the same rights and privileges, of course the word *all* is to be understood in the abstract; an idiom in modern democracy signifying *white*."[107] More frequently, black newspaper editors made the argument simply by underscoring the phrase "all men," as did Henry Highland Garnet in 1848 when he noted of the Declaration that "[i]t asserts that '*all men*' are entitled to 'life, liberty, and the pursuit of happiness,'" or as did the *North Star* in demanding the "Equal and Inalienable Rights of ALL MEN."[108]

Nineteenth-century black egalitarians thus launched a multipronged rhetorical assault on the dominant Anglo-American political culture to embrace and promote Human Equality. Their argument was substantiated by both universal rights and the implicit promises of the new nation's Constitution. They employed the Declaration of Independence as a rhetorical fulcrum to give leverage to Equality as a primary commitment of the community, promoting it to the status of the prevailing and competing constitutive values of Liberty and Property. The case they built for Equal Liberty was persuasive, but it was not without serious political opposition, and its full enactment as a principle of American governance would have to await the outcome of the Civil War. Its importance notwithstanding, however, Equal Liberty was not the black egalitarians' sole demand.

Equal Rights

As soon as fugitive slaves became "nominally free men," they turned their attention to building upon their Equal Liberty.[109] They quickly realized that Liberty meant little in a society where the distribution of rights was not equal. Therefore, after 1817 free blacks turned their attention to extending the natural rights basis for Equal Liberty to the inculcation of Equal Rights. While there had been profound disagreements about the universal application of Equal Liberty to all persons, there was even less of a consensus on the meaning and role of Equal Rights.

Some African-American writers repudiated the claim to Equal Rights altogether. Seeking to avoid pushing inegalitarian Anglo-Americans too far and too fast, they reassured the white power structure that freedom from slavery was their solitary goal. As one writer put it in *Freedom's Journal* in 1827, "We do not wish them to elevate our people, in their rude and unqualified state to equal rights."[110] This position appeared relatively infrequently in the early national period, and by 1827 it was all but completely obliterated as the demand for the "equal rights of all men, irrespective of birth, color, or condition," became a virtual rallying cry for the growing African-American community.[111] The quantity of its usage notwithstanding, the scope of its application never achieved full consensus.

The first problem derived from the ambiguity between the word "equality" and the phrase "equal rights." To begin with, Equal Rights might be taken simply as a concretization of Equality, as in the parallels that contrasted "freedom over slavery, equality over caste."[112] By contrast, however, Equal Rights could also be used in ways that represented an actual narrowing of the demands linked to the broader claim to "*perfect* Equality." This narrowing resulted in part from the fact that non-egalitarians ridiculed the feasibility of absolute Equality. This encouraged black egalitarians to restrict the scope of their demand for Equality so as to make it seem more plausible. Hence they claimed "that all men are equal— not in stature, intellect, morals or manners, (for we colored Americans know that we have better manners than our white fellow-citizens generally), but equal in rights."[113] Such narrowing of Equality to Equal Rights may also have represented the authentic preference of many black leaders, who typically promoted merit as a standard of Equality. This is indicated most clearly by *Freedom's Journal*, which maintained that "[w]e have never contended, that there should be no distinctions in society: but we have, and are still determined to maintain, that distinctions should not exist merely on account of a man's complexion."[114]

Whether it was a defensive move resulting from argumentative strategy, or simply the result of underlying beliefs, the usage of Equal Rights generated by nineteenth-century African-Americans was not the function of a commitment to a generalized Equality. It did not imply a lack of all distinctions between individuals or groups, and it did not call for governmental guarantees for an absolute equality of respect and rewards. Instead, it merely claimed an "equality, not of property or favor, but of rights."[115]

The dominant metaphor that concretized this insistence on Equal Rights in the public vocabulary of African-Americans was the demand for placement "upon an equal footing" with other citizens.[116] Its persuasive force came from the hearty self-confidence of black leaders who faithfully believed that if they could have "the same advantages" as whites, they would be competitive and successful in the "great race we are running."[117] The "equal footing" metaphor envisioned a black race, naturally equal to the white race, living in conditions of slavery and prejudice that caused it to sink "below the level of a common equality [with whites]."[118] African-American leaders thus assumed that if they could start on an equal footing in this race, they would naturally reap "an equal benefet" [sic] from the laws of the republic.[119] There can be little doubt that the ultimate interest of the leaders was in achieving a substantive equality, not merely formal equality. However, the overwhelming majority of black leaders wanted to *earn* that substance, not receive it as a grant or entitlement.[120] This left three different interpretations of the government's role in "putting us on an equality," and they produced three different specifications for the meaning of Equal Rights: equal ability, equal opportunity, and equality before the law.[121]

Equal Ability

The first version of Equal Rights assumed that black people themselves, not the government, must take the lead by demonstrating their ability. Martin R. Delany argued, "We have speculated and moralised [sic] much about equality—claiming to be as good as our neighbors, and every body else—all of which, may do very well in ethics—but not in politics. . . . By the regulations of society, there is no equality of persons, where there is not an equality of attainments."[122] Some speakers assumed that the need to prove one's equality was a matter of fact, not right. The black citizens of

Philadelphia argued, for example, that equality of achievement was simply a pragmatic means for convincing whites to give them what they deserved; it was *not* a logical requirement of political equality.[123] The goal, therefore, was to work hard enough to "show himself equal."[124]

A second inflection on the call to demonstrate individual and group abilities implied that the enactment of competence was a requirement of political equality. Frederick Douglass suggested that a society would grant Equal Rights only to those who earned them by the contributions they made:

Men are not valued in this country, or in any country, for what they *are;* they are valued for what they can *do.* . . . We must become valuable to society. . . . The individual must lay society under obligation to him, or society will honor him only as a stranger and sojourner.[125]

The demand for achievement rested on the firm assurance that African-Americans possessed merit, but it prescribed ever so tightly the link between performance and equality.

Equal Opportunity

The call for equal ability presumed an essential relationship between equal rights, merit, and achievement. However, black advocates also used Equal Rights so as to invert the relationship between merit and achievement by calling for "equal opportunity."[126] When focusing on Equal Opportunity, black rhetors assumed that merit was proportional to the opportunity that governments guaranteed their people. This usage was similar to the Jacksonian call for equal economic opportunity, but it contained one significant difference: Whereas President Jackson sought to prevent government from creating new and unfair advantages for some wealthy citizens, African Americans sought to influence the government's role in redressing long-standing conditions of unfair advantage.[127] Three different versions of Equal Opportunity existed.

The simplest version of the call for positive government action to elevate "colored people to equal right," requested changes in those laws which proscribed the basic rights of free blacks. They asked "to be freed from all unnatural burdens and impediments with which American custom and American legislation have hindered our progress."[128] Black leaders here presumed that legal barriers were the sole impediments to the Equal Opportunity that would allow their people to demonstrate their merit, and thus legitimately earn the privilege of Equal Rights. This most limited version of equal opportunity nonetheless required governmental activity, since the federal government would be required to counter state and local actions.

The presumption that the only barriers to equality were legal ones was excluded from the second and third usages of Equal Opportunity. Rather, these usages incorporated the claim that slavery and prejudice had suppressed the innate and natural equal abilities of blacks. When those who employed these usages characterized their people as "degraded," they did not simply mean to describe them as "lowly" but to emphasize that they had been *actively taken down* from their natural place. As David Ruggles noted in his call for Equal Opportunity: "Now we are degraded and ground to the very dust by prejudice."[129] The active process of "degradation" required an equally active process to counter it on the part of the government.

The usages by black rhetors isolated the source of degradation in two different places. First, they located it in white prejudices that prevented African-Americans from attaining education or positions that allowed them to develop and reap the rewards from enacting their equal abilities. Second, they traced it to the institution of slavery and other past discriminations that had produced deleterious and enduring effects on blacks. The most powerful examination of this effect came from Hosea Easton, who explained in detail how something as basic as the diet and living conditions of an enslaved mother could seriously undermine the natural abilities and potential of her child.[130] Frederick Douglass and others, appealing to the economic interest of Northern capitalists, similarly emphasized that harsh working conditions could destroy the liveliness of the mind and body, not only among black workers but among the Irish and English as well.[131]

Finally, African-American rhetors realized that any effective change in their Equal Opportunity would require a change in public opinion as well as law. The reason for this was all too obvious, for the prejudiced image of African-Americans that dominated the mainstream Anglo-American discourse posed a self-fulfilling prophecy, convincing blacks that they could not succeed and thus discouraging them from even trying.[132] Given these factors, Hosea Easton concluded:

emancipation embraces the idea that the emancipated must be placed back where slavery found them, and restore to them all that slavery has taken away from them. Merely to cease beating the colored people, and leave them in their gore, and call it emancipation, is nonsense. . . . Let them rather act the part of the good Samaritan.[133]

There is a clear materialist insight here, but Easton and others failed to tie it to specific concrete remedies, although they did carry it to the point of demanding reparations for past harms by way of restoring blacks to an "equal footing" with whites. Neither did they envision the process of restoration as a permanent or multigenerational commitment. Their call for such accommodations always referred directly to the real people who had experienced slavery.

There was a third version of Equal Opportunity, but it neither presumed nor argued that equal merit would result from its guarantees. Indeed, it admitted the unequal abilities of human beings, simply declaring that a social system ought to allow and encourage the growth and development of all of its members to whatever degree their abilities would allow. As a letter by "AFRI" noted, "if I understand the principle for which we contend, they are neither an intellectual nor physical equality. We contend only for an equal chance to develop these natural gifts."[134] Equal Rights in this sense of Equal Opportunity thus suggested a government that insured the chance for all its citizens to develop to the best of their ability, whether or not that chance ultimately resulted in substantive Equality.

Equality before the Law

The final usage of Equal Rights neither rested on merit nor concerned itself with empowering merit. It called neither for substantive Equality nor Equality of Opportunity. Rather, it was a demand for formal Equality that reduced Equal Rights to Equal Law. The identification of Equal Rights with Equal Laws emerged from statements that sought to eliminate laws that favored the interests of whites.

Egalitarians of both races opposed themselves "to all discriminations, by the Government in the distribution of rights or privileges, having any other bases than character and conduct."[135] As such, they declared themselves for the "equal political and civil rights of all men, . . . recognizing no legalized prerogatives on account of birth, wealth, learning, or complexion."[136] In so doing, they cited the "wickedness of creating distinctions among equal citizens on account of complexion"[137] and asked for the government to "guarant[ee] to all their citizens equal rights and privileges, without any distinction whatever."[138] The outcome of such statements was an argument, frequently summarized in the phrases "Equal Laws" and "equality before the law," which called for blacks and whites to "stand equal in the eyes of the law."[139] Charles Sumner's thunderous argument before a Massachusetts court related the argument to the Anglo-American heritage by maintaining that "the same anathema which smites and banishes nobility must also smite and banish every form of discrimination founded on birth."[140]

This usage sounds similar to the version of Equal Opportunity that required the government to "eliminate existing barriers" so that black people
might show their merit. But it was not identical with that usage, for it did
not assume that the elimination of barriers should be premised on allowing
merit to show; instead, its solitary premise was the formal principle of equity. It also contrasted directly with the other usages of Equal Opportunity, for it ignored historically generated differences of condition that
might have required special treatment for blacks to help them to achieve
"equal footing." Those who applied this usage asked only for "equal participation," "the same" educational facilities, "the same" education, and so
on. If it led to substantive inequality or even meant self-extinction, that
was of no matter. [141] As Frederick Douglass argued:

> Let ignorant and degraded negroes be placed everywhere upon the same footing,
> and receive the same offices of charity which are extended to ignorant and
> degraded people of other varieties of mankind—no more, no less—and if they can-
> not stand up under this equal and just treatment, let them fall down. [142]

This last usage for Equal Rights was the most acceptable to the Anglo-
American population, both because of its abstraction and because it required the least in terms of social and political change. That would give it
additional potency in the process of ideological change that would occur in
the American mainstream in the years following the Civil War.

Human, Civil, Political, and Social Equality

The efforts to define Equal Rights in terms of substantive achievement,
opportunity, and the law extended throughout the period from 1827 to
1860. After 1848 disagreements about the fields to which equality should
be applied accompanied such efforts. The debate explored whether equality was a function of human, civil, political, or social rights. The first three
terms appeared frequently in African-American public discourse, but the
phrase "political rights" clearly dominated the other two. One can find
few direct challenges to these three terms, and very little in the way of careful distinctions drawn between and among them. By contrast, the standing of Social Equality became the focus of heated controversy. Some
argued vigorously for social rights, while others altogether disavowed the
search for Social Equality. In part, the difference involved strategic considerations. Anglo-American whites had frequently opposed Equal Liberty
and Equal Rights on the grounds that it would lead to the amalgamation of
the races. Some black rhetors were sensitive to the alienating potential of
this argument for otherwise supportive white audiences, and thus they did

as much as they could to allay the fear that they sought Social Equality of any kind.[143]

There was, however, another consideration involved, and that was the conflict between assimilationist and separatist visions. Those who sought Social Equality tended to be those who promoted the similitude of all human beings under the metaphor of "one human family." This went beyond a demand for the recognition of a common humanity, to the desire for broad similitude. Social egalitarians thus tended to envision a homogeneous America, saying "[W]e believe in human equality; that character, not color, should be the criterion by which to choose associates."[144] It was not their desire "to build ourselves up as a distinct and separate class in this country, but as a means to a great end, viz: the equality in political rights, and in civil and social privileges with the rest of the American people."[145] These advocates saw whites and blacks as having already adopted the same "habits, manners and customs."[146] Indeed, some even argued that whites and blacks shared the same blood, and that while there might be minor gradations of difference, there were no physically distinct races.[147] In portraying this homogeneity, they thus emphasized the "common origin" and "common destiny" of the inhabitants of the nation.[148] As a spokesperson for this future, Frederick Douglass literally sought to live out this vision by first marrying a black woman and then later marrying a white woman.[149]

The contrary position, which held that social equality was not desired because blacks did not wish to be involved in social life with whites, was not widely expressed in public by African-Americans in this period.[150] Given that those who held such a vision were typically separatists, seeking to escape a common destiny through emigration, the absence of this argument is not surprising. Their vision could not contribute to an American worldview, for they took it to foreign shores.

Consequently, however, in this period no authentic dialogue about culture took place between the assimilationists and the separatists, and accordingly no true Afro-American understanding of cultural accommodation developed. This does not mean that black culture disappeared or encountered strong repression. Rather, it suggests that the treatment of culture in this period was generally nonreflective. African-American newspapers routinely highlighted the travels of black musicians, favorably contrasting their native style with that of white musicians. They also covered African history and affairs. At the same time, they condemned specific aspects of black culture, such as the use of tattoos and various religious superstitions, and they emphatically urged blacks to participate in European culture.[151] A few strong voices called for the maintenance of black culture as superior to white culture.[152] However, there was no real public debate in which the issues and values at stake could be carefully examined. Most important, there was no overt effort to address the relationship between Social Equality and social interaction. So, for example, the argument to "advance the slaves to an equal social and political condition with the white race" might have implied only a numerical equivalence, not an identity or interaction of cultures.[153]

Some rhetors foresaw the possibility of separate cultures in a shared polity. The New York Convention of Colored Citizens, arguing from the examples of Jewish and Quaker history, maintained that "men may be *politically* equal, and yet remain socially distinct: this grand problem it has been the glory of American institutions to demonstrate."[154] This possibility was further reflected in the popular saying of the 1850s, "A Man's A Man For A' That," indicating that a base of similarity could co-exist with a plenitude of difference.

It would take many years before the public usage of Equality in the realms of politics and culture would engender a thorough exploration of the issues posed by cultural and social relations. In the years prior to the Civil War, however, where the most pressing topics for blacks were survival issues, the concern for cultural and social relations was left in the world of the polarized universal ideals of homogenity or separatism.

Although the issue of social equality was largely set aside, after 1848 black egalitarians specified with great precision new areas of political rights to be included under the concept of Equal Rights. First, they helped formalize the inclusion of voting rights under the heading of foundational and universal Equal Rights. The revolutionary era, for all its talk of "the consent of the governed," had not included universal (white) manhood suffrage in that list. Several states had eliminated property restrictions from their suffrage requirements since that time, but such decisions had not received much national attention. Consequently, when the Convention of New York Colored Citizens insisted on "the right to vote on an equal basis with other citizens," they were among those providing the basis for the first national discussion of the role of suffrage as a material component of Equal Rights for all citizens.[155]

Of similar importance was the demand for Equal School Rights.[156] Public education was not widespread in the revolutionary era. Although the movement toward universal public education had begun, the topic did not develop beyond the state and local levels. The African-American demand for Equal School Rights thus provided the basic framework for America's understanding of this right on a national basis. This constituted a most significant revision of the laissez-faire doctrines of Anglo-

American political theory. Rather than to specify the role of a republican government solely as a matter of the protection of individuals from each other (the Lockeian/Hobbesian version) or from tyrannical governments themselves (the Federalist version), the argument for Equal School Rights assigned affirmative responsibilities to the government for the development of its people.[157]

In addition to suffrage and schooling, African-Americans explored issues of equal treatment on public conveyances, broached the issue of equal economic opportunity, and reasserted Anglo-American concepts such as the right to serve on juries, to testify before a court of law, to exercise free speech, etc. These issues, however, achieved far too little development to have any serious effect on the nation's constitutive framework. The issue of public conveyance was developed through anecdotal narratives of mistreatment rather than through formal argument about the essential character of those facilities. As such, it never became an issue of public rights.[158] The issue of economic opportunity likewise found expression only in terms of private relations, not in the vocabulary of public law and the Constitution.[159] Although the age left several issues to future generations, African-American rhetors had expanded the possible usages of Equality in several directions.

The fundamental premise of the African-American rhetors who responded to the Anglo-American interpretation of the Constitution enshrined in the rhetoric of the American Colonization Society was unassailable: "[T]he black and the white—the Negro and the European—. . . will ever remain the principal inhabitants of the United States."[160] Change in the public vocabulary, therefore, was imminent, but the form in which it would occur was clearly open to debate.

For their part, America's African descendants constituted themselves as a collective people and offered a worldview that included an alternate and expanded vision of Justice. The African-American people had not been constituted biologically, for there was no pure race in America. Neither had it been constituted by cultural identity, for such issues achieved only sparse attention. Nor had it been constituted economically, even though economic issues were a crucial concern. The African-American people had been constituted politically, and in that context the revision of American society that they offered was a political one that emphasized the equal sharing of political rights.

There were difficulties built into the situation. White Americans did not wish to share their power, while blacks demonstrated their determination to "equalize the laws in reference to our people, so as to give them power and influence in this country."[161] There were also significant difficulties built into the African-American alternative. African-American rhetors proposed usages of Equality that would eventually eliminate their status as a politically constituted people, but to develop such usages they had to constitute themselves as a separate people. That left open the question of whether the U.S. government would remain a federation of "one people" or become a federation of many. More important, the descendants of Africans and Europeans could not yet fully foresee all of the issues involved in sharing a continent under the rubric of Equal Rights.

To produce a functional rhetoric of Equality for all Americans would require more experience in living together. This was, however, a significant beginning. African-Americans did not simply point out a contradiction in the Anglo-American usages of Liberty and Slavery. They crafted that contradiction by materializing the usage of Equality, adding it to Liberty in a way that might curtail the scope of Property. In so doing, they employed several creative rhetorical strategies. First, they extended the usage of Equal Liberty to include themselves by emphasizing that the similarities among human beings as rational creatures were not only greater than the dissimilarities but also were fundamental to the concept of rights. Additionally, they employed the stunningly efficient tactics of adding or emphasizing the word "UNIVERSAL" in front of usages of Liberty or Equality, and of enumerating a broad and specific range of human groups who fit under Liberty's umbrella. After transforming Equal Liberty from a general to a universal value, they asserted their Equal Citizenship by transforming citizenship from a birthright based on lineage to one based on territory. They also promoted the Declaration of Independence to constitutive status. Finally, they expanded the repertoire of usages available for Equal Rights by accentuating the political rather than social, cultural, or economic usages of Equal Opportunity and Equal Laws.

These creative and often powerful rhetorical constructions stood as a serious challenge to the Anglo-American system of government, and they demanded a response. To force the response, African-Americans exploited their physical and persuasive power to exacerbate the growing conflict between the North and the South. Gradually, more and more Anglo-Americans attended to the issue, and, at least in the North, they appropriated selective bits and pieces of the African-American vision. But the rhetorical process of national development was complicated, for the Anglo-Americans themselves did not speak with one voice. And the war came.

PART TWO

*Rhetorical
Integrations*

CHAPTER FIVE

Separate But Equal
1865–1896

"It is utterly and totally impossible to mingle all the various families
of men, from the lowest form of the Hottentot up to the highest
Caucasian, in the same society."

Senator Edgar Cowan, 30 May 1866

"America has been and will be, despite legislation, the gathering
place of the nations and races of the whole earth. Its future must be
worked out by a harmonious working together of its heterogeneous
population. All must be uplifted together."

W. S. Scarborough, *Arena,* 1890

The Civil War succeeded in preserving the Union, at least in name, but
it did nothing to guarantee that the North and South would share a
national vision of constitutional values. During the antebellum period
each region had confidently expressed a sense of what it stood for and how
it imagined the union of states to share in a common worldview. In the
immediate postbellum period, however, Northerners and Southerners
alike suffered from what one erstwhile rebel described as "indecision, confusion, chaos."[1] Many on both sides of the bloodstained battle lines
wanted to return to "the Union as it was, the Constitution as it is." But
such aphorisms aside, the Emancipation Proclamation made the enactment of such a vision a virtual impossibility. The public vocabulary that
had sufficed to join the North and the South in common government
when four million Africans were in chains was altogether inadequate to
govern a nation that harbored four million free African-Americans. Unable to expatriate free blacks as they had once dreamed of doing, the competing voices within America's white political culture could not agree on
the desirable or viable alternatives.

From 1865 to 1895 the nation struggled to find a way to integrate in
practice the broader usages of Equality consecrated by the Civil War and
mandated by the reconstructed Constitution. The public discourse of this
period marks clearly the constant shifting of argumentative positions as
white supremacists, republicans, and African-Americans actively negotiated the problem of living in a legally constituted egalitarian society.[2] And

in so doing, each in its own way strove to influence the mainstream political and cultural interpretations of Equality. White supremacists sought to limit its meaning in the narrowest possible terms to "the right of every man to eat the bread his own hands had earned."[3] This indicated a partial return to the minimalist, natural rights provision of Equal Rights established by the War for Independence, albeit with extension of those minimal rights to all persons. White republicans, influenced by the abstract Christian idealism of the pre–Civil War era, countered with a broader, more encompassing doctrine of Political Equality, but this generally did not include equality in schools or in the workplace; it almost never included equal access to elected office. African-Americans, seeking in some ways to assuage fears and prejudices of the dominant white political culture, proposed a usage of Equality that expanded the range of political rights, but that also treated individual merit as the test of persons and eschewed social interaction.

Neither racists nor egalitarians ever held full sway over the national consciousness in a way that allowed them to control the legal scope of Equality. At all times, the prevailing legal enactment of Equality functioned as a compromise among the competing voices and their diverse views of what American government should be. The national consciousness was thus literally crafted from the argumentative grounds that the warring parties shared, or from which they were willing to acquiesce. These grounds never achieved a settled state, and so from the 1870s to the 1890s an active process of public debate and negotiation resulted in a series of uneasy—and often unsound—compromises, with the national consciousness see-sawing from Political Equality to Legal Equality to the "separate, but equal" doctrine.

This debate did not occur in a historical vacuum. As we demonstrated in Part One, the political value of the word "equality" is at least as old as the nation. And while the founders made a point of minimizing the scope of its public usage, they also established its rhetorical foundations in a way that gave both black and white abolitionists a powerful source for critiquing the institution of slavery and the efforts to promote African colonization. Additionally, during the Jacksonian era the white Anglo-American usage of Equality underwent two limited but ultimately significant rhetorical transformations. The first was the expansion of the suffrage in Northern states and Western territories to all white males regardless of economic station.[4] Equality thus appeared to be more inclusive than the rights to life, liberty, and property, incorporating at the state and local levels the rights to vote and hold office. The second transformation was Andrew Jackson's appropriation of the phrase "equal protection." Jackson employed the phrase in vetoing the proposal for a national bank in 1832, arguing against the disproportionate economic advantage such an institution would afford some citizens over others.[5] Equal protection thus came to be affiliated with the principle of laissez-faire government, the claim that the state should not act so as to favor the property rights of some groups or individuals over those of others.

Both of these usages authorized the federal government's passivity in enacting Equality, and while they seem modest by the standards a century of progress would bring, at the same time they constituted the most pragmatically egalitarian government on the face of the earth. The Civil War and the ideological contest that preceded it put a severe strain on that government, literally testing the durability of the nation's constitution. However, both the test and the contest cleared a discursive space for moral growth, and it was the public debate occupying that space in the thirty years immediately following the war that set the stage for the rhetorical integrations of Equality in the twentieth century.

That debate unfolded between 1865 and 1896 in three stages that we identify roughly as reconstruction (1865–70), redemption (1871–80), and separation (1881–96).[6] The three dominant voices in this debate were expressed by inegalitarian white supremacists, egalitarian republicans, and African-Americans.[7] They articulated their positions in a thousand locales and public fora, including public lecture halls, the floors of state legislatures and the U.S. Congress, local newspapers, books, and pamphlets.[8] In what follows we first chart the competing arguments of each of these voices for each stage of the debate, and then we identify the ways in which they achieved rhetorical integration in official compromises that constituted a national public consciousness of Equality.

RECONSTRUCTION (1865–1870)

The end of the war brought not only an end to slavery but loud and vociferous proclamations of universal freedom. This marked a significant change in public attitude, but the change was not nearly as monumental as some commentators suggest.[9] The nation had originally committed itself to eliminating slavery if it could be done without violating Property or States Rights.[10] As numerous Northern agitators pointed out, by seceding from the Union the Confederate states abrogated their right to any protection of their property; hence, practical or philosophical barriers to enacting the commitment to Universal Liberty no longer existed.[11] Nonetheless, there is a profound sense of bewilderment, awe, and humility in Abraham Lincoln's Second Inaugural Address, as he looks backward upon the forces of change to discover "that the cause of the conflict might cease with or even before the conflict itself should cease."[12]

The nation was changing at breakneck speed, and it caught even the leaders of that change entirely by surprise. Once they assured personal freedom, they had to turn their attention to the underlying problem in the national consciousness: What status should we grant America's erstwhile "aliens"? Recalling the problems of free, but not equal, blacks in the antebellum period, the question was: Would the freedpersons share Equal Rights with the nation's European descendants? And if so, which rights would they share? Crafting an answer to these questions was the key task facing America in the age of Reconstruction. White supremacists, republicans, and African-Americans all approached it in characteristically different ways.

White Supremacists

White supremacists sought to reestablish slavery in everything but name and property rights. The visible product of this was the Black Codes, which enacted the belief that whites should use "severe legislation . . . to compel negroes" to engage in "coarse, common manual labor, and to punish them for dereliction of duty or nonfulfillment of their contracts with sufficient severity, to make the great majority of them useful, productive laborers."[13] Northerners saw this as the reestablishment of slavery, and given that the Southern states had not yet been readmitted to the Union on equal terms, the Republican minority quickly wielded its military superiority and squelched any effort to revive the past.

Fear and confusion reigned throughout the white South, as former slave owners were forced at gunpoint to establish a new relationship with their former slaves. Some white Southerners responded by adopting fully egalitarian positions, but the more typical response declared itself in the vocabulary of white supremacy.[14] The central principle of this ideology was a belief in the inherent racial inferiority of the "negro," and as a result, white supremacists devoted a great deal of rhetorical effort to characterizing blacks as incompetent, ignorant, and unworthy of republican government.[15] The *Atlanta Constitution*, hardly a voice of extremism, asked in 1868 if "a million precious lives of the white men of America were sacrificed to appease the greasy, filthy, lazy, brutish negro?"[16] Additionally, white supremacists argued that the Negro's inferiority was fixed and certain, not solely a matter of the present condition of the race but inexorably demonstrated by its lack of achievement in any condition throughout human history: "We do not trace to him any of the achievements in art, science and literature, which mark the progressive developments of mankind."[17] Racial hierarchy was a natural and divine condition.[18] For whites to enter into equality with blacks was thus to lower their own status.[19]

More so, it was to risk losing everything, for white supremacists joined the argument of racial inferiority with a fear of "negro domination."[20] Revisionist historians tend to deprecate this fear, characterizing it as an ingenuine ploy. Thus, for example, they point out that blacks never actually dominated the governments of the South.[21] However, in the years before redemption, "negro domination" was as much a fear about what might happen as it was a description of existing conditions. Those defeated by Yankees, economically destitute, and surrounded by a black majority only recently freed from the brutalizations of slavery might reasonably balk at a future in which the people they had so completely degraded held substantial political power. *De Bow's Review* stirred this fear, warning that blacks "hold incendiary meetings, caucuses, and conventions every day. They are all around; they are continually drilling in defiance of law. They have everywhere secret military organizations."[22]

The fear of domination was not only a fear of violence but also a recognition of the power that a republican government could put into the hands of an alien people. *De Bow's Review* continued its warning: "[T]he negro tenants, next year, will claim half of our lands, and negro judges, jurors, justices, etc., will sustain their claims."[23] White supremacists were not willing to take this risk, and so they concluded that a government based on Equality was not possible. Senator Thomas A. Hendricks of Indiana supported their judgment in the U.S. Congress: "I can say to the Senator that they never will associate with the white people of this country upon terms of equality. . . . If they are among us as a free people, they are among us as an inferior people."[24] In a system historically premised on homogeneity, the existence of difference coded as "inferiority" signaled the absence of the necessary "genius" for republican forms of government. It thus became an adequate barrier to political equality. For, as *De Bow's Review* concluded, "We must quite expel nature before we can make the negroes the equal of the whites, or even so elevate them, as to fit them to be governed by a code so mild as that which suffices to govern whites."[25]

Republicans and Egalitarians

White supremacists found strong, though not diametric, opposition in the public discourse of egalitarian republicans. The commitment of Republicans to Equality was limited, for most restricted the right to Political Equality, and even then they treated it as an "experiment." Both white and black republicans writing in the mainstream press agreed with white supremacists that the ex-slaves were *currently* inferior to whites, but they generally believed that this condition was mutable. The *Monthly Religious Review* asked, "Is it possible that the former can be so educated, elevated, and civilized as to take their place on equal terms with their lighter-complexioned fellow-citizens?" They concluded that it was possible but offered no prediction about the completeness of this equality, arguing only that "the negro be allowed to stand in the position to which he is entitled by whatever intelligence and integrity he may possess."[26] The *Nation's* E. L. Godkin was even more stern, warning, "The negro race must, in short, win a good social position in the way other races have won it; and when it has its roll of poets, orators, scholars, soldiers, and statesmen to show, people will greatly respect it; but not till then."[27] It is important to note that unlike white supremacists, republicans did not see inferiority of education, civilization, or attainment as a disqualification for Political Equality. Rather, recalling the tones of Jacksonian rhetoric, they claimed, "Distinctions in society will always exist under every just government. Equality of talents, of education, or of wealth cannot be produced by human institutions." Nonetheless, they concluded, "every man is equally entitled to protection by law."[28]

Generally speaking, however, reconstruction republicans were willing to do something distinctly non-Jacksonian, that is, to support governmental activities such as the Freedman's Bureau, designed to elevate freed blacks. Godkin quoted Frederick Douglass's request that the white man "leave the black man alone" but warned that this could only be done at an appropriate time, when everything had been done "to make the difficulties with which the negro has to contend no greater than those with which poor white men have to contend."[29] Most republicans saw this as a temporary expedient, justified solely by the conditions of militarily induced emancipation.

Although republicans supported Political Equality, they were split over the desirability of Social Equality. Most simply refused to contemplate the issue, as though it resided beyond the realm of government consideration. They argued that it was a "bugbear" and that "the negro in the south does not want social equality." These rhetors often interpreted Social Equality as including both intermarriage and access to public accommodations.[30] A few writers entertained the possibility of social equality, but even they indicated that the process of achieving it would be long and arduous.[31] Moreover, like the white supremacists, they tended to speak in terms that emphasized the race as an organic whole rather than as a collection of individuals. Godkin continued the argument cited above by focusing on the collective when he suggested that "[p]eople won't dare to sneer at a black skin when they have become familiar with the spectacle of a black skin covering sages and heroes and jurists and millionaires."[32] White rhetors did not propose individual merit as the test of recognition; rather, they believed that elevating the status of the race as a whole might encourage popular acceptance of the race's Political Equality.

African-Americans

By 1890 African-Americans had gained substantial access to the national arena through the periodical press. However, during the years of reconstruction and redemption, black national discourse occurred primarily at black conventions and in black newspapers. It should come as no surprise that this black national discourse differed substantially from the prominent white voices speaking in this early period. The most notable difference was the virtual unanimity among African-Americans with regard to the necessity of *immediate* Political Equality, including the full range of civil and political rights for which they had agitated before the war. This included "equal schools," "equal rights to be sworn as a witness," and "equality and perfect franchise" as well as "equal accommodations for equal pay" and "equal justice before the law." In short, they insisted on "complete equality—legally and politically . . . without regard to race or color."[33] They not only wanted formal Political Equality, however, but the social "recognition" of equality that they could bequeath to their children as "the most precious [of] legacies."[34] All of this aside, they nonetheless entered delicately into the brawl over their desire as a race for Social Equality.

Black advocates frequently denied that they wanted "social equality," but they meant something different by this than did most whites. In this early period, there was a general lack of specificity on all sides about the meaning of "social equality." African-Americans highlighted three aspects of the term. First, they characterized social relations as regulated by a "higher" law.[35] They argued that the government could neither control the respect that one person held for another (wherein Social Equality meant "social recognition") nor compel personal intimacy between people who did not seek it (wherein Social Equality meant "social interaction"). Second, they emphasized that they had no desire for interracial marriages or social relationships, for they found white Americans to be no more socially desirable than their own people. Finally, they insisted that they would not concede their access to public accommodations by giving up "public rights."

This was the primary definitional problem facing African-American rhetors. They wished to draw a line between Social Equality, which the government could not and should not regulate, and "public rights," which the government should insure for all. At the 1866 State Convention of

Colored People of Georgia, those present insisted they were "disavow-
ing 'any desire for social equality beyond the transactions of ordinary business life, inasmuch as we deem our own race equal to all our wants of
purely social enjoyment.'"[36] Frederick Douglass's marriage to a white
woman suggested that this position was not universally shared, but most
black newspapers castigated his choice. The near consensus of black opinion, however, indicated that marriage should be a matter of individual
choice and that they were not going to force themselves "unwanted" upon
anybody, white, black, or otherwise.

The issue of Social Equality was vital to the formulation of a national
compromise. The white supremacist's insistent drumming against "amalgamation" and "miscegenation" as the necessary end result of Social
Equality kept blacks from claiming full Equality. And indeed, it was the
unified opposition of white leaders to Social Equality that guided black
leaders when they carefully qualified their demands, concluding, "Freedom, justice and equality (that is equality before the law,) must be the
motto."[37] Thus, in this period, the most frequent usage of Equality as a
constitutional value became the phrase "Equality Before the Law." As will
become increasingly clear, this proved to be a consequential concession.

The African-American's demand for Equality was also substantially
different from that of most liberal whites, who drew upon the Christian
concept of the universal brotherhood of humanity. Such abstract Christian
rhetoric held out a vision of Equality that treated all individuals as equal "in
God's eyes," making them all "of the same blood." This vision had been
vital to the antislavery argument, but beyond positing a baseline for human dignity it failed to offer a model for enacting human political interac-
tions.[38] Although clearly motivated by Christian principles, the African-
American vision was far more concrete. It forecast a version of human
equality based on a model that allowed one to continue to discriminate
among people, so long as one did not judge with "distinction as to race."

This usage of Equality arose in part because of the particular character
of the black leadership. As any number of commentators have pointed out,
the black political leadership in this period emanated largely from elite,
middle-class mulattoes.[39] The vision of equality they sponsored was similar to that of their white middle-class counterparts in that it emphasized
the value of individual merit. They did not argue that all persons should be
treated equally in all ways nor did they support economic equality as a substantive end. Rather, they promoted the antebellum interpretation of
Equality contained in the phrase "equal opportunity." Continuously they
repeated, "We ask no special privileges; we only ask for a fair chance in the
race of life, and recognition according to our personal merits. To ask less is

not manly—to ask more is foolishness."[40] Having achieved a degree of economic success themselves under the worst of circumstances, they faithfully believed that other blacks were equally capable of earning wealth, of contributing to the production of high culture, and of advancing the boundaries of scientific knowledge.

The preference for earned wealth extended to land ownership. August Meier argues that the upper- and middle-class leadership, much to the contrary of the black peasantry, placed more emphasis on rights and less emphasis on land.[41] This is only partially correct, for the significant difference between classes concerned the way in which they argued for acquiring land. Immediately after the war, the newly created black peasant class, prompted by a minority leadership of people like Martin R. Delany, publicly supported proposals that would confiscate the plantations and redistribute them to former slaves. By contrast, the majority black leadership enthusiastically emphasized the value and necessity of *earning* and *purchasing* one's own land and homes. Indeed, such encouragement quickly equaled and rapidly outweighed the commitment to political rights.[42]

Black leaders thus typically asked for nothing more for their people than what their "ability and importance in the State demand, of that they [whites] may be judges, provided they judge us by the same rules that white men are judged."[43] And with the faith that in time merit would erase the color line, they relied on the phrase "without distinction of race or color" as the key to unlocking the riches of Equality. This is not to say that they argued for a completely laissez-faire government. They did not simply apply the Jacksonian notion of Equal Protection to people of all colors as a means of producing equal opportunity.[44] Although they generally disavowed requests for "special privileges" in view of past suffering and denial of rights, they recognized the need for "protection" and frequently pleaded for "legal protection against every species of outrage."[45] They keenly recognized that Equal Protection would involve substantial government activity. They warned that "the concession of rights in a legal form is comparatively valueless and often a mockery unless supported by the whole judicial and military power of the country."[46] The issue of federal enforcement became the crucial point on which they and their white allies would eventually part company, and once that happened, it would take a full century before whites caught up with the black view.

African-Americans thus advocated the most extensive version of Equality in the Western tradition to that time. The usages were not yet as extensive as they would become in the 1960s, but they included Equality before the Law, Equal Chance, Equal Justice, Equal Footing, Equal Opportunity, and Equal Rights. These usages would require substantial government action to bring them about, for they framed a far more vigorous interpretation of the changing Constitution than even that which the mainstream republicans were willing to acknowledge.

Official Compromises

The array of worldviews in the postbellum era was as large as at any time in American history. Yet most of these views stood upon some common ground. Almost all agreed that slavery should be abolished and that the claim "all men are created equal" indicated that persons could not be reduced to property. If we remember to count Southern blacks, a majority also came to believe in the necessity of a broader sense of Political Equality; but there was no consensus on the scope of that Equality, whether, for example, it should include voting rights or the rights to hold office, serve on juries, use public accommodations, and so on. Most also agreed that the government should not act to create Social Equality, although there was little agreement on what actual role the federal government should play.

The nation's law was built upon the common grounds among these various positions, just as were the national directions articulated by the various presidents as they addressed the American people. The outlines of national law carved in this period are broadly familiar: the Freedman's Bureau was implemented to assist the slaves in their transition to free labor; the Thirteenth Amendment enacted a permanent and universal proscription against slavery; the Fourteenth Amendment granted citizenship to all freedpersons, simultaneously protecting their rights and threatening to penalize any states that withheld enfranchisement from them; the Fifteenth Amendment proscribed voting rights discrimination. All of this was accomplished before the end of 1870. Historians have so frequently rehearsed this program of reconstruction that it does not bear close scrutiny here.[47] For our present purpose, however, it is worth noting how these laws steered among the three prevailing participants in the public debate.

The Thirteenth Amendment posed no serious rhetorical or ideological problems. While many white supremacists would have preferred to retain chattel slavery, even they widely conceded its provisions as the price of defeat. And in this context many claimed that the South has "abolished slavery by an astonishing unanimity."[48] The Freedman's Bureau developed as a war measure, and it rapidly lost favor on the grounds that it cost too much, provided special privileges to blacks, and encouraged black dependency rather than self-reliance. It thus neither directly challenged the assumption of black inferiority nor provided a precedent for enacting the African-American's notion of government protection and Equal Rights. It served primarily the white republican concept of Equality, and then only under the extraordinary conditions of the war.

The Fourteenth and Fifteenth Amendments are somewhat more difficult to place. With the benefit of hindsight, it is tempting to read these amendments as an effort to guarantee full equality to America's black population. There is much textual support for such a sweeping interpretation in the public statements of those who drafted these measures and shepherded them through Congress. Locating intent in this way, however, ignores the fact that each of these amendments underwent multiple revisions designed not only to insure their passage in Congress but to present an ideological compromise that would earn them popular ratification. So, for example, each amendment intentionally hedges the issue of equality so as to allow both a narrow and a broad reading of its applications and implications. The Fourteenth and Fifteenth Amendments thus constituted neither an egalitarian outpost established by an enlightened minority and later forsaken by a depraved majority, nor merely a sham form of Equality. Each amendment represented a compromise between regnant, competing ideologies, and they embodied this competitive tension in strategic ambiguity.

This shows up most painfully in the equal protection clause. The country was still bound to the model of state sovereignty, and so the Fourteenth Amendment prescribed federal action only against state violations.[49] Perhaps if the authors had known how this would get played out in the 1890s so as to provide absolutely no equal protection, they would have worked harder to overcome the objections of their contemporaries and written to foreclose such a narrow interpretation. But of course that is pure speculation on our part, and we cannot know that if they had done so it would have been successfully passed and ratified.

The linking of citizenship to place of birth rested on firmer ground, for it followed the ideal proposed by antebellum black rhetors. After vigorous debate, the Fourteenth Amendment enshrined the assumption that African-Americans were a part of "the people." This concession, however, did not wholly embody the African-American interpretation of equal rights. Although white republicans and African-Americans agreed on a very broad range of citizenship rights, white supremacists, adamantly opposed to such an interpretation, proposed a counterinterpretation in which citizenship did not even entail full political equality for whites. The Fourteenth Amendment thus provided no definitive answer to the scope of equal citizenship rights.

In the coming years, strength for the narrow interpretation of citizenship rights would evolve from the fact that in a laissez-faire government the line between the public and private (or social) spheres is vague at best, generally favoring a large degree of freedom in a large private sphere. Citizenship clearly guaranteed Equality in the rights of Life, Liberty, and Property. What other rights it entailed, if any, was much less clear. Suffrage? Jury duty? Civil service jobs? Access to all businesses and travel facilities? Many came to see citizenship as tantamount to an equality of all rights, arguing that there could be "no safe middle ground" between "slavery and full citizenship."[50] Yet, as a matter of fact, women provided an obvious model of a class of citizens who lacked political equality as well as a broad range of other rights. Moreover, there was nothing clear or obvious about the claim that all persons should have governmentally protected access to restaurants, inns, parks, schools, and the like. The Fourteenth Amendment's declarations of citizenship and Equal Protection did not self-evidently guarantee that all persons would be treated in all respects without regard for their race. As the political debate of the reconstruction period began, the narrow, white supremacist interpretation of citizenship had distinct political advantages, and it would take a century of experience with interracial citizenship for the nation as a whole to conclude that a fuller Equality was the most tenable meaning of this amendment to the Constitution.

The Fifteenth Amendment came close to providing the mechanism for guaranteeing all other forms of "equality before the law." If one could control the legislature, one could insure equal access to facilities and equal protection of rights. This is why African-Americans asked for the franchise, declaring "give us the ballot and the country is safe."[51] In so speaking, they voiced that unique combination of self and general interest that defines representative government. From their view, the largest threat to the Union came from a group of rebel secessionists who demonstrated no allegiance to the government or its prevailing vision of freedom and equality. Giving the blacks electoral supremacy in the South would presumably prevent the reestablishment of the conditions that led to the Civil War. This was not a merely partisan matter. For black republicans, the confluence of personal survival and principle made it a matter of the first order, and necessarily so. Nonetheless, the amendment left open a crucial loophole, and many at the time knew that they were doing so.

The particular form of the Fifteenth Amendment accurately reflected the lack of political consensus characteristic of the period. It sought to protect the democratic ideal of voting from discrimination based on racial prejudice. While not all Northerners approved of granting "ignorant blacks" the vote, the majority was willing to accede access to the franchise for accomplished and propertied blacks. Many Southern patriarchs also supported this position. The phrasing of the Fifteenth Amendment, which prohibited discrimination based on race rather than guaranteeing the right to vote, institutionalized this middle ground in the Constitution. It left open the possibility that blacks and whites could be disproportionately disenfranchised to the extent that African-Americans in fact diverged from whites in some systematic way. Meanwhile, the South, while still largely under the force of coercion, could at least acquiesce to the amendment. Moreover, the contemporary African-American conception of Equality was compatible with such a perspective, and many black leaders openly agreed to such a qualification of voting on the grounds of "character" or "culture."[52] Ultimately, the nation refused to accommodate such restrictions on the franchise, but the formulation of such a case would take time. The Fifteenth Amendment, written to allow a wide construction, enacted a vague and loose compromise among the agreements and disagreements of the time. Those who call it the high-water mark of equality or a cynical ploy are equally wrong. It was simply the entering wedge in the debate.

The development of a national ideological compromise that offered a restricted political equality with little amelioration of basic living conditions can also be traced in more direct form in presidential epideictic speaking.[53] Lincoln's ceremonial speeches featured two striking elements. The first was the widely celebrated shift from tolerance of slavery to abolition, and the second was a commitment to colonization.[54] It seems strange to many that the Great Emancipator was also the great colonizationist, but as we demonstrated in Chapter 3, this simply illustrates the extent to which Lincoln spoke directly from the heart of the dominant Anglo-American worldview. It is not clear that Lincoln ever came to believe that blacks and whites could share America as equals under the form of government he loved. Gradually, however, he ceased to tie emancipation to colonization, and the thought disappeared from his later State of the Union addresses and his Second Inaugural Address.[55] Although whites would not cure their urge for separation for many years, Lincoln was the last president publicly to support colonization as a final remedy.

In many ways, Andrew Johnson simply picked up where Lincoln left off, although with far less dignity. In his first State of the Union Address, Johnson endorsed the Thirteenth Amendment, rejoicing that "slavery, the element which has so long perplexed and divided the country," would be effaced. He also represented the unified mind of the nation when he espoused the principle that "[t]he American system rests on the assertion of the equal right of every man to life, liberty, and the pursuit of happiness, to freedom of conscience, to the culture and exercise of all his faculties."[56] He violated the opinions of only the most extreme white supremacists when he further extended these rights specifically to former slaves, noting that "good faith requires the security of the freedmen in their liberty and their property, their right to labor, and their right to claim the just return of their labor."[57]

It is not insignificant that as a Southerner he also endorsed the Jacksonian ideal of "'equal and exact justice to all men,' special privileges to none," and embraced public education, while denouncing forced colonization. This reads like a progressive list, and it was. But it was also sharply limited, both out of commitment and the political necessity to walk a balanced line between the progressive North and the regressive South. A careful reading of the statement indicates that although he evoked the broad tones of Equality, his list included only personal rights to freedom, life, and property, ignoring all civil or political rights. Further, he expressed the sense in which the nation looked to the new, limited egalitarianism as an "experiment." Although he opposed deportation and urged Southerners to "avoid hasty assumptions of any natural impossibility for the two races to live side by side in a state of mutual benefit and good will," he also echoed the white supremacist sentiment that blacks might face extermination if left in open competition with whites, suggesting that "if they fail, and so perish away, let us be careful that the failure shall not be attributable to any denial of justice."[58]

Historians often treat Johnson as a backslider, but his Third State of the Union Address, fully consistent with his First, articulated the shared ground between white republicans and supremacists.[59] In the later speech, he placed the need to restore the Union as a more pressing matter, but he was hardly inconsistent in urging repeal of the Reconstruction acts on grounds that "these are powers not granted to the Federal Government," or that such acts "trample down all those rights in which the essence of liberty consists."[60] When he insisted on the "dignity, equality, and rights of the States or of individuals," he explicated the reigning balance between the concern with individual rights and States Rights. For ultimately, in the South as for much of the North in this period, the old Jeffersonian vision still obtained: the best protection of Liberty resided in the absence of a strong and centralized federal government. The strengthening of the federal government, even on the grounds of the protection of individual rights, could only threaten that individual Liberty. As Johnson warned, "It is the curse of despotism that it has no halting place."[61] Hence, as the war ended, it was not a "waning interest" of the Republicans or of the nation that led to a retrenchment of rights commitments. Rather, it was the end of war powers that brought about a shared inactivity by both egalitarians and white supremacists. Egalitarians wanted Equal Rights for blacks, but assumed that the freedmen were so situated that they could make their own way. White supremacists did not believe that they were so situated, but they also did not care that their former slaves would be unable to achieve equality.

The story is the same with regard to other elements of Johnson's Message to Congress, which represented equally jarring and uncomfortable compromises. He offered an extended defense of his opposition to a national mandate to enfranchise former slaves. He defined the "glory of white men" as resting in his having exhibited the necessary qualities "in sufficient measure to build upon this continent a great political fabric and to preserve its stability for more than ninety years, while in every other part of the world all similar experiments have failed." By contrast, he argued that "negroes have shown less capacity for government than any other race of people."[62] He once again, however, struck an ideological compromise. Rather than argue explicitly for disenfranchisement as a permanent and universal condition, he left the matter to the states, thus accommodating the goals of the white supremacists and the sensitivities of the egalitarians.

The final compromise Johnson struck was to support the white supremacists in drawing the line at "negro domination," claiming that "the transfer of our political inheritance to them would, in my opinion, be an abandonment of a duty which we owe alike to the memory of our fathers and the rights of our children."[63] He repudiated the worst tendencies of the racists, however, supporting the republicans in "[his] willingness to join in any plan within the scope of our constitutional authority which promises to better the condition of the negroes in the South, by encouraging them in industry, enlightening their minds, improving their morals, and giving protection to all their just rights as freedmen."[64]

Andrew Johnson left office under a dismal cloud. His sin, however, was not his failure to articulate a reasonable compromise on racial equality among the rhetorics of various white constituencies. Rather, he disagreed about the time at which the state of war should be ended, and the relative powers of the president and Congress. However, in balancing State Rights against individual rights, in casting the negro as inferior, and in seeing the desirability of assisting and elevating the status of African-Americans, he clung to a narrow compromise that represented the opinions of the most articulate and vocal white Americans. In the period of redemption that followed, the speeches of Presidents Grant and Hayes would sound far more egalitarian, but this shift was caused by the inclusion of African-Americans in the national audience.

Redemption (1871–1880)

The decade of redemption was a period of intense and confounding legal contradictions. When Congress passed the Civil Rights Bill of 1874 it made an effort to institute a broad and encompassing conception of Equality that would protect both the political and civil rights of all citizens, including assured equal access to all public accommodations, without regard to race or color. Additionally, Congress buttressed its work with a variety of enforcement provisions. This Congress was not in tune with the prevailing national consciousness, however, and when it was soon replaced by one more compatible with the nation's perceived needs, America's most radical reformers lost the forum from which they might effectively have lobbied their proposal. Sadly, while the Congress of 1874 sat in session, the bills it crafted did not provide an adequate compromise among the competing ideological positions vying for control of the constitutional value of Equality, and as such it achieved no support from the president, the Supreme Court, or the people.

At the other end of the spectrum, Southern Democrats employed violence, intimidation, and fraud to remove Republicans from power. Just as the radical Republicans could not effectively claim to speak for the nation, so too Southern Democrats had difficulty identifying a national audience. Their violent treatment and disfranchisement of African-Americans alienated Northerners, who found such behavior repugnant, but the Northern response was relatively mild and never very sustained. One might have expected liberally inclined presidents like Ulysses S. Grant and Rutherford B. Hayes to intervene forcefully, but they did not. And as a result, those who sought to redeem the white South won the day.

To explain these apparent inconsistencies historians have sometimes simplified the problem by focusing on the shift from a national Republican government to state Democratic governments. This explanation has much to recommend it, but ultimately it conceals a number of larger issues, including both how and why the shift occurred, and, more important, why it entailed the specific set of public usages that came to the fore. In order to answer these questions it is once again necessary to chart the arguments of white supremacists, republicans, and African-Americans before considering how they achieved integration in an official compromise.

White Supremacists

As soon as white Southerners recaptured control of their political community, the supremacist argument split into two different voices. One voice spoke an essentially elitist, romantic patriarchalism; the other voice sounded the racial chauvinism of a group of belligerent "fire-eaters."[65] Both voices concurred on several fundamental points as necessary to the redemption of the South. First, the Redeemers agreed on the vital need for the South to control its own political destiny.[66] Second, they agreed that to allow the kind of Political Equality that granted black control of government risked the stability and security of both Liberty and Property.[67] And finally, they agreed that the "negro" was inferior to the "white race." Beyond these three points, their beliefs and public usages differed in significant ways.

Fire-eaters like Montgomery Blair and Henry Watterson constituted the dominant political force in the daily commercial life of the South. They expressed a form of white supremacy that rationalized the white South's pillaging of the labor and goods of African-Americans, openly justifying a socioeconomic system that replicated the former slave system in every way except for the literal ownership of individual blacks.[68] To that end they denied the possibility of elevating blacks from their "naturally" debased and subservient position, adamantly maintained that "the races could not live together as equals," and explicitly rejected any possible sense of equality in government.[69]

The fire-eaters' version of white supremacy might well have chilled the hearts and steeled the resolve of Yankees and Unionists had there not been another voice emanating from the South. It too articulated a firm commitment to white supremacy but it did so in more compromising and accommodating tones, and as such it was heard more clearly in the national arena. The romanticized paternalism of Lucius Quintus, Cincinnatus Lamar, Alexander H. Stephens, and even the early Wade Hampton offered a very different picture of the white South. These men assured their readers that they supported the national commitment to equality before the law, and they further agreed with the republican belief that, though inferior, the negro race could be helped to achieve an elevated position in society.[70] As Lamar argued in 1879, "[W]hat we of the South have borne, our friends of the North must bear with us, until the negro has become what we both want to make him."[71]

A key problem confronting the patriarchs was to find a way to defend their violent and fraudulent appropriation of Southern government. They argued by parallel analogy that the election frauds that had most recently run the Republicans out of office were no different than those that had originally helped them to gain office during the reconstruction period.[72] Moreover, they justified the violent shift in governments as a necessary means of eliminating the "wanton misrule" of black Republicans. Thus it was, for example, that the *Atlanta Constitution* railed against "ignorant negro officials who have ruled and robbed the city [of Vicksburg] for years," and insisted on the right of "tax payers to protect themselves against the rapacity of the negro thieves."[73]

Unlike the fire-eaters, the patriarchs wanted to enhance their identification with Northern white audiences, and so they went to great pains to emphasize the reasonableness of their position. Cincinnatus Lamar underscored the "intellectual culture," "moral strength," "material interests," and "political experience" of the region before going on to ask, "[I]s not this result [rule by elites] exactly what the intelligence, character, and property of the country are striving to effect in every Congressional district in the Union?"[74] Moreover, they argued, blacks recognized this right to rule, for as Wade Hampton put it, "As the negro becomes more intelligent, he naturally allies himself with the more conservative of the whites."[75]

Not content simply to rationalize their own behaviors, Southern patriarchs went on the offensive. They accused the Northern press and legislators of exaggerating "Southern Outrages," and dismissed such stories as a "tissue of exaggerations and misrepresentations from the beginning to the end."[76] They even denied that blacks had experienced wholesale disenfranchisement. As Lamar pointed out in 1879: "[T]he statistics of election will show that the negro vote throughout the South has not been suppressed. That there have been instances of fraud and force I admit and deplore, but they have been exceptional."[77] Some went so far as to argue that the invidious segregation of public accommodations in the South was a myth.[78] And whatever the case might be, they insisted that individual violations of rights—and those were the only kind that they conceded might exist—could and should be remedied through the courts, for the states themselves had not acted to violate the rights of anyone.[79]

The patriarchal voice of the white supremacist promised Northern moderates that "[we] are more than prepared to guarantee that there will be no serious breaches of the peace; [we] are more than ready to give assurances that the law will be respected and maintained . . . to guarantee protion [sic: protection] of life, liberty, and property to every human being within its borders."[80] With these assurances, and with the apparent congruence of republican and patriarchal positions on issues such as State Sovereignty, black inferiority, the respect for rights, and the need to elevate the status of blacks, it is not difficult to see how men such as President Hayes could come to believe that Southerners would honestly enact the nation's embryonic egalitarian creed, however gradually. Egalitarian republicans certainly offered nothing to counter such a position, and in that context Hayes withdrew the last of the federal troops from the South in 1877.

Republicans and Egalitarians

Republican egalitarians offered only minimal resistance to the Southern patriarch's persuasion. Republican newspapers continued to publish stories documenting violence and fraud against blacks, and Northern whites and Southern blacks challenged the patriarchal vision of the white South on the floors of Congress.[81] However, most of this was dismissed as partisan propaganda. Most Northerners had no direct access to life in the South, and so one claim was as likely as the next. Without the means to assess the accuracy of competing claims, the Southern patriarch's romantic vision was undoubtedly more appealing than the republican's "bloody shirt."

This is not to say that the republicans capitulated completely to the burgeoning Southern myth of Reconstruction. D. H. Chamberlain challenged the notion that black leadership had destroyed the region, arguing that "the colored race gave to the Southern States wise, liberal, and just constitutions."[82] Generally, however, in the face of the Southern patriarch's reassurances, republican rhetoric was more or less nonresponsive, merely reiterating in general terms the importance of "equality in all civil and social rights, immunities, duties and obligations."[83]

Republican inaction sealed the convergence of patriarchal rhetoric and the national consensus in yet another way. The protection of blacks required reconstituting the government in an entirely new form, and this was something that republicans refused to do. The *Nation* explained the painful dilemma the country faced:

The negro voters being for the most part a poor and dependent and credulous class, how is the subtle and effectual intimidation of creditor, landlords, and employees to be <u>legally</u> met? How is the practice of spreading frightful stories among them about the consequences of voting to be put down? How are juries to be got to punish infractions of Federal election laws, except by packing them?

The editor answered this litany of daily experiences with the sober conclusion:

It will submit also to the people in black and white the momentous question, whether they are willing to make a fundamental change in their system of government in order to put an end, in four or five States out of thirty-eight, to disorders which there is strong reason to believe are transitory, and the chief causes of which are gradually disappearing before our eyes.[84]

As Harold Hyman amply demonstrated, in 1880, the new nation had no conception of itself as a centralized government. Moreover, it had no conception of statistical measures, proportional representation, or any of the

other machinery it would gradually invent as the accoutrement for constituting a heterogeneous "people." Hence, the problem was not so much
a vehement resistance to equal rights per se but the inability to imagine
how such rights could be enacted without simultaneously destroying personal liberties.

African-Americans

While white republicans came to trust the Southern patriarchal vision, and
thus failed to push aggressively for radical reform, African-Americans dis-
trusted it absolutely. Their distrust was of course born of their day-to-day
experience with the patriarchs, and this led them to ponder and debate
ways to reconfigure a government so as to make equality under the law a
literal fact of life. African-American leaders addressed this problem on
multiple national fronts.

To begin, African-American rhetors employed their first-hand experience with Southern life in testimonials designed to contradict the rosy portrait of white Southern government that had captured the national
consciousness. The difficulties of this task were many, especially given
that the Redeemers destroyed most Southern black newspapers, and
Northern black newspapermen lacked the immediate experience to make
their accounts compelling. Nevertheless, there were national venues in
which the case could be made, and African-Americans took full advantage
of them. So, for example, Congress held hearings on the "outrages" of the
South and on the Ku Klux Klan, and Senator John R. Lynch of Mississippi
used these and other occasions to characterize his personal experiences of
discrimination while traveling.[85]

Simply characterizing the terms of violence and degradation under
which they lived was not enough to satisfy the black community. African-
American leaders offered a variety of rhetorical responses ranging from an
appeal for the use of retaliatory violence to the promotion of migration to
the North.[86] The most important and prominent of such responses, however, was an argument for blacks to "elevate" themselves from their ignorance and poverty. In the words of the San Francisco *Elevator,* frequently
repeated in other forms, blacks needed to "put our own shoulders to the
wheel, and no longer complain of hard times."[87]

This rhetorical effort has been widely derided by those who consider
this campaign as little more than a form of Uncle Tomism. Black leaders
clearly urged the sacrifice of popular black culture and the appropriation of
middle- and upper-class bourgeois values.[88] It is equally possible, however, to judge this rhetorical campaign positively, as a grand and successful
effort to redefine a fragmented black slave culture as specifically African-

American.[89] However we finally judge it, there can be little question that it gradually worked profound changes on black and white culture. It is the dynamic of those changes that draws our attention.

The campaign began by acknowledging the inability of existing political methods to solve the problem of blacks and whites living together. In the South the problem was in large part a function of the superior political and economic power of whites.[90] In the rest of the country, it was a matter of sheer numbers. In any case, the experiences of black leaders rapidly led them to the conclusion that holding political office would not be sufficient to achieve any kind of substantive Equality. As with one voice, they began to articulate the necessity for the cultural and economic development of African-Americans:

. . . they are tired of risking their fortunes upon the uncertainties of politics. They recognize the fact that their only salvation lies in work. The right to franchise alone cannot elevate us to respectability among men. If we would win a name and a fame among nations, we must hew out our own fortunes.[91]

This, of course, required a change in the "ways of life" of black people, and that entailed a change to those social values that would lead to the acquisition of wealth: "Let us then be up and doing with a mind for any fate still achieving, still pursuing, learn to labor and to wait. Let us begin to cultivate virtue, temperance, industry—and be sparing."[92] At times, such appeals directed blacks to imitate white culture and business practices.[93] As the *Colored Citizen* harshly admonished its readers in 1878: "Never mind making excuses, do like other people, get a farm and suffer on it a few years, till you get a start and then by good management get rich. It pays to suffer a few years in this world, if that suffering ends finally in prosperity and plenty."[94]

The adoption of wage labor values inevitably clashed with the popular values of a people accustomed to their double heritage as Africans and slaves to work without wages. Based in their prior experiences, American blacks valorized a life-style inimical to the demands of industrial capitalism (e.g., displays of a zest for life, a love of spectacle, and an appreciation of the revelry of large social gatherings).[95] The national voices of the race actively discouraged these values, deriding excursions, parades, excessive fashion, emotional religious demonstrations, and short-term thinking.[96] "Nothing is worse than contentment in degradation," chastised the *Colored Citizen*.[97] Hence, most black newspapers launched a campaign against beggars or "loafers," and also set out to separate the upper and lower classes on the belief that the latter exerted an excessively negative moral influence on the former:

[O]ur colored papers throughout the land are advocating a dividing line, in our society. A line drawn between the moral and immoral of our race. . . . The managers of our entertainments should drive out the loose characters both male and female. There is none of us that have children, want them to associate with the loafers, thieves, bummers, harlots, street-walkers and prostitutes.[98]

The campaign for economic and cultural improvement led to a two-sided portrait of African-America in the nation's black press. On one hand, these newspapers featured columns that extolled the progress of the race, evidencing its claims with statistics, testimony, and illustrative examples of blacks who had made good.[99] This provided a counterbalance to the portrait of black ignorance and barbarism that prevailed in the white press and that was the basis for the national consensus of the last third of the nineteenth century. On the other hand, the specific task of black newspapers was to elevate their people, and so they frequently portrayed black Americans as saddled with nonproductive habits and values.[100] Characterizations such as these fed the national consensus by duplicating the claims of white egalitarian republicans. Booker T. Washington would eventually become the preeminent spokesperson for this view, but as August Meier demonstrates, his voice merely echoed the dominant black rhetoric of the era.[101]

This is not to say that African-American leadership in this period simply matched republican rhetoric point for point. Indeed, they pushed beyond in a number of important areas to explore the potential grounds for an even more radically egalitarian nation. Their first call for action came as an opposition to separate schools. Segregated education has always been a primary sticking point for civil rights propositions, for then as now, too many whites were unwilling to send their children to integrated schools.[102] While some black leaders saw separate schools as the only practical option for avoiding harsh treatment by white pupils or for securing employment for black teachers, most typically opposed them in principle.[103] Indeed, it was the black leaders of this period who first claimed that separate schools inevitably result in unequal appropriations for black and white students, and further that separate was not only inherently unequal but it reinforced prejudice by implying the inferiority of blacks.[104] Because the stigma of inferiority inhibited equal opportunity, and thus the chance to achieve wealth, black leaders treated this as the extremely important issue that it was.[105]

A second point of African-American opposition came in the more abstract demand for "respect." Haunting almost every black speech and newspaper of the era was the quest for the holy grail of "manhood" and "recognition." Speaking on the floor of Congress, Representative James

T. Rapier framed the demand in this fashion: "Mr. Speaker, nothing short of a complete acknowledgement of my manhood will satisfy me."[106] The *Colored Citizen* agreed, claiming, "[W]e are entitled to respect, and that due attention should be given to our deeds."[107]

Ultimately, "respect" was the reason that black leaders responded to the issue of social equality in such a disunified voice. Blacks were unwilling to concede their inferiority to whites in any way, but the realities of the Social Equality issue virtually trapped them into doing so. If they agreed to a federal ban on Social Equality, they implicitly acknowledged their inferiority in a system that placed being white at the top of the hierarchy, an implication that white supremacists in particular would quickly seize. If they challenged such a proscription, they would be interpreted as aspiring to the top of the hierarchy. Congressman Thomas Whitehead, for example, suggested that there was "this longing on the part of the colored man," but that "[y]ou have not the power to make him white, and he never will be satisfied short of that."[108] The real complication was that in the vocabulary of white supremacy, Social Equality functioned as a code word for interracial marriage and racial amalgamation. Black leaders skirted the paradox by denying either the desire for interracial marriage or for a law that would enforce social distinctions. Congressman John Lynch gave the most extended, cautious, and thoughtful response to the issue in a speech before Congress in 1878 that is notable for its effect upon republicans. Drawing on the doctrine of individualist merit he began:

That the passage of this bill can in any manner affect the social status of any one seems to me to be absurd and ridiculous. I have never believed for a moment that social equality could be brought about even between persons of the same race. I have always believed that social distinctions existed among white people the same as among colored people. . . . I cannot believe that gentlemen on the other side of the House mean what they say when they admit as they do, that the immoral, the ignorants and the degraded of their own race are the social equals of themselves [sic] and their families.

Having thus drawn a wedge in white solidarity on the basis of culture and class, he continued, "[T]here are hundreds and thousands of white people of both sexes whom I know to be the social inferiors of respectable and intelligent colored people." He went so far as to attack explicitly the racists on the other side of the aisle, asserting his superiority to some of them: "[I]f at any time I should meet any one of you at a hotel and occupy a seat at the same table with you, or the same seat in a car with you, do not think that I have thereby accepted you as a social equal. Not at all." His conclusion was a resounding no: "No, Mr. Speaker, it is not social rights that we desire. We have enough of that already. What we ask is protection in the enjoyment of *public* rights." And when such rights have been achieved, he promised, "[You] will find that there is no more social equality than before. That whites and blacks do not intermarry any more than they did before the passage of the bill."[109]

Lynch's arguments failed. The sticking point was the schools. Congressman John Storm of Pennsylvania, arguing to the middle segment of the nation who might have tolerated most such public rights, claimed that if consistency was important, the adoption of this position meant integrated schools. No one truly trusted the children of the nation to make their own distinctions on the basis of racial solidarity. Few believed that they should be allowed to make distinctions otherwise. Even black leaders, in denying that they sought social rights or social equality, agreed that some distinctions made on the basis of race might be appropriate if made at the individual level. Inasmuch as children were denied the status of individuals capable of making major decisions on their own, at least in the schools, governmentally imposed segregation seemed defensible. The schools case thus served as the issue that allowed white supremacists to defend the plausibility of their position. The generalization of social equality to other public facilities must not in themselves have carried logical or persuasive force, but the supremacists lumped all of the cases together. The failure of most black leaders to endorse Social Equality and to deny social distinctions on the basis of race meant that there was no voice articulating the practical equality of all races on earth. White men, however low their particular individual merits, remained happily content to think themselves superior as a race.

Had the majority of white Northerners accepted Lynch's argument, and even gone so far as to accept Social Equality, it is not clear that this would necessarily have led to Equality in the South. As we noted above, most whites generally agreed that the active involvement of the federal government in such matters crossed the boundary to despotism. Blacks, drawing from their radically different experience of the federal government as the agent of Liberty and the protector of individual rights, argued otherwise, vigorously supporting federal action. The *Colored Citizen* claimed, "We want no other laws than those made for every other class of citizens; neither do we want such discriminating laws as are passed by most of the former slave States. . . . All we ask is the interposition of national authority against the usurpation of such power by States."[110] John Mercer Langston pushed the argument further, claiming that "should the State fail to give such protection, it is the duty of the General Government to give it."[111] Years would pass before the wisdom they had gained from their experience could be shared, but by that time even more radical proposals would occupy the attention of African-Americans.

The forerunner of one of these proposals—affirmative action and economic quotas—was also developing in the black press of this time period. Black leaders began tentatively to express the idea that society ought to proportion its goods on the basis of race. Eventually, this idea would conflict with the ideology of individual merit, but at the time of its introduction it emphasized the relatively narrow redistribution of political goods, not the broader, social redistribution of economic goods. Blacks appealed to the Republicans to provide patronage jobs and minor electoral offices in recognition of the contribution of blacks to the party. This demand was surprisingly visible and sustained in black newspapers; nevertheless, the party refused on both grounds of principle and political expediency.

By the 1870s blacks had grown intolerant of this posture and demanded the opportunity to hold office themselves. They concluded, "If we are to take any part whatever in politics then we have just as much right to ask that colored men be placed in office, as any other element of the party has."[112] This position rapidly extended to patronage jobs, articulated in this fashion by the *Colored Citizen:*

There are several negro voters in this city, several negro property holders, and several negro tax-payers, and they have as much right to representation in these little matters [the appointment of a black policeman], as the other classes of people that go to make up the town.[113]

This is a long distance from the late twentieth-century idea of quotas, but it stirred the debate.

The black rhetoric of the Redemption era thus contributed in some ways to the consensus about limited Equality through its omissions and descriptions, but it also began to think out new possibilities and discover new paths.

Official Compromises and National Consensus

The Southern patriarchs successfully persuaded the North to withdraw from the South, and the issue of race relations reverted back to the State governments. A variety of factors motivated this change: the North tired of supervising the South, political maneuvering favored Southern Democrats, business interests preferred normalcy, and Southern white supremacists exercised greater will and the selective use of violence. Historians have duly noted all of these factors. Of equal importance, however, though far less remarked upon, is the fact that Southern patriarchs produced a public rhetoric that made them appear as if they occupied a national common ground between all of the competing parties.

White supremacists, republicans, and African-Americans all agreed that black abilities and accomplishments were currently inferior. Each group also agreed that government-sanctioned Social Equality was undesirable, although they disagreed on the meaning of social equality. Additionally, all but the fire-eaters agreed that blacks should be elevated—although again there were differences about how high—and that violence against blacks and election fraud should be ended. The only substantial disagreement separating the parties concerned the scope of federal power, but the only group to argue for federal control was the African-Americans. Southern patriarchs regained control of the issue by portraying their position as representing the common ground.

The appearance of compromise notwithstanding, serious disagreements lurked just beneath the veneer of public discussion. The white supremacists defined opposition to Social Equality so as both to exclude blacks from all white public facilities and to deny them a sense of common respect or dignity in their daily encounters. They allowed for the need to elevate blacks and to guarantee legal equality, but they meant this in the most imperialistic and minimalist ways possible: blacks should be socialized to the Puritan work ethic as a means of making them a more efficient work pool, not so they could become political equals. Moreover, while they opposed violence against blacks, the commitment was not deep enough to engender the necessary enforcement to convert the principle into policy.

These differences were not obvious, for they were never explicitly expressed. Nevertheless, their presence in the tone and details of patriarchal rhetoric mark it as an essentially antiegalitarian position, inherently at odds with republican commitments and more radical black interests. The presidents of the period featured a different tone in their version of the compromise. While granting the task of implementing Equality to the Southern patriarchs, they opted to use their office and station as a bully pulpit from which to articulate an egalitarian rhetoric.

The inaugural addresses of Rutherford B. Hayes and Ulysses S. Grant are practically indistinguishable with regards to the race issue. Both men agreed that "a moral obligation rests upon the National Government to employ its constitutional power and influence to establish the rights of the people it has emancipated, and to protect them in the enjoyment of those rights when they are infringed or assailed."[114] Their State of the Union addresses also expressed similar views, favoring "the full enjoyment by all classes of persons of those rights to which they are entitled under the Constitution and laws" and invoking "the aid and influence of all good citizens to prevent organizations whose objects are by unlawful means to interfere with those rights."[115]

Given these similarities it is perhaps odd that Hayes has suffered condemnation as the traitor to Reconstruction, while Grant is simply remembered as a political incompetent. Part of this may emanate from a small difference in their positions: Grant actually held out for slightly greater "constitutional power" in the federal government than did Hayes. However, in our judgment, a larger difference emanates from the fact that Hayes's presidency fell at that point in America's history "when such government [return to State sovereignty] is the imperative necessity required by all the varied interests, public and private, of those States."[116]

Both Grant and Hayes spoke the official compromise and national consensus of their decade. The first element of that consensus was their shared opposition to slavery, both in the United States and throughout the world. The second element of that consensus was their commitment to education as a primary mechanism for elevating blacks to a position where they might be worthy of citizenship. In fact, both of these presidents were actually progressive leaders, going beyond the national consensus to propose specific measures to insure education on a national basis and to give additional responsibility to the federal government. Most important, both men accepted both sides of the terrible ideological dilemma of their day: they believed that black men were citizens and that their rights ought to be protected; but they also agreed that the responsibility to insure such protection rested foursquare in the hands of the States. Their expression of that dilemma deserves attention.

Grant and Hayes both significantly surpassed their predecessors in the breadth of rights they assigned to all men equally, including not only Equal Liberties but the promise of equal accommodations and the vote. They even appeared in places to recognize as a necessity that citizens must share *all* rights. As Grant noted, "[T]he effects of the late civil strife have been to free the slave and make him a citizen. Yet he is not possessed of the civil rights which citizenship should carry with it. This is wrong, and should be corrected."[117] Similarly, Hayes called for "a civil policy which will forever wipe out in our political affairs the color line and the distinction between North and South."[118] By the same token, however, Grant took great care to deny that he would promote Social Equality:

Social equality is not a subject to be legislated upon, nor shall I ask that anything be done to advance the social status of the colored man, except to give him a fair chance to develop what there is good in him, given [sic] him access to the schools, and when he travels let him feel assured that his conduct will regulate the treatment and fare he will receive.[119]

Hayes sounded even more egalitarian, claiming in a speech that rested on the plane of high abstraction that blacks had been lifted "from a condition of servitude to that of citizenship, upon an equal footing with their former masters."[120]

At the same time that Grant and Hayes expressed these egalitarian commitments, they recognized the flip side of the dilemma in acknowledging that ultimately government must rest in the hands of the states. Grant, who had the Enforcement Acts at his disposal, nonetheless espoused his great "reluctance to exercise any of the extraordinary powers thereby conferred upon me." He later declared, "The whole subject of Executive interference with the affairs of a State is repugnant to public opinion. . . . Unless most clearly on the side of law, such interference becomes a crime. . . . I desire, therefore, that all necessity for Executive direction in local affairs may become unnecessary and obsolete."[121] Hayes located "honest and efficient local self-government as the true resource of those States for the promotion of the contentment and prosperity of their citizens."[122]

How then did these presidents reconcile these two conflicting tendencies? In some ways, the conflict of values that Grant and Hayes faced was precisely the conflict faced by the nation before the war. Prior to the war the conflict was between States' Rights and Property versus Freedom and Liberty. Now it was a conflict between States' Rights and Equality before the Law. The common denominator was racial conflict. Both resolved the dilemma in favor of States' Rights, and thus contravened the interests of egalitarians and African-Americans. Both decisions were also eventually overthrown by a change in the balance of power and values. In each instance, however, the fundamental values themselves survived, even though their relative place in the political hierarchy changed or the scope of their application expanded or contracted.

A great deal of attention has centered on the fact that both Grant and Hayes turned the matter over to the state governments and that this resulted in an outrageous step backward for African-Americans. It must be remembered, however, that they did so with the voice of the Southern patriarch in their ear, reassuringly promising that the Constitution would be respected and that African-American rights would be protected. They did so also with the insistence of white republicans that the freeman required cultural and economic uplifting before he could in fact be equal. And, finally, they did so within hearing distance of African-Americans who confidently asserted that while they had not yet achieved equal abilities with Caucasians, they could do so if given the chance to learn and earn.

Faced with this conjuncture of rhetorics, Grant and Hayes enacted a faithful compromise among the disparate elements of the fractured national will. They did not, however, stop there. For each, and especially Hayes, used his national office to promote broad egalitarian principles. And while their proclamations of these principles cannot be taken as an indication of the state of the nation, they provided a direction and marked a trail. As Hayes warned his fellow Americans in 1877:

But it must not be forgotten that only a local government which recognizes and maintains inviolate the rights of all is true self-government. . . . The Evils which afflict the Southern States can only be removed or remedied by the united and harmonious efforts of both races, actuated by motives of mutual sympathy and regard.[123]

The nation, however, still had much to learn.

Separation (1880–1896)

The redemption of Southern white power interests occurred at different years in different states.[124] Once it achieved completion, the revolutionary rhetoric instrumental in bringing it about was no longer viable. In its place there developed a maintenance rhetoric that sought to specify and routinize the social and political relations central to the new way of life. Southern patriarchs, finally once again ruling their own destiny, did not want to have to employ violence as the primary means of repressing black citizens on a daily basis.[125] The reason for this, of course, is that they feared provoking the federal government into changing its mind and reasserting its authority over the states. While the white supremacist voice dominated the process of redefining the contours of daily living in the South, its ultimate success relied upon the acquiescence of republicans and African-Americans; constant violence would make such acquiescence highly unlikely. Additionally, once white Southerners made it obvious that they had no intention of enacting the Northern vision of a limited Political Equality, they had to provide a public rationale for their way of constructing interracial relations. That justification emerged in the closing years of the nineteenth century as a new national consensus on the phrase "separate but equal" as a doctrine of political governance.[126]

White Supremacists

As the era of separation unfolded, the voices of the patriarch and the fire-eater gradually merged in the national public arena. As the need to seduce the federal government into relinquishing its power waned, and as the control of Southern blacks required an increasingly intense rhetoric, the tone of the fire-eater came to predominate the white supremacist voice. What it spoke was the now aging refrain that the white South must decide the issue of racial equality. Protecting this claim was no simple task; it required defending the constitution of the "Southern people" as inherently white, and this required the abrogation of the principle of majority rule.

As in the previous era, the denial of majority government entailed the proposal by those such as Henry W. Grady that the "domination of the white race in the South" was a legitimate assertion "of the right of character, intelligence, and property to rule."[127] It further depended on the claim that prior to Redemption the "ignorant negro" masses had dominated Southern state governments. This was numerically incorrect. However, supremacists justified this position by explaining that "negro domination" encompassed a wide range of eventualities that went well beyond simply holding political office. Walter B. Hill defined the opposition to Negro domination in this broad way: "She [the white south] is not to be ruled by the blacks, nor by white men at home or from abroad who owe their election exclusively to the blacks."[128] The word "exclusively" was important here, for it did not mean that only blacks had voted for an official but that blacks had held the balance of power in the election. It was precisely this that led H. H. Chalmers to lament the Fifteenth Amendment, with its "instant elevation of so much of ignorance and pauperism to complete equality with wealth and intelligence," for its effect "has been to give them the balance of power in all our recent political struggles."[129] "Negro domination" thus represented virtually any counting of black votes that did not corroborate the white vote. Following such logic to its inevitable conclusion, white supremacists resolved that "partnership [with other races] itself was impossible."[130]

If there could be no partnership, they further concluded that the nation's government was theirs by right of conquest. As Senator Wade Hampton put it, "This continent belongs to those who conquered the wilderness, who have taught to the world how a people can govern themselves, and who want no foreign element, white or black, to control their destiny, or to debase their civilization."[131] The argument eventually evolved into the claim that superior force equaled superior right, but there was more here than the simple rhetorical appeal to a shared principle that might makes right.[132] White Southerners were appealing to Northern whites on the basis of a shared civilization. They argued that "whites have not substantial grievances against them [blacks], except their claim to an equality in political rights, which, as experience shows, deteriorates civilization."[133] In one sense, this attack was no more than a form of blaming the victim. So, for example, when H. H. Chalmers held the negro vote responsible for the "demoralization of our politics which has sprung from the debasement of the elective franchise," he referred to the fact that the only way Southern whites could regain power was by resorting to fraudulent behaviors that debased the ballot, thus effectively creating a destructive tradition of tolerating ballot abuse.[134] Blaming the victim developed into a primary rhetorical strategy for white supremacists, as they required blacks to bear the guilt for the wrongs entailed by the imposition of white supremacy.

The most frequently mentioned of these "wrongs" was the growth of taxes. Much has been written about the reality of the white Southerner's claim that Reconstruction governments undermined the capacity for economic redevelopment through excessive taxation. Whatever the economic reality was, it could not have been known to most white supremacists. What they did know was that for a period of twenty years they had to pay these taxes against their will.[135] In their collective mind Liberty had been destroyed and Property had been threatened by removing the legislative and taxing powers from the sole control of those who would pay most of the taxes. They, therefore, felt justified in expressing "the profound conviction that neither life, liberty, nor property is safe when it is in the power of the ignorant negro masses."[136]

There is a more fundamental aspect to the complaint about "Negro domination" and its relationship to the protection of white civilization. Twentieth-century scholars have treated the almost routine depiction of emancipated blacks as a "barbarian" race as nothing more than a highly freighted metaphor.[137] While it is no doubt true that Southern white supremacists failed to appreciate or value any dimension of black culture, hasty disparagement of their rhetoric may lead us to an incomplete understanding of their motivation. While we agree that white supremacy was misguided, and even that it was exacerbated by economic advantage, we also believe that it must be understood as the attempt of a culture to protect and preserve all that it valued. Southern whites saw clearly the difference between black and white culture, and they feared the effect that this other culture would have on their own. Numerous speakers and writers referred to the "degradation and decay" that occurred when blacks were in a situation to select their own culture, identifying this barbarism in specific terms, as a loss of major Anglo-American institutions, a "loss of civil government, and loss of the Christian religion."[138]

We cannot say with any confidence that the white supremacists were wrong, for they may have correctly understood that when black culture developed outside of and apart from white rule it followed a different path than the one prescribed by white civilization.[139] To whatever extent this occurred, it was virtually inevitable (in this historical period) that whites would perceive the obvious differences in behavioral norms between the two cultures as a disconcerting threat to the survival of their own culture.[140] This perception became all the more intensified by reminders of the historical pattern of young and lower-class whites adopting black cultures, values, and norms when intercultural contact occurred.[141] To some extent, therefore, we should understand the white supremacist desire to place blacks under white control as, in fact, a sincere call to preserve and protect white culture and civilization as they knew it.[142]

Difference was the end point of the white supremacists' argument. Contrary to the egalitarian's belief that all persons were similar because they were born in God's image, the white racists insisted that human difference was greater than similarity and, therefore, more important.[143] The vision of social separatism was, accordingly, as important to white supremacy as was political inequality. The principles of the American Colonization Society did not die with the Civil War. Instead, colonization simply had to change its form. As Wade Hampton put it in 1890, "[T]he prosperity and the perpetuity of government depend most on the homogeneity of its people."[144] In order to preserve government and prosperity, nonhomogeneous elements would have to be cast out. As the nineteenth century came to its end, some white supremacists argued that blacks should be given a separate territory within the United States; others urged the government to support with a "lavish hand" the transportation of former slaves and free blacks back to Africa or to any other distant venue.[145] Some insisted, "The separation of the races under different governments will alone cure this flagrant evil, by giving to the negro race an opportunity for self government; and to the white race an unobstructed course in the accomplishment of their high destiny," but they offered no plan at all to achieve this separate government.[146] A few urged that the effects of separation be mitigated through the diffusion of Southern blacks across the nation.[147]

Ultimately, territorial separation of any sort proved to be impossible. And once that became clear, white supremacists settled on the option of segregation. Segregation allowed them to exclude blacks from contact with whites in the public sphere, including on streetcars, and in parks, inns, restaurants, legislative galleries, theaters, and so on, legally precluding all possible contact between the races except in those situations where the lines of power and merit reproduced the relationship of white overseer and black servant. Of course, they had to persuade Northern egalitarians and African-Americans that this did not violate the fundamental national principle of Equal Rights, and so they gave their segregation a special name: "equal accommodation for each race, but separate."[148]

At this point one can understand the crucial role of the white supremacists' repugnance toward Social Equality. White racists not only opposed biological amalgamation, they opposed cultural amalgamation as well. In order to maintain both separation and cultural integrity, they had to deny that the black race offered anything of equal merit to what the white race had already built. Only in this way could they discursively forestall members of their own race from even considering the incorporation of black and white culture. Therefore, it was precisely the "social recognition" sought by the blacks that the white supremacists refused to offer.[149]

Given such an understanding of the cultural bases of white supremacy, we can better understand the rhetorical nature of the argument against biological homogenization. To see, in operation, the discursive closure that made integration unthinkable, we need only observe the circularity and internal contradictions built into Henry W. Grady's classic and pivotal defense of the permanence of racial and cultural differences:

Without it, there might be a breaking down of all lines of division and a thorough intermingling of whites and blacks. This once accomplished, the lower and the weaker elements of the races would begin to fuse and the process of amalgamation would have begun. This would mean the disorganization of society. An internecine war would be precipitated. The whites, at any cost and at any hazard, would maintain the clear integrity and dominance of the Anglo-Saxon blood. They understand perfectly that the debasement of their own race would not profit the humble and sincere race with which their lot is cast, and that the hybrid would not gain what either race lost.[150]

Grady's argument is incoherent if we view the issue from the perspective of individual contact and biological fusion. However, if we see Grady as an elite white Southerner desperately struggling to maintain his culture, his line of argument is comprehensible. He must control both blacks and lower-class whites, and he must do so while preventing the "disorganization" of his society by the incorporation of competing values, behaviors, and relational patterns. The alternative is "unthinkable" because there is no reason outside the culture itself to want to preserve it. In responding to George Washington Cable's egalitarian counterclaim that no race instinct would *necessitate* conflict as an alternative to integration, Grady thus fell back on pure prejudice:

We hold that there is an instinct, ineradicable and positive, that will keep the races apart. . . . We add in perfect frankness, however, that if no such instinct existed, or if the South had reasonable doubt of its existence, it would, by every means in its power, so strengthen the race prejudice that it would do the work and hold the stubbornness and strength of instinct.[151]

Why would Southerners seek to strengthen such prejudice? Grady gave no answer. With the advantage of historical perspective we now know that the cause was simply prejudice that fed and maintained itself. Ultimately, for the white Southerner, race instinct served as an irreducible assumption, because it was central to their cultural identity. It was neither challengeable nor rethinkable. As William Breckinridge wrote, "[A]ssimilation was believed to be, first, impossible, and secondly, intolerable; the very contemplation of it was unendurable."[152]

The inability of white Southerners to contemplate the similarity between themselves and African-Americans as a culturally constituted people became an underlying cultural assumption that manifested itself in their daily linguistic usages. "Americans" and "Southern people" stood in contrast to "Negroes," just as "us" and "them" were culturally coded to distinguish whites from blacks in ordinary conversation. It also showed itself in frequent and direct challenges to the claim that blacks were "the posterity of the white race."[153] Hence, the Redemptive solution to emancipation after the Civil War turned out to be a modification of the antebellum consensus. Instead of geographic separation, Southerners resorted to segregation.[154]

This segregationist policy was not a manifesto for extermination.[155] Many white Southerners willingly granted blacks what they thought of as legal equality. They did not argue for the right to treat blacks unfairly, cruelly, or tyrannically, nor even the right to take their lives, property, or personal liberty. They promised "equal accommodations" and "equal comfort."[156] They also repeatedly promised Equal Justice in the law courts.

The promise to provide Equal Justice was of course an essential element in their justification of segregation as a legitimate democratic institution. Nonetheless, the Southern patriarchs who touted the promise of Equal Justice the loudest could not guarantee that the courts would actually make it a reality for African-Americans. In fact, they admitted that while a black defendant might receive a fair judgment, a black plaintiff would in all likelihood not fare so well, especially if the accused party was white.[157] The historical record indicates clearly that the patriarchal vision of supplying legal equality without substantial Political Equality was doomed, for white judges and juries simply did not treat those without political, social, or economic power justly. The insufficiency of the compromise over Equal Justice was exacerbated by regional and cultural misunderstand-

ings. Republican and white Southern notions of Equal Justice clearly differed. Hence, republicans simply could not understand how a white
supremacist could treat a black person's request for "respect," that is, to be
treated equal, as "insolent," and thus deserving of severe and even violent
"correction." Yet, for white Southerners this was simply an example of
Equal Justice in action.[158]

Similar problems surrounded the white Southern conception of Equal
Protection. From the very beginning of the Reconstruction period white
supremacists railed against the provision of what they saw as special laws
or special privileges for blacks.[159] The Freedman's Bureau was only the
first and most obvious of such targets, and when its charter lapsed, the
anger it had generated toward "special privileges" for blacks continued.[160]
From the white Southern perspective, any attempt to provide what egalitarians called "equal protection" was by definition inherently unfair and
unequal, for it presumably offered special privileges to blacks that had
never previously been offered to whites. To understand this complaint it is
important to recall that in white Southern culture the prevailing expectation was that men would protect their own life and liberty, literally engag-
ing in duels if necessary. To rely on the government for such protection
was unmanly.[161] Southern whites projected the same for blacks. As unfair
as this might seem—given the different character of hostility among equally
empowered individuals and between differently empowered groups—it
nonetheless led white supremacists to conclude that blacks did not deserve
individual liberty, for they were not able to protect it as individuals.[162]
And from here it was only a short step to conclude that the very request
itself threatened liberty in general, for it threatened the local control of
government that was liberty's essential prop.[163]

In the end, the age of separation represented a significant advance beyond the periods of reconstruction and redemption for Southern white
supremacists. They had firmly regained political power, and in order to retain it they veiled their racial reign of terror under the rubric of a "separate
but equal" doctrine and an intricate rhetoric of self-justification. According to that rhetoric, whites and blacks were inherently and inexorably different from one another, this difference should not be ameliorated or
accounted for in establishing or enacting the government, and the integration of the races should be specifically disallowed, as should the inclusion
of African-Americans in Southern social and political culture.

Republicans and Egalitarians

The voices of white supremacists, though numerically dominant in the
South, were more than balanced in the national arena by egalitarians.

Nonetheless, with few exceptions, the egalitarian rhetoric of this period failed to offer any substantial resistance to the policy of segregation and racial dominance being articulated by the white supremacists. One might conclude from this that Northern republicans had changed their principles and softened their commitment to Equality. Actually, the softer voice in which they spoke is more closely related to their conclusion that it would take time to enact those principles, and to their subsequent decision that in the meantime they needed to face up to certain realities about the social and political world in which they lived.

There can be no doubt that this compromise between final goals and present policies produced an altogether ineffective rhetoric. Many republicans wrote articles in which they adopted so much of both the egalitarian *and* white supremacist positions that they now sound wildly contradictory.[164] Moreover, egalitarians had not yet come to see blacks as "like" themselves. Otherwise egalitarian authors routinely published articles that characterized blacks as amusing, dependent, lovable, superstitious, poverty-stricken, quaint, or in some other way different from whites.[165] Perhaps the sole important difference between the national consensus and white supremacist doctrine was that the latter characterized the inferiority of the black race as permanent, while the former was willing to undertake an "experiment" on the presumption that inequality was temporary. Consequently, even those authors who clearly argued in favor of a form of government that included active and extensive equality, such as George Washington Cable, acknowledged that blacks were currently both different and inferior and that it would take time to constitute any sense of real equality. In a highly sympathetic article William Mathews maintained that it was obvious that "the elevation of the mass of freedmen must be slow . . . "[166] A few thought that, in the meantime, formal political and civil equality should be maintained. Most, however, evaded the issue altogether.

The overwhelming chant one finds in the mainstream press at this time was that the solution to the Southern problem would take time.[167] "Patience!" was the cry of the egalitarian voice, as republicans sat back to wait upon the day when blacks might become similar enough to whites to make Full Equality a practical option.[168] Even those articles authored by blacks and published in the mainstream press tended to agree with this perspective. Frederick Douglass, ordinarily no shrinking violet when arguing for Equal Rights, declaimed that "an abnormal condition, born of war, carried him [the black man] to an altitude unsuited to his attainments. He could not sustain himself there. He will now rise naturally and gradually, and hold on to what he gets."[169] Booker T. Washington's familiar words were similarly reassuring to those who feared too quick and precipitous change when he noted in the *Atlantic Monthly* in 1899: "We must therefore find some basis of settlement that will be constitutional, just, manly; that will be fair to both races. . . . This cannot be done in a day, a year, or any short period of time."[170]

The rhetoric of gradualism had significant consequences for the fate of African-Americans, and they were consequences that would extend well into the next century. Once egalitarians conceded that racial equality was a goal to be achieved at some unspecified future date, and further, that America's blacks had thus far failed to overcome their inferior status, it was difficult, though not impossible, to argue that they should be allowed the opportunity to hold political office. It was likewise difficult to argue that whites should hire them, or let their children attend schools with white children, or for that matter simply to interact with them as equals in a social context. The claim that "time equals progress" thus functioned as a rationale for eliminating the conditions of political control and cultural contact that would otherwise have increased the chance of effecting the changes that it promised. The egalitarian rhetoric of gradualism conceded the upper hand on all policy decisions to the view of the world characterized by the white supremacists.[171]

There were a few variations to this pattern of egalitarian argument in the national press, and it was most frequently offered by younger African-Americans. In a brief article, T. Thomas Fortune vehemently attacked Senator John T. Morgan, a leading white supremacist, for his attitude of "prejudice and hatred."[172] W. S. Scarborough vigorously countered attacks on black character by pointing out that whites had a far greater record of mismanagement of government than had blacks and by citing individual negroes who had achieved excellence as scholars. He argued as well that whites must consider these issues from the perspective of blacks, suggesting that one was "right when he said that the solution of this question should be left to time," but wrong when he further added, "and to the sound judgment of the Southern people."[173] These voices, although indicative of an important change to occur in the future, were in a small minority at the time.

The one issue on which the egalitarians spoke in relatively united opposition to the white supremacists was Social Equality. Most egalitarians agreed on two things. First, they agreed that to the extent that Social Equality referred to social recognition or intercourse it was not a matter that could be regulated by law. Second, they agreed that Social Equality was different from civil or public rights. This was born of the belief that the line beyond which governmentally guaranteed Equality could not reach should be drawn on the other side of public accommodations. They thus insisted, "Men have understood, from time immemorial, that the province of social equality and that of civil rights are separate and distinct."[174] From this perspective, the law could rightfully insure equal access to the same public facilities without distinction of color.

As in the previous era, the persuasiveness of this argument rested on the assumption egalitarians shared with the white supremacists that both races had a racial "instinct" that led them to prefer contact with people of their own kind in social matters.[175] Because of this instinct, the egalitarians argued, racial mixing in public places would not lead to miscegenation. That argument would be used against egalitarians by the Supreme Court, when it upheld the "separate but equal" doctrine on the grounds that both races desired separation, and, therefore, separation could not be an imposition upon the black race.

The second weakness in the position that mainstream egalitarians took on the issue of Social Equality was their failure to explain convincingly why blacks wanted to have access to the same accommodations when they had the opportunity to enjoy separate ones. In the most extended discussion of the issue in the era, J. C. Price argued:

When a person of Negro descent enters a first-class car or restaurant, or seeks a decent stateroom on a steamer, he does not do it out of a desire to be with white people. He is seeking simply comfort, and not the companionship, or even the presence, of whites. Frequently his course is an effort to escape from the unpleasant odor of tobacco, or from the more undesirable presence of foul men and vile women. When a train stops for refreshments, and the Negro enters a dining room, he does not go there because he is seeking social contact with the whites, but because he is hungry.[176]

This line of defense was faulty, for Grady and his compatriots had already offered a reasonable solution to it. The Southern patriarchs promised not only separate facilities, but ones of "equal comfort."[177] The nation, especially in the North, did not yet have the experience to prove that racial separation would lead inevitably to inferior accommodations for blacks. *In 1890, it was at least plausible that separation might be compatible with Equality.* If the Southern patriarchs actually had been able to maintain equal comfort, then the line of argument accepted by the republican leaders of the period might have made the doctrine of "separate but equal" legitimate down to our day.

The rhetorical posture of the egalitarians in this period thus offered little resistance to the white supremacist's proposal of "separate accommodations, but equal." That position would come to occupy center stage as the national compromise during this period, especially once the Supreme Court legitimized it in its decision in *Plessy v. Ferguson* (1896). But that decision was only the culmination of several decades of argument and discussion, the ground for which was prepared most importantly by republican egalitarians, who failed to demand Social Equality, and who shared and expressed the white supremacist belief that America's black population was at least temporarily inferior.

African-American Rhetorics

On many issues, the black press of this period simply mirrored the positions of the republican-oriented magazines that circulated across racial lines. At the same time, however, they tended to promote the themes with which they had affiliated themselves in the 1870s. We thus find them frequently exhorting retaliatory violence, encouraging their readers to engage in business ventures as a means of achieving wealth, and demanding proportional patronage from the Republican party.

The most notable change in the black press of this period is the significant reduction of the appearance of the word "equality" and its various forms, including "equal rights" and "equal opportunity." After white Southerners achieved redemption, the life conditions for Southern blacks became highly unstable. As that instability increased, the plea for protection accelerated and shifted forms as African-Americans worried less about Equal Protection and more about the simple protection of life, liberty, and property.[178] One feature of this shift in rhetorical usages was the quite substantial campaign against lynching led by Ida B. Wells [Barnett], an indication of how central the issue of mere protection was in that day. Another feature of this shift was the way in which black leaders stilled their voices on the issue of the franchise, virtually acquiescing to the Southern enactment of discriminatory restrictions based on literacy.[179]

The tendency in the latter half of the twentieth century has been to criticize this rhetorical track as an insidious form of "Uncle Tomism." But such a critique fails to account for the very real obstacles faced by black leaders in this time period. Additionally, it fails to recognize that the shift in public usages affected by black leaders served to move the passive, Jacksonian notion of Equal Protection away from its laissez-faire roots.[180] Finally, and most importantly, it ignores the very strong and progressive development of a rhetoric of racial pride that began to emerge in the black press during this period and that would have a significant impact on a later generation of African-Americans.

Even prior to the Civil War, America's black communities expressed a strong sense of racial pride. Until the 1880s, however, its presence in black newspapers had been sporadic and tenuous. From the 1880s forward it grew steadily, centering on the claim that African-Americans constituted a unique race that offered its own special contribution to humanity. So, for example, the *Washington Bee* reported a lecture by John H. Smythe in which he proclaimed the "peculiar genius" of America's African population:

Blood—not language and religion—makes social distinctions. We are therefore bound by every drop of blood that flows in our being, and by whatever of self-respect you and I individually and collectively possess, to make ourselves—not on the pattern of any other race, but actuated by our peculiar genius in literature, religion, commerce and social intercourse—a great people.[181]

Some newspapers argued that blacks had a responsibility to patronize black-owned businesses and newspapers as a means of helping the race to develop more rapidly.[182] Such efforts were not a conservative call to return to the past to discover a purified and homogeneous cultural identity. The black leadership clearly cast a forward-looking gaze to a future in which it could enjoy the new and vital contributions being generated out of their multiple heritages.[183]

The growth of the rhetoric of race identity served an important function in counterbalancing the characterization of blacks as inferior that frequented the mainstream press. At the same time, however, it functioned also to validate the "separate but equal" compromise. By admitting that there was a uniqueness to race, a special value—perhaps an instinct—that moved counter to and above individual merit, it put the argument on the white racist's ground. By making the matter a group issue, the rhetoric of racial pride set itself over and against the rhetoric of individual merit that African-American leaders had worked so hard to make the focus of their vision of Equality. By emphasizing racial identity, they undercut the claim that individuals should be treated with regard to their own merit. As such, it appeared to support the conclusion that different races ought to remain distinct from each other. In this way, the blacks of the period, though generally in favor of civil rights and equal access to accommodations, nonetheless contributed to the national consensus that unfolded in *Plessy* v. *Ferguson*.

Official Compromises

Writing in the aftermath of the Supreme Court's ruling in *Brown* v. *Board of Education*, it is quite common to find authors who characterize *Plessy* v. *Ferguson*, with its legal institutionalization of the "separate but equal"

clause, as a racist decision.[184] As we have suggested, however, *Plessy* v. *Ferguson* was not a simple reiteration of the white supremacist position but rather a common ground among the range of existing positions. It encom- ⎱ β./Ken~?
passed the white supremacist's desire to preserve white civilization by restricting black political power and social presence. It further encompassed the Northern republican's uncertainties about integration and their willingness to allow Africans the time to achieve "elevation" before pushing for Full Equality. Finally, it also incorporated the decision of the African-American leadership to emphasize economic and safety measures over electoral ones, to concede "social equality," and to promote racial distinctiveness. *Plessy* v. *Ferguson* thus represented a combination of "separatism" and "egalitarianism" that merely required a minor revision of the prewar Anglo-American commitment to the principles of colonization, albeit a form of colonization designed to fit the impossibility of full-scale black emigration. To understand the nature of the decision as a national compromise, we need to examine it as a discourse produced in the context of a constraining national rhetorical culture.

The first section of the decision deals with the relationship of segregation to slavery. In it, the Court found that "a statute which implies merely a legal distinction between the white and colored races—a distinction which is founded in the color of the two races . . . has no tendency to destroy the legal equality of the two races, or reestablish a state of involuntary servitude."[185] Thereby, it concluded that, contrary to the claims made by African-Americans, slavery had not been the cause of racial prejudice. By arguing that the Thirteenth Amendment did not include civil rights, the Court enabled itself to identify a livable and, indeed, desirable middle ground between full equality and slavery. Historically, Americans have tended to view this section of the decision as altogether noncontroversial, and even at the time, the Court thought it "too clear for argument."[186] The insistence of Reconstruction radicals notwithstanding, the belief that there could be "no middle ground" between slavery and full citizenship was not a dominant position in the national psyche.

The second section of the decision was more clearly and immediately controversial. It found that the Fourteenth Amendment did not proscribe state laws which compelled separate public facilities for each race. The Court rested its decision on the presumed natural distinction between the races:

The object of the amendment was undoubtedly to enforce the absolute equality of the two races before the law, but in the nature of things it could not have been intended to abolish distinctions based on color, or to enforce social, as distinguished from political equality, or a commingling of the two races upon terms unsatisfactory to either. [187]

Here, all of the components of the national compromise converged: the natural distinction between races, the difference between social and political equality, and the desire to preserve racial difference. The Court then concluded that the African-American's version of "Equality before the Law"—that there should be no "distinctions based upon color"—was impossible, given "the nature of things." A form of Equality which encompassed distinction without implying inferiority would thus constitute the national commitment. The Court announced, "Laws permitting, and even requiring, their separation in places where they are liable to be brought into contact do not necessarily imply the inferiority of either race to the other."[188]

Of course, the Court betrayed its position in a number of ways. First, it drew its example from the different relationship between adults and children, a relationship that it contended did not imply legal inferiority but which clearly did replicate the paternalistic relationship of white and black. Further, in discussing the property right one might have in a reputation that might be injured by segregation, the Court framed the issue so as to assume black inferiority, arguing that a black person might not seek damages for segregation because "he is not lawfully entitled to the reputation of being a white man."[189] Finally, the Court identified blacks as the sole object of the legislation under review, noting that such law "neither abridges the privileges or immunities of the colored man, deprives him of his property without due process of law, nor denies him the equal protection of the laws."[190] Clearly, the Court viewed segregation through the lens of social inferiority whose existence it denied. But this should not be surprising, for we know what "separate but equal" came to mean in practice. Nevertheless, it created a doctrine that allowed both the Court and the nation as a whole to imply that their commitment to separation was not a repudiation of the value of Equality.

Making this formal determination required the Court to take sides between the white supremacists and the blacks by deciding that the sharing of public accommodations was a social rather than political or civil matter. It based this conclusion on the precedents established by state laws that had long identified schools and marriage as social rather than political matters, in which separation could legally be maintained. When challenged that the State power to make such distinctions among the people would lead to the proliferation of pernicious distinctions, the Court responded by claiming that "every exercise of the police power must be reasonable" and that given the "established usages, customs, and traditions of the people" the distinction between races is not "unreasonable."[191]

Finally, the Court bolstered its decision by co-opting the African-American argument that Social Equality cannot be legislated, insisting,

The argument also assumes that social prejudices may be overcome by legislation, and that equal rights cannot be secured to the negro except by an enforced commingling of the two races. We cannot accept this proposition. If the two races are to meet upon terms of social equality, it must be the result of natural affinities, a mutual appreciation of each other's merits and a voluntary consent of individuals.[192]

It then concluded its description of the American vision of nineteenth-century Equality by noting:

"When the government, therefore, has secured to each of its citizens equal rights before the law and equal opportunities for improvement and progress, it has accomplished the end for which it was organized." . . . If one race be inferior to the other socially, the Constitution of the United States cannot put them upon the same plane.[193]

The Supreme Court, of course, constituted only one of the three official national voices. The U.S. Congress became progressively more silent in this period, proposing and passing little monumental legislation. The authority of the presidency was another matter, however, and the presidents of this period—Grover Cleveland, Chester A. Arthur, James Garfield, and Benjamin Harrison—were not yet willing to be silent. Each expressed a combination of the elements of the national compromise, in addition to urging the white South and the nation to do their best to support and protect America's new citizens.

In his 1881 Inaugural Address, for example, Garfield insisted both that the "supremacy of the nation and its laws should be no longer a subject of debate," and that "there can be no permanent disfranchised peasantry in the United States."[194] The former statement was limited by the phrase "so far as my authority can lawfully extend . . . acting always within the authority and limitations of the Constitution, invading neither the rights of the States nor the reserved rights of the people," just as the latter was limited by the issue of time, for, indeed, the South included a disfranchised peasantry.

By contrast, Cleveland emphasized Liberty as the central national value; and although he employed the Southern phrase "equal and exact justice" in place of the broader notion of egalitarianism one finds in Northern discourse, he lectured his Southern constituents:

All discussion as to their fitness for the place accorded to them as American citizens is idle and unprofitable except as it suggests the necessity for their improvement. The fact that they are citizens entitles them to all the rights due to the relation and charges them with all its duties, obligations, and responsibilities.[195]

Cleveland himself was not certain about the ultimate potential of blacks. He held that "[i]n my opinion it is yet too early to judge the colored race either one way or the other," but he sought to convince America that there should be no backsliding to the days before the postwar constitutional amendments.[196] Moreover, he also resisted the casting of African-Americans as aliens:

I see that considerable discussion has been going on of late over what shall be done with the colored man, but I wish to enter my protest against this parcelling of him as though he were a distinct element in our body politics. He is an American.[197]

Harrison continued the theme and may have left a high watermark when he asked the South:

Shall the prejudices and paralysis of slavery continue to hang upon the skirts of progress? How long will those who rejoice that slavery no longer exists cherish or tolerate the incapacities it put upon their communities?[198]

Harrison argued that giving the black man the ballot and making him an ally would be good for business, and further that mob rule discouraged progress and commerce. He thus promoted federal action to educate the former slaves, declaring: "The colored people did not intrude themselves upon us. . . . They have from a standpoint of ignorance and poverty—which was our shame, not theirs—made remarkable advances in education and in the acquisition of property.[199] Moreover, he recognized that America's colored people were "deprived of any effective exercise of their political rights and of many of their civil rights," and he urged the nation to mend its ways, even if that entailed federal control of elections.[200]

As a group, the presidents of this period celebrated the end of slavery and worked toward its worldwide elimination. They urged the nation to exorcise the evil habit of lynching. And, in an ironic twist, on the eve of the Supreme Court's "separate but equal decision," Cleveland signaled the end of the dream of colonization by requesting congressional appropriations to retrieve the victims of a failed Mexican colonization scheme. It is obvious that the nation did not listen too closely to the chastising it received from its presidents, and it is equally obvious that the presidents remained bound by a vow of inactivity. Nevertheless, as a group they refused to give up on a rhetoric of racial progress, and they consistently urged the nation ever forward to a more encompassing understanding of "equality before the law which it guarantees to every citizen . . . unimpaired by race or color."[201] The presidents who followed in the wake of the "separate but equal" doctrine would prove to be far less uniform in their sentiments.

The Civil War ended nearly a century of uncertainty and bickering about the possibility of transforming the proposition that "all men are created equal in a state of nature" into a social compact that preserved that equality to all men in the governed state. However definitively the war enshrined Equality as a central value for the nation, it did not settle the question of the range of usages the term would have within the social compact. The outer limits of its meaning remained a matter of great contention and unease. In the years between 1870 and 1896 the nation participated in an ongoing public debate to decide how the word "equality" could be effectively integrated into the national public vocabulary now that it had been officially identified as a constitutional value.

Traditional histories typically begin the story of this period by noting the effort of radical Republicans to insure an expansive egalitarianism under the rubric of "political equality" in the 1870s, and then shift attention to the ultimate control arrested by the white supremacists who effected an oppressive separatism under the rubric of the "separate but equal" doctrine in the 1890s. This way of telling the story not only ignores the important role played by African-American advocates in this debate, it also implies that the final outcome was simply the result of the superior strength of white racists and the moral cowardice of republicans and egalitarians. None of these assumptions is altogether accurate, and they lead us to ignore the role that rhetoric plays in the process of social and political change.

As this chapter demonstrates, three voices dominated the debate that occupied the nation as it moved from reconstruction to Southern redemption to separation, and each voice was active in each phase of the debate. While the national consensus that emerged at each stage more closely represented one of these voices rather than the others, it is altogether incorrect to say that any one voice was ever wholly identified with the national consensus. In the Reconstruction era, the national compromise worked against the wishes of the white supremacists by both freeing the slaves and granting citizenship to African-Americans. All the same, the national policy did not go as far as egalitarians of either race preferred, for it failed both to define citizenship as entailing an adequately broad range of rights and to insure federal enforcement of those rights. The era of Redemption likewise featured policies built on mutual ground. The national compromise reflected the propositions, shared by white supremacists, white egalitarians, and African-Americans alike, that blacks were currently inferior, that Social Equality was neither necessary nor desirable, and that ending the violence against blacks was important. Combined with the laissez-faire view of government shared by most whites, these beliefs effected a return of political control to Southern whites, who promised to elevate blacks for their future role in the society and to protect their life, liberty, and property. The insincerity of the promise led to a renegotiation of the compromise in the 1880s and 1890s. In return for the promise of simple protection and consideration of a separate American identity, blacks decreased their demand for Equality. As white egalitarians temporized, white supremacists offered a formula—"equal accommodations but separate"—for preserving both the value of Equality supported by white and black egalitarians and the Separation desired by white supremacists and some black leaders.

When Equality was thus finally integrated into America's public vocabulary as a commitment to the "separate but equal" doctrine, it reflected yet another compromise crafted from the struggle among different groups to enhance their own well-being and to define a common good. If Separate But Equal had not represented a compromise position, if white supremacists had actually controlled the national discourse without interference, as some have claimed they did, the public commitment to Equality would have been absent altogether. Under such circumstances the silencing of black America would have been far more comprehensive and enduring than it turned out to be. That the national consensus articulated through the Congress, the presidents, and the Supreme Court emphasized Equality before the Law provides clear evidence of the presence and force of competing voices demanding to be heard on this issue; and, indeed, that it preserved the public space for continued dissent was essential to the demise of the compromise wrought in the "separate but equal" doctrine. As the nineteenth century gradually gave way to the twentieth, the voices of dissent grew louder and more vociferous, for with each passing decade every one of the parties to the national compromise became increasingly uncomfortable with the concessions they had made.

CHAPTER SIX

Integrated Equality
1896–1960

There will be peace and security only if we share our institutions together.

Pittsburgh Courier
22 March 1941

Most ideological compromises are unstable. The national compromise founded on the Separate But Equal doctrine was inherently so, for its underlying predicate was the claim that "time" would bring change. White supremacists and egalitarians exacerbated that instability through their competing interpretations of Equal Justice. Consequently, even as *Plessy* v. *Ferguson* lent legal legitimacy to the Separate But Equal doctrine, and Southern states feverishly incorporated the doctrine in scores of segregational laws, the ground upon which the compromise had been struck began a gradual but profound shift. This shift was initiated by a dramatic polarization of the public positions of African-Americans and white supremacists between the end of the nineteenth century and the Great Depression. By 1948, this polarization forced egalitarians to promote and defend a bold new vision of integrated Equality. Between 1948 and 1960 the commitment to that vision initiated a battle for full Equality that would set the stage for the tumultuous 1960s.

As in Chapter 5, we will chart the way in which the primary interested parties talked about Equality during these three time periods. Unlike Chapter 5, however, where we reported on a time period in which the differences in the competing voices were relatively discrete, here we find the word "equality" becoming gradually integrated in the public vocabulary, and thus we find ourselves forced to characterize the various interested voices in gradually broader and more diffuse categories. We identify three periodic stages in the development of this discursive integration: polarization (1896–1930), the initial public commitment to an integrated equality (1930–48), and an increasingly aggressive fight for equality (1948–60).

Polarization, 1896–1930

In the first third of the twentieth century, African-Americans began to force a national transition from a commitment to a world in which "separate" was "equal," to a world of integrated equalities. White supremacists made this shift possible by indulging themselves in an intensifying spiral of racist rhetoric that they colorfully and proudly displayed in the national arena. White egalitarians were thus forced to choose from between a virulently racist caste society or integrated Equality, and gradually they made the choices that moved the nation away from legalized segregation. The polarizing interplay of African-American and white supremacist rhetoric thus motivated the mainstream egalitarian response, which functioned as a national compromise that reconstituted America's public commitment to Equality.

African-American Rhetoric

As the new century dawned, a new generation came to maturity, and it was the first generation in which the majority of America's African descendants had been born free. Although they were still economically poor and inadequately educated, black Americans at least now had an educated leadership, a small middle class, and a relatively sophisticated national communication network.[1] All of this allowed the formation of effective national organizations, such as the Brotherhood of Sleeping Car Porters, the Urban League, and, most visibly, the National Association for the Advancement of Colored People (NAACP). These organizations fostered a new African-American rhetoric that quickly achieved a greatly amplified public force.[2]

Most of the themes from the separatist period continued to permeate the national discourse of blacks in this era, but gradually their vision shifted as new emphases and ideas began tentatively to evolve and find public expression.[3] One of these trends included the resurrection of many long dormant Reconstruction themes, including the right to vote and the importance of national sovereignty over states rights. However, there were also substantially new themes being expressed. The most important new position was caused by the experience of the harsh realities generated by the Separate but Equal doctrine. These experiences effected a reversal in African-America's acceptance of segregation. In the words of William Pickens, "a generation of experience has taught him the meaning of successful segregation."[4] African-American leaders thus vigorously repudiated the compromises that had led to *Plessy* v. *Ferguson* and its aftermath. Repudiating segregation required African-Americans to demand both the right to interact with whites as equals in the public sphere and the recognition that whites and blacks were "equal races." Given the nation's rhetorical history, this meant an endorsement of the most controversial phrase of the post–Civil War periods: "social equality."

When an ideological group reverses its position on an issue, the shift is often slow to show itself fully in public discourse. The first voices articulating the new position are typically tentative and isolated. Hence it was that even before the turn of the century some African-Americans cautiously suggested their support for Social Equality. After seeing the results of repudiating Social Equality, the *New York Age* concluded, "Deny social equality to a man and political equality and industrial opportunity will be denied him sooner or later. Inequality in one thing will carry with it inequality in all things in a Republic."[5] In a front-page editorial cartoon the paper mocked the Southern patriarch and his social equality with black women by asking: "Social Equality is it? Well, who created 3 million 'African-Americans' and denied them fathers by law?" In insisting upon Social Equality, many African-American leaders were careful to maintain that they did not mean to imply that blacks sought white interaction because whites were superior. Rather, they argued that it was their intention to destroy the demeaning lines of segregation. They promised that if treated as "a social and political equal," black people would become more "clanish" than ever.[6] In this spirit, Reverend A. J. Carey, concluded:

. . . the liberty which civilization is quite willing, theoretically at least, to accord, almost everywhere today involves something else which civilization is more reluctant to grant; that something is EQUALITY. . . . Social Equality . . . means simply that all sorts and conditions of people in this country, must live side by side in a spirit of mutual helpfulness and Good Will.[7]

Other African-Americans in this period would continue to disavow Social Equality,[8] but between 1920 and 1929 it became the single most frequently appearing usage of Equality in the African-American national press.[9] The defense of Social Equality against staunch white resistance took many forms.[10] *The Crisis,* the official organ of the NAACP, provided two different extended accounts exploring the links among social recognition, individual manhood, Racial Equality, and Social Equality. In the first, formal version, W. E. B. Du Bois, the journal's editor, dealt thoughtfully with the issue on the social scale:

We believe that social equality, by a reasonable interpretation of the words, means moral, mental and physical fitness to associate with one's fellowmen. In this sense THE CRISIS believes absolutely in the Social Equality of the Black and White and

Yellow races and it believes too that any attempt to deny this equality by law or custom is a blow at Humanity, Religion and Democracy.[11]

In a later essay Du Bois took a more individualistic, experience-centered perspective when he asked:

Do I want Social Equality? Certainly I do. Every normal decent human being wants to associate with his fellowmen on terms of equality. We like to be invited out. We want people to want us. . . . We will surely never stultify our souls by seeking those who despise us, but equally we will refuse to lie and to say that we *wish* to be despised. . . . Of course, we want social equality and we know that we will never be real men until we get it.[12]

In order to gain "manhood" recognition for the race, African-American leaders knew that legally mandated segregation would have to be exorcised.[13] Many of the black voices in this period endorsed voluntary black separatism in the economic and cultural spheres, but most also widely repudiated legal segregation as "a law that will make and keep one man superior to another, whether he is intrinsically superior or not."[14] The "Boston Colored Men" thus resolved:

We ask no favors that are withheld from other citizens, ar[sic] to which they are not entitled, but we do ask for that civil and political homogeneity which invades no man's private social rights, but which does lie at the foundation of national unity. . . . We contend for the contact with our white brethren which elevates and does not degrade either them or us.[15]

The African-American leadership thus inaugurated the argument that would be picked up fifty years later by the Supreme Court in *Brown* v. *Bd. of Education*, by claiming that "segregation is in itself an injury and denial of the equality of citizenship . . . humiliating and degrading."[16]

The repudiation of segregation also had its pragmatic side. Based in a compromise with white supremacy that conceded political control to white racists, separate accommodations for blacks quickly had become wildly and inherently unequal accommodations. A variety of statistics summarized these differences in financial support for white and black institutions.[17] Accordingly, the African-American leadership extended the argument against segregation to all facilities where visible qualitative differences had emerged, including schools, railroads, recreational facilities, hospitals, theaters, restaurants, and inns. The argument went further, however, to suggest that even without racist control, unequal accommodations were an inherent feature of segregated facilities. The *Western Appeal* noted, for example, that separate schools could not be equal, because "everyone knows that no two things are equal or alike and separate schools are no exception to the rule."[18] Equality, they argued, was incompatible with difference.

The heightened demand for Equality extended to economic concerns with an insistence on equal industrial freedom and equal opportunity.[19] This demand had not previously been expressed on a popular scale, and it represented a subtle but important shift from the previous era. Black newspapers and magazines in both the eras of redemption and separation had preached the importance of accumulating money. So, for example, the *Colored Citizen* counseled: "Get all the intelligence, property, and money you can."[20] The leadership of this earlier era assumed that the only necessary requirement to achieve such wealth was individual initiative. The difficulty of finding employment for those educated either in the classical liberal arts or in the trade schools overturned these assumptions, even as it stilled the squabble over the "best" type of education for the race.[21] The barriers that prejudice and segregation put in the way of the success of any individual initiative gradually became obvious. Black Americans came to realize that white prejudice would prevent the accumulation of economic goods, even where blacks had skills to offer. The leadership thus came to recognize the political nature of economic activity and began to include it in their demands.[22] Hence the phrase "equal opportunity" was frequently employed between 1895 and the 1920s, as African-Americans determined to fight for "equal opportunity, opportunity to labor and opportunity to enjoy."[23] This was neither a Jacksonian conception of equal opportunity nor a Marxist version of economic equality. It was not Jacksonian, because it requested an active government to remove those barriers preventing a "fair chance in the race of life." It was not Marxist, for the majority never abandoned the assumption that substantive equality was to be earned, rather than guaranteed by the government.[24] Even *The Messenger,* the most leftward leaning of the black magazines on economic issues, urged personal acquisition of wealth and provided encouragement and advice on how to achieve it.[25]

In discussing a wide variety of subissues, the leadership of the black community soon realized the need to replace limited, adjectival versions of "equality," such as Equality before the Law and Equal Rights, with broader and largely unqualified versions.[26] As George Frazier Miller put it, "I want every kind of equality I can have."[27] John Hope agreed, asking, "If we are not striving for equality, in heaven's name for what are we living?"[28]

African-American leaders not only supported Equality, however, but also began to argue that America's black community had elevated itself. Numerous articles in the black press touted the equal achievements of black soldiers, ministers, dramatists, musicians, and teachers as "equal to any that exist."[29] The press went even further, suggesting that in some areas, such as music and drawing, colored schools and their pupils exceeded the accomplishments of their white counterparts.[30] It is in this context that Booker T. Washington's rhetoric can be seen as a sustained campaign to demonstrate the worth and accomplishments of blacks.[31] A number of black leaders even suggested that in some respects the natives of the Congo were equal to or better than Americans. The expression of this argument was extremely tentative, but it foreshadowed the much later multiculturalist position that different cultures are meritorious in different ways.[32] Finally, the leadership took on the argument that blacks were "mental inferiors" by challenging both the validity of IQ tests and the claim made by nineteenth-century scientists that biological difference was the root of social difference.[33]

In addition to promoting black achievements, the national black press emphasized negative characterizations of "the proud, haughty caucasian."[34] White Southerners were commonly labeled "crackers," and white racists were depicted as "brutes" or "lazy." The *New York Age* declared that "The American people are to a large degree semi-civilized."[35] The indictment stretched to Northern white racists as well, so that those living above the Mason-Dixon line received a hint of the denunciation they would face in the next decade.[36] In view of the barbarity of the lower-class white Southerner and the moral blinders worn by Northern whites, it was not unrealistic for black newspapers to conclude that the African-American "compares, class by class, very well with his white neighbors"[37] and that "today [he] stand[s] upon equal footing with them among the races of earth."[38] It was with a sense of confidence, then, that the *Washington Bee* denounced "the poor white man and woman who want the Negro to admit his inferiority to them." And it was with pride that it announced: "This the Negro will never do."[39]

The assertion of equal achievements did not produce a self-satisfied complacency. Black advocates constantly exhorted their audiences to enact the social virtues of work, thrift, and family, and frequently criticized them harshly for embodying the "typical faults of the race." The *New York Age,* for example, declared that "the average Afro-American wage-earner spends too much of his wages on eating and drinking and on wearing apparel."[40]

There was a second and more profound dimension to this self-criticism. Black leaders described America as a "composite" nation, constituted by the blood of a multitude of races.[41] For some this implied amalgamation.[42] For others, like W. E. B. Du Bois, the preservation of the "mighty human rainbow" of American culture was a cause for celebration.[43] This celebration was not without its costs, however, for it implied a duty to generate a unique African-American contribution to American life. It was in this context that Booker T. Washington noted the existence of a "dawning race consciousness" that included the desire to do "something which will demonstrate the right of the Negro, not merely as an individual, but as a race, to have a worthy and permanent place in the civilization that the American people are creating."[44]

Faced with this duty, turn of the century black leaders expressed a distinct feeling of inadequacy. Alexander Crummell anguished over the condition when he noted that "as a race in this land, we have no art; we have no science; we have no philosophy; we have no scholarship. Individuals we have in each of these lines; but mere individuality cannot be recognized as the aggregation of a family, a nation, or a race; or as the interpretation of any of them."[45] The *Washington Bee* quoted a concurring opinion, complaining further that "the Negro in America has no specific social forms, but invariably copys [sic] what is known as American of which he is not the projector."[46]

These laments pointed out the next pressing task facing the African-American community, and in so doing they virtually called the Harlem Renaissance into existence. By the 1920s the "Africa for Africans" sentiment motivated a new and sophisticated self-assessment of African-American culture, and with it a reconsideration of the value of Anglo-European culture. *The Crisis* suggested, for example, that African nations "must distinguish between those Western habits which are good for them and those which are not."[47] In like fashion, Bishop C. C. Alleyne indicated:

The cultured African investigates; and his investigations create in him a disposedness to conserve the best in his native civilization. He learns to discriminate and this leads to the rejection of many features of Western Civilization which he at first worshipped [and] sympathy with the best customs of his fathers.[48]

A similar process of selectivity was going on in America as black newspapers and magazines urged the rejection of some African-based customs and practices, such as faith healing, while simultaneously urging the acceptance of others such as African religions and music, Dahomayan proverbs, and so on.[49]

Even within the black community, there was no consensus on most cultural issues.[50] Some black voices called for the creation of a new civilization to replace "that European civilization which is now rushing furiously to its doom," arguing that "the war has shown us the cruelty of the civilization of the West. History has taught us the futility of the civilization of the East. Let ours be the civilization of no *man*, but of *all men*."[51] Others sought "equal, *parallel* and *distinct* development" or an independent black nation.[52] At the same time, however, many black leaders continued to emphasize the essential similarity of people of different races.[53] It was not clear whether or how being culturally distinct *and* American could be developed in tandem with one another, nor was it clear what the relationship between political, economic, and cultural difference might be.[54]

As the twentieth century matured, African-America's leadership spoke in a voice that clearly distinguished itself from its late nineteenth-century precursors by challenging all of the bases of *Plessy* v. *Ferguson*. Drawing upon the tremendous progress made by a significant portion of the race, black advocates denied the existence of racial inferiority as a justification for withholding rights. They further denied the undesirability of social equality between the races, rejecting any limits on Equality. They also assembled the organizational tools necessary to give public force to their rhetoric. The black press had been well developed, and it informed the black community in detail about the variety of strategies employed by whites to empower the vicious racism that contributed to the development of negative black self-images. The black press told the horrifying truth about race riots and lynchings and about the causes of black crime. It also revealed the hideous effects of such popular cultural agencies as the cinema, demonstrated most fully in the racist rendition of the reconstruction period presented by D. W. Griffith's *The Birth of a Nation*. The black national press thus offered both a widely available critique of America's prevailing racist creed and a compelling alternate vision.

In addition to the press, local and national organizations offered assistance in defining the African-American community.[55] The migration of blacks from the South to the North, especially to Northern cities where they could freely exercise the franchise, added strength to these sources of communal identity. World War I also provided blacks with jobs as the military and increased munitions production required additional labor power. Finally, blacks turned increasingly to violence as a means of defending themselves against white threats, thus giving a new meaning to the phrase "race riot."[56] This "Rising Tide of Color" opened onto a cacophonic debate within the nation's mainstream between white supremacists and egalitarians.[57]

The Mainstream Response

Unlike the period of separation, during the early years of the twentieth century both the national press and the U.S. Congress listened to what the

voices of African-Americans had to say. The effect was to heighten the
public tension between African-Americans and white supremacists, and
thus to force white egalitarians into the position of choosing from between
them. So, for example, mass distribution magazines attended equally to
African-American and white supremacist voices. As the century wore on,
however, the journalistic treatment of the ravings of white supremacists
became unfriendly, as the increasingly moderate and thoughtful writings
of mainstream journalists expressed outrage at the inhumane treatment of
Southern blacks. In like manner, egalitarians, although not dominant in
the U.S. Congress, managed to moderate the brazen and hostile tones of
racism expressed by white supremacist legislators. Whether in the pages of
the popular press or on the floors of Congress, then, the public argument
of white supremacists and egalitarians evolved in radically different directions. In the process, the uneasy compromise they had agreed to in the
1890s, woven within the fabric of the Separate But Equal doctrine, began
to unravel.

White Supremacists

By the end of the nineteenth century, white supremacists had achieved an
entrenched, de facto control of the race issue in America, especially in the
South. As the new century unfolded, however, the emergence of an increasingly assertive and aggressive African-American people stood as a
potential threat to their control. Together, these two conditions led white
supremacists to intensify the virulence of their racist rhetoric.

White supremacists sought first to turn back the African-American
challenge by increasing the hostility of their characterization of blacks and
by stridently insisting upon the superiority of the "Anglo-Saxon" race.[58]
In the 1890s characterizations of racial difference had been largely non-
threatening.[59] As time wore on, however, the characterizations became increasingly vicious and malignant, so much so that M. L. Perry's depiction
of an "outburst of insanity" among the negroes because their brains failed
to "sustain the mental strain" of advanced civilization "as well as that [the
brain] of a white man" was not atypical of the period.[60]

The most frequent means of discrediting blacks was to depict them as a
criminal race. Statistical crime tables appeared with some regularity to
demonstrate that blacks were statistically far more likely to break the law
than whites.[61] The impression of blacks as hateful and unredeemable savages was compounded and accentuated by claiming that the black man's
peculiar crime was the pernicious rape of white women.[62] Lynching provided the popular response to this crime, especially in the South, and in the

years 1890–1920 there were more lynchings in the United States than the total number of executions.[63] Moderate racists conceded that lynching was incompatible with social order, but they mitigated their position by insisting that it was a local problem and ought to be handled by local authorities.[64] Extremists lauded the practice of lynching in florid terms: "Swift vengeance upon the criminal who in this heinous manner outrages God's law and the sacred rights of virtue will ever be the rule, the right, and the duty of the white man that is loyal to his race."[65] Some went so far as to defend lynching on the grounds that white women victims should not have to face the humiliation of telling their tales in court.

As a part of this storm of violent stereotyping, racist extremists nurtured a new theme in the national public arena when they maintained that education was bad for the black man, because it "unfitted him for his place in life."[66] As time wore on, the Separate But Equal doctrine began to come true in a way the white supremacists had not expected. Blacks had rapidly educated themselves in the way of the dominant culture, thereby providing living counterevidence to the white supremacist position that blacks were inherently inferior. To stem this tide, whites sought to stop the education of blacks. In order to justify this, they argued that education increased black criminality by raising the social and economic expectations of black people to unrealistic levels.[67] The schools, they concluded, "are turning out thieves and vagrants in companies, battalions and armies."[68] Only a few argued that there should be no schools at all for blacks, claiming that "most of the theories for the improvement of the negro are chimerical."[69] More tolerant racists wanted merely to refuse blacks access to higher education, replacing it with an industrial education that would produce more competent and passive workers. Others wanted to eliminate "book learning" for blacks, replacing intellectual culture with moral training in obedience.[70]

White supremacists did not rely solely on the prevention of black education. In order to contain the social, political, and economic effects of the increasing numbers of able African-Americans, they developed the argument for a racial caste system based on averages. To this end, they reduced all African descendants to a single group or class, dismissing able individuals as exceptional. Next, they established the principle that "policy must be built on what is usual, not upon what is exceptional."[71] From this premise they then concluded that "however individuals of one race may appear the equals of individuals of the other race, the races themselves are essentially unequal."[72] Making policy based on the supposed "average" of the race would effectively cut off individual, and therefore group, advancement. Hence, in order to rule out blacks from consideration as

skilled laborers, Walter L. Hawley reasoned from "the indolence and unre-
liability of the negro as a race" to the conclusion that

[t]he average negro cannot become a skilled artisan. He is devoid of the intelligence
necessary to master a trade requiring skill in the use of tools, and without the patience requisite to successful apprenticeship. . . . Employment in factories and
machine-shops, where skill and intelligence are required, is closed to the average
black.[73]

The irony here was that blacks had constituted the Southern artisan class
during slavery. Nevertheless, such considerations were categorically rejected, for whatever the abilities of individual blacks, their destiny as a
class had been racially determined. As J. C. Hemphill wrote in *Harper's
Weekly*, "In the South the negro has always been a hewer of wood and a
drawer of water and he will always continue to be: that is what he was
made for, and the decrees of God are not to be changed."[74]

The racial caste argument functioned somewhat differently in political
matters, but even there it worked effectively to exclude blacks from political representation. Whites refused to be "ruled by ignorant negroes," as a
racial caste, even though they expressed a willingness to allow the few exceptional blacks to vote.[75] By thus setting the presumption against blacks
as a class, white voting registrars were empowered arbitrarily to exclude
worthy black voters. They thus insured that the only blacks who would be
deemed "exceptional" would be those who voted with white interests. As
a result, they made it impossible for even exceptional blacks to represent
their people.[76]

The racial caste argument went even further than basic voting rights,
for it functioned to exclude exceptional blacks from serving in government posts. The argument against appointing blacks to government office
in the South was a violent one, for it went straight to the heart of segregation policy. Such appointments created black political power and provided
highly visible examples of black ability.[77] Ultimately, however, the an-
imus of such hostility arose from the fact that racism could not survive if
whites were required to treat *any* black person with the respect due to a
peer or superior. Individualized treatment was inimical to maintaining a
racial caste. The white supremacists thus indicated that placing blacks in
positions that required respect would destroy the social order of the South.
Samuel McEnery explained:

. . . the South does object to placing negroes in official positions, where they will
have to come in contact with white men and women for the reason it is degrading
to them to have to accord to the negro that personal respect that is due to one holding a high official position, such as collectors of ports and postmasters.[78]

Even worse, they worried that "white women in the service of the Government may be placed under them."[79] Here, as in the case of lynching, the white supremacist relied upon his duty to "protect" white women as a reason for denying equal protection to blacks.[80]

Although they were not much troubled by arguments that sought to eliminate the equal rights of African-Americans to education, economic reward, and political representation, white Southerners in general were nonetheless increasingly discontent with what Separate But Equal had wrought. They felt "the nagging tensions of daily life" inherent in the segregation system, and they worried that segregation was reducing the control that whites held over black communities.[81] As the difficulties of life in a segregated society piled up, white supremacists expressed perplexity, asking, "[W]hat are we going to do about it?"[82] Fearing that segregation could not be permanent, some dreamed "of an airship" to spirit the blacks away.[83] But they also admitted no such airship would come.[84]

The responses to this situation varied. As a unit, white Southerners continued to put a brave face on the problem, claiming that they were providing "fair treatment" to blacks. They thus insisted that "in the South he [the Negro] is treated with every consideration. The laws are enforced in his behalf just the same as they are in behalf of the white man. His school and church privileges are the same; his rights of property are respected."[85] Some shifted back to a romantic patriarchalism that entertained minimalist egalitarian notions.[86] By 1907 a small number of Southerners even began to urge enlightened policies in the national forum.[87] However, more vocal racists sought to improve conditions in the same way they had during the days of slavery, by intensifying restrictions and exclusions, even to the point of disfranchisement and the use of corporal punishment.[88]

To preserve segregation, racists argued for ever-increasing white control of the social and political order. Seeing that their authority in this context required the careful cultural reproduction of white racist values, they sought to replace black teachers and ministers with whites who could assume the role of providing moral guidance and instruction to the black community.[89] The fire-eaters portrayed the "experiment" of Equality as a failure, announcing that the inability of the "Negro to hold up his own in the struggle of competition" had now been demonstrated.[90] They thus repudiated all forms of Equality, including Political Equality, suggesting that "[e]very schoolboy knows that full political equality carries with it social equality."[91] In the end, they found themselves trapped into denying that America was a "government of the people" and to arguing instead that Sovereign States, when led by the best elements, formed the soundest basis of government. It was in this vein that Representative Charles F. Reavis insisted that the American government "was never a government by the people, nor was it intended by the fathers to be such a government," for the Constitution had worked by "safeguarding the Government from the direct control of the people."[92]

The spiral of oppression that had played itself out in the development and preservation of slavery was once again in action. As in the antebellum period, the effort to oppress a minority required repudiating the political rights to vote, hold office, and act as a juror. White supremacists articulated the argument with abandon, declaring that such so-called rights are really only "mere privileges."[93] Thus forced by the march of events and the inherent tendencies of their own rhetoric, white supremacists found themselves in this period literally abrogating the grounds upon which the Separate But Equal compromise had been built. As such, they could not even point to a future equality in their program of separation. This continued march down the path of extremist racism was not only evil but, as it would turn out, rhetorically ineffective as well.

Egalitarians

The extremist rhetorical position of ultraracists made it impossible for egalitarians to continue pretending that white Southerners could be trusted, or that in time Southern white supremacists would allow African-Americans to achieve Political Equality. They had gone too far, and as a result they provoked a bitter response from more liberal elements in both the national media and in Congress.

The egalitarians of this period strongly denied the claims that education was deleterious to the black person and that blacks were destined to menial labor. They also indicated that "given equal opportunities, all Negroes are not necessarily the intellectual inferiors of all white people."[94] Du Bois further argued that the disagreements between North and South, white and black, supremacist and egalitarian, arose precisely because "[t]he teachers in these institutions come not to keep the Negroes in their place, but to raise them out of their places where the filth of slavery had wallowed them."[95]

Egalitarians likewise repudiated the extremists' defense of lynching. Their refutation was not fully effective, for even within the black press it was many years before the campaigns launched by Ida Wells [Barnett] succeeded in leading Americans to realize that lynching was not, in fact, performed solely or primarily to punish rapists.[96] For far too many years, the national media continued to accept the claim that rape was the issue behind lynching.[97] Even given that false assumption, however, the national press generally denounced lynching on the grounds that "lawlessness is no remedy for crime."[98] Similarly, egalitarians deplored race riots and chastised whites who participated in them, characterizing them as "ruffians—as low and contemptible as the lowest in the quarter which they sacked."[99]

The egalitarian voice also rose in opposition to the white supremacists' new openness in proclaiming that the superior accomplishments of the white race were a permanent feature built on natural necessity. Egalitarians denied the presumption of the argument, indicating that superiority "is not to be instantly assumed, but is to be proved" and concluding that "[n]o evidence has yet been adduced which proves that the negro is physically, intellectually, essentially, necessarily an inferior race, and that he must remain so." They went further to characterize prejudice in hostile terms as "provincial, unintelligent, and unchristian."[100] Finally, they emphasized the root similarities among peoples, highlighting the progress black people had made and their contributions to the nation. Chief among such contributions was their role as soldiers in the U.S. military.

The egalitarian position was bolstered additionally by the efforts of a steady stream of congressional representatives who took advantage of their opportunity to speak as members of the national legislature by insisting that the United States was founded on a substantial commitment to Equality. Representative Theodore E. Burton was fairly typical of egalitarian congressmen when he noted, "The most striking feature of both the Declaration of Independence and the Constitution of the United States and its amendments is equality, the right to life, liberty and property, the absence of all discrimination. These are great American ideas."[101] More important, egalitarian legislators also argued that the federal government had the power to enforce this vision, even over the objections of states. Where the state governments abdicated their responsibility to provide equal protection, they asserted, the federal government had a legal duty to step in.[102]

Finally, mainstream egalitarians denied the legitimacy of restricting access to the political process.[103] This does not mean that they all disapproved of the white Southerner's enactment of ballot qualifications. However, the egalitarians did draw a line between those measures that rested on educational or property qualifications and those that drew a distinction on items unrelated to "merit."[104]

When experienced cumulatively, this barrage of refutations and arguments effected a shift in the underlying public characterizations that had rhetorically motivated the Separate But Equal compromise. And as this happened, white supremacists came in for ever-rougher treatment. The publishers of national magazines began to print editorials that criticized and refuted the white supremacist articles they published, declaring white Southerners "impossible on this issue" and accusing them of a "blindness that will not see."[105] Du Bois's characterization of the South as "an armed camp for intimidating colored folk" gained an edge of plausibility.[106] The stories offered by the mass media increasingly suggested that contrary to its promise the white South had not honestly sought to elevate the colored race. Rather, it had actively engaged in keeping all black people in an inferior place. Some rhetors accused white supremacists of seeking to "keep him [the black man] what he is in relation to the white man; how to prevent his ever achieving or becoming that which would justify the belief on his part, or on the part of other people, that he and the white man can stand on common human ground."[107]

At the same time, the positive depiction of blacks in the mainstream press increased significantly.[108] These portraits were frequently paternalistic, and they emphasized differences between whites and blacks, but they also offered an increasing variety of favorable images for blacks to emulate and for whites to recognize. Most important, the mainstream press enthusiastically undertook the task of introducing black culture to white America through a rhetorical process we call cultural interbraiding. These black cultural forms were often extremely different from those to which whites were accustomed, and the process of introducing them may have heightened the sense of distance between the two peoples, but it also enriched the nation's culture immeasurably. There can be no question of the importance of this cultural interbraiding in setting the nation on the road to "social recognition" and "racial equality."

During this period the predominant voice of the national media became a mild egalitarianism; it attacked Marcus Garvey and his promotion of black nationalism, and it expressed a decided preference for the doctrine of fair treatment over full equality, but on the whole it supported the black demand for "equal industrial opportunity."[109] The media were joined by an increasingly vocal group of congressional representatives. Together they began to denounce the principle and practice of separation, and to work for equality of opportunity and equal treatment before the law.[110] Their efforts imposed a significant pressure against the official Separate But Equal doctrine, and this required a careful response from both the presidency and the Supreme Court.

The Supreme Court and the Presidency

The unraveling of a national compromise often requires decades before it produces changed laws and customs, for no matter how severe the disagreements underlying it, alternate visions must mature before changes of habit can occur. This was certainly the case with the Separate But Equal doctrine. Even as the foundations of the compromise began to erode, numerous laws designed to formalize and extend segregation successfully passed through Southern state legislatures.[111] The unresolved question was whether or not the Supreme Court would legitimize such measures.

Throughout the immediate post-*Plessy* period the Supreme Court supported fully neither the advocates of white supremacy nor of egalitarianism. In practice this meant that the Court would do whatever it could to preserve the Separate But Equal compromise. Consequently, it systematically overturned cases where state legislators directly attacked Equality. So, for example, in 1915 the Court begrudgingly found in *Guinn and Beal* v. *US* that the "Grandfather clause" violated the Fifteenth Amendment, noting that "we seek in vain for any ground which would sustain any other interpretation."[112] Similarly, in *Neal* v. *Delaware* the Court ruled out trial procedures that excluded the possibility of black jurors, denying Delaware's claim that no black person met the qualifications to be a juror.[113] In *McCabe* v. *Atchinson, Topeka and Sante Fe R. Co.,* the Court focused on the personal nature of individual rights when it mandated supplying separate but equal services to black persons, even if that required making first-class passage available to blacks on routes where there was little or no demand for it.[114]

Where attacks on Equality were less direct, the Separate But Equal doctrine permitted separation that allowed the Supreme Court to produce racial exclusions. The ruling in *Williams* v. *Mississippi* exemplifies this side of the balance struck by the Court. The core of the decision was the Court's willingness to accept as fact the existence of basic, characteristic differences between blacks and whites, and to conclude that discrimination based on these differences, rather than on race per se, was not in violation of the Fifteenth Amendment. The Court's decision endorsed the Mississippi Supreme Court's rationale for enacting voter qualifications that excluded black citizens from political participation. According to the Mississippi Supreme Court:

By reason of its previous condition of servitude and dependencies, this race had acquired or accentuated certain peculiarities of habit, of temperament, and of character, which clearly distinguished it as a race from the whites; A patient, docile people; but careless, landless, migratory within narrow limits, without forethought; and its criminal members given to furtive offenses, rather than the robust crimes of the whites. Restrained by the Federal Constitution from discriminating against the negro race, the convention discriminates against its characteristics, and the offenses to which its criminal members are prone.

The United States Supreme Court concluded:

But nothing tangible can be deduced from this . . . the operation of the constitution and laws is not limited by their language or effects to one race. They reach weak and vicious white men as well.[115]

The justices on the Supreme Court recognized that this interpretation ran contrary to the intent of the Fifteenth Amendment, and so they denied the standard of intent. Their decision relied on the finding of the 1883 Civil Rights Cases that the Fifteenth Amendment applied only to active discrimination by state law. Accordingly, the plaintiffs would have to demonstrate that either the law itself was directly discriminatory, or that state administrators had actively discriminated in applying it. The court concluded that the plaintiff had failed to demonstrate its case.

It is revealing that the Court supported its findings by comparing *Williams* v. *Mississippi* to the case of *Yick Wo* v. *Hopkins*.[116] In the earlier case, the Court argued that the intent to discriminate solely on the basis of race was obvious, because a San Francisco law had clearly operated to exclude only Chinese launderers. The use of this comparison is telling, for the briefs in *Williams* v. *Mississippi,* like in *Yick Wo* v. *Hopkins,* relied on a numerical tally to demonstrate the discriminatory effect of the law. In *Williams* v. *Mississippi* they cited the massive shift in eligible voters that accompanied the law. However, while the Court concluded that undue discrimination existed in *Yick Wo* v. *Hopkins,* they denied it in *Williams* v. *Mississippi*. The reason was that in *Williams* the Court believed that the "characteristics" of blacks had led to the discrimination, and that, they concluded, was altogether reasonable. Because the Court was less aware of the Chinese "characteristics" that led white San Franciscans to enact discriminatory laws, they literally could not imagine a reasonable justification for such laws. Racial characterizations thus played a significant role in the Court's rulings, and it was only after whites stopped depicting blacks as a class with a fixed set of "characteristics" that the Court could perceive the existence of discrimination in such instances.

While the Court worked to preserve the national compromise, the presidents headed off in distinctly different directions from each other, literally pulling the compromise apart. William McKinley typically evaded issues concerning race and equality, or, when necessary, he displaced them to the foreign realm. Theodore Roosevelt, William Howard Taft, and Calvin Coolidge struck clearly egalitarian poses, while Woodrow Wilson and Warren G. Harding moved the country deeper into the recesses of the Separate But Equal doctrine.[117]

McKinley's epideictic oratory matched the lukewarm and minimalist egalitarianism of the early part of the twentieth century. He addressed the lynching issue and affirmed the principle of equality, but argued sparingly for any additional change. Thus he declared to Congress in 1906:

Equality of rights must prevail, and our laws be always and everywhere respected and obeyed. We may have failed in the discharge of our full duty as citizens of the great Republic, but it is consoling and encouraging to realize that free speech, a free press, free thought, free schools, the free and unmolested right of religious liberty and worship, and free and fair elections are dearer and more universally enjoyed today than ever before. These guaranties must be sacredly preserved and wisely strengthened. The constituted authorities must be cheerfully and vigorously upheld. Lynchings must not be tolerated in a great and civilized country like the United States; courts, not mobs, must execute the penalties of the law. [118]

Roosevelt and Taft both extended these claims.

As in everything else, Roosevelt's rhetoric was aggressive; rather than adopt the role of national compromiser he frequently cast himself in the role of moral leader. First, his commitment to egalitarianism was not simply a vague and abstract pledge. He spent almost three pages excoriating lynch law, explaining why it was unacceptable even for a crime like rape. [119] When he insisted on education for blacks, he also insisted that financial support should not depend on the percentage of their tax receipts. When he supported industrial education, he did so not with arguments about its fitness for blacks but with his typical Bull Moose gusto, preferring "good citizens" to "scholars." [120]

Roosevelt's rhetoric was not only concrete, it added important usages to the mainstream discourse of Equality. The first was his adoption of the African-American's conception of Equality as a relationship of humans founded on "no distinction on the basis of color." In appropriating this phrase he identified the importance of individual merit over group classification in determining discriminatory practices. As Roosevelt argued:

There is but one safe rule . . . to treat each man, whatever his color, his creed, or his social position, with evenhanded justice on his real worth as a man . . . [hewing to the] question of relentlessly punishing bad men, and of securing to the good man the right to his life, his liberty, and the pursuit of his happiness as his own qualities of heart, head, and hand enable him to achieve it. [121]

The second step Roosevelt took was to deny the inherent opposition between Equality and Liberty. African-Americans had asserted the necessary link between Liberty and Equality, while white supremacists portrayed the effacement of white Liberty by black Equality. Roosevelt repudiated the white South's definition of Liberty, maintaining that there cannot be "a liberty to wrong others."[122]

Building on this ground, Roosevelt placed another foundation stone for later usages of Equality. He agreed with African-American rhetors that a centralized, national government was essential, basing his argument on interstate commerce and the control of the increasingly national scope of business corporations.[123] He did not particularly apply the principle to issues of race, equality, or segregation, but his emphasis on the "interdependence" of modern life, and his launching of the initiative in favor of the federal government over "the old doctrine of State's Rights," was a historically crucial measure in the development of an integrated Anglo/African Equality.[124]

President Taft took up this banner in his Inaugural Address in 1909, arguing, "The scope of a modern government in what it can and ought to accomplish for its people has been widened far beyond the principles laid down by the old 'laissez-faire' school of political writers, and this widening has met popular approval."[125] Taft's construction of the national compromise was mildly egalitarian. Although he accepted the restrictions on voting suggested by Southerners, he portrayed them as consistent with the egalitarian principles of the nation.[126] Taft also supported Liberian development, the Freedman's bank, and the national Negro exposition, all the while touting the progress of the Negro race in America. Echoing the antebellum rhetoric of black Americans he declared a national commitment to more inclusion and elevation:

The Negroes are now Americans. Their ancestors came here years ago against their will, and this is their only country and their only flag. They have shown themselves anxious to live for it and to die for it. Encountering the race feeling against them, subjected at times to cruel racial injustice growing out of it, they may well have our profound sympathy and aid in the struggle they are making. We are charged with the sacred duty of making their path as smooth and easy as we can.[127]

Most remarkably, Taft declared, "Personally, I have not the slightest race prejudice or feeling."[128] It had been a long route from the Great Emancipator's freely professed prejudice to the renunciation of such prejudice as an inaugural principle of the nation. Whether Taft was accurate in his self-assessment or not, in proclaiming the illegitimacy of prejudice he was a moral leader, not merely a mirror of the national consensus of his time. The extent to which this was the case became patently obvious with the election of Woodrow Wilson.

Wilson represented the other trajectory in American ideology.[129] His ceremonial inscriptions of the national values were largely silent on the racial issue, but his quiet policies spoke volumes. Wilson's Southern cabinet attempted to introduce segregation into the federal government. This was a momentous policy, implying that segregation was not simply tolerated because the federal government had no power to preclude such state action but rather that segregation was a national preference. Following Wilson in the presidency was Warren G. Harding, a former newspaperman who either naively or maliciously proclaimed that "in the United States, equality of opportunity has been obtained, though not all are prepared to embrace it."[130]

President Coolidge would return the nation to a mildly egalitarian track in 1925, repeating the arguments of the earlier, more egalitarian presidents. He called the rights of colored people sacred, deplored lynching, and pleaded for mutual understanding and full participation, Equal Opportunity and Equal Protection under the law. He also endorsed the principle of "liberty and equality before the law without distinction of race or creed."[131] Additionally, Coolidge affected a small advance in 1928, when he countermanded Harding's demand that all peoples assimilate to a single, homogeneous "American way" with an alternate vision of America built on diversity and variety: "Our country has many elements in its population, many different modes of thinking and living, all of which are striving in their own way to be loyal to the high ideals worthy of the crown of American citizenship."[132]

The presidency of the first half of the twentieth century was nearly as polarized as the rest of the nation, but its more progressive leaders seemed to have the edge. And as the nation unknowingly prepared itself for an era of national crises, those leaders moved additional and expansive egalitarian usages into the mainstream public vocabulary. It would remain to be seen if and how they would be integrated with the events of the coming era to enhance the position of America's black population.

But this might be to put too rosy a cast on the circumstances confronting the nation at this time, for even in the face of the most progressive national leadership, America's mainstream remained trapped within the limiting prejudices of culturally codified stereotypes. President Theodore Roosevelt's handling of the Brownsville affair illustrates the problem. In 1906, a violent racial conflict occurred between black soldiers and white citizens in the small town of Brownsville, Texas. Roosevelt, discharging his duty as the commander in chief, immediately dismissed three companies of black troops without trial, hearing, or honorable discharge. He had once pronounced the necessity of distinguishing between "good men" and "bad men," but in this instance he made no such effort. Eventually the soldiers would have their case heard, but Roosevelt's autonomic reaction reflected the deep chasm in the American public vocabulary, undermining the best intentions of the best of leaders: Roosevelt reacted to blacks as a caste rather than as individuals.

The problem, of course, was that even when they were fully committed to the idea of Equality, white Americans still responded to blacks as some distant, alien other, a fact clearly expressed in their rhetorical distinction between "them" and "we, the people." Whether whites perceived blacks paternalistically, as docile, fun-loving and dependent, or with hostility, as dangerous, bestial predators, they *always* perceived them as "of a type," and that type was fundamentally different from white people. In order to conceive of full Equality and to enact any part of it, a great deal of rhetorical work would have to be done to remove that sense of distance and difference. And in the meantime, America tottered on an old and unsatisfactory compromise, sadly ignorant of what Equality could come to mean.

COMMITTING TO INTEGRATED EQUALITY, 1930–1948

The Great Depression and World War II revolutionized America. In a span of less than twenty years the federal government evolved into a powerful and sophisticated central government, taking on the responsibility of making a better life for all its citizens, regardless of race, creed, or color. The presidency and the Supreme Court made the first firm efforts to replace Separate But Equal with an Integrated Equality that included political equality, equality of economic opportunity, and integrated public facilities. A simple majority of Congress joined in this effort, but they did not do so wholeheartedly, and when confronted with public resistance and intense localized hostilities they usually backed away from any kind of strong action. Nevertheless, by the time America entered the era of the Cold War, its egalitarian public vocabulary had continued to expand, moving the nation ever closer to the national upheaval of the 1960s.

African-American Rhetoric

The 1930s and 1940s were years of moderation and persistence for the now flourishing Afro-American press. Having resolved themselves to a course of social, political, and economic equality, both local and national groups went about the task of effecting it through local community action and the courts in an orderly yet forceful manner. For its part, the press continued to keep the black community informed of current problems: attention to lynching shifted to include more focus on police brutality; stories were told about peonage or the injustices of federal employment projects; and the papers and magazines reported exciting achievements in athletics that demonstrated once and for all that the white supremacists' claim to "physical superiority" was laughable.[133] The press also attended to African history, as most publications ran a regular series teaching African-Americans about their past.

A string of legal successes and the increasing appearance of white goodwill enhanced the confidence and optimism of the black leadership.[134] The key devil term of the era was "race hate." The term "interracial" proliferated as in both the North and the South mixed groups of blacks and whites worked together, albeit cautiously, on racial problems. Black newspapers celebrated heterogeneity, but they saw room in it for both intermarriage and black pride.[135] Langston Hughes wrote of being "black and beautiful," and the NAACP and other community groups ran "beautiful baby" contests.[136] It was within this milieu that Thurgood Marshall, a young black lawyer working for the NAACP, provided what was probably the quintessential definition of Equality for the day: [T]he only way to get equality is for people to get the same thing at the same place and at the same time."[137]

This was clearly an era of goodwill and moderation, but it did not totally lack either a hint of militancy or a determined effort to affect change.[138] *Opportunity* set the tone, arguing that "there is no one guaranteed over-all method of disposing of racial discrimination," that "the Negro is 'demanding' not just 'asking' for justice," and that "it is possible to maintain self-pride and to challenge any form of prejudice and discrimination without assuming a chip-on-the-shoulder air. Neatness and cleanliness, energy and efficiency are proved essentials regardless of one's race or station."[139] *The Crisis* agreed, urging "race pride" without "racial chauvinism," and suggesting that "it would be equally unwise to accept the leadership of the overzealous who desire and expect to overcome racial inequalities over night."[140]

This was, of course, the voice of the active middle class speaking, and in this period, tensions between the middle and lower classes simmered. Unlike the period from 1895 to 1930, however, the tension did not manifest itself in major battles between the leaders of the different classes. In the late teens and twenties the black bourgeoisie and its leadership widely condemned Marcus Garvey, a charismatic leader of the mass poor operating from New York City's Harlem. In the 1930s and 1940s, however, there was no sustained, black national leader exclusively serving the poor.[141] Disapproval focused instead on those members of the middle class who were comfortable and unwilling to make sacrifices for the advancement of those who were not so comfortable.[142] In general, there was only minor overt conflict between the middle-class leaders and the poorer classes.[143] This relative harmony occurred because the target of the leadership— enforced segregation—harmed colored citizens of every class, whether by forcing them into crowded and dangerous residential ghettos, denying them a decent job, or restricting their access to higher education.

The African-American rhetoric of the period thus proclaimed that "Segregation must go."[144] As black advocates frequently argued:

Negroes, no matter what fancy language may be used to dress up the proposition, can *never* accept a plan of segregation. The record shows that whenever such agreements are entered into, inevitably the chickens of proscription, limited opportunity, and inequality come home to roost.[145]

The decision to target segregation was influenced by the two major events of the era. The growth of the federal government had been catalyzed by the Great Depression, and black leaders argued for a "proportional" share of the benefits, especially in the burgeoning federal works projects. As long as the money involved was federal, the white supremacists could not rely on their age-hardened argument that the federal government had no power to force integration.[146] In fact, the presumption rested in favor of integrated efforts, as black leaders complained when Tennessee Valley Authority (TVA) work did not go to blacks on a "proportionate share." Thus, they argued, "These men are used to segregation and prejudice. But they are not used to it at the hands of the federal government."[147]

The approach in the TVA case was typical. It premised Equality on mathematical proportions within the population. It thereby assumed that equality was a transitive relationship; as "equals," black and white people were interchangeable. However, even at this early date, this form of equivalence was problematic. The resort to "proportion" did not resolve the issue, for the basis of proportion was always negotiable. Should percentages be based on national population? Local population? Or on the basis of need? In the case of the TVA, the blacks objected to the goal "to employ Negro workers in proportion to their population percentages in the Valley area," because it "did not take into consideration the excessive proportions of Negro workmen to be found among the jobless in the Valley."[148] Additionally, there were problems with equivalence in wage levels and types of work. After pointing out that blacks received only "9.5% of the payroll as contrasted with 11 percent of the total number of workers employed," they complained of the "failure to include a fair proportion of Negroes in skilled work."[149] The problem, in part, was that at this point in time Negroes and whites were not "equally skilled," so that transitivity was a false assumption.[150] For many years, whites maintained an argumentative circle in which they *refused to train* blacks on the grounds that jobs in skilled trades were not open for them, and then they *refused to hire* them on the grounds that blacks were not adequately trained.

It was for this reason that a central focus of the desegregationist efforts during the periods from 1935 to 1939 and from 1945 to 1954 was education.[151] The school debates similarly relied on mathematical proportion as a test of equality. Time and again egalitarians demonstrated that there was not a "fair and equitable spending of school funds," by citing the number of black and white students and the gross discrepancies in per pupil spending, in funds for busing, and in teacher's salaries.[152] Of course, the case was strengthened by federal aid to education. Perhaps states could discriminate, but the federal government should not. In other areas where federal funds were spent, a similar argument was applied. In health and housing, as well as in the Civilian Conservation Corps, arguments based on proportion were central.[153]

The case was further strengthened by World War II. Even more than World War I, World War II required large quantities of human power to make the war machine run. That meant a need for both soldiers and factory workers to increase the production of munitions and other war-related items. To match the demand, America needed to rely on its entire surplus labor pool, including both black persons and white women. So strong was this need, that even the white Southern members of America's official establishment were willing to concede to at least some of the equity demands of black people in order to gain cooperation.[154] Consequently, long-standing black demands for inclusion, integration, and promotion in the military achieved a toehold.

Equally significant was the Fair Employment Practices Commission (FEPC). By threatening a massive and embarrassing demonstration in Washington D.C., A. Philip Randolph, the leader of the Brotherhood of Sleeping Car Porters, forced President Franklin Roosevelt into concessions on defense-related employment.[155] Additionally, the FEPC was formed. Although it was not effective in achieving absolute parity in wages, jobs, and skill levels, it provided a highly visible prototype that moved many companies toward integration. It was integrated at high levels itself, and it worked out the methods of proportional assessment and federal supervision of private contracts that would provide the basis for general fair employment laws of the future. A similar model was at work in federal housing efforts, which evolved from the need to house the large numbers of workers who migrated to defense jobs. In time, the focus on proportion as a working definition of Equality became the litmus test of Equal Justice.[156] This did not mean, however, that blacks were now committed to placing race above merit as a criterion of equality. *Opportunity* demonstrated the careful balancing of these issues:

Is there any such thing as Baptist science, or Negro science, or Jewish science, white science, or colored science? These are contradictions in terms. When we seek a professor for the faculty of Howard University we seek the best obtainable; we do not lower our ideals. When two persons of equal ability are available—a colored man and a white man—we choose the colored man. . . . But I should oppose to the bitter end, taking a second-rate colored man to a first-rate white man.[157]

The African-American rhetoric of this period thus evolved a new meaning of Equality to replace what they called the "invalid hypothesis" of Separate But Equal.[158] The new vision assumed that although there might be important cultural differences, similarity outweighed difference. Individuals were, therefore, interchangeable in the market as well as in political and educational institutions. Accordingly, equality necessitated equal access to the same material conditions for blacks and whites as measured by the simple mathematical process of transitivity. This usage of "equality" required the nation to meet two tests. First, Equality existed if, on a particular list of items, the same proportional quantity of blacks and whites appeared (i.e., if there were equal percentages of blacks and whites in housing, health, school, and employment by wage and type). Second, Equality existed when blacks and whites shared side by side in the same facilities. Of course, white supremacists resisted this definition, but by the end of the period it had been widely endorsed in the mainstream mass media and legitimated by both the Supreme Court and the presidency.

Mainstream Rhetoric

Until the arrival of World War II, the message one finds in the mass distribution national magazines regarding matters of race and equity remains pretty close to what one finds in the earlier period of polarization. The war, however, revolutionized the way in which Americans talked about Equality. The emphasis on "world democracy" that had effectively justified World War I became even more potent in World War II. Of course, part of the motivation for this was the material need to incorporate black labor and lives into the war effort. Additionally, Hitler's program was directly and openly identified with racism, and this allowed American egalitarians to oppose racism and democracy as inherently antithetical to one another. Concerns about international ethos greatly amplified the issue of internal consistency. As long as it treated colored people inequitably, the nation was highly vulnerable to foreign propaganda challenging the sincerity of its claim to democracy. This concern achieved wide circulation during the war, and the character of the Cold War that followed continued to make international opinion vitally important.

If democracy was the key term justifying integrated equality, the key narratives envisioning it depicted various injustices perpetuated upon colored people. The routine story recounted how America had expected colored people to give their lives and effort for the nation during the war, but now denied them the privilege of living in the nation as free and equal citizens. *Harper's* led off a series of such stories in this manner:

When the first load of bombs exploded on the deck of an American man-of-war lying in Pearl Harbor on the morning of December 7th a black boy raced up from the galley and on to the deck of his ship . . . he unhesitatingly manned a machine gun and fired it at the enemy until his ammunition was spent. And when the fight had stopped and the smoke had cleared away from the harbor, he returned to his galley quarters, where, because he is a black American, he must remain—in spite of heroism, ability, or the need of the Navy for first-class fighting men.[159]

Accompanying these stories was an effort to recharacterize the public image of blacks. Older stereotypes—those that portrayed blacks as essentially good but distinctively different from whites and in need of paternal protection—were replaced with two new and different sets of characterizations. The first was a depiction of blacks as having the ability to work effectively in factories. Wiping out the white supremacist protest that blacks were incapable of factory work, news magazines reported that "Negroes were found to be satisfactory workers" or that Negro women were "superior workers who are displaying remarkable aptitude."[160]

The second set of characterizations emphasized the similarities between members of the two races and their ability to live and work together peacefully.[161] At the same time, the mass media unleashed a tidal wave of negative characterizations of the "racial bigot." The postwar period signaled the end of *vicious* African-American stereotypes in the print press, although such images would continue to appear in Letters to the Editor or in places where they were framed as clearly unacceptable usages.[162] The shift away from negative black stereotypes was not total, however, for the recharacterization effort allowed the presentation of black Muslims as black racists.[163]

None of this added up to uniform support for full equality. There was still a fairly broad range of opinions represented in the popular press. The range now ran from the moderate paternalist, bent on gradualism, to the advocate of Integrated Equality, leery of black nationalism. There was no overt public support for Social Equality, for the issue itself had been simply omitted from the national discussion. Even the phrase "racial equality" appeared only sparsely. The phrase "equal opportunity" was used more frequently than "equality," and the use of phrases like "full equality," "absolute equality," or "complete equality" were rare at best. Ultimately, while the white mainstream press expressed concern with the same list of issues as the black press, they were as likely to view them as matters of basic decency or fairness as they were to see them as entitlements based on Equality. The Negro deserved an undefined "fair treatment" with regard to housing, health, jobs, and public accommodations. This fair treatment clearly required vastly improved facilities, but only with reference to schools did the popular press of the period frequently and consistently demand Equality. Moreover, the use of mathematical proportion as a test of fairness was more rare than in the black discourse. It was clear that the existence of proportionally skewed employment patterns or housing patterns could be taken as a sign of a lack of fairness or Equal Opportunity, but the resort to proportion in these contexts did not mean that the nation had committed itself to a guarantee of proportional goods in all areas.[164]

The national press thus underwent a substantial, though still circumscribed, shift toward egalitarianism during World War II, and it maintained its new posture in the postwar era. Two discursive factors were central to this shift: a new portrait of blacks as essentially similar to whites, and the elimination of the extreme white supremacist pole of the debate. This is not to say, however, that the white supremacist voice was silenced, for the debate remained radically polarized in the U.S. Congress.

The Congress

Members of Congress represented local and regional perspectives rather than national ones. Consequently, throughout the depression and war years there remained a strong representation of racist fire-eating rhetoric in the halls of Congress. In the 1930s, Southern congressmen continued to misrepresent the record of the South on education and equal protection, even as they claimed that they were the "best friends" of the Negro. Nevertheless, they were adamant in their continual assertion that the white race was superior and that efforts at integration would destroy Anglo-Saxon civilization.

One of the most outrageous figures of the period was Senator Theodore Bilbo of Mississippi, who scandalously proposed a colonization scheme that recalled the efforts of the nineteenth century. He asked Congress to provide a large sum of money to settle blacks "voluntarily" outside of the United States. While Bilbo's efforts garnered sensationalized attention, his rhetoric and that of the fire-eaters was convincing to no one but the white racists themselves. Moreover, black congressmen such as Oscar DePriest responded in no uncertain terms to the white supremacist's claim that blacks were "happy" in the South: "I am making these remarks because I want you to know that the American Negro is not satisfied with the treatment he receives in America, and I know of no forum where I can better present the matter than the floor of Congress."[165] Black congressmen were not the only legislators to represent black interests, for the great migration had given many Northern white congresspersons substantial black constituencies, and many of these representatives defended the interests of these constituents by expressing strong egalitarian sentiments.

The combination of enhanced egalitarian interests and the demands of World War II were simply too much for the fire-eaters to survive. Egalitarians mandated American unification against Nazi-style racism in favor of democratic government and thus declared prejudice "un-American."[166] They also insisted that the war effort required the use of black workers and troops and that to obtain that use greater fairness was necessary. Finally, they were able to transcend the rhetoric of black/white difference with the broader concept of "minorities." This was an extremely important move, for it incorporated religious groups, such as Jews and Catholics, with other racial groups, such as Hispanics and Asian-Americans, into a much larger coalition.

The fire-eaters did not give up white supremacy in view of these developments, but in order to protect segregation they agreed to "bettering [the] social conditions" of black people.[167] They insisted, however, that segregation itself was an unerasable line. As Senator Eastland declared:

I know the South must spend more money on Negro education. . . . We must improve his hospital facilities. There must be better housing. Every decent southerner believes in these things. . . . Mr. President, the racial agitation in this country today is not over equality of economic opportunity for the Negro. It is not over a program to raise the Negroes' standard of living and better their condition. The issue is the destruction of segregation.[168]

Throughout the period, white supremacists sought to reinforce the idea that activities like eating and sleeping together were familial activities, and thus by insidious implication associated with marriage and racial purity.[169] They were not public activities. Consequently, the military forces could not be integrated, nor could restaurants and inns accommodate black and white together.

Although white supremacist representatives were claiming less and less ground, they were speaking in far more openly racist tones on the floor of Congress than in the mainstream press. They continued to insist that Negroes were inferior and different and that they could not, therefore, be included in American political and social equality. And in point of fact, white supremacists continued to hold sway in terms of the laws they could affect. They filibustered or killed in committee federal antilynching legislation and bills to eliminate the poll tax, just as they managed to shelve the establishment of a permanent Fair Employment Practices Commission. They achieved much of this by exploiting parliamentary tactics that allowed them to turn their minority position into an effective legislative posture. They could do this, in part, because the intensity of the commitment to Equality held by the majority of Americans was far weaker than the intensity of those who opposed it. The change in public usages were nonetheless important, and the official positions of the national government would be dramatically altered by the virtual unification of the victims of the Supreme Court and the presidency.

The Supreme Court

The period between 1930 and 1948 represents the key turning point in the reconstitution of American law by the Supreme Court. Although the 1930s provided a mixed bag of race-related decisions, the Court signaled a sharp new turn, which it further accelerated in the 1940s.

Juries, the all-white primary, and higher education provided the crucial issues of the 1930s. In *Norris* v. *Alabama* (1935), the court extended its proscription against the exclusion of blacks from juries in *Neal* v. *Delaware* to the Southern states. This case is noteworthy for its use of proportional arguments. The Court found that, in the face of the proportional makeup of the population, the fact that no blacks at all had ever appeared on a jury in the district at issue represented a prima facie case for the existence of racial exclusion. It rejected the testimony of the jury commissioner that "I do not know of any negro in Morgan County over twenty-one and under sixty-five who is generally reputed to be honest and intelligent and who is esteemed in the community for his integrity." Instead, it concluded, such a statement is not sufficient to outweigh the statistical argument, especially in the face of concrete testimony of other "men of intelligence" as to the existence of nearly 200 "qualified negroes."[170] White supremacists would no longer have an easy time branding all blacks with negative characterizations.

The Court seesawed back and forth on another important issue. In 1926 it began its agonized consideration of the "white primary." In *Nixon* v. *Herndon* the Court concluded that a state law prohibiting blacks from being members of the Democratic party, and, therefore, from voting in the all-important primary election, violated the Fourteenth Amendment. The decision read: "States may do a good deal of classifying that it is difficult to believe rational, but there are limits, and it is too clear for extended argument that color cannot be made the basis of a statutory classification affecting the right set up in this case."[171] The white Texas Democrats continued to seek for the "limits" of the law. Two more cases would reach the Court, and in the latter the Court upheld the exclusion of blacks.[172]

By 1938, however, the Court set off in a definite egalitarian direction in the case of *Missouri ex rel Gaines* v. *Canada*.[173] The state of Missouri did not provide graduate legal training for blacks. It did, however, provide tuition for blacks who wished to pursue graduate training at schools in other states. Considering the contortionism the Court had used in the past to support white supremacist preferences, it would have been easy enough for the majority to find that this position provided separate but equal education. For the first time, however, the justices chose to wield the weapons of technical legalism in favor of egalitarianism. Thus, they ruled: "The question here is not of a duty of the State to supply legal training, or of the quality of the training which it does supply, but of its duty when it provides such training to furnish it to the residents of the State upon the basis of an equality of right."[174]

With this decision, the Court signaled a new commitment to attach increasing substance to the term "equality." This commitment would rapidly carry it beyond Separate But Equal. First the Court marched against indirect evasion of constitutional provisions for Equality. In *Smith* v. *Allwright,* it ruled against all white primaries on the grounds that "Constitutional rights would be of little value if they could be thus indirectly denied."[175] Then, in *Shelly* v. *Kraemer* (1948), the Court extended the concept in its first direct strike at the underlying notion of Separate But Equal. In this case the Court decreed that any State enforcement of restrictive covenants was impermissible because the mutual exclusion implied in segregation statutes violated the Constitution:

The rights created by the first section of the Fourteenth Amendment are, by its terms, guaranteed to the individual. The rights established are personal rights. It is, therefore, no answer to these petitioners to say that the courts may also be induced to deny white persons rights of ownership and occupancy on grounds of race or color. Equal protection of the laws is not achieved through indiscriminate imposition of inequalities. . . . The Constitution confers upon no individual the right to demand action by the State which results in the denial of equal protection of the laws to other individuals. And it would appear beyond question that the power of the State to create and enforce property interests must be exercised within the boundaries defined by the Fourteenth Amendment.[176]

In this series of cases in the 1930s and 1940s the Supreme Court took a new direction, one that would soon make Equality a substantial condition of the American Constitution. Its movement in this direction was strengthened and accelerated by the fact that the presidency was moving in a similar direction.

The Presidency

Herbert Hoover's concept of a largely passive federal government guaranteed that his would be an administration that made little change on race and equality, but then his inability to deal with the depression also guaranteed that his would be a short-lived administration as well.[177] Franklin Delano Roosevelt and Harry S. Truman, however, created the conditions that would invite substantial egalitarian rhetoric. Dramatically reversing the presumption of federal inaction across the board, Roosevelt opened up the possibilities for presidential and congressional action to stamp out state-enforced inequality, even though his own achievements in racial equality were modest.[178] His successor, Harry S. Truman, rapidly utilized the latitude Roosevelt had created.

In the postwar era, Truman moved to employ the link between Hitler's concept of race superiority and the white supremacist's concept of segregation.[179] He then chastised the nation when he noted:

We have recently witnessed in this country numerous attacks upon the constitutional rights of individual citizens as a result of racial and religious bigotry. Substantial segments of our people have been prevented from exercising fully their right to participate in the election of public officials, both locally and nationally. Freedom to engage in lawful callings has been denied.[180]

Truman, however, did more than simply demand "equal opportunity for education, for jobs and economic advancement" as well as "equal protection under our laws."[181] He adopted the African-American's notion that to be equal was to share equally in the concrete conditions of life. He promoted this usage to national status as a central component of the American creed, saying, "In this Nation, the ideals of freedom and equality can be given specific meaning in terms of health, education, social security, and housing."[182] Breaking a seventy-year logjam, he announced the national government's power to insure the enactment of these promises in the lives of the people, and he appointed a Civil Rights commission to investigate the problem and to locate solutions.[183]

The Civil Rights Committee's report, *To Secure These Rights,* was a far reaching document. In its opening pages it proclaimed that the "American way" is a "heritage of freedom and equality for all men."[184] It denied the opposition of Liberty and Equality, asserting the interdependence of the two on the grounds that "[w]ithout this equality [equality of opportunity] freedom becomes an illusion."[185] It also defined America as a "diverse" nation, not a homogeneous one, and found strength in that diversity: "The cultural diversity of the United States has flavored the whole political, economic, and social development of the nation. Our science, our industry, our art, our music, our philosophy have been formed and enriched by peoples from throughout the world."[186] The report then enumerated a broad range of basic American rights, chronicling the way in which they had been violated through lynchings, police brutality, faulty trials, peonage, military and job discrimination, the denial of suffrage, the mass detention of Japanese citizens, and so on. Finally, and perhaps of most importance, the committee attacked the Separate But Equal doctrine, concluding that "reason and history," as well as "experience," "substantiate the argument against segregation."[187] Thus, it announced:

The separate but equal doctrine stands convicted on three grounds. It contravenes the equalitarian spirit of the American heritage. It has failed to operate, for history shows that inequality of service has been the omnipresent consequence of separation. It has institutionalized segregation and kept groups apart despite indisputable evidence that normal contacts among these groups tend to promote social harmony.[188]

The report concluded with a call for sweeping action that rejected the underlying warrant of the original separate but equal compromise, that "time equals progress," by proclaiming that the "time for action is now."[189]

President Truman moved on several fronts to begin executing this agenda. He began the desegregation of the military, he inaugurated the desegregation of Washington, D.C., and he submitted civil rights legislation to Congress. This last effort would prove immediately unsuccessful given the makeup of the national legislature, but it nevertheless effectively established the expectation for future presidents who would lay claim to the constituencies of African-Americans and white egalitarians. It also reorganized the executive branch's effort to effect nondiscrimination requirements in federal contracts. Although the enormity of the task, the rigidity of his opponents, and other substantial demands on his time meant that only the smallest beginning was made, in his last annual message he could fairly conclude:

There has been a great awakening of the American conscience on the issues of civil rights. And all this progress—still far from complete but still continuing—has been our answer, up to now, to those who questioned our intention to live up to the promises of equal freedom for us all.[190]

By 1948, the nation's leadership had endorsed a substantial portion of the African-American version of the code of Equality. This new code incorporated Equal Opportunity in all public walks of American life, and it defined the public arena to include privately operated public accommodations, educational and health facilities, and so on. Nonetheless, the nation's leadership, black and white, faced intense opposition from a variety of sources, including both the private racist attitudes of many Northern whites and the public racist rhetoric of the white Southern leadership. The commitment of the presidency and of the Supreme Court was not a solution to the race problem, but it was a long-delayed reengagement of the battle for racial equality.

THE FIGHT FOR EQUALITY, 1948–1960

Our cultural memory of the 1950s plays back to us the vision of a quiet, happy, "do-nothing" era, inviting us to recall the later 1960s as the decade of conflict and violence. In actuality, the 1950s served as an important transition period between the rejection of the Separate But Equal compromise and the rhetoric of black nationalism and separatism that would come to fruition in the later 1960s. The earliest part of the 1950s did indeed mark a fairly quiet time for the nation as far as civil rights were concerned. But the middle years saw an aggressive movement from restrained legal action to the militant enforcement of legislative measures. For black Americans it encompassed both the end of the interracial period and the first inklings of a militant black response to racial inequality. For white Americans it inaugurated the period in which the costs of Integrated Equality would begin to surface, and with them it brought the desperate, last-ditch efforts of the segregationist South to preserve the old order.

The Presidency and the Supreme Court

Dwight D. Eisenhower dominated the presidency during the 1950s. His record on civil rights, as on so many other issues, was static. He did not try to retract the egalitarian rhetoric of his forebears, but he enunciated it with less clarity and firmness.[191] When confronted, he employed federal force against segregation in Little Rock, Arkansas, and he signed a minimal civil rights bill. However, he did not actively lead the country toward Equality.

By contrast, the Supreme Court not only continued its attack on the circumvention of voting rights, it also disallowed the legal legitimacy of the Separate But Equal doctrine.[192] The issue of equal education provided the vehicle for the Court to overturn the legal doctrines of *Plessy* v. *Ferguson,* and it did that most completely in 1954 in *Brown* v. *Board of Education,* where it announced decisively that "the doctrine of 'separate but

equal' has no place. Separate educational facilities are inherently unequal."[193] In *Brown* v. *Bd. of Education* the Court openly agreed with what
by that time was the ancient claim of nineteenth-century African-
Americans that "[t]o separate them from others of similar age and qualifications solely because of their race generates a feeling of inferiority as to
their status in the community that may affect their hearts and minds in a
way unlikely ever to be undone."[194]

The *Brown* decision was neither unanticipated nor unprecedented. Following the lead of a group of innovative black lawyers, including Charles
Houston Hamilton and Thurgood Marshall, the Court laid the ground-
work for *Brown* v. *Bd. of Education* in two prior cases decided in 1950.[195] In
Sweatt v. *Painter,* the Court looked to "intangible factors" to rule that
Texas's separate law school for blacks was unequal. These factors included
both the higher status of the University of Texas law school, and the exclusion of black law students from interaction with 85 percent of the future
white lawmakers of the state. In *McLaurin* v. *Oklahoma* the Court also
placed interaction with other members of the community as an intangible
factor denied to segregated blacks.

These cases made clear that at least in higher education separation generated inequality. Southern white supremacist lawmakers knew well what
was coming. They scrambled to upgrade black schools throughout the region, and in South Carolina they passed a provision that would enable the
legislature to abolish public schools if and when the Court applied this rationale to elementary and secondary education. In 1954, the Court did
exactly what white Southerners feared most. However, it offered white
supremacists an important concession in granting them "time" in the
doctrine of "all deliberate speed."[196] This proved to be a major concession,
and one that allowed substantial maneuvering room for the many lower
court judges who would seek to preserve segregation. Such maneuvering
notwithstanding, the Supreme Court constructed a new ground of national compromise that diametrically opposed the Separate But Equal
doctrine. The national common ground now rested between the patriarchal white supremacists' profession of egalitarian politics and the request
for more time to implement them, and the African-American and white
egalitarian insistence on immediate desegregation. The national press
chipped away even at this ground.

The Popular Press

The major topic of the mainstream press in the 1950s was equality in education. The mass magazines almost universally supported equalization of
education and the *Brown* decision.[197] They also kept up their efforts at re-

characterization, pitting the "loud-mouthed bigots of the South" against "the Negroes," who were making "themselves worthy of the respect of men of any race."[198] Many journalists also claimed that "the cultural difference between colored and white American groups now appears to be so narrow that in a few more national elections any distinctions between the Negro and White vote will be little more than academic." Consistent with this prophecy, they portrayed a "new" Negro:

The average Negro today is an urban dweller, probably a grammar or high school graduate, a newspaper reader, a televiewer and a radio owner. . . . He is, doubtless, a church-goer, maybe is one of 1,500,000 Negro labor-union members, has served in the armed forces at home or abroad, has a savings account, could be one of the million homeowners and not unlikely is one of 200,000 colored who have graduated from college since World War I.[199]

The reinforcement of the egalitarian discourse of the 1930s and 1940s and the seconding of the Court's desegregation decisions were important, but the print media of the 1950s also featured one small but critical discursive shift. They stopped depicting Equality as a distant possibility in an obscure future and began to treat it as a present necessity. The new sense of time was best articulated by Carey McWilliams in an article entitled "The Heart of the Matter." Here he posed the "clear majority" of Americans who "feel that the time has come to eliminate the national disgrace of Jim Crow" against the "vocal minority" who hope that "integration is now 'a long way off—years and years and maybe never.'"[200] Like many others, McWilliams pointed out that it had already been a hundred years since the Emancipation Proclamation. He thus argued that gradualism could no longer be a means of permanent deferral, and that "a special burden rests on the proponents of gradualism to present a program and a timetable."[201] Some writers portrayed the new order as "inevitable," but at least they placed segregation in the past, as an "an outmoded and thoroughly discredited social pattern."[202]

The regional resistance of the white South remained strongly set against this "new era," however, and the U.S. Congress remained the white supremacists' bastion of strength.

The Battle in Congress

During the 1950s Southern racists continually gave up previously attained ground in congressional debates. Most significantly, they no longer attacked Political Equality as a goal, but instead claimed that it already existed as a fact of life. When egalitarians argued that Southern Negroes did not vote, white supremacists simply asserted that they did not want to vote.[203] Consequently, they concluded that any legal changes would be either redundant or unnecessary. In addition to shifting the ground of their argument on Political Equality, they adopted new arguments or modified old ones to continue their attack on the egalitarian alternative. For example, while they did not concede States' Rights, they felt support for the phrase crumbling, and so they supplemented it with the notion of "local control."[204] It is of particular note, however, that they arrayed Liberty against Equality by highlighting the liberties or rights of whites that would of necessity be sacrificed in order to achieve integration or Equality.[205] Attacking the Supreme Court's decisions, for example, they suggested that integration violated the "right of preference" that whites might have to choose their associates, the right of white school children to an education untrammeled by political influences, and the right of private property that allowed business people to exclude those they did not want to serve from their premises.[206] They portrayed the antisegregation movement in catastrophic terms, with whites literally facing eviction from their homes. In the words of Representative John Rankin, "white Americans are being driven from the restaurants and hotels in the District of Columbia in the same way. They are being driven from the Federal pay roll, to escape the humiliation that is being imposed upon them under the present regime."[207]

This new segregationist rhetoric added an individualist ground to earlier arguments based in racial caste. Fundamentally, however, the group rights argument persisted as the mainstay of the segregationist's position, for they juxtaposed the general concept of majority rights against minority rights, indicating that the former outweighed the latter.[208] They argued further that as a group blacks had already received more than their proportionate share of public goods. Representative Rankin insisted that "these racial minorities that are always whining about civil rights have a hundred times as many of their own members on the Federal pay roll as they are numerically entitled to."[209] Finally, they continued to argue in defense of white culture, insisting that integration would "destroy those great institutions and the great culture which are now in full flower in the Southern States—the culture of the Anglo-Saxon."[210]

As in the past, these arguments accompanied negative characterizations of African-Americans. Congressmen frequently emphasized the "pronounced differences" between the two races, especially detailing the high incidence of crime, illegitimacy, and venereal disease in the black community.[211] White racists were nonetheless increasingly sensitive to the charge that they were hatemongers, promoting a system of oppression that identified them as unearned aristocrats. Hence, their depictions both lacked the vicious and virulent edge of an earlier age and were accompanied by avowals of good intentions. For example, after portraying blacks as deserving of "second class citizenship" because of their inferior moral behavior, Senator Williams of Mississippi insisted, "[I]t has not been my purpose in presenting the foregoing to establish one race as a super race or to present the other as a race of degenerates. I do not hold to either of these beliefs."[212] By asserting their good will, Southern congressmen sought to create the appearance of a basis for continuing to claim the right to represent both black and white Southerners. As Williams had earlier avowed, "Our Negroes know that we have their interests at heart."[213]

In order to generate strong negative affect, without directly attacking blacks, the segregationists adopted another strategy. They laced their rhetoric with virulent attacks on Communists and other "outside agitators" who motivated the forces behind integration. Representative Bryson, for example, described the FEPC as "the darling of every radical Negro, Communist, and socialistic organization in the Nation."[214] He thereby was able to link the attack on the "American way of life" that communism represented with the attack on the Southern "way of life" represented by integration.[215] Both groups, after all, called for "equality."

If the Communist threat failed to generate adequate fear, the segregationists could also invoke the threat of violence. Southern patriarchs frequently warned anyone who would listen that the failure to respect the limits they set could lead to the return of the fire-eaters; and with that, they claimed blood would flow in the streets, for integration would "lead to the eventually destructive methods of secret organizations."[216] Indeed, the claim that segregation was necessary as a means of preventing social violence was to continue as a mainstay of white supremacist rhetoric throughout the 1960s.

The segregationists' final argument was perhaps the most telling, and for Northerners the most difficult one to disavow, for it attacked the hypocrisy of white Northerners who sent their children to private schools and otherwise evaded the vision of Equality they purported to support.[217] Southern legislators thus insisted that racism was not simply a Southern white view but comprised a dominant view in the North as well.[218] If anything, the fact that they were correct was to prove the ultimate limit of what Congress could do.

In response to these rhetorical maneuvers, the egalitarians in Congress continued their attack on "un-American discrimination," noting that "[t]he one premise which is the very cornerstone of our democracy is that all men are created equal."[219] They touted the progress made by the Negro race, recognizing that the meaning of Equality was shifting and expanding. As Representative Emmanuel Celler noted in 1956: "We cannot maintain for long the concept of aristocracy of one color or another. The principle of equality of opportunity so long a standard of definition for these United States is expanding, and this we must recognize."[220]

Congressional egalitarians also rejected the racist's appeal to white rights, noting that government efforts to prohibit legally enforced segregation did not take away the liberty of whites. Finally, they reversed the presumption of the argument, suggesting that racists could choose not to attend mixed public establishments, while concurrently insisting that the white South had had enough time to adjust to the progress of the Negro: "[T]he South has had all the time since the War Between the States to make this adjustment. That is why I am not greatly moved by the last hour pleas of the South, 'We need more time, more time, more time.'"[221]

For the first time in many decades, egalitarian words were legislatively effective. In spite of stalwart resistance by the white racist minority, the national legislature passed the Civil Rights Act of 1957, designed to increase federal authority to investigate and prosecute voting rights cases. It was the first such legislation in over eighty years, and its provisions were mild, but they were not to be the last.

African-American Rhetoric

As the nation's white leadership adapted itself to the abolition of legal segregation, African-American leadership was once again keeping one step ahead. As the 1960s approached, the black community was gearing itself up to demand enforcement of the new legal configuration imposed by *Brown* v. *Bd. of Education* through mass protest. Mass protest was not a new tool for the descendants of Africans in America, for throughout their history they had engaged in boycotts, marches, and "freedom rides." The methods, however, were now transformed from a sporadic response to local problems to a national campaign. And they were to be directed toward the Deep South. The Montgomery Bus Boycott gained the greatest national attention in the period, and it set a model of peaceful, collective activism for black communities. The attempt to integrate the schools in Little Rock, Arkansas, set the opposite example. Both were important for the evolution of the movement.

Mass efforts, whether violent or peaceful, were absolutely essential to the success of the desegregation campaign. The federal government might rule that segregation was unconstitutional, but Southern whites were not going to comply voluntarily with those rulings. Black Americans had to force compliance physically. Their first line of attack was to boycott and march, but if that failed, they would provoke the violence necessary to compel federal military intervention. The federal government would not use its police power to enforce its laws unless forced by state violence to do so, and so it became the task of the African-American community to create the conditions under which such intervention would be understood as essential to maintaining law and order. Their efforts worked, and by the end of the decade the process of federal enforcement was ready to begin in earnest.

Accompanying these actions was a new rhetoric. The NAACP, with its commitment to the strategy of working through the courts, came under attack from the "new young leadership" for its inadequately militant methods. The new leadership, boldly guided by groups such as the Southern Christian Leadership Conference, chose to allow others to work through the courts, while it literally stepped over the segregationist line and dared the white supremacists to deny them their legal and equal rights. Rev. Martin Luther King, Jr.'s program of peaceful, nonviolent resistance provided the model for this action. King's style was an eloquent blend of militancy and dignity. Following his lead, other black leaders insisted that NOW is the time for a new order, and that the clock had run out on the old order.[222] America's Negro people demanded "AFFIRMATIVE ACTION" to address the problems of the race.[223]

The "new militancy" continued to be an interracial matter. As *The Crisis* noted, "[E]very major gain in race relations has been accomplished by militant Negroes and courageous whites."[224] *Ebony* and *Jet* gave a great deal of attention to interracial marriage, and all of the black magazines provided models of interracial living by telling stories about places where integration worked harmoniously.[225] They also continued to recognize individual merit, not racial castes. As *The Crisis* reminded its audience, "The Constitution does not guarantee any right to any racial solidarity or to the protection or preservation of any race."[226]

As in earlier periods, however, this did not mean that black people gave up their African roots. Extensive coverage of Africa continued in black newspapers and magazines, as did the call for blacks to retain a sense of their African identity. However, there continued to be a balance between cultural distinctiveness and interaction with the larger human community. "The right of her peoples and their civilization to retain their own identity" was combined with the effort to add "the distinctive attributes of the Negro—those specific characteristics which are his alone—to the 'common treasure-house of culture.'"[227]

This militant interracialism was not black separatism, but it did open up room for a respectful hearing for separatists in the national public arena. The national press covered Black Muslims with far more tolerance than their forerunner, Marcus Garvey, had ever received.[228] Nonetheless, in the 1950s, the Uncle Toms were the black middle-class, prosegregationists who had put their own jobs ahead of the interests of the race's advancement, and they were declared largely extinct.[229] The black separatists had not even begun to attach the label to the militant integrationists as they would in a later era.

The 1950s produced little significant change in the ways African-Americans employed the term "equality." The decade, however, inaugurated the movement of this discourse out of the distant realm of national politics and into the local realms of daily life.

A hundred years after the commencement of the Civil War, the national debate had changed decisively. African-Americans had chosen to endorse Social Equality, offering a vision of it that allowed a fluid interplay between cultural distinctiveness and cultural interaction. They had come to demand Full Equality, and they defined it as the receipt, side by side with whites, of mathematically proportional goods such as jobs, education, and housing. They then moved forward, seeking to achieve implementation of this Equality through direct action and governmental programs such as affirmative action. Meanwhile, the voices of the white supremacists faded as their thunderous offering of vicious depictions of blacks and the vigorous repudiation of Political Equality and popular government became a muffled request for white majority rights, local control, and the denunciation of Communists. White supremacists still yelled loudly, but they were relatively isolated, and their voices were dampened rather than amplified by the cultural milieu. These changes, combined with the white egalitarian decision that the time for Equality had finally arrived, manifested themselves in the nation's mainstream press as positive characterizations of blacks, the visible incorporation of black culture into mainstream American life, and strong support for equality of education. The new usages of equality produced a new national compromise as well. At the beginning of the century, the Supreme Court employed literalist definitions and legal technicalities to hew carefully to the doctrine of Separate But Equal. By mid-century it had redeployed similar technicalities to overthrow Separate But Equal for its failure to provide equal accommodations. The presidency, divided and polarized at the beginning of the period, became uniformly tolerant and sometimes strongly supportive of a vision of Integrated Equality.

At the end of this period, America's white and black leadership came as close as they had ever been in their vision of the nation's goals and purposes, and their joint understanding of Equality reflected this consensus.

Both agreed, although not unanimously, to an Integrated Equality. For white leaders, equal employment, education, housing, public accommodations, and health provided the test of its embodiment. These material conditions constituted measures by which the nation would know that "equal opportunity" existed in fact. For blacks, these proportionate measures of material goods were likewise tests, but the goods also constituted goals in themselves. That was a small difference, and in an otherwise perfect world the black and white egalitarians might have been able to make their visions continue to overlap with one another.

There was, however, another difference. Black leaders demanded racial Equality or Negro Equality or Social Equality. By this, they meant not only individual interracial relationships but also respect for the dignity and achievement of their African heritage and their race qua race. Whites never fully endorsed Negro Equality when they accepted Equal Opportunity. In the case of white supremacists, this failure to endorse "the equality of the two races" as races arose both from hostility to the Negro people per se and out of a desire to protect "Anglo-Saxon" culture. Even for many white egalitarians, there was estrangement from this ideal of equality based in a studied ignorance of the riches of African culture and in a vigorous pride and defense of what European culture had wrought. And in this particular, at least, Southern white racist leaders remained fully in tune with the rhetorical culture of ordinary white Americans.

This difference between African and Anglo-European culture would be responsible for the writing of yet another chapter in the tale of American Equality.

CHAPTER SEVEN

The New Equalities
1960–1990

> Someday . . . every black man, woman and child in America will
> get back the same name, the same language, and the same culture
> that he had before he was kidnapped and brought to this country and
> stripped of these things.
>
> Malcolm X, 1962

> The Negro need not yearn to be assimilated into American
> culture—he is and determines American culture.
>
> Kenneth Clark, 1967

The Americans who will live to see the next millennium are people of
the post–*Brown* v. *Board of Education* generation. Among other
things, this means that their socialization has led them to think of integrated public Equality as a legal foundation of national life. Nevertheless,
many persons of all colors are racist, and America's African descendants
continue to face daily discrimination. Most also experience a standard of
living that is lower than the national average.[1] Consequently, over the last
forty years the nation has continued to grope for a viable plan of racial
Equality. At the forefront of that search have been the efforts of America's
black leadership, which has come from a variety of places and played a
number of different roles in shaping the national public life of all Americans. During the 1960s this leadership consisted largely of racial activists of
one sort or another, during the 1970s it consisted of mainstream political
leaders, and in the 1980s it incorporated a contingent of public intellectuals, including scholars and filmmakers. Each of these groups has offered
a different set of discursive possibilities for enlarging the rhetorical culture
from which an American Dream of Equality might be crafted.

We conclude our story about American Equality by examining a time
period in which we are contemporaries, and so we proceed cautiously to a
consideration of the range of new equalities that seem to have occupied the
national mind in each of the past three decades.

The Sixties

The transformation in the civil rights movement that occurred during the 1960s has been cast widely as both a shift from a Southern-based campaign to a Northern or national offensive, and as the radicalization of nonviolent massive protest into self-consuming riots. This transformation has also been portrayed as a shift from a concern for citizenship rights to a struggle over economics.[2] The 1960s wrought all of these things as movement activists superimposed a mythic image of Malcolm X over a similarly mythic vision of Martin Luther King, Jr.[3]

It is important to remember, of course, that during the 1960s this shift occurred primarily among movement members; it did not represent a wholesale endorsement of Malcolm X's philosophy by the majority of black Americans. Indeed, it would take more than a decade before the mainstream of African-American thought adopted more than bits and pieces of the black power agenda. Nonetheless, the redefinition of Equality offered by the radicals of the era ultimately had enormous influence. In large measure, of course, these new versions of Equality were a product of the success of the civil rights movement in attaining its original goals. By 1960, the Supreme Court's new stance had virtually erased legally mandated segregation from the nation's statutes; and as the Court was making eminently clear, the NAACP's campaign for equality before the law had achieved its objective.[4]

After living under this new legal equality for several years, however, many African-Americans concluded that it would not bring about all of the changes that they sought. First, as white supremacists had warned, American life was dictated by culture as well as by the law. Indeed, in many instances, white supremacist culture was more of an imposition upon race relations than the law, a condition amply demonstrated by the fact that whites continued to mob and kill blacks solely on the basis of their skin color.[5] Second, the *absence* of legal barriers against equal opportunity was not the same thing as the *presence* of equal opportunity itself. Even had it been, the brute fact of the matter was that the majority of blacks faced severe poverty, and under the best of circumstances it would take many years, perhaps generations, before the heritage of poverty could be erased. As Martin Luther King, Jr., noted in 1964, "[T]he law pronounces [the black man] equal, abstractly, but his conditions of life are still far from equal to those of other Americans."[6]

Blacks thus turned their attention from "civil rights" to "human rights," from "legal equality" to "substantial equality."[7] Adjusting itself once again to the flow of history, *The Crisis* proclaimed in 1963 that "real emancipation involves more than the granting of mere legal freedom."[8] Rather, it announced three years later, blacks sought "not just equality as a right and a theory, but equality as a fact and a reality."[9] There were two fundamental elements of this Equality: the first and most immediate was economic equality, the second was cultural equality.

The emphasis on economic issues grew throughout the decade. The increasing prominence of the phrases "equal opportunity," "equal employment opportunity," "equal job opportunities," and "equal pay" reflect this concern. It was reflected most singularly in a growing emphasis on "poverty," even by mainstream integrationists like King. In 1968, just before his untimely death, King wrote that "the economic question is the most crucial" for black people.[10] The search for economic equality was, as in earlier eras, not a Marxist demand for the total redistribution of wealth, although it was routinely cast in a Marxist vocabulary.[11] The movement's mainstream continued to demand jobs, not government handouts. Militants, such as Representative Adam Clayton Powell, Jr., argued for a governmentally mandated minimum wage floor, but the focus was to "strike down the barriers of the economic blockage. We not only want to sit at the lunch counter, we want to work behind it!"[12] Even King's suggestion for a guaranteed, minimum annual income was not a demand for a government controlled economy. It was, rather, an insistence upon what Ronald Reagan would later call a "safety net." It asked that the government guarantee jobs only where the market did not provide them, and that it grant welfare only for those who were unable to work.[13]

The insistence upon a safety net made the demand for economic Equality more than a demand for Equal Opportunity. Building upon the proportional concept of Equality established in the New Deal era, African-Americans expressed the expectation that within a short period of time, certainly within a generation—if not "NOW!"—the economic profiles of black and white Americans would equalize. What this meant was that the distribution of wealth, the size of the middle class, and the occupation of professions would represent the proportional distribution of blacks in the general population. Jesse Jackson would eventually call this concept "parity," and he would work for it through efforts such as Operation Breadbasket and PUSH/Excel.[14] Parity, however, involved the government as an employer, for blacks conceded that "the natural functioning of the market does not by itself ensure every man with will and ambition a place in the productive process."[15] Government was to make up for what the market could not provide. Given that black workers were disproportionately excluded from the marketplace, government would be required to show "special preference" for black persons.

This vision of substantive economic equality was Janus-faced. It resulted from the fundamental tenets of the movement for Integrated Equality, but it fed the fires of separation. The expectation of substantive Equality arose from the assumption that if blacks were the same as whites, and if equal opportunity existed, then one would logically expect mathematical proportionality in any economic arena. It might have been excessively optimistic to expect it within ten years after equal opportunity was legally mandated, but "Freedom NOW!" had been the watchword of the integration movement, and the demand for immediacy was all but irresistible. Moreover, it was also immediately obvious that the abolition of white supremacy as a public doctrine did not abolish white supremacy as an important belief for a large segment of the white population. Quite simply, many whites engaged in both overt and covert racist behaviors that froze blacks out of the economic marketplace. African-Americans, therefore, had reason to be immediately discouraged about the prospects of laissez-faire equal opportunity to bring about the substance of equal economics.[16] Consequently, programs for government enforcement of antidiscrimination statutes were immediately supported, and they were based on proportionality and preference. Similarly, "affirmative action" was mandated to overcome both the heritage of legalized inequity and the ongoing private discrimination colored persons faced.

The concept of preference, however, required the repudiation of both the goals of color-blind justice and integration. This in turn necessitated a massive revision of the century-old black national rhetoric. From Frederick Douglass onward, black leaders had rejected the white racists' claim that they sought special privileges. After a very short experience with federal government support programs, however, the new black leadership endorsed special preference, arguing that in order to overcome both the legacy of "separate but equal" and current discriminatory practices, they needed special governmental protection.[17] The new militants endorsed the use of goals and quotas, declaring that "[w]e have found the cult of colorblindness not only quaintly irrelevant but serious[ly] flawed."[18] This not only meant the end of the notion of the "color-blind Constitution," it also required maintaining at least enough racial separation to perpetuate a stable group identity that would allow for assessment and assignment by racial group. The concept of cultural equality constructed this identity and perpetuated the separation.

Black Muslim separatists were the most responsible for invigorating the concept of cultural equality. Muslims had long been interested in emphasizing separatist means to build up black economic strength, and their leadership created a mythic vision of African cultural superiority. Elijah

Muhammad, the head of the Muslims, presented a prophetic account of America in which white persons played the role of "devils" soon to be exorcised from power by Allah, who would then return the black man to his rightful stewardship of the planet. Information about the history of Africa and the great kingdoms that had once flourished there bolstered this mythic view of the world. From these materials, Black Muslims and others constructed a heritage of which black people could be proud, including a rich black culture and powerful black nations.[19]

Malcolm X brought that worldview to the civil rights movement with wit and force. In doing so, he constructed a substantially different vision of equality from that which had been offered by Martin Luther King, Jr. King's signification of Equality was generally abstract, as in his contrast between the Negro's past as a "sweltering summer of . . . legitimate discontent," and the inevitable future as an "invigorating autumn of freedom and equality."[20] His usage of Equality rested in the Anglo-American, Judeo-Christian tradition of equal creation:

So I say to you, my friends, that even though we must face the difficulties of today and tomorrow, I still have a dream. It is a dream deeply rooted in the American dream that one day this nation will rise up and live out the true meaning of its creed, "we hold these truths to be self-evident, that all men are created equal."[21]

This vision highlighted the fundamental, irreducibly shared nature of all human beings. It did not require complete sameness, but it focused on the shared basic humanity of all persons, what King called the "beloved community."[22] In opposing desegregation to integration King noted:

We do not have to look very far to see the pernicious effects of a desegregated society that is not integrated. It leads to "physical proximity without spiritual affinity." It gives us a society where men are physically desegregated and spiritually segregated, where elbows are together and hearts are apart. . . . It leaves us with a stagnant equality of sameness rather than a constructive equality of oneness.[23]

As one studies King's discourse, it becomes increasingly clear that the commitment to Equality he articulated presumed a world in which extensive assimilation and integration of the races was both necessary and desirable.[24] Thus, for King, Equality rested in the assumption that human beings possessed a basic spiritual nature, and that nature was identical and interchangeable among specific individuals in the same way that one might say "1 + 1 = 2." It was a notion of formal similarity, underlayed with love.

By contrast, Malcolm X described an Equality based on power. He committed himself to a vision that saw relationships of equivalence resting only between two or more clearly separate entities, each of which possessed its own identity, but was similarly powerful, as one might say that Great Britain and France were equally strong nations. For Malcolm X, $A = B$ was not a relationship of identity, it was a statement about resources; A has as much power as B, and can, therefore, resist B. In his *Autobiography* he characterized the formal commitment to Equality voiced by Northern white liberals as an empty deceit:

. . . [H]e grins with his teeth, and his mouth has always been full of tricks and lies of "equality" and "integration." When one day all over America, a black hand touched the white man's shoulder, and the white man turned, and there stood the Negro saying "Me too . . . " why, that Northern liberal shrank from that black man with as much guilt and dread as any Southern white man.[25]

A few pages later he replaced this deceitful conception of Equality with one grounded in the functional equivalency of power which, he argued, could only be enacted through separation and opposition:

The American black man should be focusing his every effort toward building his *own* business, and decent homes for himself. As other ethnic groups have done, let the black people, wherever possible, however possible, patronize their own kind, hire their own kind, and start in those ways to build up the black race's ability to do for itself. . . . *The black man never can become independent and recognized as a human being who is truly equal with other human beings until he has what they have, and until he is doing for himself what others are doing for themselves.*[26]

For Malcolm X, then, Equality was a form of respectful reciprocity between two equals in power. The separateness of the equals was vividly apparent in his definition: "We believe in equality," he warned, "and equality means that you have to put the same thing over here that you put over there."[27]

The success of Malcolm X's definition of Equality relied on the Afro-American community's acceptance of black separatism. Few blacks came to believe the most extreme versions of separatism expressed in Elijah Muhammad's programs calling for a "back to Africa" movement or "separate states" for blacks in America.[28] Fewer still bought James Forman's notion of black supremacy.[29] But the oldest element of the vision, the romantic interest in African culture as a heritage, rapidly and powerfully pervaded the black community. Even Malcolm X's amplification of the long-tenured notion that "black is beautiful" and that the descendants of Africans ought to keep to themselves and retrieve their cultural heritage gathered large adherence.[30] Having succeeded in legalizing the formal equality that asserted their similarity with whites as "American citizens," African-Americans now had the luxury of exploring the African half of their heritage. Hence, the topic of difference, once the tool of the white supremacist, became a prominent subject among black egalitarians. Expanding earlier strands of black cultural nationalism, 1960s black activists emphasized the differences between the cultures of American whites and blacks. John O. Killens made the point in this fashion:

We are not fighting for the right to be like you. We respect ourselves too much for that. When we fight for freedom, we mean freedom for us to be black, or brown, and you to be white and yet live together in a free and equal society. This is the only way that integration can mean dignity for both of us. . . . My fight is not for racial sameness but for racial equality.[31]

The emphasis upon difference was immediately influential in mass culture, where young Afro-Americans sought to borrow from contemporary African dress and art. It included a broad-based return to respect for things black, including African hair styles and naturally dark black skin. For a few, however, the differences represented in being "black" or "brown" were more than matters of daily life-style. Robert S. Browne called attention to a fundamental difference in values between the two cultures:

Negroes are demonstrating that they do not accept the common core of values that underlies America. . . . The alleged disproportionately large number of Negro law violators, of unwed mothers, of illegitimate children, of non-working adults *may* be indicators that there is no community of values such as has been supposed, although I am not unaware of racial socio-economic reasons for these statistics also. But whatever the reasons for observed behavioral differences, there clearly is no reason *why* the Negro should not have his own ideas about what the societal organization should be.[32]

Browne's argument would not be fully developed for another decade, so the precise boundaries of the differences between "African," "African-American," and "Euro-American" culture remained to be debated, but the issue had clearly made its appearance, and it would simmer just below the level of national public discourse. — Not well supported

The leaders of the civil rights movement quickly rejected both the sound and principles of "black power."[33] By the middle of the 1970s, however, the notion of "black power" had been adopted by most activists, although it came to mean different things to different people. For the mainstream black newspapers, "black power" simply meant collective, focused, and determined efforts at achieving nondiscrimination, along with feature stories on black standards of beauty, and African art, food, and dress.[34] For a minority of activists, black power meant the thrill of "Burn, baby, burn!"—a threat used to intimidate whites into providing economic resources for the black community or to face the economic consequences. For the black academy black power constituted a license to explore African roots and slave culture in ways that would bear new fruit in two decades time.

Whites reacted with horror to the rise of black power and separatism for a variety of reasons. One important reason was that the collectivization of black racial identity was paired with the collectivization of white identity as racist. Black rhetors gradually began to shift their attack away from "bigoted individuals" and toward "institutional racism."[35] The concept of institutional racism was vague and broad. The fact of disproportional representation or wealth was taken as incontrovertible proof that a given institution was racist. Since such disproportion existed in profusion in most American institutions, America as a collective entity, therefore, was condemned. "The nation itself [is] racist," declared James Farmer.[36] Indeed, "racism" became a trump card, for the attack on institutional racism allowed no white person to escape from its indictment.[37] Collective identity on the part of victims resulted in a collectivized identity for whites as oppressors.

Collectivization had other concomitants as well. If blacks were to share a collective identity, they needed a single image of themselves as a race or culture. An equation between the "black person" and the "poor black person" quickly evolved. Projecting the image of an "underprivileged" and "oppressed" mass, the black leadership insinuated a collective identity of black poverty. As part of this effort, there were sustained and hostile attacks on the black middle class, which was excluded from the allegedly authentic community of black culture for its adoption of white middle-class values.[38] At the same time, the traditional leadership of the black community, which had typically arisen from the well-educated, hard-working, successful women and men of the black middle class, was repudiated. Those who came to perform positions of leadership emerged from impoverished and deprived backgrounds—or at least they postured themselves as such. This issue of class identity linked directly to the issue of black separatism. The conclusion was patent: the black masses had never wanted integration; that always had been a middle-class dream. "Real" African-Americans wanted racial purity and separation, not the dilution of their "African" culture and identity that would result from interracial marriage and assimilation.

This collectivized image of blackness gradually eroded the long-established African-American concept of individual Equality. The vision of the equal merit and dignity of all individuals was incompatible with a collectivized identity of poverty and victimage. In its place, the concept of meritless equal dignity was offered. The Student Nonviolent Coordinating Committee (SNCC) praised what they took to be Malcolm X's position: "He recognized the true dignity of man—without the white society prejudices about status, education and background that we all must purge from our minds."[39] The older usage had defined equality within the law as compatible with inequality outside of the law. The new definition denied the legitimacy of any judgments of inequality.[40] This more thorough usage of equality never achieved universal acceptance, and it was rarely articulated in full, but it provided an increasingly important background against which black expectations would be shaped.

The collectivization of African-American identity had its roots in many sources, not the least of which was the long history of American black nationalism. The dominance of collectivity over individuality in the historical moment, however, was in large measure due to the vivid successes achieved through collectivization. America's African descendants had eradicated de jure discrimination only when they unified, formed a militant movement, and aimed together at a singular target. The importance of unity and collectivization became a standard topic of all civil rights leaders, and black people reminded themselves repeatedly of "the victory of the concept of collective struggle over individual achievement as the road to Negro freedom."[41] Collectivization also served as an effective way to deal with the psychological rejection of blacks by many whites. Repudiating the need for white "acceptance" provided a means to avoid the damning rays of white supremacy, which private individuals and organizations continued to impose with great ferocity.[42]

When the 1960s spilled into the 1970s, a new range of black-fostered definitions of Equality became available for public usage. The Christian notion that "all men are created equal" by a God who made them in His own image retained its baseline force, especially among older activists who remembered its sonorous intonation by Martin Luther King, Jr.'s "beloved community." Superimposed upon this definition was a usage of "equal Opportunity" that presupposed a government that would work actively to create equality of opportunity for wealth and merit. However, these two visions, premised on homogeneity, had been joined by a set of usages premised on difference. "Equality with difference" could mean merely the possession of an equal or proportional number of material goods, or it also could mean equal power or the presumption of the equal merit of different cultures.

The bridge of government action made this extension of the usages of Equality viable. However, the three-step transition was not smooth. It began with the relatively easy task of attacking the government programs of the New Deal, which had inequitably distributed public goods. That economic focus and the attendant calculus of proportionality energized the conversion of discriminatory private economic activity into a government responsibility. The transformation concluded with the demand that the government create economic parity between two separate cultures. The significant shifts from one stage to the next unfolded with relative ease because the overwhelming legacy of oppression became so highly visible once the tower of *Plessy* v. *Ferguson* and the citadel of white supremacy crumbled.

White Reactions

The collapse of white supremacy as a public doctrine continued throughout the 1960s. This is not to say that many individuals did not continue to hold to it and act on it directly in their private and public lives. Nonetheless, its rout represents one of the most successful radical shifts in a nation's public commitments ever recorded in human history. The effect of that rout is most visible in the 1960s in presidential discourse and Supreme Court decisions. In cases far too numerous to explore here, the Court handed down ever more far-reaching declarations that the principle of "equality under the law" had replaced the notion of white supremacy.[43] The court not only expanded the areas in which Equality would apply beyond education to include housing, transportation, and voting. It also expanded the amount of activity it would condone on the part of government agents seeking to insure that Equality.

The presidency also endorsed an accelerated application of Equality. President Kennedy has been widely chided for his failure to take adequately forceful action. Be that as it may, his use of the oval office as a national bully pulpit was eloquent and ultimately effective. He sought to persuade the nation to adopt Equality and to repudiate white supremacy through three different lines of argument. The first was the age-hardened appeal to the notion of "equal opportunity." Kennedy declared that "the policy of this administration is to give to the individual the opportunity to realize his own highest possibilities."[44] Kennedy's second theme was that the white race needed to learn to identify with other races by ignoring or reducing the significance of skin color. He thus implored white Americans to engage in the same exercise William Lloyd Garrison had long ago undertaken: to imagine themselves in the place of their human fellows. He called upon them to live up to the Golden Rule by offering "the kind of equality of treatment which we would want ourselves."[45] At the same time he endorsed the acceptance of diversity as a third topic, reassuring a frightened America facing a multicultural world that "[w]e can welcome diversity."[46]

substantive
equality (214)

The usage of Equality that Kennedy employed was that of Martin Luther King, Jr., not that of Stokely Carmichael and the black separatists, but this should come as no surprise, for black nationalism was not widely approved even among the Afro-American community during the early 1960s. Kennedy thus focused on political equality, equal education, and government guaranteed equal opportunity.[47] He did not offer substantive equality, but his concern that poverty not be inflicted upon the undeserving was compelling and not altogether irrelevant to the direction the nation was slowly moving. He did not encourage separatism, promising instead that "the constitution will be color blind."[48]

Much to the surprise of many, Lyndon Johnson extended this vision and was instrumental in enshrining it in national legislation. Johnson too emphasized equal opportunity in housing, education, employment, and public accommodations.[49] Additionally, he moved the usage of Equality closer to that of the black culturalists in at least two respects. First, he internationalized the perspective, proclaiming that "our ultimate goal is a world without war, a world made safe for diversity, in which all men, goods and ideas can freely move across every border and every boundary."[50] Second, he also advocated legislation that shifted immigration priorities away from color-based considerations, thus extending equality "*to those in other lands seeking the promise of America,* through an immigration law based on the work a man can do and not where he was born or how he spells his name."[51] This immigration act was an important one in the demographic reshaping of America, for it would eventually lead the country to imagine for itself a future in which the majority was no longer of northern European heritage.[52]

Johnson also reflected the later, more radical themes of the civil rights movement through his focus on the poor. His "War on Poverty" was shaped as such for a variety of reasons, but it dovetailed nicely with the black community's shift from race per se to poverty.[53] Like them, Johnson did not offer a guarantee of substantive equality; his program remained a "safety net," designed to prevent or ameliorate the effects of poverty under specific conditions.

The degree to which the presumption in the argument had shifted is only evidenced the more by the fact that leaders like Kennedy and Johnson, whose actions were more progressive on race issues than the overwhelming majority of presidents had ever been, could be legitimately chided for their slowness, reluctance, and inactivity. Most notably, in this era, even conservative presidents such as Richard Nixon felt compelled to chime in on the side of human Equality, though they would routinely reject specific implementation measures.

The national triumph of Equality over White Supremacy did not silence all the voices of white supremacy, and the national Congress remained a place where one could hear them. Congressman Jack Miller, in the age-old tradition of the slaveocracy, was willing to sacrifice free speech to supremacy as he denounced Malcolm X, insisting that "irresponsible statements designed to promote bloodshed and violence should not be permitted in the name of free speech."[54] He also rejected Equality on the grounds that it required the elimination of Liberty, reading into the *Congressional Record* an article from the *US News and World Report* that warned the nation against the "terrible equality that is slavery."[55] Congressional racists continued to use many of their arguments from the previous decade, but they replaced older attacks on the character of Negro people with tirades against the new black nationalists. They described the black power advocates as Negro "hate groups," casting them as a frightening alternative to white supremacy.[56] They also indulged themselves in a Second Reconstruction fantasy which, in the most purple prose, analogized federal civil rights efforts to the federal "Bayonets" of the 1860s.[57] In fits of pique, they even generated a new colonization scheme to send Negroes North so as to give Northern liberals "a taste of their own medicine."[58]

The foundation of the conservative argument, however, gradually came to rest on historically unusual ground: the concept of "equality before the law."[59] For conservatives, this clearly represented a major advance toward egalitarianism, but the meanings they attached to this principle still varied. Although many willingly acceded to political equality, most still sought to oppose "the concept of cultural, economic, or social equality."[60] All drew an absolute barrier against "biological intermixing."[61] The persuasive heart of their campaign to defend "equality before the law" as the maximum allowable usage for "equality" rested on the revitalization of the resistance to special privileges.

In earlier decades, the argument against special privilege had not been a particularly strong one for white supremacists. Their insistence that the use of federal forces to prevent lynchings or insure voting rights was a "special privilege" had not been persuasive to Northerners and Westerners who saw federal action as a simple compensation for the failure of Southern legal officials to do their jobs. In the era of Affirmative Action, as black leaders began openly to demand special preference and quotas, the case gained force with mainstream whites. These tools could be easily portrayed as giving special privileges to individual blacks, privileges which came at the expense of individual whites.[62] They also could be attacked because they destroyed the criterion of merit. As Representative John M. Ashbrook complained, "Merit will not count, only the likes and dislikes, the whims of those in authority who feel they are divinely endowed."[63]

The opposition to any active federal efforts to achieve substantive economic equality was summed up in the phrase "reverse discrimination."[64] Although federal programs such as job training, affirmative action, and Head Start would have an effect on only a tiny proportion of individuals, the complaint was no chimera. Merit and individuality were being sacrificed for racial equality. Federal judges openly stated as much. As one judge noted, "I am not requiring that persons be hired who are incompetent. Rather, in order to achieve a racial balance, I am saying that it may be necessary to hire the second best."[65] Consequently, the opposition to affirmative action and quotas received the support not only of old-fashioned Southern white supremacists but also of those committed to individualism and the principle that one should "judge a man on his individual merit."[66]

Congress thus was fractured along a wide spectrum of thought ranging from reparations–oriented egalitarians to reactionary, heel-stomping segregationists. On the extremes, both right-wing and left-wing groups wanted to recognize collective, race-based rights in preference to individual rights and integrated equality. The right wing believed that these rights and privileges belonged to whites only, but they were willing to permit formal recognition of them to blacks because they also believed that under a laissez-faire government whites would win the political, economic, and social competition.[67] The view of the far left was not yet fully evolved, but their position demanded these rights for both whites and blacks. Sharing the opinion of the political right about the likely outcome of laissez-faire government, however, the far left would come to support the governmental guarantee of substantive Equality between racial groups.[68] The majority of Congress, however, supported neither of these positions. The liberal plurality voted for federal activism to redress historically created imbalances because they claimed that such measures were only temporary expedients that would allow the nation to return soon to the root principle of an individually based, integrated equality. They were willing to incur temporary sacrifices of individual rights for the longer-term goal of protecting individual rights.

The dominant congressional position that integrated social and political Equality with Equality of Economic Opportunity reflected a reaction against the black power movement. Very few legislators defended black separatists, and when they did so, it was not to adopt their position but rather to explain the source of black activist wrath as resulting from economic conditions and the history of discrimination.[69] The Congress of the

1960s was not tightly unified, but its position was clearly in the center of
the newly plotted discursive terrain. It did not endorse substantive equality, but it accepted substantive economic equality as a measure of Equal
Opportunity. It did not endorse equal cultures, arguing instead for integration and individual human equality. And when all was said and done, it
promoted legislative programs built around the idea of achieving political
equality and promoting equal economic opportunity.

The Mass Media

The centrist or liberal position that carried the day in Congress was even
more dominant in the national mass media. White supremacists could get
no hearing in mass magazines, although they were able to speak through
regional and local newspapers. At most, the statements of would-be racists tended to be based on the affirmative defense of individual rights rather
than on claims to white supremacy or opposition to political equality.[70]

With regard to particular measures for implementing integrated equality, such as busing, the media maintained a balanced hearing of "both
sides" of the issue. But even in such cases, the voices of opposition insisted
that their rejection of particular policies did not constitute opposition to
the value of Political Equality as a whole. When the race riots came in the
later part of the decade, the press reveled in sensationalism, conjuring up
threatening images of black hoodlums and terrorists, but generally it accepted and reproduced the liberal portrait of the riots as based in historical
inequities.

As the decade closed, the Vietnam War became the central national issue
and civil rights faded as the primary topic of national debate, but by then
America had constructed a new rhetoric of Equality. As always in the past,
common usages of "equality" varied greatly, and deep tensions undercut
the compromises that produced the law. And, as always, there was a substantial group of racists in the nation. Still, for the first time in its history,
the majority of Americans declared invalid the claim that this was a "white
man's country." White supremacy had become a rump minority view.
Now that most Americans recognized the nation to be the property of all
its inhabitants, a new negotiation among those groups about what its
character should be was ready to commence.

THE SEVENTIES AND BEYOND

The new American rhetoric of Equality did not solve all of the problems of
black people. At its best, however, it gave America's black population a
new dignity that included the right to walk in public as equals, to share

public facilities as equals, and to enjoy equal voting rights. At the same time, however, it unleashed a new class of leaders and a new set of programs that would seek additional concessions from white America.

The programs of the civil rights movement during the 1970s focused on jobs, housing, and welfare. These programs employed long-standing movement strategies and tools but on a much larger and more effective scale. During the 1960s, Operation Breadbasket, and efforts modeled after it, used boycotts, pickets, and negotiation to force many corporations to increase their hiring of black persons, to support black products and banks, and to include an Afro-American component in marketing and advertising.[71] That project, combined with new legislation, had a ripple effect during the 1970s. Seeking good public relations, attempting to avoid lawsuits, or acting out of conscience, corporations that were not directly the target of these campaigns nonetheless followed the model, instituting affirmative action efforts. During the 1970s, PUSH/Excel followed on the heels of Operation Breadbasket as the large-scale organization stumping for black involvement in the American economy. PUSH/Excel added a strong component of self-help for ghetto children, serving as a cheerleader by promoting mass assemblies designed to keep young people off drugs, and to encourage them to develop industrious study and work habits that would pay off in the economy.[72]

In addition to these largely private initiatives, Afro-American leaders were active in the public realm, building and protecting the economic programs of the Great Society, especially those such as job training, food stamps, Aid for Dependent Children, Medicaid, and various housing programs. These publicly directed efforts gained the most attention in the mass media. Reporters generally ignored the central interest of black leaders in securing good jobs and enhanced job training for their people, so that they could successfully participate in the market. Instead, the mainstream media, as well as conservatives in general, depicted the Great Society as a welfare system pandering to the lazy and irresponsible, a group predominantly depicted as black. Meanwhile, the inner cities deteriorated as drug addiction increased, crime flourished, and schools disintegrated.

African-Americans Leading the Mainstream

Alongside the struggle of the black inner city for economic progress and social stability was a second, more heartening development. For the first time in the nation's history there arose a group of African-Americans who provided political leadership for all America, not merely for persons of dark skin. In the past, there had been a few government appointees with public responsibilities that transcended their racial constituencies, but these new dark-skinned national leaders had built their own political base from racially mixed constituencies, and they exercised powerful and visible national leadership on important issues other than race. Shirley Chisholm, Andrew Young, Barbara Jordan, and Thurgood Marshall were the earliest and most visible of these new leaders, but dozens, and then hundreds were to follow.[73] The rhetoric of these leaders was egalitarian, but while it was informed by their experiences as black Americans, it transcended race, producing broad new visions of social and political inclusion.

Barbara Jordan provides perhaps the paradigm case of a black person serving as a national leader with a compelling American vision of Equality. Jordan began her career as a Texas legislator in a predominantly black district. However, she refused to play the role of "black caucus" in the Texas assembly. Unlike Adam Clayton Powell, Jr., another highly visible elected black legislator, Jordan was a consensus builder. She sought power through existing channels rather than repudiating the establishment. More important, she did not make blacks her sole constituency but spoke to and for all the people of Texas. She was remarkably successful and quickly moved from the Texas assembly to the U.S. Congress.

Jordan is most remembered for her highly effective address before Congress supporting the impeachment of Richard Nixon, a speech that the national news media reported and touted. Jordan's Watergate address, like most of her speeches, was built on a rock-solid base of deductive logic. It was carefully researched and her evidence was presented in confident, strong, and authoritative tones. Jordan's speech was also significant as a "coming of age" ceremony for African-Americans. Jordan began her speech by endorsing the new Constitution of America:

"We, the people."—It is a very eloquent beginning. But when that document [the Constitution of the United States] was completed on the seventeenth of September in 1787, I was not included in that "We, the people." I felt somehow for many years that George Washington and Alexander Hamilton just left me out by mistake. But through the process of amendment, interpretation and court decision, I have finally been included in "We, the people."

She then made the transition from outsider to insider:

Today I am an inquisitor. I believe hyperbole would not be fictional and would not overstate the solemnness that I feel right now. My faith in the Constitution is whole, it is complete, it is total. I am not going to sit here and be an idle spectator to the diminution, the subversion, the destruction of the Constitution.[74]

Once inside she used her authority to elucidate the premises of American government, to outline the constitutional grounds for impeachment, and to place the violations of the sacred trust of office committed by President Nixon side by side with those constitutional grounds. She thereby effectively demonstrated the case for impeachment, and she did so as a black person who had entered the mainstream and arrived as a national leader of all the people, not as a leader of blacks.

Jordan served a similar role in the Democratic National Convention in 1976. Her address there also began by recognizing her identity as a black woman:

One hundred and forty-four years ago, members of the Democratic Party first met in convention to select a Presidential candidate. Since that time, Democrats have continued to convene once every four years and draft a party platform and nominate a Presidential candidate. And our meeting this week is a continuation of that tradition. . . . But there is something different about tonight. There is something special about tonight. What is different? What is special? I, Barbara Jordan, am a keynote speaker. . . . I feel that not withstanding the past that my presence here is one additional bit of evidence that the American Dream need not forever be deferred.[75]

Here again, Jordan provided leadership for all the people, not solely for black people. Rather than pillorying the Republicans, easy targets in the aftermath of the Watergate affair and the hapless presidency of Gerald Ford, Jordan humbly apologized for the failings of the Democratic party, proposing an affirmative agenda rather than a fault-finding platform. The center of that agenda was Equality. She defined the common national goal by saying that "We are attempting to fulfill our national purpose; to create and sustain a society in which all of us are equal." Her vision was informed by her own experiences of oppression, and she defined equality by saying, "This is a belief that each American regardless of background has equal standing in the public forum, all of us." The bounds of that Equality denied special privilege, for as she proclaimed, "[W]e believe in equality for all and privileges for none." This did not, however, mean passive government: "We believe that the government which represents the authority of all the people, not just one interest group, but all of the people, has an obligation to actively underscore, actively seek to remove those obstacles which would block individual achievement . . . obstacles emanating from race, sex, economic condition. The government must seek to remove them."

Jordan did not speak merely as a representative for her constituents but actively sought to teach the American people that they could transcend group oppression by a dual agenda of government-assured individual achievement and a vision of common interest. She warned:

> But this is the great danger America faces. That we will cease to be one nation and become instead a collection of interest groups: city against suburb, region against region, individual against individual. Each seeking to satisfy private wants. If that happens, who then will speak for America? Who then will speak for the common good? . . . Are we to be one people bound together by common spirit sharing in a common endeavor or will we become a divided nation? . . . there is no law that can require the American people to form a national community. This we must do as individuals and if we do it as individuals, there is no President of the United States who can veto that decision.[76]

Representative Jordan spoke in this manner in many other settings. It was not "integrated" talk if integration meant that one forgot one's past and one's identity, for she repeatedly gave explicit attention to her identity as black and female. When necessary she spoke primarily as a representative of blacks and women, as in her testimony against the nomination of Robert Bork to the Supreme Court.[77] But Barbara Jordan's vision was also not separatist. She offered, instead, a model of "interbraiding," a nation unified via the harmonious intertwining of different groups, each group itself composed of individuals.[78]

Other dark-skinned leaders shared in this rhetoric of interbraiding. Shirley Chisholm spoke often in support of the Equal Rights Amendment in the 1970s, drawing analogies with the black experience in civil rights.[79] She did not receive the hearty support of the black male establishment, who wanted a male as the representative of the black race, but she was an early candidate for nomination as president of the United States.[80]

Another model of the black-skinned leader of mainstream America was provided by Andrew Young, who served as the mayor of Atlanta, a member of the House of Representatives, and U.S. ambassador to the United Nations. He was not a popular ambassador among conservatives for he insisted on opening talks with the Palestinian Liberation Organization, and he worked to include black Africa as a vital consideration in American foreign policy. What is important to notice about his leadership, however, is not simply that he turned out to be ahead of his time on these issues but how he arrived at them.

Young's ability to see further down the road of international affairs than others was a function of his ability to reflect on his African-American heritage. As one who had experienced both the American dream of opportunity and the America nightmare of racial oppression, he recognized that America had literally created a "new man."[81] If Young had *only* experienced the dream *or* the nightmare his vision would have been limited and restricted. If he had been like Martin Luther King, Jr., whose vision was dictated by the dream, Young might have continued to imagine a world in which integrated equality was the salvation of all; if he had been like Malcolm X, whose vision was dictated by the nightmare, he would have rejected all that America had to offer.[82] But Young knew of both worlds, and more, his experience led him to see beyond the tension that held them together. He was an example of the "new man," a unique product of America's fusing of diverse cultures, and it was this that led him to have a broader vision of the possibilities in the world.

Young brought his dual heritage to bear in one arena when he recognized the importance of Africa in America's foreign policy. He did so in other arenas by applying the model of his civil rights experience to generate the vision of a new world in which cultural diversity and economic vitality intermix in internationally open communities. Young played a central symbolic role in obtaining the 1996 Olympics for Atlanta as he portrayed the city as a crossroad for the world: an open community that used peaceful methods, celebrated cultural diversity, and prospered on the resulting free trade.[83] Young's vision of a peaceful, diverse, and prosperous Atlanta offered a vague but nevertheless stirring addition to American notions of Equality.

But Young paid a price for this vision with his black audience. In his run for governor of Georgia in 1990 he lost significant black support by employing mainstream themes such as business development, environmental reform, and higher education. In refusing the increasingly popular pieties of black militancy and separatism he cast himself as an interracial consensus leader, and his black audiences recognized the implication that he was not a "black leader." To win he thus needed to gain enough white support to compensate for the loss of separatist blacks, and this was something that eluded him. And therein rests the dilemma of black-skinned leaders today: African-Americans who would lead an interracial America face repudiation as Uncle Toms from Afrocentrists, and are still rejected as "black" by a majority of whites.

Interracial political leaders were not alone, however, in their efforts to combine both halves of a dual heritage. Visions of interbraided Equality also dominated the black press. Magazines such as *Ebony* gave serious and sophisticated attention to specific problems of black people, incorporating components of the 1960s black power movement, without endorsing full-blown separatism. In most black newspapers, moderation and integration remained central throughout the 1970s and well into the 1980s, even though black reporters and editorialists were angry with the white establishment for its lack of progress. They still offered, however, the hope of a black middle-class America, contentedly going about its business side by side with white America. In academe, black articulate opinion behaved differently.

The African-American Academy

The black academy of the 1980s and early 1990s adopted a cultural separatist posture, becoming increasingly firm in its support for a combination of absolute economic equality and absolute cultural equality. This occurred for several reasons. First, by the 1980s it had become apparent that the civil rights legislation of the 1960s had not significantly improved the economic condition of a large sector of the black community. Federal efforts during this period were limited largely to affirmative action programs and the effort to locate and promote qualified minorities. But affirmative action was not a "quota system," for it did not require racial balancing. Even where such balancing had been attempted, as in some public schools, white recalcitrance precluded the ability to achieve the proportional distribution of social goods. After 1971 economic progress halted, and by 1980 serious regressions occurred in black income relative to white income, in crime, in drug use, and in school performance.[84] The black academy quickly became disillusioned with the concept of integrated Equality.

A second factor was the promotion of black leftists by whites in the academy. Conservative whites tended to oppose the inclusion of African-American and Black Studies programs, and so they typically lost any effective input in the selection of which blacks would enter and attain power within the academy. White marxissants were the allies of blacks in the academy, and they tended to encourage and promote those blacks who were most friendly to Socialist and Marxist approaches to social and political change. Consequently, the center of the African-American academic agenda became a function of class-based concepts and visions of government-mandated, substantive economic equality.

Third, black scholars focused their attention on the success of black students. They sought creative approaches to improve black student achievement, and part of their method was to exhort black students to higher performance. The other strategy that evolved was to blame the curriculum. Black students, the argument went, needed motivation, and they would not find that motivation in the lily-white curriculum that dominated American universities in the 1970s. Therefore, university committees went to work to include more African and African-American content in the curriculum. These efforts rapidly spread to all areas of student life.

In order to improve black student retention and academic performance, universities created black student events, dorms, fraternities, and recreational facilities.[85]

Black separatism provided the handy and obvious rationale to justify the garnering of these resources. Because Malcolm X was the most visible author of black identity, he became the hero of the hour.[86] At the same time, black nationalism became a central theme of research. The output of articles and books on the black nationalist tradition was not only out of proportion to its place in African-American history, it was also often distorted to suit the needs of contemporary ideologues.[87] In the process, a black establishment developed in the academy. This establishment, however, was not interested in offering leadership to the national mainstream. Rather, it offered to represent blacks as a minority group. Like the teachers in segregated black schools of the past, the prestige and existence of these scholars and administrators came to depend on the maintenance of separatism; and black academies now had the resources both to elaborate the rationale and to pass it on to future generations of students (always an idealistic group, ready to hear the tones of militancy).

The move toward separatism was further enhanced by two basic dynamics of the university community. First, academic careers are made and broken on the advance of "new" discoveries. After thousands of papers on Shakespeare arcana, Shakespeare himself might be fresh, but finding new and interesting things to say about him can be extremely difficult. And so it was with the much codified, overly refined, "Western canon." But there was almost a whole world to be discovered outside the boundaries of the Western canon. Many of the inquisitive minds of the academy thus set to work on these sparsely combed treasures.[88] However, they had to justify studying something that was "outside the canon" and, therefore, lacked the presumption of being important. The politics of inclusion offered a readily available rationale, but it was often interpreted in terms of the separatist rationale about the impact on student identity.

Second, the academy places significant value on purity and specialization. Universities organize themselves around groups of cloistered and insular disciplines, each of which values a unity of theory. Cloistering has the effect of excluding groups that are not part of its cluster. As a result, Afro-American scholars frequently found themselves excluding non–African-Americans from their dialogue. Such institutional separation reinforces separatist ideas. If one only talks to blacks, one rarely worries about whites who get factored out of the intellectual equation. This is exacerbated by the university's tendency toward a unity of theory. For a variety of reasons, messy arguments that incorporate multiple facets and perspectives do not play well among scholars. Success comes to those who specialize, pick a very narrow train of thought, and follow it to its ultimate extension, however out of touch with reality or common perspectives such extensions might be. Humanists in particular indulge this tendency, because their intellectual foundations are so deeply rooted in theory and philosophy. And African-American departments are humanities.

As a consequence of these two separate dynamics, the African-American academy of the 1970s and 1980s produced two currents of thought. First, it generated a treasure-trove of new knowledge about African and African-American history, literature, and art. It achieved this both on its own and by stimulating scholars in other social sciences and humanities to consider the effect of Africa and African-Americans on the subjects of their disciplines. Second, it articulated a new discursive structure that, at its most benign, supported multiculturalism and, in its purist form, expressed a commitment to Afrocentricity.

Multiculturalism refers to the significant rewriting of American educational curricula at all levels, so that they no longer exclusively tell the story of the rise of Anglo or European society as the roots of American thought and culture.[89] It entails teaching all students about the basic history of the planet, not just about Europe and the United States, and it requires exposing them to models of excellence in art, literature, music, oratory, and the other liberal arts, as they derive from all human cultures, not just from eighteenth- and nineteenth-century Europe.

Afrocentricity extends the principle of multiculturalism to its furthest conceptual extreme. The Afrocentric perspective takes the differences between the descendants of Africans and Europeans and magnifies them to their purest, most heightened imaginable form. It treats these descendants as wholly beholden in this historical moment to values and conditions that existed hundreds or even thousands of years ago. Moreover, it holds that these European and African traditions were based on fundamentally different root values.[90] Europe is generally portrayed by Afrocentrists as individualist, ambitious, future-oriented, ruthless, and intellectual. Africa is generally portrayed as communal, experientially rich, presentist, humane, and emotional. The two cultures are thus characterized as diametrically opposed to one another.[91]

If the differences between cultures are this great, Afrocentrists hold, then individuals must be taught from curricula that are consonant with their own cultures. Black students need an Afrocentric curriculum, while white students need . . . well, there lies the problem. Unlike multiculturalists, who portray all cultures as equal, Afrocentrists have yet to take a clear stand on the relative equality of African and European cultures.

Like any ethnocentric system, Afrocentrism is fundamentally a critique of other cultures, specifically European culture. Its supporters tend to portray Western society as offering humanity little more than a series of dead-ends that lead individuals to oppress one another. Afrocentrists have not yet fully spelled out the solution to the problem, the replacement of European culture with African culture, but their opponents have been quick to take the hint. At the turn of the decade, an energetic coalition of scholars had arisen to defend the "Western tradition."[92] Meanwhile, coverage of the issue of race and equality in the mass media changed as well.

The Mass Media

As the 1980s came to a close, the mass media offered an increasingly two-sided picture of race relations in America. The central oppositions in the race issue shifted from white supremacy versus equality to integration versus separation and preference versus sameness. This allowed the media to once again present a debatable set of issues related to the subject of Equality with at least two apparent sides. The left defended compensatory efforts to preserve black culture and to give it equal economic weight and political power with white culture. The right opposed the placing of collectivized Equality over other values such as local control, individual rights or merit, and a defense of European-based American culture.[93] A center voice, which might have supported the idea of a mixed American culture and the reallocation of resources to insure equal opportunity for individual development, was rarely heard, or was mixed by reporters into one side or the other. The treatment, of course, depended to some extent on the subissues at stake.

In general, the media presented a balanced view of the debate over quotas and affirmative action; the more liberal magazines (*New Republic, Time, Christian Century*) were only slightly more favorable to programs of special preference than the more conservative magazines (*US News and World Report, National Review*) that preferred color-blind equality.[94] The story is different with regards to the issue of multiculturalism.

Few mass media treatments of the issue of cultural equality have separated multiculturalism from Afrocentricity.[95] In terms of resources, there is a very good reason for this. Both multiculturalism and Afrocentricity demand a reallocation of intellectual resources, replacing at least some of the resources allocated to the study of things European with resources allocated to the study of things African. This explains why the debate in the academy itself has been so irrationally vicious. Everything scholars value is at stake: their jobs, their status, and the cultural and intellectual heritage to which they have dedicated their lives.

This does not provide an excuse for bias by the media. Too frequently, the mass media's conflation of Afrocentrism with multiculturalism was the precursor of an absolute condemnation of Afrocentricity that served to delegitimize multiculturalism as well.[96] At base, this occurred because white journalists tended to work from the assumption that the good elements of American culture derived from Europe.[97] The media cannot provide a balanced treatment of a fundamental subject when its human agents believe that objective conditions favor one side over another.

This bias left the important issues raised by multiculturalism largely unexplored. For multiculturalism raises the difficult question of cultural equality: At what levels and to what degrees do we, should we, must we, or can we describe different cultures as Equal? And what are the consequences of doing so? How do we decide what cultures or cultural elements are superior? Is American culture superior to those of other cultures? Can these other cultures be improved by mixing them with the American heritage? What will happen to the American heritage if such mixing takes place? The defenders of European culture vehemently reacted to these questions. While these issues have not yet been worked out, one voice in particular has dramatized a multicultural vision on the national political scene.

Jesse Jackson

Jesse Jackson took a different route to national leadership than that of other black leaders who sought power in the dominant political establishment. Like Jordan, Jackson sought a base in commonality. Instead of envisioning a common national community, however, Jackson offered "common ground" among disadvantaged groups. Like Jordan and Young, Jackson worked creatively from his heritage instead of repudiating it. Hence, he appropriated W. E. B. Du Bois's image of the "rainbow of humanity" and adopted the chant "I Am Somebody." But Jackson's agenda was fundamentally different from those of Jordan and Young. Instead of a color-blind constitution, Jackson offered a multicolored quilt. Instead of seeking out a mainstream, middle-class constituency, Jackson sought to build a coalition of the oppressed.

The rhetoric of Jesse Jackson in this era was complex and ambiguous. It addressed two different audiences: black America and the whole marginalia of Americans who characterized themselves as oppressed minorities. In addressing the issues and concerns of black America, Jackson's rhetoric combined the century-old themes of the black press with the more leftist themes of the black power movement. His speeches were laced with references to the work ethic and individualism. The chant, "I Am Somebody," the maxim "[Y]ou're not responsible for being born in the gutter but you're responsible for getting yourself out," and the attack on television, drugs, and the educational establishment were vintage middle-class African-Americana. Jackson also repudiated the "victim identity" adopted by militant blacks in the post–civil rights era by trying to persuade young blacks to imagine themselves as creative agents of opportunity rather than passive victims of oppression.[98]

Jackson accompanied these traditional themes with those of the black power movement, sometimes through a unique synthesis with more mainstream values, and sometimes simply by allowing opposed concepts to work creatively on different fronts. Thus, although he urged black Americans to focus their attention on gaining middle-class riches, he accepted the identity of black America as poor America. He also combined his individualist emphasis on achievement with the idea that group identity is fundamental. He railed against "institutionalized racism" and claimed that "the personality of the culture is anti-black."[99] He integrated these black culture themes, however, with support for integration, not separatism. Thus, for example, he supported integrated schools and the teaching of African history to all students on the grounds that it is important to expose all children to cultural diversity.[100]

The central issue for Jackson was also that which had been defined by black leaders in the late 1960s: economics. Focusing on "economic and political equity and parity," he adopted Malcolm X's notion of equality as "reciprocity."[101] He insisted, "[W]e want our share. . . . We want 10 percent."[102] In order to achieve that "fair share" Jackson argued for a series of four increasingly aggressive stages of economic development, which included antidiscrimination laws, affirmative action, goals and timetables, and minimum quotas.[103] When put on the spot he denied that these represented reverse discrimination, defending them as just and necessary both because a history of discrimination had built up disadvantage, and because racism was still active in America. That the government was responsible for countering this racism was a fundamental assumption of the story of equality that he told to America.[104]

Jackson's combination of traditional and black power themes provided creative leadership to the black community. He embedded these themes in captivating metaphors, rhythmic phrasing, and collective chants, all of which combined to provide a particularly eloquent vision of America. Moreover, in the 1990s, filmmakers like Spike Lee and John Singleton began to translate his mixed verbal images into even more compelling visual images.[105] This rhetoric, however, spoke to and for black people. When Jackson sought the presidency, he needed a more inclusive rhetorical base, and he located it in black power's leftist rhetoric of oppression. The key theme in his bid for the presidency in both 1984 and 1988 was the transition from "racial battlegrounds" to "economic common ground."[106] Throughout both campaigns he openly referred to the coalition he would build by terms signifying their oppressed status. Consequently, even when speaking to the mainstream, Jackson openly endorsed special preference for historically oppressed groups, especially racial groups, and he placed his identity not among "all Americans" but among poor Americans.[107] It was as such that he proclaimed, in his 1984 Rainbow Coalition Address before the Democratic National Convention, "My constituency is the damned, disinherited, disrespected and the despised."[108]

To build this coalition, Jackson sought common ground of two sorts. The first was in economic programs, since the one thing shared by most marginal groups was poverty. Like most black leaders before him, it was not a proletarian revolution that Jackson urged. He wanted government job programs to step in where the private enterprise system failed, but he usually talked about getting a larger share of the products of private enterprise for those who were poor. At the bottom line his emphasis was on guaranteeing "a good job at a good wage."[109]

The second strategy Jackson used to build coalition, especially in his second campaign, was to try to get members of various oppressed groups to support the particular dimensions of each other's causes.[110] In order to provide a metaphor that captured the mutuality involved in a simultaneous respect for commonality and difference, Jackson turned to the "rainbow" and the "quilt." He thus emphasized the composite beauty that is created by multicultural difference, but in so doing he nevertheless had to preserve and perpetuate difference.

Ultimately, Jackson's rhetoric of oppression failed to provide an effective national leadership. The downtrodden are not active voters, and Jackson's efforts at voter registration simply could not overcome the ignorance and despondence that creates political apathy. Additionally, his rhetorical posture contained its own paradoxical limitations, for his strategy of adding up minority groups to create a majority required a leader who could transcend his own minority identity. But under the dominant image of a rainbow, with fixed different colors, no one can transcend their own group identity. And Jackson's emphasis on difference was a component in forestalling the crossover votes he wanted and needed. But the matter ran deeper than voting behavior.

For Jackson, group difference was represented in a quilt of multicolored patches held together by nothing more than a single, narrow thread.[111] To his national audience, Jackson offered a coalition and a minimalist common ground of shared wealth rather than a program of integration and common good. Any national vision that demands both cultural and economic equality for members of all cultural groups runs into Jackson's problem. The desire for economic equality in common runs counter to the demands of one's ethnic community for economic advantage. The tendency for an identity of cultural difference to swamp common goals was brutally illustrated by the fact that Jackson tangled himself in the trap of denigrating other cultural groups (e.g., his reference to New York City as "Hymietown"). Jackson's refusal to repudiate Black Muslim Louis Farrakhan and his use of Farrakhan's language is simply another example of the same dilemma.[112] The problem was not a simple human failing on Jackson's part, for the goal of establishing economic equality between cultural groups necessarily sets them against one another. If one's stake in the economic system is determined by one's cultural group, then cultural identity and the struggle for economic advancement of one's group tend to preclude common ground with other groups.[113]

Jesse Jackson's campaign rhetoric represented a creative effort at crafting a vision of Equality for America, one which took into account the cultural and economic thrusts produced in the late 1960s and refined throughout the 1980s. In so doing, it illustrated yet another version of the potential tensions implicit in the rhetorical culture of Equality. Even a rhetoric that mandates absolute and full equality comes to face a central problem of consistency in the inevitable tension between substantive economic and cultural equality.

FUTURE EQUALITY

In the decades of the 1960s, 1970s, and 1980s the transformation in American usages of Equality continued. In the 1960s African-Americans began to argue for a substantive version of Equality that focused on culture and economics and that culminated in Equal Power. As in the past, white conservatives resisted their offerings, but in this time period they finally conceded the principle of Equality before the Law, although they nonetheless continued to oppose biological intermingling. In the mainstream press, visions of Integrated Equality and Equal Opportunity presented the compromise between these two groups, and multiple measures were taken to enforce Political Equality. The 1970s saw continued, largely unsuccessful, efforts to implement policies designed to improve the jobs, housing, education, and general welfare of black persons as well as the rise of a national leadership class who used their African-American heritage to provide creative options to the nation as a whole. In the 1980s, the debate changed again as the conflation of Afrocentric and multicultural concepts short-circuited deeper analysis of the concept of cultural equality. Throughout the decade, creative black leaders like Jesse Jackson struggled to find a rhetoric for the shifting conditions in racial life that arose as the century headed toward its close.

As the 1990s arrived, Congress, the president, and the nation's schools woke up to find that the temporary expedient of federal preference for blacks was transforming into something new. Rather than to compensate blacks for historical disadvantages, or to restore the nation to an "equal playing field," it was becoming the permanent installation of "group rights" or "entitlements" to substantive cultural and economic equality. The nation at this point seems to be facing two problematic options. It can preserve an individually based meritocracy in which the members of different races have different opportunities to achieve merit because of their different cultural backgrounds, or it can produce a society with fixed and hostile racial castes to which economic funds are constantly reallocated so that they may be equally shared.

In the 1990s, leftists seem to be supporting the latter vision, while conservatives have come to support Equality under the Law and the maintenance of a vision of human brotherhood and integration. Conservatives now admit the evils of the past, but they propose a vision of the future in which difference regardless of skin color and a color-blind Constitution are the solutions to the national problem of different groups living together.[114] Conservatives also seem to be gaining substantial new resources for forwarding their agenda. Having come to accept formal equality, they are now free to play catch-up with the leftist establishment. Now they can promote black conservative leaders to places from which they can respond to the black leftist leadership earlier promoted by leftist and liberal whites.[115] As we write this, Clarence Thomas has just been confirmed as a justice on the U.S. Supreme Court, Douglas Wilder has announced his candidacy for the presidency, and Shelby Steele is becoming a prominent fixture in the academic world. Such rhetors are slowly but effectively beginning to bring the traditional black American voice to bear against the liberalizing and leftward leaning tendencies of the likes of Cornell West, Molefi Kete Asante, belle hooks, and Henry Louis Gates, Jr. That the conservative blacks tend to operate in the public sphere rather than in the academic realm may well give them a boost in the debate, but that is something only the future will tell.

It does not, of course, seem likely that the voice of black nationalism will soon return to its place as the marginal voice of black intellectual America, but probably it will lose the pervasive influence it has held for the past twenty-five years. This is not to suggest that the battle over the future vision of Equality will be equitable or fair. Presumably struggles for Equality would not exist in the context of a truly just society. But America is not yet that. Moreover, we are not even sure what Justice and Equality should mean. It is impossible to predict the next plot twist in the story of American Equality. It is nonetheless certain that it is a central story for our nation, that it is a story from which we learn and create how to be who we are, and that it will, for the foreseeable future, continue in some measure to be the story of an Anglo/African word.

AFTERWORD

The Negro is the acid test of the American democratic system. It may be, God forbid, that after 179 years we are to discover that the Declaration of Independence will not work as to "all men." Our Western world may founder on the problems of the color line. It does not have to do so.

Roy Wilkins
The Crisis, 1955

. . . for a lasting solution, the meaning of "American" must lose its implicit racial modifier, "white."

Lewis Killian and Charles Grigg
Racial Crisis in America, 1964

B ooks must end, and as authors we face a powerful impulse to write a concluding chapter that would bring together all of the various strains of our analysis of the word "equality." If we were to follow contemporary conventions, we would provide a summary of all that has preceded and then suggest some grand scheme for how American Equality should *now* be understood. Such a conclusion, however, would be inconsistent with the subject and focus of our project. The public meaning of Equality has undergone perpetual transformation since the time it was first introduced as a key term in America's rhetorical culture in the 1760s. As the story we have woven in the preceding pages indicates, it would be unreasonable to assume that the meaning of Equality in 1992 represents a final locus for its potential range of meanings. To offer a traditional conclusion at this point would be to suggest, if only by implication, that the egalitarian foundations of the nation are somehow set in the present. This would be no different than assuming that they were inexorably fixed in 1776 or 1865 or 1954, and it would be equally as wrong.

We began the project by identifying our perspective as rhetorical, and we have played the role of rhetoricians throughout, seeking to elaborate the history of Equality as a discursive foundation of American public life. A rhetorical history is not only a description of the role that public discourse has played in a community's past, it is also an affirmative, critical reconstruction of that past as it actively impinges on the present life of the

217

community. It is thus a vital engagement with the rhetorical culture from which both the past and the present are constituted, and out of which the community's future will emerge. From the Isocratean perspective on rhetoric that we assume, the crafting of a communal future that promotes the values of freedom and autonomy requires a collective memory of the "past" that can serve analogically in public argumentation as a rough guide to present actions and future possibilities.

The United States of America is almost certain to become increasingly multicultural in the years ahead, and such a future will necessitate historical exemplars that can guide the development of a culturally diverse, democratic polity. Until the 1960s, the majority population in the United States was clearly of white, European-based, Caucasian extraction, and it was practical—arguably even desirable—to recall a univocal, melting pot history of American Equality. As we approach the millennium, however, this will no longer be the case. The statistical trend is clear in indicating that America's population is becoming an ever more complex admixture of racial and ethnic origins. As this trend continues, Americans will find themselves confronted with the need for historical analogies that will help them to address the changing nature of American society and the problems that it will face. The words of Thomas Jefferson, Daniel Webster, Henry Clay, Abraham Lincoln, etc., regarding Equality will be important as we face the social and political exigencies in a multicultural world, but *only* if we remember that these men were actively involved in a public, rhetorical dialogue with a range of competing voices that included the likes of Absalom Jones, Maria Miller Stewart, Henry Highland Garnet, Martin R. Delany, Sojourner Truth, Frederick Douglass, and so on.

The story of American Equality we have crafted is different from the conventional narrative, then, in two important respects. First, we have emphasized the role of public argumentation in the developmental process of America's commitment to Equality as a foundational principle of governance. It has been our intention to accentuate the fact that terms like "equality," "liberty," and "property" are not "mere words" masking underlying ideas that can somehow be abstracted from their usage and left intact. There is no *necessary* and *natural* form of equality. Whatever the word "equality" turns out to mean, then, it is necessarily a function of the interaction between its past and present usages for a particular rhetorical culture. To eliminate those usages—or at least the collective memory of them—is essentially to eliminate the term itself. It is also to risk eliminating an important dimension of one's cultural identity. To understand *and* employ such terms in a way that is consistent with the life of a democratic polity is to recognize their rhetorical substance, and this, we believe, will become all the more important in the years ahead.

Second, and perhaps more important, we have offered an understanding of America's egalitarian past that identifies the role that a variety of competing voices have played in affecting its public usage. When the founders of America's revolution employed the word "equality" as a strategic wedge against what they perceived as an intolerable British imperialism, they had only a very weak sense for what the term could mean. In America's subsequent history, we have seen the ways in which a variety of groups have engaged in the process of public argumentation in order to settle upon a meaning for Equality that would presumably represent the best interests of the nation. What is important about the way we tell the story is that rather than rest our understanding of Equality on the apparent conclusions arrived at by leaders subsequently recognized as the great and near great, we have undertaken to rewrite the history of Equality so as to acknowledge the significant contributions made to its public meaning by a full range of Euro- and African-American advocates. As such, we hope to have presented a narrative that acknowledges the roots for negotiating the multicultural interests and exigencies in the historical past of our national rhetorical culture.

We believe that such an understanding of Equality is becoming increasingly important with each passing day. Expression of racial and ethnic superiority persist among a substantial portion of both America's white and colored populations. In the present decade, a black man was lynched in Idaho, the home ground to the revived Aryan Nations. In New York City, Italian-Americans murder African-Americans for infringing on "their" turf and women, while Hasidic Jews and blacks retaliate against one another with violence and vicious insults. In Miami and throughout California, Hispanic-Americans and African-Americans do battle, both physical and symbolic, for economic and political power. The L.A. riots of 1992 were tragic, but not really all that surprising. No one familiar with the facts can claim that the elimination of legal segregation or the manifest advances in Political Equality have brought about either racial harmony or the fact of racial equality. Today, many even deny Racial Equality as a goal, while others have begun to promote it to a constitutional "group" right. To chart a course for the nation that is just and decent and advantageous for all its citizens requires careful consideration of the rhetorical dynamics of Equality, both in the past and in the present. We have already provided a diachronic analysis of Equality that brings us to the present. As rhetoricians, however, it is necessary that we consider the implications of such an analysis for how we might craft an increasingly egalitarian future. We thus close with a brief consideration of three pairs of terms that we believe will become increasingly important to the synchronic locus of Equality in American public discourse in the years ahead: heterogeneity/homogeneity, culture/economics, and Liberty/Equality.

HETEROGENEITY/HOMOGENEITY

Heterogeneity and homogeneity are both important to our understanding of Equality. The public usages of American Equality must be able to encompass some component of heterogeneity because cultural difference is a fact of the national landscape. A nation populated, in a few hundred years, by immigrants from every spot on the globe cannot avoid heterogeneity. America has traditionally accommodated that heterogeneity in a variety of ways. Had it failed to do so, we would already be a graying people, lacking the vibrancy that has made us a perpetually youthful nation, a land of innovation and variety.

There are, however, limits on the extent of heterogeneity that can be tolerated in any system. When heterogeneity becomes "oppositionality," it turns destructive. The problem with the black power movement of the 1960s was not its emphasis on the beauty of black culture, or even its insistence on the right to violent self-defense for black persons. As we have demonstrated, black militancy, black self-defense, and black cultural pride are old and recurrent themes in African-American public discourse. The problem was that the generation of militants who grew up in the 1960s was the first generation of black militants to define white people and white culture as "the enemy." When Malcolm X made slavery the paradigm case of white/black relationships, he characterized the interaction between blacks and whites as inherently and permanently antithetical, freezing the past in the present, and creating a pessimistic vision of the future. The current appeal to Afrocentrism, which posits not merely difference, but the diametrical opposition between European and African cultures, hinting at African supremacy, is merely the intellectualized development of this earlier position.

It is clear today that a democratic government can encompass substantially more diversity than the Anglo-Americans of the eighteenth century thought either possible or desirable. A nation cannot, however, encompass *oppositional heterogeneity*. Such oppositionality breeds hostility in an escalating spiral of response and counterresponse. Already, black oppositional discourse has spawned successful white racist political commercials and tactics. Additionally, it has generated both a vehement defense of the

elements of American culture derived from European antecedents, and a
virulent attack on the claim that African culture has *any* valuable contributions to make to the Western world.[1] The apparent increase in racial violence, now perpetuated "equally" by both blacks and whites, may also be
related to the authorizing of this oppositional stance.[2]

To preserve a democratic heterogeneity we must envision a nonoppositional difference between cultures and groups. This may ultimately mean
that the concept of group rights is as unworkable and destructive as is
Afrocentricity. The concept of group rights holds that different cultures
have rights per se. That is, they are *entitled* to both the preservation of their
own culture and a certain share of all of the material goods in a particular
community. The amount of such goods generally reflects the particular
group's quantitative proportion in the community. The notion of group
rights is destructive for a wide variety of reasons.[3] The most important
problem with group rights is that it imagines communal life as a zero-sum
game in which groups must contend with one another *as* groups for scarce
resources. Individual group members are thus implored to put their efforts
into group practices that proceed only at the cost of other groups. It is precisely this that has generated the white backlash against Affirmative Action. Whether or not Affirmative Action has actually "taken jobs away
from whites" as a matter of fact, it has reified the racial struggle, thereby
calling forth and legitimating white America's defense of its group interests. As we observed in Chapter 5, the concomitants of the intense
nineteenth-century effort among white Southerners to preserve their culture from the encroachment of freed slaves suggests that the legitimation
of racial cultures may not be a particularly salutary idea.

Advocates of African-American group rights defend their perspective
by claiming a "special privilege" on the grounds that they have experienced unique disadvantages that justify the existence of black group rights
but not white group rights. In addition to the difficulty of persuading the
plurality of white citizens to assent to such a claim, it is a temporary rationale at best. At some point, that debt will have to be declared paid or can-
celed. Hence, on the grounds of "special privilege," group rights can at
their best be little more than a temporary palliative to political, economic,
or cultural inequalities.

The second defense of group rights holds that such a legal usage merely
recognizes a phenomenon that has been going on covertly for centuries.
Accordingly, group rights advocates note that whites have always played
the group rights game, and they claim that publicly sanctioning the game
is the only way to give blacks an equal opportunity to play. We do not believe that this is a correct assessment of the situation. Whites played the

group rights game until the late 1950s, at which time the game was no longer constitutionally sanctioned. However, there has been no time at which the nation has enacted the possibility of a government in which there are no legal sanctions for any groups. By the end of the 1960s, black power advocates had instituted equal group rights as the replacement for white group rights. A rhetorical culture in which group rights are declared illegitimate deserves a trial. This is especially desirable given that the alternative entails the permanent pitting of one group against the other in encounters that will be at least locally and sporadically violent, and which will possess a strong potential for sustained and organized violence as has been the case in Northern Ireland, South Africa, the disintegrating Eastern European nations, and Lebanon.

Abrogating the group rights perspective, however, must not entail the refusal to redress the inequities generated by prior group rights. One-third of the nation's black population is trapped in a cycle of poverty that derives from the legacy of the white rights game, and the problems of these particular people must be addressed. Rather than addressing them as a matter of "race," however, we can move toward solutions based on territory (the "urban problem" is one that impinges on many Americans in some fashion) or upon economic justice ("equal opportunity" requires equal schools for all the nation's children, if not superior school/community services for economically disadvantaged children).

Our last objection to group rights is philosophical. The concept of rights was built around the existence of individuals. Individuals are materially and discretely identifiable. Cultures are not. It is virtually impossible to identify and define the *essential* characteristic of racial cultural groups. If they are defined on the basis of individual members, it becomes impossible to identify who is a "black" person and who is a "white" person without ludicrous laws. The current efforts to define "Hispanic" are only the latest example of such absurdities, long represented in the struggle to define who counts as a "native American" and whether octoroons and quadroons are "really black."

Cultures themselves, once distanced from embodied persons, are even more difficult to define. What is "black culture" in America? Michael Jackson's music? The wearing of dreadlocks? The practice of Voodoo? That which white scholars like Lawrence Levine say it is or black scholars like Henry Louis Gates, Jr., and Molefi Kete Asante say it is?[4] The concept of group rights is philosophically incoherent because cultural identity is never fully discrete. Cultures are rhetorically constituted, their boundaries fluid and permeable.[5]

The usage of heterogeneity should, therefore, be set within the concept of individual rights, and it must be shaped in a nonoppositional fashion. It must also be compatible with areas of homogeneity. To say that African-Americans have different elements in their heritage than do Irish-Americans is not to say that Irish-Americans and African-Americans have no common traditions, for by definition they share a common *American* rhetorical culture. Each must learn something of the traditions of the other as well as about their common heritage. There are fundamental values that members of America's cultural groups agree upon, and these include a respect for democracy, for individual autonomy and freedom, and for economic well-being. Members of these groups respect these values *in spite* of the fact that their countries of origin were almost all antidemocratic. Hence, African-Americans are no different from Irish-American descendants of monarchy or Italian-American descendants of the Fascisti in their repudiation of part of their heritage in order to be American.

Some scholars have envisioned this combination of shared culture and separate culture in the notion of a "third culture." This model indicates that two cultures come together, maintain their own identity, and yet participate in a common third culture.[6] The image, however, suggests that the two original cultures remain apart from the common culture, and that is neither an adequately precise nor practical description of cultural development. Because cultures are not discrete entities, they change upon contact with other cultures. Only those who have vested interests in preventing cultural change object to the evolution of a culture upon contact with new influences.[7] Hence, whether we presume a "third culture" conception of heterogeneity and homogeneity, or a more fluid vision, in which contact in the middle creates a homogeneous core about which various diversities swirl, heterogeneity and homogeneity can be envisioned as compatible.

We believe, therefore, that it is probably important that Americans maintain an image of themselves as "one people," but it is equally important that we recognize that as a collectivity "the people" do not require their component parts to be identical. "One people—many cultures" is a rhetorically sound and morally compelling formulation.[8]

CULTURE/ECONOMICS

The likelihood of combining homogeneity and heterogeneity has been undermined, since at least the 1960s, by the tensions between culture and economics. As we indicated in Chapter 7, during the 1960s there was a concerted effort to conflate these two terms by characterizing African-Americans as the poverty-stricken race. Black nationalists, white socialists, and holdover white supremacists all conspired in this definition. Poor people, however, constitute no more than a one-third minority of the African-American population in the United States. It is time to stop identifying black culture with the culture of poverty. As the black middle class has begun to explore its own identity, it has also begun to parse out different elements of culture and identity.[9] As a result, culture begins to become more than simply a matter of "race." Rather, cultural identity is the function of a multiplicity of factors, including class, gender, regional location, and so on. More important, race increasingly shows itself to be more a *product* than a *cause* of culture. Biological race does not define black culture in America today. People who are half- or three-quarters "white" routinely identify themselves with black, rather than with white, culture. If they did not they would be accused by self-proclaimed "pure" blacks of being traitors to "their race," or they would be refused by whites for a lack of "purity."

Two factors that currently hold together this diffuse sense of a common black culture are a shared history of oppression and a desire for economic gain. Even middle-class blacks perceive themselves as economically disadvantaged, and to some extent they believe that the most effective route to economic advantage is by attaining racially based economic privileges. Hence, although black middle-class culture is in some ways at odds with economic imperatives that have defined black people as poor, it is also defined and sustained by that same notion. This push you–pull me relationship is complicated by the tensions between cultural equality and economic equality, and the inherent weakness of the very idea of racial economic equality itself.

The terms "cultural equality" and "economic equality" tend to come in conflict with one another. To imagine why, consider two different, hypothetical cultures: *A* and *B*. Assume that culture *A* is oriented to individual economic advancement, the future, the production and consumption of material goods rather than intangibles such as art and entertainment, and the mind rather than the body. By contrast, assume that Culture *B* is oriented to honoring the past and making the most of the present, collective survival, the production of intangibles such as spirituality and entertainment, and the body rather than the mind. The "products" of these two cultures would surely be radically different from one another. On any given measure, such as income or spirituality, one culture is likely to exceed the other. Indeed, the very idea of cultural difference presumes that different cultures will produce different material products. Hence, even where there is no economic discrimination based on race, cultures with different values will live with differences in economic wealth. Respect for cultures as equals, that is, allowing them the greatest possible autonomy, and valuing what it is they produce, requires tolerance of economic inequality.[10]

There is a second incompatibility in the usages of economic and cultural equality, one that is more directly a product of the discursive dynamics of the particular way that these terms have evolved as part of the public vocabulary. The rhetorics of economics and culture envisage different mathematical quantities as equal. Hence, it is possible for economic equality to require a "12 percent" solution to a problem, whereas the dynamics of cultural equality require a "50 percent" solution.

The first part of the problem, as we see it, is that usages of "economic equality" have been defined according to a mathematical formula that assumes uniform proportionality based on population.[11] Hence, economic equality establishes the expectation that blacks will be 12 percent of any measurable group. In our current climate, this is a difficult expectation to satisfy. The fact that African-Americans constitute only 12 percent of the population would make them a lonely minority if they were distributed evenly across the board. More important, the culturally focused rhetoric of black power works against such a distribution. By arguing for the clustering of blacks in "separate" communities, it makes a 12 percent across-the-board standard unattainable.

The problem is even more complex than this, however, for the black power agenda also creates an expectation of 50 percent parity rather than a 12 percent proportion. Black power rhetoric is framed with the assumption that racial relations are a dualistic, black/white dynamic. Black power rhetors in the 1960s spoke about this dialectic in such a way as to suggest that because black and white constituted "equal" alternatives, American culture should be "50 percent" white and "50 percent" black across the board. This perspective generates troublesome expectations, as in the case of the black sports commentator who recently complained that "20 percent" was too low a proportion for blacks in baseball.[12] Similarly, the black power definition of "equal power" between equal cultures leads to the expectation of "equal coverage" of the black and white heritage in the academic curriculum. The proportionality standard, however, would call for only 12 percent. The discourses of the mathematical standard of population proportionality and the black power standard of cultural parity thus lead to a whirl of conflicting expectations about the nature of equality in those many cases where culture and economics overlap.

At the same time, contemporary demographic shifts are beginning to undermine both the proportionality standard and the black power image. African-Americans are rapidly losing their status as the primary American minority. Hispanic-Americans are currently immigrating and reproducing at a higher rate than America's black population. The number of Asian- and Native Americans is also on the increase. Hence, the problems of the proportional standard, if applied to all minorities, will eventually work against African-Americans. Proportional and cultural equality standards collapse under the weight of pragmatics when they are applied to multiple cultures. And in like manner, the black power image of a dialectic of black and white is already crumbling under the weight of multiculturalism and a "rainbow America."

We should probably not be surprised at the demise of the proportionality standard. People are not identical. Mathematical processes that treat humans as substitutable units simply cannot provide an adequate notion of Equality. This does not mean that we should stop measuring unequal economic conditions, but we must recognize such measurement as an instrumental prod to help us in moving away from past discriminations, not as the final and ultimate goal of a free and autonomous democracy.

We need, therefore, to continue to explore the relative desirability of cultural and economic Equality as well as to craft public usages that might transcend or transform these incompatibilities. This task requires, finally, that we consider the relationship between Equality and Liberty.

LIBERTY/EQUALITY

When Americans first began to use the term "equality," in the eighteenth century, they opposed it to the term "property." Slaves could not possess Equality because to do so would be to violate the slaverholders' Property Rights. Eventually, Americans stopped seeing Property as more important than Equality, and the burden of the struggle shifted to a tension between Equality and Liberty. In the twentieth century the public opposition to Equality has been predicated on the fact that it destroys Liberty.[13] This, at least, is the conclusion drawn by myopic ideologues.

The relationship between Liberty and Equality is not a simple antithesis. In the Anglo-African American experience, at least, they have been related in a complex mixture of mutual dependence and tension. It is true that a system of absolute enforced Equality in every particular is only possible with the destruction of personal Liberty. It is also true, however, that without Equality, Liberty cannot exist. If one does not recognize the fundamental equality of human beings, one cannot imagine this right to be free from tyranny. It was for this reason that when conservative colonists decided to demand their Liberty from Britain, they were dragged against their preferences to employ the term Equality. True, their usages of the term were minimalist, and they would be expanded by others with less blue blood running in their veins. But even colonial business leaders were forced to concede, both by their actions and their cautious pronouncements, that Liberty and Equality are interdependent values. The experiences of both the American South and South Africa are fairly conclusive in demonstrating that the conditions necessary to maintain oppressive inequalities destroy personal liberty. Under such circumstances, even the oppressors are required to give up individual Liberties to protect the collective enterprise of oppression; freedom of speech, freedom of conscience, even free economic enterprise are rapidly sacrificed to the psychological demons generated by a rhetoric of racism (or religious persecution or sexual exploitation).

This mutual dependence, of course, does not deny the tension between Liberty and Equality. Just as we know that Liberty cannot survive absolute Equality, we have also learned that Equality cannot survive total Liberty. Worldwide experience has taught us that when left unconstrained, human beings persecute one another both economically and violently with a distressing degree of uniformity.

In like manner, truly effective Liberty requires Equality. The term "equality" loses its positive force if our usage of it is not grounded in the materiality of individual human lives. What could it possibly mean to be Equal in a world where one had no Liberty? Even though a collectivist usage of Equality is logically possible without personal Liberty, it is nonetheless undesirable. In spite of how cultural essentialists frequently end up talking, few believe that a culture is more important than the persons who create and sustain it.[14] Most arguments for the importance of cultures rest on the negative impact that the failure to attend to culture has upon the living, breathing people who constitute these cultures. A culture has no value as an empty shell devoid of the individuals who create and sustain it. To sacrifice personal Liberty to achieve cultural Equality is to make a deal with devil. This does not mean that cultures have no importance, for we have learned well and often that individuals come to adulthood as enculturated beings, and therefore we cannot neglect cultural specificity. However, it is important to treat individuals as at least of equal importance to their cultures. Ultimately, the sacrifice of personal Liberty for collective Equality does not make sense.

What then, can Equality mean? America is still a young culture, and we are still exploring the balance of Liberty and Equality. Our history, however, has taught us a few things. We have learned, for example, that the basic Christian concept of human dignity is one important ingredient to a shared culture, but that it is not *enough*. The Christian ideal is too abstract and insubstantial to construct the best possible world for our species. We know, for example, that Equality before the Law and Equal Protection are minimal necessities, and that the Political Equality of individuals is vital as well. We have also learned that the portion of Social Equality that we call "public accommodations," or that we might call "public equality," is also mandatory. We may not yet be over the divide on the dimension of Social Equality that allows people to select their friends and mates based on individual rather than racial or ethnic traits. Lighter-skinned Americans bitterly battle the inclusion of blacks in their neighborhoods and country clubs, while separatist black leaders insist that African-Americans should exclude whites from many of their affairs as well.

Other usages of Equality stand on less firm ground. We have discarded Separate But Equal as a viable compromise of competing interests, but the status of the concept of "equality without regard to race or color" is still undetermined. We have not yet decided if Justice should be color-blind or a dispenser of Rainbow fairness, for we do not know whether it is confined only to the present or accountable to the distant past. Neither do we know what conditions are possible for the future. If it is possible for people to outgrow their racial prejudices, then after a short period of special preference to restore African-Americans to an "equal footing," we can return blithely to a formal, color-blind equality that includes only a modicum of economic proportionality. But what if racial prejudice continues to glow brightly, so that white employers, school teachers, and social workers refuse opportunity to their dark-skinned fellow citizens? Are we then saddled forever with "special preference" by the government to make up for private hostility?

The most difficult permutation of equality to negotiate is "racial equality." This phrase no longer refers primarily to biological essentialism. America is a "mongrel nation." While some Americans can trace their ancestry completely to one continent, very few can trace it to one linguistic or cultural group, and fewer still to one nation or tribe. Biological studies of racial characteristics are thus virtually irrelevant. Even in the case of so-called racially pure groups, biological origins remain inconsequential as long as we are concerned with individual merit, ability, and rights. Intra-group variance on such matters is always greater than intergroup variance.

The question with regard to equality of cultures remains, likewise, a twisted one. We do not yet know what we mean when we say that two cultures are "equal." At the least, it should mean that we grant all cultures presumption on their own terms. Accordingly, to the extent that we find cultural practices such as foot-binding, slavery, conspicuous consumption, etc., to be perverse, we must commit ourselves to persuading those who practice them to change rather than to using military might to force their compliance. But cultural equality should not, we believe, mean that cultural autonomy is sacred, inviolate to outside influence or disagreement. No culture today participates in human sacrifice, but it seems ludicrous to argue that should such a culture be discovered, we should not endeavor to persuade its members to alter their practices. All cultures have equal dignity, but all cultural practices are not equal. The problem remains, of course, that ethnocentrism thrives in most cultures throughout the world. It is very difficult to work through a critique of one's own culture by distinguishing between those cultural practices that, though different from one's own, are harmless or meritorious, and those that are both different and inhumane.

Some representatives of minority cultures would argue that a belief in intercultural argumentation of this sort is itself an ethnocentric Western bias. After all, many cultures base their decision-making processes on either historical precedent or authority. They would not willingly open themselves to a debate about those practices with outsiders. Even were it desirable to maintain cultural autonomy at this level, however, it is simply no longer possible. One can no more "opt out" of the global dialogue than one can opt out of acid rain, the pressures of overpopulation, or a nuclear winter. The land-based, low-material life-style of a group of Peruvian aboriginals is a worthy life-style. The ancient ways of Native Americans were also of value. But to preserve those cultures requires restraining other cultures from *developing* their cultural preferences, that is, to farm the land, to mine the mountains, to tap the oil field, etc. In the past, such decisions were made without discussion, on the simple principle of might makes right. Presumably, rhetorical decision-making processes that allow principles and values to intervene are preferable. But that requires that we generate some kind of international, or perhaps transnational, rhetorical culture through which to engage such a dialogue.

The problem is only slightly more tractable if we focus on more narrow issues, closely related to the story of Equality in America. It is clear that cultural equality means at least this much: that the contributions of members of all the nation's subcultural groups should be recognized. Again, however, we cannot yet say what it is to be "equally" recognized. An Afrocentric school might provide a curriculum that is evenly divided in its discussion of African and European culture. Does that provide its children an "equal curriculum"? Does a social studies and humanities curriculum that is 10 percent African-American provide an "equal" curriculum? And what does it do to our judgment to realize that the 10 percent comes out of only 50 percent of the curriculum? And, again, is the African-American heritage represented by an *African* curriculum? And how do we know

what is really "European" and what is "African"? It seems odd to attribute
mathematics, for example, to a particular culture, in spite of the fact that
Europeans, and more recently Asians, clearly made the most of mathematics in the last few hundred years. And why are Mesopotamians and
Egyptians either white or black?

Such questions of ultimate adequacy should not stymie our efforts to
broaden our curricula. While we do not know how much is enough, we
certainly know that what we have in most schools and classrooms is not
yet adequate. But we do not yet have ultimate answers.

That also leaves us with the issue of Economic Equality. There is broad
agreement, we believe, that "equal economic opportunity" ought to exist,
and that this entails an African-American usage of the phrase, not a Jacksonian one. That is, government must have some role in insuring against
economic discrimination. It is also the case that most informed people recognize that equal economic opportunity, however we might ultimately
define it, does not currently exist. Nevertheless, some prefer an even
stronger version of "economic equality" that is articulated typically in one
of two forms. In the first form, the phrase sneaks in through the back door
of equal economic opportunity. From this perspective the measure of
equal economic opportunity is treated as if it were literally the standard
against which to measure economic equality. In the second form, American leftists support a vaguely defined concept of economic equality. Some
in this group would overthrow capitalism to achieve economic parity between whites and blacks. Nevertheless, economic equality has not yet
been enshrined in the nations' laws and constitutional structure.

The expression of Economic Equality as a cultural value remains potent, and it drives extensions of Equality into such areas as culture because
economic conditions for one-third of the black population are so rank and
bleak. As long as public perceptions of this kind of inhumanity persist,
Americans, who remain morally sensitive as a public, will be susceptible
to persuasion. To bring about an end to the threat to Liberty posed by ex-
pansions of Equality, we must, ironically, deal with the basic economic
problem pointed to by those demanding Economic Equality. However,
this does not mean that we must deal with it in their way. Injustice always
calls forth answers in one form or another. In part, this means perhaps the
need for yet another rhetorical revision of Equality.

Today, in the United States of America, many African-Americans live
in a nation within a nation, just as their ancestors did in the 1830s.[15]
However, after much travail by brave African-American orators and

writers, the usage of Equality has spread across the nation and has grown in strength and application. Additionally, in spite of the increasing radicalization of Afrocentricity, and the persistent racial hatred by some, there is much more discursive interaction across interracial boundaries than ever before in America's history. Most of America's lighter skinned inhabitants no longer claim that the United States is a "white man's country." They have recently come to recognize that the United States could not have become the economically wealthy nation it is without the years of hard labor contributed by African-Americans. They have additionally begun to recognize that the nation could not be the culturally vital place it is without the rich aesthetic contributions of African-Americans. Finally, they have begun also to recognize that the nation would not have the Constitution it has without the important political contributions of African-Americans. In fact, America has never been a white man's country. African-Americans do not need a "separate nation" or a "back to Africa" movement in order to inhabit a country in which they can point to the political constitution as one they participated in building. The United States of America satisfies that condition. Clearly, America is not wholly beholden to Africa, but then America is not wholly beholden to any nation. It is the product of the descendants of multiple lands.

This leaves us with a rhetorical problem. How do we characterize this America and the rhetorical culture in which it participates? The current public arena seems to be littered with metaphorical depictions of what America is: a melting pot, a rainbow, a quilt, a tossed salad, a family, and so on. The use of metaphors can be a dangerous move, especially if we forget that every metaphor is no more than an invitation to consider limited comparisons between otherwise different phenomena. But therein, too, lies the special value of metaphors for constituting a rhetorical culture, for as long as we remember that metaphors invite an audience's assent and participation rather than dictate a recalcitrant worldview, they provide a site at which competing voices and interests can negotiate the meaning of their common world. America is not a melting pot you insist? Well, then, let us consider the available possibilities. A melting pot implies the reduction of variety to a homogeneous mass. We would probably do well to avoid such blandness. But neither is America a tossed salad, as some have recently suggested. As a nation we are far too interdependent for that. Our history and language represent a shared and common heritage. We owe too much to each other to be conceptualized as a set of isolated elements that can be picked through and discarded like individual pieces of lettuce, tomato, and broccoli.

Our own preferred metaphor is the genetic one. We see the human family as a culturally and biologically interbreeding species. Both racial supremacists and cultural supremacists have rejected this possibility on grounds that it would reduce the human species to a common denominator that would guarantee mediocrity. Such, we believe, is not the case. Interbreeding three distinct groups produces a complex diversity where there was once only three simple options. The kind of regression toward a gray and featureless mean imagined by rhetors as different as Theodore Bilbo and Ursula K. Le Guin is at most a very long-term possibility that will take thousands of years to evolve. Even then, it would require a uniformity of experiences and environments that seem unlikely at best.

We find ourselves, however, in public debate with others whose disparate experiences we respect, and so we recognize the need to compromise our preferences. Many advocates prefer an image of America that preserves rigid cultural distinctions. For our own part, we are also cautious of a metaphor that relies on passive biological motion rather than human choice and action. Therefore, perhaps the American experience is best characterized as a hearty stew. In such a stew the individual ingredients remain identifiable throughout the eating, but the tempting broth whose flavor permeates the whole is the product of all of the ingredients. A stew also requires careful and constant human attention. If it is overcooked, we end up with a bland and tasteless gruel. If it is undercooked, we get a raw mass without any interaction of flavors and blending. The image of "cookery" is indeed a rhetorical image of America, is it not? We are not the separate units we were when our ancestors started out, but then who would want to be? Why live in America if you want to be European or African or Asian? And yet, the various cultural and ethnic groups in America have retained a certain distinctiveness that indicates that the job of cooking the stew never reaches an end.

Our struggle over metaphors only confirms what our earlier story suggested. As Americans we have not yet constructed our nation as the promised land of Equality. We don't even know yet what it is exactly we are supposed to construct. What *is* Equality anyway? As at our beginning, we continue to ask the question, and in asking it we hope to set the stage for enacting another chapter in the life of a nation that must continually reaffirm and recraft its commitments to Liberty and Property, to heterogeneity and homogeneity, and to Equality for all.

RESEARCH AND
BIBLIOGRAPHY ESSAY

We title this section a "Research and Bibliography Essay" because our goal here is to help the reader to understand the methodological approach we employed in selecting documents for analysis, as well as to provide a description of the particular materials we used in our various samples.[1] The purpose of this study is to chart the development of the usages of the term "equality" in American public discourse from the nation's founding to the present, focusing in particular on the contributions of African-American rhetors. For most of the time periods covered in the book, there are significant scholarly debates about what constituted the core political "ideas" of a particular era. For example, in the revolutionary period, there is the debate between those like Bailyn who place a highly egalitarian and libertarian cast on American revolutionary discourse, and those like Greene and Nedelsky who argue that the discourse was tightly constrained to the interests of a narrow group of elites with a compelling interest in "property."[2] Critics and historians from both perspectives can offer a substantial list of quotations to support their arguments, making it clear that each position has some claim on the truth of the matter. Nevertheless, two important questions remain: Which public advocates, egalitarians or propertarians, were more influential in affecting social and political change? And what kind(s) of influences did they have? Answering these questions requires a new set of scholarly tools designed to examine the rhetorical structures and functions of public discourse. We hope to contribute one of these tools by providing a survey of public discourse that strives for an accurate representation of the distribution of public usages of key terms such as "equality," "liberty," and "property." While this will not answer all of the questions scholars currently face regarding the influence of rhetoric on social and political change, it should help to answer two particular questions: How frequently were particular key terms used? And with what frequency did particular usages of those terms occur?

Our particular purpose, of course, is to examine the rhetorical usages of the word "equality." To this end, we have tried to survey the most relevant public discourse in both the national arena and in the African-American community from approximately 1760 to 1990. For each time period that we examine we have examined relevant official texts, including presidential speeches and Supreme Court decisions, mass media in the form of newspapers and magazines, and public political pamphlets and oratory generated by social movement participants. Our sample of African-American discourse focuses on public speeches, and newspapers and magazines.

The criteria of "relevance" are inevitably nebulous, but we here define the relevant texts as political discourse concerning issues on which some substantial portion of the populace has employed the term "equality" in any contexts where African-Americans might claim that term. This still leaves an enormous body of discourse to examine. We have, therefore, sampled this discourse, employing two different selection protocols: significance and representativeness.

The criterion of significance is necessary because some documents in history have had more impact than others, and these ought, therefore, to receive greater attention. For example, the Declaration of Independence and John Wise's *Vindication* both use the term "equality," and Wise does it more fully. It is Jefferson's work, however, that had more direct impact on American governance, and so obviously it can not be excluded from consideration. In addition to developing our own judgments about what documents have and have not been significant, we have relied heavily on the judgments represented in the secondary literature produced by historians for each time period. The books and articles we cite in the following pages are not intended as a comprehensive bibliography on our subject but rather a listing of those works that have guided our selection of documents.[3] There are, however, problems in the use of significance as a criterion. Precisely because the scholars we have relied upon work out of long-established plot lines that tell them which documents are significant, they tend to devote a disproportionate amount of time to some documents rather than others. Over time, even the experts in each subarea lose sight of the terrain of original discourse by concentrating on exceptional documents that a history of selection has enshrined. Therefore, some measure of the representativeness of discourse is necessary, particularly where the goal is to establish research in new areas with new plot lines.

In order to gain profiles indicating which discourses were representative of various epochs, we have relied on a variety of sampling procedures, hewing as closely as possible to standard social scientific methods. For a variety of reasons, we do not use statistical measures in this volume, but we believe that borrowing social scientific sampling procedures is reasonable where an accurately representative portrait of discourse is desired. Accordingly, for each time period we survey, we use (1) a set of scientifically rendered samples, (2) samples structured to suit particular features of the time period being considered, and (3) our own intuitive sampling. Our procedures vary by time period (as reflected in the chapter-by-chapter organization of the book) because the character of the American public arena changes substantially across time. In the colonial period, there is no "national" discourse but rather many local and colonial discourses. Until after the Civil War, there are essentially two public discourses, one Northern and one Southern. After the Civil War, the reconstituted United States only gradually established a national public arena that dominated over regional arenas. Our sampling attempts to take these changes into account.

To guide our selections, we have employed a few secondary works that span several time periods. General studies that provide legal-political surveys of equality include Pole's *The Pursuit of Equality in American History,* Redenius's *The American Ideal of Equality,* Nieman's *Promises to Keep,* and Bell's *Race, Racism and American Law.*[4] The two era-spanning black historical studies that have been most influential on our selections are Franklin's *From Slavery to Freedom* and Meier and Rudwick's *From Plantation to Ghetto.*[5] Our work in the black press has been guided by Bullock's *The Afro-American Periodical Press,* Dann's *The Black Press 1827–1890,* and Suggs's *The Black Press in the South 1865–1979.*[6] Jordan's *White over Black* provided a survey of the ideology of race relations, and Howard-Pitney's *The Afro-American Jeremiad* provided an all-too-rare extended rhetorical analysis of African-American discourse.[7] Several collections of speeches and other public documents also spanned the time periods of multiple chapters. Shockley's *Afro-American Women Writers 1746–1933* anthologizes the rhetorical works of black women, emphasizing literary works of the early period, while Lerner's *Black Women in White America* provides the most expansive collection of political works by black women from 1811–1971.[8] We also employed a number of general multiple volume collections, including the *Afro-American History Series,* Aptheker's *A Documentary History of the Negro People in the United States,* and Foner's *The Voice of Black America.*[9] Single volume anthologies include Foner and Lewis's labor-oriented collection *Black Workers,* Woodson's classic *Negro Orators and Their Orations,* oriented to official and ceremonial discourse, and anthologies by Fishel and Quarles, and by Hill.[10]

CHAPTER TWO: THE BRITISH RHETORIC OF REVOLT, 1760–1774

This chapter describes the English discourse in America upon which both Anglo-and African-Americans would build. In selecting a representative body of discourse, we attempted to get as wide a survey of the colonies as possible. This is made difficult by the fact that the majority of political discourse that has been preserved was produced in Boston, Pennsylvania, Virginia, and New York. Southern colonies lacked well-developed "public spaces"—a consequent, no doubt, of their manorial character—and hence produced less public discourse. Our sample here, therefore, is more representative of the public discourse that was *reproduced* as a sum total in the colonies than it is of the "public opinion" that existed in all of the colonies.

Our samples of discourse include all of the documents of the *American Archives* for the period as well as the Boston Massacre Orations, one-half of the election sermons from Connecticut and Boston (Boston, 1748, 1768, 1770–1774; Connecticut, 1773–1775), and samples of newspapers and pamphlets. It was difficult to get a sampling basis for pamphlets. We employed a 20 percent sample of those works indexed in Charles Evans's *American Bibliography* under the titles "Political Rights" and "Slavery."[11] This proved to be largely unsatisfactory, for these categories included too much extraneous material. Thus, though we have done so cautiously, we relied more heavily on the "significance" criteria for pamphlets than on this sample.

We drew three different types of samples for newspapers (for a complete listing of all newspapers by dates see the Appendix). First, we chose the *Maryland Gazette* and the *Connecticut Courant* to read completely for the period from 1765 through 1776. The *Maryland Gazette* represents an "ideal type" for the colonial newspapers. It was not extremely slanted in its editorial selections printing both Whig and Loyalist, and radical and conservative documents through most of the period. It was not consumed by the prerevolutionary debate but gave it ample coverage. Geographically and ideologically, it seemed to provide elements of Southern and Northern colonies. In the end, we concluded that reading it completely, for the entire period, provided a fairly representative condensation of colonial discourse. The *Connecticut Courant,* by contrast, was extremely hostile to the entire discussion of revolt. Its primary method of dealing with the controversy was to ignore it. Where that became impossible, the *Connecticut*

Courant only gradually shifted from Loyalist to Whig discourse, and it held on to the possibility of reconciliation until late into the war. In addition to complete readings of these newspapers, we have employed a 20 percent sample of the discourse of the *Pennsylvania Chronicle*, the *Boston Evening Post*, and the *Virginia Gazette*, for the years 1772, 1774, 1776, and 1778 (not all papers were available in all these years). In this sample we focused particularly on culling out the precise number and character of the usages of the word "equality." Third, we examined the following newspapers for the following dates (where available): *Georgia Gazette*, the *Massachusetts Spy*, the *South Carolina and American General Gazette*, the *New York Gazette and Weekly Mercury*, and the *Connecticut Journal and New Haven Post Boy*, for March–April 1770, November–December 1772, all of 1774, June–July 1776. These dates were selected to include active periods in which major events occurred and periods of repose. The selections sought to balance both Northern and Southern, and loyalist and rebellious newspapers. Finally, we leavened the whole with a good dose of curiosity reading among other newspapers, including the *Pennsylvania Journal*, the *Weekly Monitor*, and the *Boston Gazette*.

The contents of the documents selected for significance clashed noticeably with that of our representative sample. We are indebted to Sydney James, University of Iowa, for his guidance in our selection of significant secondary sources. From what we can discern, historians working in this period have focused on describing the elements in the prerevolutionary period that later were drawn out and acted upon in the revolutionary period. As a consequence, they have tended not to provide a representative description of the range of discourse that existed in the revolutionary period.[12] Their interests are particularly reflected in the pamphlet anthologies. Bailyn's *Pamphlets of the American Revolution* reflects well the religious roots of the period, some of the egalitarian strains, and the discourse of natural rights.[13] Jensen's *Tracts of the American Revolution 1763–1776* emphasizes economics and some of the tensions between Loyalist and "Americanist."[14] The selections in Commager and Morris's *The Spirit of 'Seventy-Six* highlight the persons and events of the period.[15] Two anthologies are much broader in their content: Gravlee and Irvine selected their collection, *Pamphlets and the American Revolution*, on the basis of the frequency of publication reprintings, and Morison's *Sources and Documents Illustrating the American Revolution, 1764–1788* offers nondominant perspectives. Both collections cover a broader time period than we focus on in this chapter.[16] Potter and Thomas's *The Colonial Idiom* offers an even broader anthology of colonial discourse, incorporating an accurate reflection of a wider range of issues such as religion and education.[17]

For conceptual background and selection of significant works we have relied especially on Bailyn's *The Ideological Origins of the American Revolution* and *The New England Merchants in the Seventeenth Century,* Conkin's *Self-Evident Truths,* and Morgan's *Inventing the People* for the dominant Whig account.[18] We also have been strongly influenced by Douglass's *Rebels and Democrats,* Becker's *The Declaration of Independence,* Nash's *Red, White and Black* and *Race, Class, and Politics,* and Williamson's *American Suffrage* in understanding the other voices who supported the Revolt on more egalitarian grounds.[19] Nedelsky's *Private Property and the Limits of American Constitutionalism* provides an excellent analysis of the issue of property (although not from a perspective that places linguistic precision as central), and Becker et al.'s *The Spirit of '76 and Other Essays* perceptively portrays the forces of revolutionary change in their portrait of the average conservative Whig-Patriot.[20] Although his focus is more strictly on legal texts than we find ultimately representative of the public discourse of the time period, Reid's *The Concept of Liberty in the Age of the American Revolution* and *The Concept of Representation in the Age of the American Revolution* provide immensely useful surveys of "Liberty" and "Representation," employing the kind of careful precision necessary to accuracy about linguistic detail that is all too rare.[21] Wills's *Inventing America* does the same for the Declaration of Independence.[22] Lucas's *Portents of Rebellion* is a model of rhetorical analysis in the period, as is Ritter and Andrews's *The American Ideology.*[23] The single volume that dovetails most closely with our own reading of the prerevolutionary period is Greene's *All Men Are Created Equal,* and we are heavily indebted to it.[24]

All of these scholars have paid major attention to public discourse, and we have, wherever the materials have been available to us, tracked down and read the newspapers and pamphlets they cite. We have also been guided by their interpretation of historical events.

Because there is a small, computer-accessible text base of an appropriate nature for this period (WordCruncher Ver. 4.1), we also ran computer word counts on the important words we refer to in this chapter.[25] Generally, we found support for the claims we had already produced by hand counting our own samples. For example, in the texts analyzed by Word-Cruncher, the word "freemen" appears more frequently than "all men" in the preconstitutional period, and as frequently in the postconstitutional period. Also, as Olsen and Harvey have noted, "Natural Rights" was a relatively rare phrase in the constitutional period.[26] The same was true for forms of "equality." According to Rodgers, there are two key problems with this computer program: First, the sample of documents employed in its data files are unsatisfactory. There are a number of reasons for this, not the least of which is that it relies almost exclusively on generally acknowledged "great texts" such as the *Federalist Papers*, and thus ignores the wide body of public opinion contained in newspapers and public speeches. Second, its method for coding documents is far too literal to be of use in studying the rhetorical dimensions of a public discourse that is fraught with all kinds of idiomatic phrases, implicit narratives, and nuances of meaning.[27] These shortcoming are ones our own study compensates for, and so the fact that there is such a great convergence between the Word-Cruncher sample and ours adds some additional weight to our conclusions.

CHAPTER THREE: THE ANGLO-AMERICAN REVOLUTIONARY RHETORIC, 1774–1789

The period from 1775 to 1789 is that in which the United States became a nation. Consequently, in selecting primary documents we have shifted our attention gradually from texts produced in the various colonies or states to the "official documents" of nationhood. To some extent, this results in a merger of the categories of "significant" and "representative" documents. We attend to the classic resources of the debates in the federal convention as reproduced by Farrand, and the state ratifying conventions as preserved by Elliot.[28] We also surveyed the *American Archives, Annals of America,* and the *Annals of Congress.*[29]

The popular discourse we examined includes the ratification pamphlets anthologized separately by Ford and Storing. We also examined the *Federalist Papers.*[30] We continued our reading of the complete run of the *Maryland Gazette,* and we added Fourth of July orations to our reading of the Boston Massacre Orations and Elections Sermons. We added popular "magazines" (or the weeklies that provided a bridge toward the concept of the magazine), employing *Poole's Index* to access all of the articles indexed under the headings "slavery," "colonization," "abolition," "emancipation," and the "slave trade" that were available to us in the rare book collection of the University of Illinois. Among primary documents we included the annual reports of the American Colonization Society.

The volume of secondary literature for this period is overwhelming. We were particularly guided by the following: On the ideology of the Anglo-Americans in the period, Wood's *The Creation of the Republic 1776–1787* offers the most thorough, least biased account of any available.[31] We have also found McDonald's *Novus Ordo Seclorum* and Morgan's *Inventing the People,* as well as Rossiter's more popular *Seedtime of the Republic,* to be particularly useful in covering the time period.[32] Additionally, Bailyn's studies of the revolutionary ideology are useful for tracing the roots of what is today the dominant American worldview, but they do not accurately describe the range of ideological perspectives existent at the time.[33] On the relationship between slavery and the Revolution, we leaned most heavily on Litwack's *North of Slavery,* which shows the power of good scholarship to endure; Robinson's *Slavery in the Structure of American Politics 1765–1820,* which provides wonderfully detailed explorations of the congressional debates on slavery; Davis's *The Problem of Slavery in the Age of Revolution 1770–1823,* which places the U.S. struggle in a useful international perspective; Zilversmit's *The First Emancipation,* which provides a thorough description of the abolition process in the Northern states; and MacLeod's *Slavery, Race and the American Revolution,* which offers additional useful perspectives on the role of slavery in the revolution.[34] Kaplan and Kaplan's *The Black Presence in the Era of the American Revolution* is a highly readable summary of the role of blacks in revolutionary America.[35]

There is a real blossoming of works in the area of African-American culture in the early part of our nation's history, but there seems to be an unevenness of quality and a great deal of repetition, caused no doubt, by the limited availability of primary documents. Nonetheless, Blassingame's *The Slave Community,* Frey's *Water from The Rock,* Genovese's *Roll, Jordan, Roll,* Greene's *The Negro in Colonial New England,* Kulikoff's *Tobacco and Slaves,* Levine's *Black Culture and Black Consciousness,* Nash's *Red, White and Black,* Sobel's *The World They Made Together,* and Stuckey's *Slave Culture* were all extremely informative and useful. Additionally, Wood's "I Did the Best I Could for My Day" offered valuable cautions and guidance.[36] There remains a continued failure to come to grips with the role and importance of the American Colonization Society. Fox's highly slanted *The American Colonization Society, 1817–1840* offers a useful resource, and Staudernraus's *The African Colonization Movement, 1816–1865* provides some valuable interpretation, but the original documents remain the necessary starting point.[37] Frederickson provides a useful analysis of the relationship between colonization and the abolitionists.[38]

CHAPTER FOUR: THE AFRICAN-AMERICAN RHETORIC OF EQUALITY: 1774–1860

This chapter focuses on the construction of Equality by African-Americans, with secondary attention to white abolitionists and the dominant, national rhetoric of the period. For primary documents, our representative sample relies on speeches and the black press. We did thorough readings and systematic samplings of the available issues of the *North Star,*

Frederick Douglass' Paper, Douglass's Monthly, the *Colored American,* and the *Weekly Anglo-African.* We also examined, although not on a systematic basis, the white abolitionist newspapers, including the *Herald of Freedom,* the *Genius of Universal Emancipation,* and the *Liberator,* to assure that the few points of contrast that we were drawing were accurate and to collect additional instances of black rhetoric. Our comparisons of white and black texts are also based on our examination of presidential inaugural addresses, Fourth of July orations, and *The Negro in the Congressional Record.*[39]

To collect those documents of particular significance, we relied most heavily on the available anthologies, assuming those items that had been collected by scholars in the area for wider distribution had passed some tests of significance. We, therefore, relied heavily on the *Afro-American History Series* and the anthologies by Aptheker; Bormann; Bracey, Meier, and Rudwick; Brawley; Fishel and Quarles; Lerner; Shockley; and Woodson.[40] There is a fair amount of duplication among these sources, and that indicates some shared criteria among scholars in the area. In addition, the state and national black conventions were of signal importance, and we used these in their entirety, as they are collected and presented in Bell's *Minutes of the Proceedings of the National Negro Conventions 1830–1864,* and by Foner and Walker in *Proceedings of the Black National and State Conventions 1865–1900.*[41] We also included all of the speeches of Frederick Douglass in *The Frederick Douglass Papers,* and we sampled the documents in Foner's *The Life and Writings of Frederick Douglass.*[42] We balanced these with the speeches of Henry Highland Garnet and Maria Stewart as collected in Ofari's *Let Your Motto Be Resistance* and Richardson's *Maria W. Stewart.*[43]

The secondary literature on this area is growing rapidly. Unfortunately, there does not seem to be a definitive analysis of the development of the ideology of the African-American people.[44] Most ideological analyses seem clouded by the on-going division between radical Pan-Africanists and mainstream integrationists.[45] There are, however, good historical sources on the development of the black community, and we have allowed these to guide our selection of significant documents: Quarles's *Black Abolitionists* is clearly central, and Litwack's *North of Slavery,* Aptheker's *American Negro Slave Revolts,* Franklin's *The Free Negro in North Carolina 1790–1860,* and Bell's *A Survey of the Negro Convention Movement 1830–1861* are also extremely useful.[46] Although we only discovered it as our own manuscript was in the final production stages, we would also strongly recommend Gary B. Nash's 1988 Merrill B. Jensen Lectures delivered at the University of Wisconsin and reprinted along with relevant primary materials as *Race and Revolution*.[47] There is a growing literature on individual black rhetors that is of substantial use, although it must be fit into the larger picture.[48] Goldwin and Kauffman's *Slavery and Its Consequences* provides some useful conceptual background.[49] There is, of course, an extensive literature on slavery and abolitionism, and although these literatures have been peripheral to our project, some sources have been useful in providing a historical framework of events and documents.[50]

CHAPTER FIVE: SEPARATE BUT EQUAL, 1865–1896

As we move into the postwar era, a fundamental shift occurs in the character of the national public sphere. Before the Civil War, one can quite clearly identify a "white" national arena of public discourse and a "black" national arena of public discourse. After the war, the "black" national arena continues, but the "white" national arena is transformed into an interracial national arena. To be sure, it is dominated in the media by white reporters and, to an even larger extent by white editors and owners. However, it circulates among a growing reading public that includes blacks. It also includes black writers. The number of black writers approaches a representation of blacks in the reading public, especially where topics of racial interest are concerned. Accordingly, we, examine two sets of discourse: one, the black national press and public speeches, which were overwhelmingly dominated by black voices; and the second, the interracial or mainstream public arena, which though dominated by whites was increasingly influenced by black voices.

The Black National Public

The core of our discourse set for this period was a representative sample of black newspapers. We read the complete available run of the *Colored Citizen* as our touchstone, from which we gained an overview of the issues and general shape of the usages of Equality we might look for at this time and in this arena. We then drew a 10 percent sample, structured by date, within decades, to insure rotation by months of all available issues of the *Western Appeal,* the *New Jersey Sentinel,* the *New York Age,* the *San Francisco Elevator,* and the *Washington Bee.* In addition, we obtained systematic, but more date-limited readings of the *Savannah Tribune,* the *Freeman,* the *New Orleans Tribune* (both French and English versions), and the *New National Era.* Finally, we obtained spotty readings of other black newspapers of which only a few issues have been preserved. Our selection of newspapers was guided by our attempt to cover every decade for each of the three major regions of the country: North, West, and South. We were largely successful in achieving this balance, though for some years there were no newspapers available from a given area, especially the South.

We added to this, reading in the *Colored American Magazine* and the *Voice of the Negro,* as well as the state convention materials from Foner and Walker's *Proceedings of the State Conventions.* We also examined a substantial cross-section of speeches. The best available speech collection is Foner's *Voice of Black America.* In addition, we used Woodson's *Negro Orators and Their Orations,* Fishel and Quarles's *The Negro American,* Cox and Cox's *Reconstruction, the Negro and the New South,* and McFarlin's *Black Congressional Reconstruction Orators and Their Orations 1869–1979.*[51] We also included collections of the speeches of John Edward Bruce, John Mercer Langston, W. E. B. DuBois, Booker T. Washington, Daniel A. Payne, Francis Grimké, and Alexander Crummell.[52]

There have been relatively few secondary works on the ideology of blacks in this period. Meier's *Negro Thought in America 1880–1915* remains the preeminent work, and though our purpose has been more narrow than his, we have found our reading of documents to be in substantial agreement with his.[53] Other works have examined the period primarily with an eye to exploring its relationship to twentieth-century ideologies, especially black nationalism. We would point in particular to Painter's *Exodusters,* but see also Moses's *The Golden Age of Black Nationalism, 1850–1925.*[54]

The Mainstream Arena

For primary materials in the mainstream we have relied heavily on a representative sample of national magazines. As we argue in the text, this medium provides the best single representation of the national argument on any issue. Our 10 percent sample was structured by decade, drawn from *Poole's Index* until 1890, and from the *Reader's Guide to Periodical Literature* thereafter. In the early years, when the discourse arena provided by the magazines was still in its childhood, it was necessary to employ a larger sample than 10 percent in order to insure the statistical power that would give us confidence in the significance of our findings. After 1880 this was no longer a problem. This sample has been checked against regional newspapers (including the *Atlanta Constitution,* the *New York Herald,* and the *New York Tribune*) and the collections provided by McFarlin, and by Cox and Cox.[55]

While national debates rage in the magazines, they are transformed into national law and policy by presidents, Congress, and the Supreme Court. We call this the "official" discourse, and to study it we have relied on the debates reprinted in the *Congressional Record,* the Inaugural Addresses and annual State of the Union messages of the presidents, and the relevant Supreme Court decisions.

The secondary literature on the Reconstruction and post-Reconstruction era is daunting. The nation has still not yet satisfied its conscience on the Civil War and race relations, and so academics have been wrestling mightily with this period. From this enormous collection, Lofgren's *The Plessy Case* has added to our study of the legal discourse, as did Hyman's *A More Perfect Union.*[56] Cochrane's *Freedom without Equality* provided an exceptionally useful analysis of Northern public opinion.[57] Fredrickson's *The Black Image in the White Mind* is a particularly valuable description of the century-long debate over characterizations of Afro-Americans from the initial attempts at colonization through the early years of the twentieth century.[58] For providing general background and indicating significant texts, in addition to those works employed for Chapter 4, we used Foner's excellent *Nothing But Freedom* and *Reconstruction: America's Unfinished Revolution, 1863–1877,* Franklin's *Reconstruction: After the Civil War;* Gillette's *Retreat from Reconstruction 1869–1879,* Perman's *Emancipation and Reconstruction 1862–1879;* Rabinowitz's *Race Relations in the Urban South 1865–1890,* Rable's *But There Was No Peace,* Ransom and Sutch's *One Kind of Freedom,* Stampp's *The Era of Reconstruction 1865–1877,* Belz's "The New Orthodoxy in Reconstruction Historiography," and Williamson's *The Crucible of Race.*[59] Finally, we examined Woodward's classic study of *The Strange Career of Jim Crow* as well as the debate that has surrounded it.[60]

CHAPTER SIX: INTEGRATED EQUALITY, 1896–1960

In comparison to the other eras studied in this book, the years 1895–1950 have received relatively little attention in regard to race relations and equality. In part, this is because most studies have parsed the time segments into "Reconstruction and Redemption," ending about 1900 or 1910, and "the civil rights movement," beginning around 1954. This situation is starting to change as Lehman's *The Promised Land* begins to indicate, but the progress is very slow.[61] Sitkoff's *A New Deal for Blacks* is still one of the few valuable books on the era of the Great Depression, but we also recommend Zangrando's, *The NAACP Crusade against Lynching, 1909–1950,* and Naison's *Communists in Harlem during the Depression.*[62] Ralph J. Bunche's *The Political Status of the Negro in the Age of FDR* was originally prepared as a working paper for Gunnar Myrdal's *An American Dilemma,* and is an invaluable resource.[63] Clearly, there is still much to be done in this time period. The majority of studies concerning the years between have focused largely on such cultural issues as the Harlem Renaissance.[64] Due to their nearness in time, however, the quantity of primary material is overwhelming. Our sample at this point comes to rely heavily on the adequacy of the assumptions of social scientific sampling techniques, since, unlike our earlier periods, our samples constitute only the smallest percentage of all available material.

The African-American Rhetoric

We have tried to balance our newspaper samples among Northeastern, Central, Southern, and Western papers as well as among radical and moderate editorial stances. Our sample, therefore, includes the *Atlanta World*, the *Norfolk Journal and Guide*, the *Chicago Defender*, the *Los Angeles Sentinel*, and the *Pittsburgh Courier*. In addition, as part of the selection process, we examined a number of other newspapers, and some of these appear in text notes. During this era, the black national arena made a transition from newspapers to magazines, so we also included in our sample *The Crisis, The Messenger, Opportunity, Jet,* and *Ebony.*

To obtain a view of those texts deemed important by experts in the field, we have continued to rely on collections by the experts, extending our reading in Fishel and Quarles, Aptheker, Foner, and Foner and Lewis.[65] We have also included Meier, Rudwick, and Broderick's excellent *Black Protest Thought in the Twentieth Century* and Roy Hill's *Rhetoric of Racial Revolt.*[66]

Mainstream and White Rhetoric

To sample the mass media, we employed a random numbers table to select a 10 percent sample of the headings under "Negro" in the *Reader's Guide to Periodical Literature.* To sample the *Congressional Record* we alternated years and surveyed the articles listed under the headings "Howard University," "Lynching," "Negroes," "Race Discrimination," and "Civil Rights." We continued to study presidential discourse by examining the State of the Union Addresses, Inaugural Addresses, and any speeches expressly concerned with Civil Rights issues.

We examined the Supreme Court decisions listed by legal and historical scholars as the most important. We relied most heavily on Bell's *Race, Racism and American Law,* but our selections also come from the historical works we have listed elsewhere in this essay and incorporated into our notes as well as several specialized legal sources, especially Tushnet's *The NAACP's Legal Strategy against Segregated Education 1925–1950,* Berger's *Equality by Statute,* and Richard Kruger's classic work on *Brown v. Bd. of Education, Simple Justice.*[67]

Other Secondary Sources

Many historical sources cover parts of this era. We have relied heavily on Franklin's *From Slavery to Freedom*, the essays in Aptheker's *Afro-American History*, the essays in Franklin and Meier's *Black Leaders of the Twentieth Century*, and Nieman's *Promises to Keep*.[67] Branch's *Parting the Waters* and Sitkoff's *The Struggle for Black Equality 1954–1980* are exemplary treatments of the late 1950s.[69] Burk's *The Eisenhower Administration and Black Civil Rights* is a judicious treatment of the immediate post-Brown era, and has the added advantage of a useful bibliographic essay on important primary and secondary documents concerning the time period.[70] The bulk of the work on the 1950s and 1960s represents the recent trend toward localism in historical scholarship, but we found Lehmann's study of migration in *The Promised Land* to be particularly useful.[71] There are very few sources that deal directly with the ideology of equality and race relations. Tushnet's "The Politics of Equality in Constitutional Law" in the *Journal of American History* seems to stand almost alone.[72] We also examined Myrdal's classic work, *An American Dilemma*, along with Southern's incisive analysis of it in *Gunnar Myrdal and Black-White Relations*.[73] Notable also are several volumes that emphasize ideological analyses of the latter part of the period, including Cruse's *Plural But Equal* and Cone's *Martin and Malcolm and America*. Clark and McKerrow's "The Historiographical Dilemma in Myrdal's American Creed" in the *Quarterly Journal of Speech* is an important rhetorical analysis of the ideological tensions of the period.[74]

CHAPTER SEVEN: NEW EQUALITIES, 1960–1990

No one should pretend to be capable of complete objectivity, especially about their own era. Scholars studying political discourse should, however, attempt to move as far as they can toward a kind of evenhandedness. They can do this by reading carefully and deeply in the multiple perspectives that surround any issue. *Rather than dispassion, scholars should seek empathy with each perspective. But then, they should move to encompass all of the perspectives in their account, being both true to each perspective and also critical of it.* We have tried to fulfill this injunction, but it is clear that we are still involved in the current "chapter" of history in a way that does not allow us to understand what the outcome of the era will be. Consequently, we offer this chapter in a more tentative fashion than the others, portraying the national public debate as still open. Therefore, we have continued our samples through 1990 with regard to the U.S. Congress as described in Chapter 6. We have also continued our samples through 1970 with regard to black magazines and mainstream magazines. For the years from 1970 to

1990 we surveyed mass circulation magazines by topic rather than in terms of the scientific sampling procedure we discussed above. We chose this approach because our readers are undoubtedly more familiar with the arguments of the post–civil rights period than with earlier periods. We, therefore, shifted our emphasis from describing the basic lay of the land to covering the most problematic issues. We supplemented our studies of black rhetoric by surveying key texts such as Carmichael and Hamilton's *Black Power*, Cleaver's *Soul on Ice*, Davis's *Women, Race, and Class*, and Asante's *The Afrocentric Idea*, as well as various collections of speeches.[75] Our speech collections start with the surveys indicated in previous chapters and add Bosmajian and Bosmajian's *The Rhetoric of the Civil Rights Movement*.[75] All of these collections overrepresent the radical voices of black Marxists, black separatists, and black supremacists. That is, the percentage of pages devoted to these voices is far higher than the percentage in other media, such as black newspapers, magazines, churches, and elected officials. However, they often include pamphlets and organizational manifestos that are otherwise difficult to find and that had an impact out of proportion to their original circulation. Thus their inclusion is essential to balance out the mainstream media and to get a full picture of the available discourse.

We have also included collections by key speakers. The best available collection of Martin Luther King, Jr.'s speeches is Washington's *A Testament of Hope*; for Jesse Jackson we rely on *Straight from the Heart*.[77] There is a volume in process by Logue and DeHart of the speeches of Andrew Young.[78] No speaker changed his ideology more times than Malcolm X, or was more variable among different audiences. Thus it is important to consult multiple collections for Malcolm X; the best are *Malcolm X Speaks* and *Malcolm X: The Last Speeches*, but also of use are *By Any Means Necessary, Malcolm X Talks to Young People,* and *Two Speeches By Malcolm X*.[79] Especially useful on his Black Muslim period are Lomax's collections *When the Word Is Given*, and *To Kill a Black Man*.[80] There does not appear to be a collection of Barbara Jordan's speeches, so it was necessary for us to consult a variety of sources. In addition there is her speech at Harvard University's commencement, in *Barbara Jordan: A Self Portrait*.[81]

The secondary historical literature we employed consists of those works listed in the section on Chapter 6, but readers should also see the Marxist perspective represented in Marable's *Black American Politics* and *Race, Reform and Rebellion*.[82] In addition, with regard to Jesse Jackson, we employed Landess and Quinn's highly critical *Jesse Jackson and the Politics of Race*, and the more balanced account in House's *Jesse Jackson and the Politics of Charisma*.[83] In addition, Reed's *The Jesse Jackson Phenomenon* supplies a critical study that ties in analysis of black political leadership in the seventies and eighties.[84] Biographical sources on Malcom X include Perry's *Malcolm*, Breitman's *The Last Year of Malcolm X*, and Goldman's psychohistory, *Death and Life of Malcolm X*.[85] On King we have relied on Garrow's *Bearing the Cross*, Oates's *Let the Trumpet Sound*, and Lewis's *King*.[86] We have also consulted the essays in the forthcoming volume edited by Calloway-Thomas and Lucaites, *Martin Luther King, Jr. and the Sermonic Power of Public Discourse*.[87]

Reference List of Newspapers and Magazines

We treated newspapers and magazines as either "core" or "sample" sources. Where we treated newspapers and magazines as core sources, we examined all issues available on microfilm for the dates included. Where we treated newspapers and magazines as sample sources, we examined a 2–10 percent sample of the issues available on microfilm for the dates included. Sample sources are identified by an asterisk (*). A more detailed discussion of the specific sampling protocols and uses of newspapers and magazines is included in the "Research and Bibliography Essay" (see pp. 233–248).

American Eagle, 1910–1968
American Negro, 1890*
Amsterdam News, 1968*
Atlanta Constitution, 1868–1880*
Atlanta World, 1932–1950, 1960–1967*
Boston Evening Post, 1765–1775*
Boston Gazette, 1761–1769*
Chicago Defender, 1921–1968*
Cleveland Gazette, 1883–1915*
Colored America, 1898–1904
Colored American Magazine, 1900–1910
Colored Citizen (Topeka, KS), 1878–1879, 1897–1900
Connecticut Courant, 1770–1778
Connecticut Journal and New Haven Post Boy, 1770–1776*
The Conservator (Chicago, IL), 1882–1886*

The Crisis, 1910–1968*
Douglass' Monthly, 1859–1860
Ebony, 1945–1961*
The Elevator (San Francisco, CA), 1865–1898*
The Emancipator (and Republican), 1835–1840*
Frederick Douglass' Paper, 1853–1855
Freedom's Journal, 1827–1829
The Freeman, 1888–1915*
Genius of Universal Emancipation, 1821–1825*
Georgia Gazette, 1770*
Herald of Freedom, 1835–1841*
Jet, 1951–1980*
Liberator, 1831–1860*
Los Angeles Sentinel, 1946–1980*
Maryland Gazette (and Political

Intelligencer), 1765–1789, 1806–
1817
Massachusetts Spy, 1770–1778
The Messenger, 1917–1927*
National Baptist World, 1894*
New Era, 1870–1874*
New Orleans Tribune, 1864–1869*
New York Age, 1883–1890, 1905–
1909*
New York Gazette, 1770–1776*
New York Globe, 1883–1890, 1905–
1909*
Norfolk Journal and Guide, 1916–1966*
The North Star, 1847–1851
Omaha National Progress, 1893
Opportunity, 1923–1948
Pennsylvania Chronicle, 1772–1778*
Pennsylvania Journal, 1774*
The People's Friend, 1894*

Pittsburgh Courier, 1911–1971*
Savannah Tribune, 1886–1888*
The Sentinel (NJ), 1880–1882
*South Carolina and American General
Gazette*, 1770–1775*
La Tribune de la Nouvelle-Orleans,
1864–1869
Virginia Gazette, 1772–1774*
Virginia Star, 1878–1882*
Voice of the Negro, 1904–1905
Washington Bee, 1882–1915
Weekly Anglo-African, 1859–1860
Weekly Avalanche, 1893
Weekly Monitor, 1770–1776*
Weekly Pelican (Los Angeles, CA),
1886–1889*
Western Appeal, 1885–1915*
Witchita Tribune, 1898*

NOTES

PREFACE

1. For examples of the resurgence of rhetoric across the human sciences see John S. Nelson, Allan Megill, and Donald N. McCloskey, eds., *The Rhetoric of the Human Sciences: Language and Argument in Scholarship and Public Affairs* (Madison: University of Wisconsin, 1987); Herbert W. Simons, ed., *Rhetoric in the Human Sciences* (Newbury Park, CA: Sage, 1989). For supportive but cautionary consideration of this revival written explicitly from the perspective of rhetorical studies see Michael Calvin McGee and John R. Lyne, "What Are Nice Folks Like You Doing in a Place Like This? Some Entailments of Treating Knowledge Claims Rhetorically," in Nelson et al., *The Rhetoric of the Human Sciences,* 381–406; Robert Hariman, "The Rhetoric of Inquiry and the Professional Scholar," in Simons, *Rhetoric in the Human Sciences,* 210–32; Dilip Gaonkar, "Rhetoric and Its Double: Reflections on the Rhetorical Turn in the Human Sciences," in Herbert W. Simons, ed., *The Rhetorical Turn: Invention and Persuasion in the Conduct of Human Inquiry* (Chicago: University of Chicago Press, 1990), 341–66.

2. The internecine academic and political battles between critical theorists, poststructuralists, and postmodernists aside, we are inclined to see the commonalities rather than the differences in their joint critique of modernity. This is born of the belief that more is gained by working toward a productive rapprochement of such perspectives than needlessly reifying (and thus replicating) their oppositions. A useful and explicit attempt at such rapprochement has begun in the separate work of Mark Poster and Scott Lash, but we would point as well to the implicit efforts of Stanley Fish and Richard Rorty who write with an American pragmatist tinge that leads them to recognize quite explicitly the necessary and practical integration of rhetoric and philosophy in the crafting of public morality. See Mark Poster, *Critical Theory and Poststructuralism: In Search of a Context* (Ithaca: Cornell University Press, 1989); Scott Lash, *Sociology of Postmodernism* (New York: Routledge, 1990); Stanley Fish, *Doing What Comes Naturally: Change, Rhetoric, and*

Leff

the Practice of Theory in Literary and Legal Studies (Durham: Duke University Press, 1989); Richard Rorty, *Philosophy and the Mirror of Nature* (Princeton: Princeton University Press, 1979); and *Contingency, Irony, and Solidarity* (New York: Cambridge University Press, 1989).

3. See, e.g., Jacques Derrida, *Dissemination*, trans. Barbara Johnson (Chicago: University of Chicago Press, 1981); Jean Baudrillard, *In the Shadow of the Silent Majorities . . . or The End of the Social and Other Essays*, trans. Paul Foss et al. (New York: Semiotext(e), 1983); Georges Bataille, *Visions of Excess: Selected Writings, 1927–1939*, trans. Allan Stoekl et al. (Minneapolis: University of Minnesota Press, 1985).

4. The number of writers in this category has grown slowly and steadily since the late 1960s. Chief among those operating in this tradition is Kenneth Burke, who has actively advocated such a theoretical posture since the 1930s. See in particular his *Permanence and Change* (Berkeley: University of California Press, 1984 [1935]); and *Attitudes toward History* (Berkeley: University of California Press, 1984 [1937]); but see also his *A Grammar of Motives* (Berkeley: University of California Press, 1969 [1945]); *A Rhetoric of Motives* (Berkeley: University of California Press, 1969 [1950]); and *The Rhetoric of Religion: Studies in Logology* (Berkeley: University of California Press, 1961). Writing more recently and from a variety of humanistic and social scientific disciplines see Michael Billig, *Arguing and Thinking: A Rhetorical Approach to Social Psychology* (Cambridge: Cambridge University Press, 1987); Richard Harvey Brown, *Society as Text: Essays on Rhetoric, Reason, and Reality* (Chicago: University of Chicago Press, 1987); Terry Eagleton, *Literary Theory: An Introduction* (Minneapolis: University of Minnesota Press, 1983), esp. 194–217; and *Walter Benjamin or Towards a Revolutionary Criticism* (London: Verso, 1981); Murray Edelman, *Political Language: Words That Succeed and Policies That Fail* (New York: Academic Press, 1977); and *Constructing the Political Spectacle* (Chicago: University of Chicago Press, 1988); Anthony Giddens, *Central Problems in Social Theory: Action, Structure and Contradiction in Social Analysis* (Berkeley: University of California Press, 1979); Jürgen Habermas, *Communication and the Evolution of Society*, trans. Thomas McCarthy (Boston: Beacon Press, 1979 [1976]); and *The Theory of Communicative Action*, 2 vols., trans. Thomas McCarthy (Boston: Beacon Press, 1987); Donald N. McCloskey, *The Rhetoric of Economics* (Madison: University of Wisconsin Press, 1985); Chaim Perelman and L. Olbrechts-Tyteca, *The New Rhetoric: A Treatise on Argumentation*, trans. John Wilkinson and Purcell Weaver (Notre Dame, IN: University of Notre Dame Press, 1969); Calvin O. Schrag, *Communicative Praxis and the Space of Subjectivity* (Bloomington: Indiana University Press, 1986); James Boyd White, *When Words Lose Their Meaning: Constitutions and Reconstitutions of Language, Character, and Community* (Chicago: University of Chicago Press, 1984); and *Heracles Bow: Essays on the Rhetoric and Poetics of the Law* (Madison: University of Wisconsin Press, 1985).

5. Michael Calvin McGee, "A Materialist's Conception of Rhetoric," in Ray E. McKerrow, ed., *Explorations In Rhetoric* (Glenview, IL: Scott, Foresman, 1982), 23–48. We find it altogether curious that with very few exceptions professional historians have been among the slowest to acknowledge and seriously consider the

fundamental role and importance of rhetoric as public persuasion in the social and political processes of historical change. This is odd, not only because history, as a discipline, is rooted in the classical tradition of oratory as a primary form of social and political power but because a growing number of historians seem to be directing their attention to the rhetoric of "history" as a sociopolitical practice. For examples of those focusing attention on the role of rhetoric in history see Hayden White, *Metahistory: The Historical Imagination in Nineteenth-Century Europe* (Baltimore: Johns Hopkins University Press, 1973); and *The Content of the Form: Narrative Discourse and Historical Representation* (Baltimore: Johns Hopkins University Press, 1987); Hans Kellner, *Language and Historical Representation: Getting the Story Crooked* (Madison: University of Wisconsin Press, 1989); Allan McGill and Donald N. McCloskey, "The Rhetoric of History," in Nelson et al., *The Rhetoric of the Human Sciences,* 221–38; Daniel T. Rodgers, *Contested Truths: Keywords in American Politics since Independence* (New York: Basic Books, 1987); Kenneth Cmiel, *Democratic Eloquence and the Fight over Popular Speech in Nineteenth-Century America* (New York: William Morrow and Co., 1990). For examples of historical case studies that demonstrate the inherent value of studying the role of rhetoric in social and political change see Karlyn Kohrs Campbell, *Man Cannot Speak for Her,* 2 vols. (New York: Praeger, 1989); Celeste Michelle Condit, *Decoding Abortion Rhetoric: Communicating Social Change* (Champaign: University of Illinois Press, 1990); J. Michael Hogan, *The Panama Canal in American Politics: Domestic Advocacy and the Evolution of Policy* (Carbondale: Southern Illinois University Press, 1986); Ronald L. Hatzenbuehler and Robert L. Ivie, *Congress Declares War: Rhetoric, Leadership, and Partisanship in the Early Republic* (Kent, OH: Kent State University Press, 1983); Kathleen Hall Jamieson, *Eloquence in an Electronic Age: The Transformation of Political Speechmaking* (New York: Oxford University Press, 1988); Stephen E. Lucas, *Portents of Rebellion: Rhetoric and Revolution in Philadelphia, 1765–1776* (Philadelphia: Temple University Press, 1976); Kathleen Turner, *Lyndon Johnson's Dual War: Vietnam and the Press* (Chicago: University of Chicago Press, 1985); David Zarefsky, *President Johnson's War on Poverty: Rhetoric and History* (University: University of Alabama Press, 1986); and *Lincoln, Douglas, and Slavery: In the Crucible of Public Debate* (Chicago: University of Chicago Press, 1990).

6. Samuel Ijsseling, *Rhetoric and Philosophy in Conflict: An Historical Survey* (The Hague: Martinus Nijhoff, 1976); Brian Vickers, *In Defense of Rhetoric* (Oxford: Clarendon Press, 1988), 148–253; Bruce Kimball, *Orators and Philosophers: A History of the Idea of Liberal Education* (New York: Teachers College Press, 1986), esp. 157–205.

7. Karl Wallace, "The Substance of Rhetoric: Good Reasons," *Quarterly Journal of Speech* 49 (1963): 239–49 (hereafter referred to as *QJS*); Michael Calvin McGee, "In Search of 'the People': A Rhetorical Alternative," *QJS* 61 (1975): 235–49; Walter R. Fisher, *Human Communication as Narration: Toward a Philosophy of Reason, Value, and Action* (Columbia: University of South Carolina Press, 1987), esp. 105–42.

8. See George Norlin, "General Introduction," *Isocrates,* 3 vols., trans. George Norlin (Cambridge, MA: Harvard University Press, 1928), 1: xvi–xviii. There

have been recent and compelling attempts to challenge this characterization of the Sophists, but such efforts have not yet successfully mitigated the classical reception of the Sophists one finds in the works of Plato and Isocrates. See John Poulakos, "Toward a Sophistic Definition of Rhetoric," *Philosophy and Rhetoric* 16 (1983): 33–85; and "Rhetoric, the Sophists, and the Possible," *Communication Monographs* 51 (1984): 215–25; Susan C. Jarratt, *Rereading the Sophists: Classical Rhetoric Refigured* (Carbondale: Southern Illinois University Press, 1991).

9. See Alvin W. Gouldner, *Enter Plato: Classical Greece and the Origins of Social Theory* (New York: Basic Books, 1965), esp. 326–60.

10. See Takis Poulakos, "Isocrates's Use of Narrative in the *Evagoras:* Epideictic Rhetoric and Moral Action," *QJS* 73 (1987): 317–28.

11. Isocrates, "Nicocles or the Cyprians," 1:81–82.

12. Michael Calvin McGee, "The Moral Problem of *Argumentum per Argumentum*," in J. Robert Cox et al., *Argument and Social Practice: Proceedings of the Fourth SCA/AFA Conference on Argumentation* (Annandale, VA: Speech Communication Association, 1985), 2.

13. See Herbert A. Wichelns, "The Literary Criticism of Oratory," in A. Drummon, ed., *Studies in Rhetoric and Public Speaking in Honor of James Albert Winans* (New York: Century, 1925), 181–216; John Louis Lucaites, ". . . at the boundaries of politics (in the broadest sense) and literature": "Reading the 'Public' in Herbert August Wichelns's *The Literary Criticism of Oratory*," *Communication Quarterly,* forthcoming.

14. See Isocrates, "Areopagiticus," 2:129–31.

15. Aristotle, *The "Art of Rhetoric,"* trans. John Henry Freese, in *Aristotle,* 23 vols. (Cambridge, MA: Harvard University Press, 1982), 22:1354a–1355b.

16. In classical Greece public argumentation was generally restricted to orations presented before the *ekklesia* or the *areopagus.* Since that time the sphere of public argumentation has broadened considerably. Oratory is still a primary source of public argumentation—though the ways in which it is practiced and experienced in the age of electronic media have changed considerably—but in addition it has come to include the use of pamphlets, broadsides, public letters, various forms of written and electronic journalism, and so on. See Michael Warner, *The Letters of the Republic: Publication and the Public Sphere in Eighteenth-Century America* (Cambridge, MA: Harvard University Press, 1990); Kathleen Hall Jamieson, *Eloquence in an Electronic Age: The Transformation of Political Speechmaking.*

17. For a theoretical discussion of the "ideograph" see Michael Calvin McGee, "The 'Ideograph': A Link between Rhetoric and Ideology," *QJS* 66 (1980): 1–17. For specific examples of ideographic analysis see Michael Calvin McGee, "In Search of 'the People': A Rhetorical Alternative"; "Not Men, But Measures': The Origins and Import of an Ideological Principle," *QJS* 64 (1978): 141–55; and "The Origins of 'Liberty': A Feminization of Power," *Communication Monographs* 47 (1980): 23–45; John Louis Lucaites, "Flexibility and Consistency in Eighteenth-Century Anglo-Whiggism: A Case Study of the Rhetorical Dimensions of Legitimacy" (Ph.D. diss., University of Iowa, 1984).

18. Celeste Michelle Condit, "The Rhetorical Limits of Polysemy," *Critical*

Studies in Mass Communication 6 (1989): 103–22. See also John Louis Lucaites, "Constitutional Argument in a National Theater," in Robert Hariman, ed., *Popular Trials: Rhetoric, Mass Media, and the Law* (Tuscaloosa: University of Alabama Press, 1991), 31–54.

19. In this respect our project is generally compatible with the work being done by those seeking to write a history of "conceptual change" by examining the discursive construction of key ideas in their historical context. We begin to part company with such authors in two places. First, their selections of public discourse tend to emphasize elite texts rather than ordinary, everyday discourse of the sort that one finds in what we define as public discourse (but cf. Pocock, below). This, we believe, distorts an understanding of the pragmatic, discursive role such "concepts" play in affecting social and political change. Second, those pursuing the history of conceptual change tend to be excessively concerned with the issue of "intentionality." From our perspective, such a focus on intention overemphasizes the sense of rhetoric as *techne* to the exclusion of "how" discourse actually operates in the rhetorical culture, i.e., how particular elements of the rhetorical culture restrict and control the ways in which individuals and groups come to understand their public life together. From our perspective, a speaker's *actual intention* is far less important than the *public motives* that get articulated. See James Tully, ed., *Meaning & Context: Quentin Skinner and His Critics* (Princeton: Princeton University Press, 1988); Terence Ball, *Transforming Political Discourse: Political Theory and Critical Conceptual History* (Oxford: Basil Blackwell, 1988); Terence Ball and J. G. A. Pocock, *Conceptual Change and the Constitution* (Lawrence: University of Kansas, 1988); Terence Ball, James Farr, and Russell L. Hanson, *Political Innovation and Conceptual Change* (New York: Cambridge University Press, 1989); J. G. A. Pocock, "The Concept of Language and the *Metier d'Historien:* Some Considerations on Practice," in Anthony Pagden, ed., *The Languages of Political Theory in Early-Modern Europe* (New York: Cambridge University Press, 1987), 19–38.

20. See Michael Osborn, *On Rhetoric Style* (Chicago: SRA, 1976), 16–17.

21. The various arguments against the "dominant ideology thesis" are elaborated amply in Nicholas Abercrombie, Stephen Hill, and Bryan S. Turner, *The Dominant Ideology Thesis* (London: George Allen & Unwin, 1980). In citing them here we do not mean to endorse the economistic account of "the dull compulsion of economic relations" (1) that the authors adopt.

22. What we have in mind here is very close to Gramsci's notion of "hegemony" as the more or less fluid relationship between power, domination, and intellectual-moral leadership which produces cultural and sociopolitical legitimacy. We avoid referring to hegemony here because of our interest in establishing a theoretical vocabulary to describe the specifically rhetorical dimensions of legitimacy, and because of the ways in which hegemony has been conflated in popular discourse with "brainwashing" and "manipulative ideologies." See Antonio Gramsci, *Selections from the Prison Notebooks,* trans. Quintin Hoare and Geoffrey Nowell Smith (New York: International Publishers, 1971), 57–58, 123–202. For conceptions of hegemony that are consistent with our understanding of a rhetorical culture see T. J. Jackson Lears, "The Concept of Cultural Hegemony: Problems

and Possibilities," *American Historical Review* 90 (1985): 567–93; Ernesto Laclau and
Chantal Mouffe, *Hegemony & Social Strategy: Towards a Radical Democratic Politics*
(London: Verso, 1985), 93–194.

23. The study of "equality" is a virtual growth industry in the past twenty
years. We have no intentions of reviewing that literature here in any systematic
way. Bryan S. Turner offers a good overview in *Equality: A Sociological Enquiry*
(New York: Tavistock Pub., 1986). This volume also has the advantage of an excellent, though now slightly dated, bibliographical essay (133–38). Our reading of
the literature suggests that philosophers and political theorists, as well as some so-
ciologists interested in demographics, tend to treat equality as an idealized concept
rather than as a word that circulates in human discourse; historians tend to limit
their attention to political and philosophical treatises or other versions of elite texts
such as diaries, private letters, and so on; and jurists tend to treat equality as it develops almost exclusively in case law—though there are some interesting and important exceptions to this. Of the three groups, legal scholarship comes the closest
to the perspective that we will develop here, though we see the formal discourse of
"the law" as only one component of a rhetorical culture. To focus on it exclusively
is to ignore the wide range of ways in which ideographic terms such as equality
function in nonlegal discourse (as employed by public advocates, the mass media,
and so on) to represent the much larger public consciousness of "ordinary"
individuals.

One recent book deserves special attention: Peter Westen's *Speaking of Equality:
An Analysis of the Rhetorical Force of "Equality" in Moral and Legal Discourse*. This is
an important work, for at the outset it recognizes that equality is precisely a word
that has tremendous power and presence in American political discourse. Unfortunately, Westen moves from acknowledging the linguistic roots of equality to the
development of a critique of the "rhetorical force" of equality in moral and legal
discourse which relies upon an analytical distinction between "descriptive" and
"prescriptive" definitions of the word. In an important sense, this replicates the
troublesome tendencies of the rhetoric-philosophy debate that we have already
indicted, for it reifies equality as a philosophical principle that gets distorted in
rhetorical practice as, in Westen's words, "an accident of history" (259). In the
end, Westen's argument fails to develop a pragmatic critique of "equality" for it
privileges the philosopher's decontextualized question of *whether* equality, as an
ideal, should have rhetorical force, over the rhetorician's questions of *how* equality
circulates in the ordinary discourse of a particular historical community, and *how* it
might be crafted to promote the agenda of a democratic polity in the present era.

We list the most recent, thoughtful and characteristic work in each of these
areas:

(1) *Philosophy and Political Theory:* Charles R. Beitz, *Political Equality: An Essay
in Democratic Theory* (Princeton: Princeton University Press, 1989); Andrew Flew,
The Politics of Procrustes: Contradictions of Enforced Equality (Buffalo, NY: Procrustes
Press, 1981); J. R. Kluegel and R. E. Smith, *Beliefs about Inequality* (New York:
Aldine, DeGruyter, 1986); William Ryan, *Equality* (New York: Pantheon Books,
1981); Sidney Verba and G. R. Orren, *Equality in America* (Cambridge, MA:

Harvard University Press, 1985); Michael Walzer, *Spheres of Justice: A Defense of Pluralism and Equality* (New York: Basic Books, 1983).

(2) *History:* Terry Eastland and William J. Bennett, *Counting by Race: Equality from the Founding Fathers to Bakke and Weber* (New York: Basic Books, 1979); J. R. Pole, *The Pursuit of Equality in American History* (Berkeley: University of California Press, 1978); Charles Redenius, *The American Ideal of Equality* (Port Washington, NY: Kennikat Press, 1981).

(3) *Case Law:* Morroe Berger, *Equality by Statute: The Revolution in Civil Rights* (New York: Octagon Books, 1978); Peter Charles Hoffer, *The Law's Conscience: Equitable Constitutionalism in America* (Chapel Hill: University of North Carolina Press, 1990); Kenneth L. Karst, *Belonging to America: Equal Citizenship and the Constitution* (New Haven: Yale University Press, 1989); Donald G. Nieman, *Promises to Keep: African-Americans and the Constitutional Order, 1776 to the Present* (Cambridge: Cambridge University Press, 1991); Peter Westen, *Speaking of Equality: An Analysis of the Rhetorical Force of "Equality" in Moral and Legal Discourse* (Princeton: Princeton University Press, 1991).— I have 1990 in my reference

24. See John S. Nelson, "Political Foundations for the Rhetoric of Inquiry," in Simons, *The Rhetorical Turn*, 258–89.

25. See Michael Calvin McGee, "Edmund Burke's Beautiful Lie: An Exploration of the Relationship between Rhetoric and Social Theory" (Ph.D. diss., University of Iowa, 1974).

26. Those who desire a chronological accounting of key individuals and events that is altogether compatible with our rhetorical history should consult Nieman's excellent recent volume *Promises to Keep: African Americans and the Constitutional Order, 1776 to the Present.*

CHAPTER ONE

1. The traditional narrative frame underlies many important academic histories, including those of Duncan J. MacLeod, *Slavery, Race and the American Revolution* (London: Cambridge University Press, 1974); Edmund S. Morgan, *Inventing the People* (New York: W. W. Norton and Co., 1988); Donald Robinson, *Slavery in the Structure of American Politics, 1765–1820* (New York: Harcourt Brace Jovanovich, 1971); Leon F. Litwack, *North of Slavery: The Negro in the Free States, 1790–1860* (Chicago: University of Chicago Press, 1961). It is also presented as the historical framework of important popular speeches such as Dr. Martin Luther King, Jr.'s "I Have a Dream" and President John F. Kennedy's, "Civil Rights Address," televised to the American people on 11 June 1963.

2. Colonial printers often signified constitutive values such as "liberty," "property," and "equality" by capitalizing them, especially when they wished to indicate their importance to a particular issue. Sometimes they capitalized only the first letter of a word, sometimes they capitalized all the letters in a word. They also used a wealth of typographical devices to capture some of the richness of vocal emphasis that is lost on the written page, such as italics, capitalization, and underlining. There was no consistency to such signification. Where we quote from primary

source material we retain the original typography. In our own writing we capitalize key words and terms when we want to emphasize their specific status as constitutive values. Thus, we might talk about the philosophical concept of liberty or the physical condition of liberty, in which case the word "liberty" would be written without capitalization. However, if we intend to refer to the public status of "liberty" as a key word or constitutive value of Anglo- or Afro-American society, we render it with a capital "L."

3. For a discussion of the procedures employed in selecting public discourse for analysis see the Research and Bibliography Essay, 233–248.

4. We do not mean to ignore the role that various white women, speaking and writing from a feminist perspective, have had on crafting the meaning of the word "equality," nor to deny the enormous influence of the white-dominated labor movement. Nevertheless, limitations of time, space, and attention force us to draw lines. For now, at least, we focus on the strand of the story that relates most directly to the relationship between white and black Americans regardless of gender.

5. Throughout the book we seek to be accurate and clear in our usages of gendered terms such as "he" and "man." When we mean to designate only males, we employ male-gendered nouns and pronouns. When we mean to designate males and females we employ terms that we perceive as inclusive, including "person," "human," and "people." Whereas those speaking and writing in previous historical periods used language that was unclear as to gender, or which designated only men where today we would designate both women and men, we leave their usages—errant from our own perspective—intact, because we are concerned to describe the linguistic record with precision.

CHAPTER TWO

1. The most sensible overview of the stasis between the conventional romance of revolutionary wisdom and its countertale of elite self-interest is Richard B. Morris, "Class Struggle and the American Revolution," *William and Mary Quarterly* 19 (1962): 3–29.

2. Gary B. Nash, *Race, Class, and Politics: Essays on American Colonial and Revolutionary Style* (Urbana: University of Illinois Press, 1986), 66.

3. See, e.g., Charles A. Beard, *An Economic Interpretation of the Constitution of the United States* (New York: Macmillan, 1921); Carl Lotus Becker, *History of Political Parties in the Province of New York, 1760–1776* (Madison: University of Wisconsin Press, 1907).

4. Garry Wills summarizes the mainstream response in *Inventing America: Jefferson's Declaration of Independence* (New York: Doubleday Books, 1978), 354–56.

5. This is summarized in Morris, "Class Struggle and the American Revolution"; Billy G. Smith, "Inequality in Late Colonial Philadelphia: A Note on Its Nature and Growth," *William and Mary Quarterly* 41 (1984): 629–45. See also the

pioneering work of Elisha P. Douglass, *Rebels and Democrats* (Chapel Hill: University of North Carolina Press, 1955); and Nash's exemplary *Race, Class, and Politics*. Herbert Aptheker provides a Marxist and Africanist summary in *The American Revolution: 1763–1783* (New York: International Publishers, 1960).

6. For historians taking perspectives that support our claims, and who base their work on careful discursive analysis although not representative surveys of discourse see Jennifer Nedelsky, *Private Property and the Limits of American Constitutionalism: The Madisonian Framework and Its Legacy* (Chicago: University of Chicago Press, 1990); Jack P. Greene, *All Men are Created Equal: Some Reflections on the Character of the American Revolution* (Oxford: Clarendon Press, 1976); David Brion Davis, *Revolutions: Reflections on American Equality and Foreign Liberations* (Cambridge, MA: Harvard University Press, 1990).

7. Perry Miller, *The New England Mind: From Colony to Province* (Cambridge, MA: Harvard University Press, 1967), 298. Note that even Wise, who goes farther than other prerevolutionaries in articulating an egalitarian theory, bounds his usages of "equality" in ways similar to the defenders of slavery. See John Wise, *A Vindication of the Government of New England Churches* (Boston, 1717).

8. For the pamphlets, and evidence on circulation, see Merrill Jensen, ed., *Tracts of the American Revolution 1763–1776* (Indianapolis: Bobbs-Merrill, 1967), 94–95, 108.

9. When we refer to "the pamphlets" or "the rhetoric of revolt," we do not generally include Tory discourse. By focusing on the battle between "Whigs" and "Tories," scholars miss the important struggles *among* the Whigs.

10. Along with the newspapers, see Allen D. Candler, *The Colonial Records of the State of Georgia, vol. XV, 1769–1782* (Atlanta: Franklin-Turner Co., 1907); William L. Saunders, ed., *The Colonial Records of North Carolina, vol. X, 1775–1776* (Raleigh: Josephus Daniels, 1890).

11. See, e.g., "A Planter," *Maryland Gazette,* 7 July 1774, 1.

12. *Massachusetts Spy,* 14–16 August 1770, 1. *Supp. to the Maryland Gazette,* 11 May 1769, and 2 June 1774. All emphasis throughout our work is in the original unless otherwise indicated.

13. *Maryland Gazette,* 23 June 1774.

14. *Connecticut Courant,* 2 October 1770, 1.

15. See also multiple papers in the *American Archives,* 4th ser., vol. 1, including resolutions for Talbot Court House, MD, 24 May 1774; Connecticut Resolutions, 2 May 1774, "The British American no. V"; and the various Virginia Resolutions. See also David Lloyd, *A Defense of the Legislative Constitution* (Philadelphia, 1728), 2.

16. See, e.g., *Boston Gazette,* 7 January 1765; and *Maryland Gazette,* 11 May 1769, 1, and 23 June 1774, 1.

17. Debt and currency issues are evident in some pamphlets, but see also Nash, *Race, Class, and Politics,* 173–210, 225–42. The period following the Seven Years War was one of rising expectations and, in all likelihood, that more than absolute wealth is the determining factor here. See Edmund S. Morgan, *Inventing the People* (New York: W. W. Norton and Co., 1988), 137.

18. See, e.g., Jensen, *Tracts;* and Bernard Bailyn, *Pamphlets of the American Revolution 1750–1765* (Cambridge, MA: Belknap, 1965).

19. We note a few important exceptions below. Reid provides an excellent analysis of liberty as a jurisprudential term. We discovered his work only after we completed our own reading of original documents, and we regard the agreement between our two accounts as something akin to verification by replication. Such support is useful for two readings that go so much against the grain of traditional historiography, so we note specific agreements with Reid as we proceed. But there are also some important differences: Reid seems to work from a Ramistic sense of rhetoric, focusing on formal and legal notions of languages; whereas we borrow from Isocrates and Aristotle to emphasize popular usages apart from systematic, philosophical, or formal language. Moreover, Reid features similarities of usage across the period, whereas we target changes. See John Phillip Reid, *The Concept of Liberty in the Age of the American Revolution* (Chicago: University of Chicago Press, 1988).

20. From the *Pennsylvania Journal,* reprinted in the *Maryland Gazette,* 13 October 1774, 1.

21. 25 May 1774, in *Maryland Gazette.* See also 26 May 1774, 2.

22. See Reid, *The Concept of Liberty,* 5, 71, 72. Contrary to Reid, we claim that the colonists used "liberty" in the sense of material property and thus invented a new meaning for the term.

23. Otis's version was, "Now can there be any liberty, where property is taken away without consent?" See James W. Otis, "The Rights of the British Colonies Asserted and Proved" (1764), in Jensen, *Tracts,* 27; and Samuel Adams, "A State of the Rights of the Colonists" (1772), in Jensen, *Tracts,* 240.

24. John Hancock, *An Oration Delivered March 5, 1774* (Newport, RI: S. Southwick, 1774), 6.

25. The *Constitutional Courant,* "Containing Matters Interesting to Liberty, and No Wise Repugnant to Loyalty" (1765), in Jensen, *Tracts,* 83.

26. Colonists could draw upon a heritage of elaborated rights concerning jury trials, search and seizure, standing armies, etc., that dated from the 1600s, and the documents articulating these rights influenced colonial conceptions of liberty, especially in the wake of such events as the Boston Massacre. Bailyn argues that these earlier documents "drop[ped] from prominence—but not from awareness." Hence echoes of these broader liberties remained in the later claim to defend "liberties." We maintain, however, that they took on greater significance in the revolutionary period than in the period of revolt. Contemporary usages were more important than earlier usages. Less contaminated by presentism, Reid argues more convincingly that *liberty* as an individual right was a later invention. In this period, it signified a government guided by a rule of law, much in line with the British custom. See Bernard Bailyn, *The Ideological Origins of the American Revolution* (Cambridge, MA: Belknap; Harvard University Press, 1967), 197; Reid, *The Concept of Liberty,* 120.

27. See, e.g., John Adams as Novanglus in Jensen *Tracts,* 277–349; Henry

Laurens, "Extracts from the Proceedings of the Court of Vice-Admiralty," in Jensen, *Tracts*, 185–206; *Massachusetts Spy*, 27–31 December 1770, 1.

28. *American Archives*, 4th ser., 1:597. See also the *Maryland Gazette*, June 1774.

29. *American Archives*, 4th ser., 1:377.

30. Stephen Hopkins, "The Rights of Colonies Examined" (1764), in Jensen, *Tracts*, 43.

31. *American Archives*, 4th ser., 1:596. Hanover County concurred, "We are freemen; we have a right to be so. . . . we shall never give up the right of taxation . . . this is the great badge of freedom," 615–16.

32. James Lovell, *An Oration Delivered April 2d, 1771* (Boston: Edes & Gill, 1771), 12.

33. See Joseph Warren, *An Oration Delivered March 5th, 1772* (Boston: Edes & Gill, 1772). This is typical of a substantial minority that emphasized the right to representation as fundamental rather than as subsidiary to the right to protect property.

34. "A Copy of the REMONSTRANCE of the Freeholders and Freemen of Anne-Arundel County," *Maryland Gazette*, 2d supp., 24 October 1765, along with the cases quoted above. See also Benjamin Church, *An Oration Delivered March Fifth, 1773* (Boston: Edes & Gill, 1773). The freeholders mixed claims to natural rights with constitutional claims, but they viewed their "natural rights" as evolving only as a natural birthright of Englishmen. Though not a "correct" appropriation of Locke, Sidney, or Pufendorf, this ambiguous importation of terms separated from another worldview was the norm rather than the exception. We discuss below how it holds for the conception of birthright as natural right. Reid confirms the sense of natural right as equivalent to the British Constitution: "What exists under the British constitution is natural, and it is natural because it exists." See Reid, *The Concept of Liberty*, 29.

35. 11 May, 1769. See also, e.g., Queen Anne (MD) Resolutions, 30 May 1774, in *American Archives*, 4th ser., 1:366; Norfolk, VA, to Charleston, SC, letter, 31 May 1774, *American Archives*, 4th ser., 1:370; etc.

36. Charleston, SC, 4 June 1774, *American Archives*, 4th ser., 1:382. See Reid, *The Concept of Liberty*, 29.

37. Andrew Eliot, *A Sermon Preached before His Excellency Francis Bernard 29 May 1765* (Boston: Green & Russell, 1765), 50.

38. Nash, *Race, Class, and Politics*, 101.

39. *Pennsylvania Chronicle and Universal Advertiser*, 11–18 October 1773. See also "We consider ourselves as FREEMEN, and entitled to all the rights and privileges of freeborn British subjects," reproduced in the *Connecticut Courant*, 16 October 1770.

40. *Maryland Gazette*, 24 October 1765; and "A Copy of the REMONSTRANCE of Freeholders Anne-Arundel County."

41. Letter, Charleston, SC, 4 June 1774, *American Archives*, 4th ser., 1:382.

42. British American, no. 5, 30 June 1774, *American Archives*, 4th ser., 1:495.

43. "The Rights of the British Colonies Asserted and Proved," in Jensen, *Tracts,* 27.

44. This is also evident in the arguments before the Continental Congress, where delegates suggested that "property" needed to be represented as well as individuals. See "Notes of John Adams on the debates in the Constitutional Convention, 5 Sept. 1774," in Henry Steele Commager and Richard B. Morris, eds., *The Spirit of Seventy-Six,* (Indianapolis: Bobbs-Merrill, 1958), 49–50.

45. Chilton Williamson, *American Suffrage: From Property to Democracy, 1760–1860* (Princeton: Princeton University Press, 1960), 3–19. For underlying issues on suffrage and democracy compare Milton M. Klein, "Democracy and Politics in Colonial New York," to J. R. Pole, "Historians and the Problem of Early American Democracy," in Paul Goodman, ed., *Essays in American Colonial History* (New York: Holt, Rinehart and Winston, 1967), 444–61, 462–85.

46. See Bailyn's discussion of the gradual dissolution of this assumption and the resistance to it in *Ideological Origins,* 301–19.

47. See John Locke, "Second Treatise," in *Two Treatises of Government,* ed. Peter Laslett (Cambridge: Cambridge University Press, 1988 [1698]), 302.

48. Reprinted in *Second Supplement to the Maryland Gazette,* 24 October 1765, 1. Note here that "natural right" is modified by "our" and confined to a special blessing rather than a universal entitlement of all persons.

49. That colonists routinely employed the term "privileges" without differentiating it from the term "rights" suggests that *rights* was less secure in this period than in our own. See Reid, *The Concept of Liberty,* 24, 29.

50. *New Year's Verses of Those Who Carry the Pennsylvania Journal,* 1 January 1774, Philadelphia, PA.

51. *Massachusetts Spy,* 14–16 August 1770, 1.

52. *Maryland Gazette,* 6 October 1774.

53. Advertisements often noted the relative English-speaking capabilities of Africans. See Allan Kulikoff, "The Origins of Afro-American Society in Tidewater Maryland and Virginia 1700–1790," *William and Mary Quarterly* 35 (1978): 231.

54. See Bailyn, *Ideological Origins,* 79; Winthrop Jordan, *White over Black: American Attitudes toward the Negro, 1550–1812* (Chapel Hill: University of North Carolina Press, 1968).

55. Kulikoff notes a death rate of 1/5 in the Middle Passage, 1/4 during first year in the Chesapeake, and 1/20 after arrival before sale, along with a gross disproportion in gender ratio in favor of males in the early period. See "Origins of Afro-American Society," 232, 233, 236, 241, 242. Goldston notes that in "the greatest migration in human history," fifteen million Africans were forcibly transported to the colonies, but by 1860 only three million slaves lived in the colonies. See Robert Goldston, *The Negro Revolution* (New York: Macmillan, 1968), 23, 90. Curtin corrects this figure, indicating ten million African-American slaves, but he notes, "The cost of the slave trade in human life was many times the number of slaves landed in the Americas," for the estimated loss of 12–33 percent of slaves in the Ocean passage was accompanied by a wide variety of other deaths, including during capture in Africa, on arrival in America, and after sale in America. See

Philip D. Curtin, *The Atlantic Slave Trade: A Census* (Madison: University of Wisconsin Press, 1969), 269, 275.

56. This happened intermittently in New York, and probably more frequently in the largely unrecorded popular oratory from western regions of many colonies. Becker notes that the divisions caused various leaders to adapt their rhetoric to portions of the populace who did not fit neatly into class divisions. Sometimes these clashes among interests encouraged persuasive competitions between elites, with rhetorical bids for popular support that resulted in elite leaders speaking popular rhetorics. See Becker, *History of Political Parties;* Carl Becker, J. M. Clark, and William E. Dodd, *The Spirit of '76 and Other Essays* (Washington, D.C.: Robert Brookings Graduate School, 1927).

57. Otis's comment that "when the pot boils, the scum will rise" is frequently cited to demonstrate the elitism of revolutionary leaders. See, e.g. Douglass, *Rebels and Democrats,* 12, 156; Bailyn, *Ideological Origins,* 302.

58. Different rhetors made greater and lesser compromises of their own interests and principles with those of the masses they hoped to motivate. Otis went the furthest, recognizing black citizens as well as white in an extremely egalitarian discourse—although he was noted for taking back some of what he was caught saying on other occasions. John Adams was far more skillful, and his rhetoric was far less egalitarian. Under the persona of Novanglus, e.g., Adams substituted an attack on character and the use of narrative for any substantial citation of principles. Hence he avoided endorsing egalitarianism or alienating the populace through expression of his own elitist principles.

59. Michael Calvin McGee, "In Search of 'the People': A Rhetorical Alternative," *QJS* 61 (1975): 235–49.

60. Undated, labeled "Which Is Not Dead, But Only Sleepeth," follows 31 October 1765. The deduction is extended to conclude that Americans are "equally intitled to Freedom," and, therefore, to taxation only through representation.

61. Cato's Letters, 8, in *Maryland Gazette,* 9 May 1776, 1.

62. Other nonconstitutive forms emphasizing magnitude were possible, as when Essex County proclaimed in its resolutions of 9 July 1774 that the colony's assembly was "equal in all respects to the purposes of legislation and taxation within this Colony," *American Archives,* 4th ser., 1:527.

63. E.g., "principles of equity" were described as grounding the colonists' revolt in Letter, Charleston, SC, 4 June 1774, *American Archives,* 4th ser., 1:382, reprinted in *Maryland Gazette,* 28 July 1774. See also the use of "equitable" by John Dickinson and Samuel Adams, in Jensen, *Tracts,* 127–63, 233–55.

64. This assertion of identity was to become a crucial sticking point in the contest between Anglo-American and African-American concepts of equality. An interesting instance of the difficulties with the mathematical concept lies in the otherwise nonegalitarian discourse of John Dickinson, who argues in his "Letters from a Farmer in Pennsylvania to the Inhabitants of the British Colonies," that "equal" means mathematically proportional. He says taxes are "most *equal,* by being proportioned to every man's circumstances. . . . Taxes in every free state have been, and ought to be, as exactly *proportioned as is possible to the abilities of those*

who are to pay them. They cannot otherwise be *just.* Even a Hottentot would comprehend the *unreasonableness* of making a poor man pay as much for 'defending' the property of a rich man, as the rich man pays himself." In Jensen, *Tracts,* 161.

65. *American Archives,* 4th ser., 1:377–78.

66. Jensen, *Tracts,* 42, 44, 45, 46.

67. "Votes and Proceedings of the Freeholders of Boston," in Jensen, *Tracts,* 236. The dominance of citations from pamphlets rather than newspapers or orations is representative. While some such usages occurred in these other forms, this was a generally rare usage that was most likely to appear in the disproportionately radical pamphlets.

68. See, e.g., *Maryland Gazette,* 24 November 1774; "Letter III to the Freemen of Massachusetts Bay," *Massachusetts Spy,* 23 April 1778. In Virginia and other Southern states, however, these usages were even more infrequent, and the phrase "equal value" dominated. See, e.g., *Virginia House Journal,* 5–26 May 1774.

69. *2nd Supplement to the Maryland Gazette,* 24 October 1765, 1.

70. From Williamsburg, VA, 7 July 1774, in *American Archives,* 4th ser., 1:519–22.

71. 14 July 1774, *American Archives,* 4th ser., 1:540. See also Hopkins in Jensen, *Tracts,* 44–62.

72. William Wirt's attribution to Patrick Henry notwithstanding, the slogan preferring death to slavery was fairly widespread long before the War for Independence was imminent. The earliest extended presentation of the ideographic vocabulary of "equality" in American public discourse occurs in John Wise, *A Vindication of the Government of New England Churches,* published in 1717. This had application to church governance rather than to civil polity and was not noticed by revolutionary orators.

73. Warren, *An Oration Delivered March 5th, 1772,* 6.

74. Church, *An Oration Delivered March Fifth, 1773,* 7.

75. *American Archives,* 4th ser., 1:542.

76. E.g., one of John Adams's strongest attacks in the Novanglus letters was launched against Governor Bernard for his consideration of establishing a hereditary American aristocracy. Some Southern proprietors viewed the matter differently, and there were a very few British nobility present in the colonies at various times. See also *Maryland Gazette,* 3 February 1774, reprint of Letter from London.

77. "The Whisperer, no. VI" 4–6 September 1770, 1. Note that the phrase limits the rights to Englishmen and thus excludes African slaves. The ability of the colonists to declare themselves equal to those in power without asserting the generality of equality is also evident in the battles for equal representation in various colonies. Pennsylvanians living on the frontiers used "equality" and its various roots with great frequency in asserting their right to a share in the colonies' government. At the same time, they asked for a reward for Indian scalps.

78. Richard Bland, "An Inquiry into the Rights of the British Colonies" (1766), in Jensen, *Tracts,* 122. Note that these rights are nonetheless limited to a "people" that as we indicate below excludes African slaves.

79. Daniel Shutes, *A Sermon Preached before His Excellency Francis Bernard, 25 May 1768* (Boston: Richard Draper, 1768), 13, 28.

80. John Tucker, *A Sermon Preached at Cambridge, 29 May 1771* (Boston: Richard Draper, 1771), 13.

81. Much energy has been devoted to tracing the familiarity of the elite colonists with Locke, Pufendorf, and Sidney. While references to these authors appeared with some regularity—although not with the frequency one is led to believe by some intellectual historians—they hardly ever occur with the term "EQUALITY." The elites cited these sources for their concern with various political rights but not "for all equally."

82. Daniel Dulany, "Consideration on the Propriety of Imposing Taxes in the British Colonies, for the Purpose of Raising a Revenue, by Act of Parliament" (1765), in Jensen, *Tracts*, 102.

83. Samuel West, *Sermon Preached before the Honorable House of Representatives, 29 May 1776* (Boston: Gill, 1776).

84. 23 February 1775; 29 August 1776.

85. See Nash, *Race, Class, and Politics*, 211–42.

86. Similar sentiments carried over to the revolutionary period. See, e.g., the comments of "Rationalis" printed in the *Gazettes* of both Pennsylvania and Maryland. See, e.g., *Maryland Gazette*, 7 March 1776.

87. On the importance of characterization see Celeste Michelle Condit, "Democracy and Civil Rights: Universalizing Influence of Public Argumentation," *Communication Monographs* 54 (1987): 1–18; John Louis Lucaites and Celeste Michelle Condit, "Reconstructing ⟨Equality⟩: Culturetypal and Counter-Cultural Rhetorics in the Martyred Black Vision," *Communication Monographs* 57 (1990): 5–24.

88. Gad Hitchcock, *A Sermon Preached before His Excellency Thomas Gage, 25 May 1774* (Boston: Edes & Gill, 1774), 20.

89. John Lathrop, *Innocent Blood Crying to God, Speech Delivered 5 March 1770* (Boston: Edes & Gill, 1771), iii.

90. Samuel Adams, "A State of the Right of the Colonists" (1772), in Jensen, *Tracts*, 235.

91. Warren, *Oration Delivered March Sixth, 1775* (Newport, RI: S. Southwick, 1775), 11.

92. "Notes of John Adams, September 8, 1774," in Commager and Morris, 51–52.

93. Lathrop, *Innocent Blood*, 8, 16.

94. Reprinted in *Maryland Gazette*, 20 July 1775.

95. Fairfax County (VA) Resolutions, 18 July 1774, *American Archives*, 4th ser., 1:598.

96. Warren, *An Oration Delivered March 5th, 1772*, 17.

97. 27 May 1774, *American Archives*, 4th ser., 1:350–51.

98. All of the Boston Massacre Orations save one employ the term; the same is true of our sample of election sermons. The pervasiveness of the term has also been noted in Paul K. Conkin, *Self-Evident Truths* (Bloomington: Indiana University

Press, 1974), 110: "Over and over again Americans indicted British policies as steps toward slavery or, in their most fervent exaggerations, as the very substance of slavery. No single word better expressed their fear." In the South the term was less frequent and was often replaced by "vassalage," but even here the usage was prevalent. See, e.g., *Connecticut Courant*'s usage of "vassalage and slavery" vs. "liberty," in 17 September 1770 or 31 March–14 April 1772.

99. Charles Turner, *A Sermon Preached before His Excellency, 26 May 1773* (Boston: Richard Draper, 1773), 36.

100. See, e.g., how *Massachusetts Spy*, 11–14 August 1770, 3, col. 1, uses "slaves" and later implies its opposition to the "Sons of Liberty."

101. "To the Inhabitants of the Province of South Carolina," 6 July 1774, *American Archives*, 4th ser., 1:511; Warren, *Oration Delivered March 6th, 1775*, 6.

102. This is the earliest date at which one might cite the beginnings of the transition from a rhetoric of revolt to a rhetoric of revolution, but the pattern was uneven, extending until the 1780s in some parts of the South and beginning before 1774 in the minds of some in Boston.

103. Tucker, "*A[n] Election Sermon*," 58.

104. 24 May 1774, *American Archives*, 4th ser., 1:348.

105. Ibid., 4th ser., 1:559.

106. Most scholars of the period offer a broad range of reasons that presumably motivated the slave trade, but generally they end up focusing attention most fully on the economic motive. For an example of the view that treats the broad range of motives see Mary Stoughton Locke, *Anti-Slavery in America* (Gloucester, MA: Peter Smith, 1965); for an example of the view that focuses most directly on the economic arguments of the period see Theodore D. Jervey, *The Slave Trade: Slavery and Color* (New York: Negro Universities Press, 1969 [1925]). John Hope Franklin interprets anti-importation sentiment as a response to the Caribbean uprisings in *From Slavery to Freedom* (New York: Alfred A. Knopf, 1948). Duncan J. MacLeod focuses on cultural purity as a motivating argument in *Slavery, Race and the American Revolution* (London: Cambridge University Press, 1974), 31–32.

107. Fairfax County (VA) Resolutions, 18 July 1774, *American Archives*, 4th ser., 1:600, call slavery "a wicked, cruel and unnatural trade."

108. *American Archives*, 4th ser., 1:530, 541. See also Surry County, 593. Hanover County walks a line between the moral focus of Fairfax County and the economic concerns of the others.

109. Bailyn, *Ideological Origins*, 234. It seems anachronistic to claim that the general philosophies of the eighteenth century on slavery "applied equally to the black plantation laborers in American colonies, for their condition was only a more dramatic, more bizarre variation of the condition of all who had lost the power of self-determination." From our contemporary perspective it applies "equally," but given the codings of the larger philosophy we elaborate here, it was not at all "obvious" to all of the colonists. Bailyn notes (238) the prominent writers who *did not* mention African slavery. This simply suggests that those who noticed the analogy saw over significant discursive barriers; they were perceptive, and that perception was important, but it was not a mass neurosis or evil that kept the majority from

seeing this analogy. Rather, it was a concrete set of discourses that shaped their perceptions and kept them from even conceiving of the possibility that *they* might be enslaved *in the way* they had enslaved the Africans.

110. *Constitutional Courant,* in Jensen, *Tracts,* 89.

111. *Massachusetts Spy,* 7 August 1770, 3, col. 1; report from *New London Gazette.*

112. Dickinson, in Jensen, *Tracts,* 138.

113. See Jordan, *White over Black,* 44–98.

114. The argument between Reid and Okoye on this subject is crucial. Both agree that the colonists frequently cited slavery in other lands. Reid correctly argues that the usage of the word "slavery" was most frequently cast in terms of political slavery and modeled on foreign countries rather than being cast in terms of chattel slavery and modeled on the domestic scene. Okoye's argument is less clear, but he indicates, and we agree, that there is a great deal of indirect discourse that shows the colonists thinking about chattel slavery. However, Okoye's argument needs to be more precise. Many of the metaphors and images he cites are applicable to political slavery as well as chattel slavery, and hence they do not conclusively indicate the colonists' reference to chattel slavery. The resolution of the impasse is to say that the colonists deliberately used the older, British rhetoric of political slavery, and less consciously attempted to sublate their own experiences of chattel slavery. They succeeded fairly well at the value level. However, images of chattel slavery crept into their discourse at the narrative level. This dual characterization of the argument helps to understand *how* the abolitionists subverted the antipolitical slavery argument, making it an antichattel slavery argument with such ease, i.e., the rhetors had experienced the similarities even when they tried not to express them. See Reid, *The Concept of Liberty,* 48–54; and Mwabueze F. Okoye, "Chattel Slavery as the Nightmare of the American Revolutionaries," *William and Mary Quarterly,* 37 (1980): 3–28.

115. Church, *An Oration Delivered March Fifth, 1773,* 9, 13.

116. "To the Inhabitants of the Province South Carolina," 6 July 1774, *American Archives,* 4th ser., 1:512.

117. *Connecticut Courant,* 16 October 1770, 1.

118. Bailyn, *Ideological Origins,* 231–46. Consider, e.g., the Vermont Constitution's antislavery clause, and the eventual emancipation in various forms in Pennsylvania, Massachusetts, Rhode Island, Connecticut between 1781–84. See Goldston, *The Negro Revolution,* 56.

119. Were our focus on a precise description of the demographic location of the various rhetorics, we would argue that the egalitarian component of the discourse (that of "human rights") of this period was located (1) in the nondominant portions of the population, i.e., those who were *relatively* less successful economically and/or were geographically isolated; (2) in those orators who motivated crowds to act; and (3) in the writings and speaking of a few exceptional thinkers. We would find the nonegalitarian portions of the discourse (that of "American rights") located in the majority of the "founders" or leaders of the revolt against Britain. Both segments of the population became antiloyalist. The former group advocated those

egalitarian components of the constitution that develop in the revolutionary period. The latter group advocated the need to preserve property interests through elite mechanisms of control.

CHAPTER THREE

1. Donald L. Robinson, *Slavery in the Structure of American Politics 1765–1820* (New York: Harcourt Brace Jovanovich, 1971), 5, 8; David Brion Davis, *The Problem of Slavery in the Age of Revolution 1770–1823* (Ithaca, NY: Cornell University Press, 1975), 82, 84, 335; Duncan J. MacLeod, *Slavery, Race and the American Revolution* (London: Cambridge University Press, 1974), 1; Bernard Bailyn, *The Ideological Origins of the American Revolution* (Cambridge, MA: Belknap; Harvard University Press, 1967), 246; Edmund S. Morgan *American Slavery, American Freedom: The Ordeal of Colonial Virginia* (New York: W. W. Norton and Co., 1975), 4.

2. Leon F. Litwack, *North of Slavery: The Negro in the Free States, 1790–1860* (Chicago: University of Chicago Press, 1961), 6. Forrest McDonald provides an exception in *Novus Ordo Seclorum: The Intellectual Origins of the Constitution* (Lawrence: University Press of Kansas, 1985), 50–55, but he is entirely too cursory in denying any ideological tension at all.

3. Davis, *The Problem of Slavery,* 85–92.

4. John Locke, "First Treatise," in *Two Treatises of Government* (Cambridge: Cambridge University Press, 1988 [1698]), para. 130. See also Ruth W. Grant, *John Locke's Liberalism* (Chicago: University of Chicago Press, 1987), 68.

5. In Bernard Schwartz, ed., *The Bill of Rights: A Documentary History* (New York: Chelsea House, 1971), 216.

6. Thomas Paine, "Common Sense" (1776), in Merrill Jensen, ed., *Tracts of the American Revolution 1763–1776* (Indianapolis: Bobbs Merrill, 1977), 413. See also 431, 433, 434, 443.

7. Wills argues that the Declaration of Independence was not widely assented to. His argument relies, however, on separating the *words* of the document from *the performative act* of declaring. Since he finds no places where the exact wording and the performative act were directly referenced together, he follows Detweiler in claiming that there was no impact. The weave of the sieve seems too small. While we would not make a casual argument (Jefferson himself was wiser than that), our analysis indicates the aptness of Jefferson's dedication of the war. At the same time we note its limited scope. See Garry Wills, *Inventing America: Jefferson's Declaration of Independence* (New York: Doubleday, 1978), 324–33; Philip F. Detweiler, "The Changing Reputation of the Declaration of Independence: The First Fifty Years," *William and Mary Quarterly* 19 (1962): 557–74.

8. Jonathan Williams Austin, *An Oration Delivered March 5th, 1778* (Boston: Edes & Fleet, 1778), 14.

9. William Tudor, *An Oration Delivered March 5th, 1779* (Boston: Edes & Gill, 1779), 5.

10. *Maryland Gazette,* 24 July 1788, 2.

11. Ibid., 23 June 1780, 1. In like fashion, South Carolina carefully worded its

1778 Constitution so as to emphasize the agreements of "the freemen of this State." See also Pennsylvania's Declaration of Rights where it underscores the rights of "freemen." In Schwartz, *The Bill of Rights*, 263–75.

12. McDonald, *Novus Ordo Seclorum*, 26–27. Gradually, however, the direct contact with chattel slavery in America would create a more direct discursive opposition between "freemen" and American "slaves." This becomes particularly evident in the more frequent usage of "freemen" in the rhetoric of the slaveocracy who preferred it to the more inclusive "all men" that became prevalent in Northern rhetoric.

13. In Schwartz, *The Bill of Rights*, 263.

14. *Maryland Gazette*, 24 July 1788, 2.

15. Allan Kulikoff, "The Origins of Afro-American Society in Tidewater Maryland and Virginia 1700 to 1790," *William and Mary Quarterly* 35 (1978): 236–37; Robert Goldston, *The Negro Revolution* (New York: Macmillan, 1968), 77–82. See also *Niles's Weekly Register*, 16 and 29 May 1819, 233–34; Peter H. Wood, *Black Majority: Negroes in Colonial South Carolina from 1670 through the Stono Rebellion* (New York: Alfred A. Knopf, 1974), 250.

16. MacLeod, *Slavery, Race and the American Revolution*, 152–154; Gary B. Nash, *Red, White and Black: The Peoples of Early America* (Englewood Cliffs, NJ: Prentice-Hall, 1974), 200; John W. Blassingame, *The Slave Community: Plantation Life in the Antebellum South* (New York and Oxford: Oxford University Press, 1979), 230–33, 237; Robinson, *Slavery in the Structure of American Politics*, 33, 36–37; *Annals of Congress*, 16th Cong., 2d sess., 83–86.

17. Free blacks probably voted in some of the assemblies for constitutional ratification in the North, but almost certainly not in the South.

18. *Maryland Gazette*, 24 July 1788, 2.

19. Jonathon Elliot, *The Debates in the Several State Conventions on the Adoption of the Federal Constitution* (New York: Burt Franklin, 1888), 4:153. See also Benjamin Hichborn, *An Oration Delivered July 5th, 1784* (Boston: Gill, 1784). John Phillip Reid characterizes this as an inherited extension of the practices of British discourse in *The Concept of Liberty in the Age of the American Revolution* (Chicago: University of Chicago Press, 1988), 25–30.

20. Moses Hemmenway, *A Sermon Preached before His Excellency John Hancock* (Boston: Edes & Gill, 1784), 29.

21. *Maryland Gazette*, 24 November 1780, 1.

22. Ibid., 1 January 1789, 1.

23. Jonathan Mason, *An Oration Delivered March 6, 1780* (Boston: Gill, 1780), 21.

24. *Maryland Gazette*, 9 August 1781.

25. Peter Thacher, *An Oration Delivered at Watertown, March 5, 1776* (Watertown: Benjamin Edes, 1776), 14.

26. Elliot, *Debates*, 2:150.

27. This is evident in Congress where some advocates explicitly denied any breadth of scope to either the Declaration of Independence or the concept of natural rights. See, e.g., *Annals of Congress*, 16th Cong., 1st sess., 1149, 1154, and 1071;

Henry Clay, *Annals of Congress,* 9th Cong., 2d sess., 227. Some eventually went so far as to deny equality altogether. See, e.g., *Annals of Congress,* 16th Cong., 1st sess., 1384.

28. *Maryland Gazette,* 26 April 1787, 3.

29. Hemmenway, *Sermon,* 9–10.

30. See Max Farrand, ed., *The Records of the Federal Convention of 1787,* 2 vols. (New Haven: Yale University Press, 1937).

31. McDonald, *Novus Ordo Seclorum,* 27. For examples see *Maryland Gazette,* 8 January 1785, 12 April 1781, 16 June 1780.

32. See McDonald, *Novus Ordo Seclorum,* 53–55. McDonald lists five different "general usages" for the word "equality" in the eighteenth century. In each instance he relies on the discourse of jurists and philosophers to define the range of meanings that the term expressed, rejecting the usages of common authors who, he claims, failed to "specify what [they] meant" by such terms as "freedom" or "equality" because they assumed that their "readers needed no instruction on the matter" (9). From our perspective, common public usages, though sometimes informed by legal and philosophical discourse, are not *determined* by them. We take it as significant, e.g., that a speaker or writer would craft their discourse on the presumption of specific audience understandings, and indeed would employ such presumptions to enhance the force of their persuasion. The meanings of such terms are a function of their specific usages in practice and not simply a function of a priori definitions. Thus, the five abstract categories for the meaning of equality that McDonald develops derive from eighteenth-century law and philosophy but do not necessarily represent the ways in which the colonists understood those terms when used in popular discourse. See Clinton Rossiter, *Seedtime of the Republic* (New York: Harcourt, Brace and Co., 1953), 1, where he emphasizes that the American ideology was not a product of imported philosophies but of indigenous American experience.

33. The editorial in the *Maryland Gazette* on 26 November 1779 argued against separating people from their governors but suggested that they must be paid at a level that maintained the dignity of their "rank." This was typical of the constitutional debates which referred routinely to the different "classes" of people. See Farrand, *Records,* 1:49.

34. Wills, *Inventing America,* 218–28.

35. Farrand, *Records,* 1:180. See also Patterson at 178, 274.

36. Eugene D. Genovese, *Roll, Jordan, Roll: The World the Slaves Made* (New York: Vintage Books, 1974), 36–37.

37. See Wills, *Inventing America,* passim.

38. See McDonald, *Novus Ordo Seclorum,* 52; John Hope Franklin, *The Free Negro in North Carolina 1790–1860* (Chapel Hill: University of North Carolina Press, 1943), 150; John Henderson Russell, "The Free Negro in Virginia 1619–1865" (Ph.D. diss. Johns Hopkins University, 1913), 88.

39. Reid, *The Concept of Liberty,* 120.

40. On the consensus of opinions concerning the meanings of Liberty cf. McDonald, *Novus Ordo Seclorum,* 10, with Schwartz, *The Bill of Rights,* 232–33.

41. This pattern is repeated in many of the state constitutions as well. The sole exceptions concern the right to a jury trial and search and seizure protection, two areas in which the rights of the free blacks were typically preserved.

42. The Continental Congress referred to equal representation as "the first grand right . . . of the people [to] share in their own government [through] representatives chosen by themselves." See Schwartz, *The Bill of Rights*, 222. The majority of the members of the Constitutional Convention imperiled this right, as they preferred representation of Property to that of people. However, in public during ratification, the sharp shift back to the concept of popular representation appears most clearly in Elbridge Gerry's "Observations on the New Constitution, and on the Federal and State Convention," which changed from a preference to property to the claim that "the fundamental principle of a free government is the equal representation of a free people." In Paul Leicester Ford, *Pamphlets on the Constitution of the United States, Published during Its Discussion by the People 1787–88* (New York: DaCapo Press, 1968), 8. See also the Massachusetts debate in Elliot, *Debates*, 2: 25, 29.

43. Elliot, *Debates*, 2: 88. See also Pelatiah Webster, "The Weakness of Brutus Exposed: or Some Remarks in Vindication of the Constitution," in Ford, *Pamphlets*, 114.

44. Elliot, *Debates*, 2:523.

45. *Maryland Gazette*, 3 May 1787, 1 and 2.

46. See, e.g., Noah Webster, "An Examination into the Leading Principles of the Federal Constitution"; and Tench Coxe, "An Examination of the Constitution of the United States of America," in Ford, *Pamphlets*, 35, 145.

47. Merit was defined in terms of commercial virtues like "industry" as well as more general notions of Anglo-Christian fairness and morality. Elbridge Gerry called for the "just preference of merit" before the Constitutional Convention. See Farrand, *Records*, 1:132. See also the satire of Aesop in the *Maryland Gazette*, 27 December 1781, 1; Coxe, "An Examination of the Constitution . . ."; Richard Henry Lee, "Observations of the System of Government Proposed by the Late Convention," in Ford, *Pamphlets*, 146, 295. See also Morris in Farrand, *Records*, 583.

48. Paine, in Jensen, *Tracts*, 410.

49. Eventually, slaveholders elaborated a paternalist ideology that characterized the fatherly role as representing the slaves' own best interests, but this was *after* Great Britain's use of the "family" metaphor to justify its oppression of the colonists had been conveniently repressed.

50. We believe the analogy is a good one, defensible on many grounds. Nevertheless, it is still an analogy, not a logically overdetermined case of identity.

51. Hemmenway, *Sermon*, 27, 37. For further details, see Robinson, *Slavery in the Structure of American Politics*, 295–346.

52. Farrand, *Records*, 2:222. McDonald argues that the colonists opposed fresh enslavement, and hence the continued importation of slaves, but that they had no difficulty with the institution of slavery itself. This is not precisely correct. It is true that there was a widely shared opposition to fresh enslavement. However, it is also

the case that a substantial group of colonists opposed continued enslavement, some on grounds of rights, others on grounds of expediency, and some on grounds of morality. Even if they held the balance of power, however, their equal respect for the "property" prevented them from acting. It is possible to oppose slavery with regard to one principle but tolerate it with regard to a separate value. See McDonald, *Novus Ordo Seclorum*, 50–52.

53. Davis, *The Problem of Slavery*, 87–89; Robinson, *Slavery in the Structure of American Politics*, 36–37; Litwack, *North of Slavery*, 3 n.1.

54. Many Southerners felt more than a twinge of regret on egalitarian grounds, but more frequently on grounds generated by the material conditions of slavery. Such reactions reflected a personal morality that stood outside the public constitutive values defined through the community of discourse in which the slaveholders expressed their collective interests. Often they were traced to religious communities of discourse.

55. In Farrand, *Records*, 2:364. The conflict between "family" responsibilities and egalitarian principles was more evident in nonofficial discourse. See, e.g., "A True Friend to the Union," *Maryland Gazette*, 25 November 1790, 3. The property principle also camouflaged a crucial shift in value premises. During the period when Southerners willingly apologized for slavery (while insisting on the necessity of maintaining it), they used the individualist right to property as a warrant. Once pushed to the point of defending slavery on moral grounds, however, they recharacterized the property interests as collective ones related to the need to develop land and territories. The turning point for this argument seems to emerge in *Annals of Congress*, 1st Cong., 2d sess., 1459–60.

56. Forrest McDonald gives property its dues in both *Novus Ordo Seclorum*, 3–22, and *E Pluribus Unum: The Formation of the American Republic 1776–1790* (Indianapolis: Liberty Press, 1979 [1965]), but it disappears in otherwise important works by Bailyn, *Ideological Origins*; Edmund S. Morgan, *Inventing the People: The Rise of Popular Sovereignty in England and America* (New York: W. W. Norton and Co., 1988); Charles L. Mee, Jr., *The Genius of the People* (New York: Harper and Row, 1987). One of the most interesting and important treatments of property is offered by Stephen E. Lucas in *Portents of Rebellion* (Philadelphia: Temple University Press, 1976), 32, where he distinguishes public discourse on the basis of "first order" and "second order" economic interests. See also Jennifer Nedelsky, *Private Property and the Limits of American Constitutionalism* (Chicago: University of Chicago Press, 1990).

57. Farrand, *Records*, 1:533, 534, 541, 542.

58. Ibid., 1:593.

59. Alexander Hamilton, James Madison, and John Jay, *The Federalist* (New York: Heritage Press, 1945), e.g., nos. 62 and 63; Elliot, *Debates*, vols. 2–5.

60. On the disruptions see Gordon S. Wood, *The Creation of the American Republic 1776–1787* (Chapel Hill: University of North Carolina Press, 1969), 234–35.

61. Farrand, *Records*, 1:422–23.

62. Delegates expressing such views directly included Gouverneur Morris, William Richardson Davie, Pierce Butler, Rufus King, John Rutledge, William

Samuel Johnson, George Mason, James Madison, Alexander Hamilton, William Paterson, John Dickinson, Edmund Randolph, Hugh Williamson, Charles Pinckney, General Charles Coatesworth Pinckney, and Elbridge Gerry. Gerry was the most outspoken proponent of what amounted to a nonhereditary aristocracy. Others, especially Madison, shifted back and forth. Only James Wilson and Benjamin Franklin seem consistently populist. Nathaniel Ghorum and Dickinson made some strong defenses of the populace. The delegates themselves seem confused about the relationship of property to wealth. Some project two classes including the wealth/propertied and the nonpropertied, and others project three classes including the nonpropertied, the nonwealthy propertied, and the wealthy propertied.

63. Farrand, *Records,* 1:150.

64. Ibid., 1:48, 49, 57, 58, 66, 80.

65. Ibid., 1:142.

66. The separation of Federalists and Anti-Federalists in the Constitutional Convention on the basis of wealth fails to recognize that most of the conventioneers were more or less of one class. There were no poor men here. More important, ideology is only indirectly related to economics. Jefferson was wealthy after the planter fashion, and yet he was one of the more egalitarian voices. That does not mean that there are not broad economic tendencies. See Charles A. Beard, *An Economic Interpretation of the Constitution of the United States* (New York: Macmillan, 1921); Raymie E. McKerrow, "Critical Rhetoric: Theory and Praxis," *Communication Monographs* 56 (1989): 94.

67. Elliot, *Debates,* 2:302, 322. For a colorful portrait of the rich and poor at war over the Constitution see McDonald, *E Pluribus Unum,* 333–71.

68. Elliot, *Debates,* 2:75.

69. Ibid., 2:102. Singletary represents the "landed" vs. "commercial" interest, but such identification relies too heavily on categories of economic well-being.

70. Elliot, *Debates,* 2:245.

71. Ibid., 2:257, 260, 276.

72. Federalism and antifederalism broke down more strictly along different lines. In the state conventions, "liberty" was the key term of the Anti-Federalists, whereas "order," "efficiency," "strength," and "stability" dominated Federalist discourse.

73. Article IV, Sec. 3 protects government Property.

74. This is both a chronological fact and a logical entailment. Before the resolution of this controversy, the term "property" dominated discussions, as did observations on class-based behaviors. Afterward both virtually disappeared. By shifting the discussion to the "equality of states," and refederalizing the Constitution, the issue of "who" was to be represented was replaced by "which states" were to be represented. The issue of individual property was thus obviated.

75. Farrand, *Records,* 1:138.

76. Ibid., 1:151.

77. *Maryland Gazette,* 27 December 1781.

78. Farrand, *Records,* 1:583.

79. The price of such accommodation is sometimes high. During the Jacksonian era the working class was able to negotiate a doctrine of "equal opportunity" precisely because aristocracy had not been formally enshrined in the Constitution.

80. For an excellent examination of the particularities of the inclusion of slavery in the text of the Constitution see Donald Nieman, *Promises to Keep: African-Americans and the Constitutional Order, 1776 to the Present* (New York: Oxford University Press, 1991), 5–24.

81. Farrand, *Records,* 1:594.

82. Elliot, *Debates,* 2:41. Many Anti-Federalists argued against this accommodation, but largely on the grounds that the three-fifths compromise increased Southern voting power. This is not to question the sincerity of their opposition to slavery but only to note that they expressed their opposition in part as a strategic play for additional Northern representation. The Northern acceptance of Property Rights as superseding Equal Rights also was widespread in the Congressional debates of the era, and particularly visible in the response to petitions seeking revision of the Northwest Ordinance. See MacLeod, *Slavery, Race, and the American Revolution,* 58.

83. *Maryland Gazette,* 18 May 1786, 3.

84. Robinson, *Slavery in the Structure of American Politics,* 27–30, 33–38.

85. E.g., *Maryland Gazette,* 15 November 1781.

86. *The Federalist,* no. 54, 366.

87. Ibid., no. 54, 368.

88. See Davis, *The Problem of Slavery,* 82. Historically, conservatives claim that liberty and equality are incompatible, but this assumes that liberty implies property. Some aspects of liberty and property are themselves contradictory.

89. Confusion about the extent of antislavery sentiment in the Upper South arises in large measure from the split between Southern leaders such as Jefferson and their more proslavery constituents. See Allan Kulikoff, *Tobacco and Slaves: The Development of Southern Cultures in the Chesapeake, 1680–1800* (Chapel Hill: University of North Carolina Press, 1986), 433; John W. Blassingame, *The Slave Community: Plantation Life in the Antebellum South,* 78; Davis, *The Problem of Slavery,* 204. In the state conventions, South Carolina expressed a proslavery sentiment (Elliot, *Debates,* 4:272–73) while North Carolina expressed an antislavery sentiment (Elliot, *Debates,* 4:30, 100). Robinson notes that the "first unqualified and extensive justification of slavery in the national Congress" occurred in 1781. See Robinson, *Slavery in the Structure of American Politics,* 104.

90. Farrand, *Records,* 2:371; Elliot, *Debates,* 2:42, 452.

91. This provides an additional explanation for the tortured responses of Southerners to the issue over time, and the misunderstandings that emerged between North and South. Both are ably described by Robinson, *Slavery in the Structure of American Politics.*

92. See the debates in the Constitutional Convention. Until the point at which the large state/small controversy arose, representation and governance were dis-

cussed on the basis of individuals. After that issue arose, however, Equal Representation was applied to the equality between states, not individuals.

93. As we will indicate in Chapter 4, the Equal Rights vocabulary was actually not the most popular public reason for abolition. The primary public warrants for abolition included appeals to Christian morality, economic expedience, and the inhumane mistreatment of slaves. See, e.g., George Mason in Farrand, *Records*, 2:370; Gouverneur Morris in Farrand, *Records*, 2:221-374.

94. See, e.g., the petition to the Virginia Assembly from Northampton City in which the signers agreed that they would neither rent to free negroes nor deal with them economically. In *New England Magazine* 2 (April 1832): 280. See also Litwack, *North of Slavery*, 101.

95. John M. Werner, *Reaping the Bloody Harvest: Race Riots in the United States during the Age of Jackson 1824–1849* (New York: Garland Publishing, 1986).

96. Elliot, *Debates*, 3:297.

97. See Randolph and Mason in Farrand, *Records*, 1:66, 101. The point is similarly made in the Virginia and North Carolina debates in Elliot, *Debates*, 3:448 and 4:29. On "homogeneity" see Wood, *Creation of the American Republic*, 58.

98. Rossiter, *Seedtime of the Republic*, 94.

99. Tudor, *An Oration Delivered March 5th, 1779*, 6.

100. Phillips Payson, "Election Sermon, 27 May 1788," *The Pulpit of the American Revolution*, ed. John W. Thornton (Boston: D. Lothrop and Co., 1876), 330.

101. Paine in Jensen, *Tracts*, 421.

102. *Maryland Gazette*, 20 January 1785, 1.

103. Elliot, *Debates*, 2:119.

104. Mechal Sobel, *The World They Made Together: Black and White Values in Eighteenth Century Virginia* (Princeton: Princeton University Press, 1987); Blassingame, *The Slave Community*, 31, 20, 41. See also Genovese, *Roll, Jordan, Roll*, 184–85, 210–13; John Hope Franklin, *From Slavery to Freedom: A History of Negro Americans*, 5th ed. (New York: Knopf, 1988 [1947]), 19–21; Kulikoff, *Tobacco and Slaves*, 347.

105. Sterling Stuckey, *Slave Culture: Nationalist Theory and the Foundations of Black America* (New York: Oxford University Press, 1987), 3–97.

106. Peter H. Wood, *Black Majority: Negroes in Colonial South Carolina from 1670 through the Stono Rebellion* (New York: Alfred A. Knopf, 1974), 138–39, 272; Sobel, *The World They Made Together*, 184.

107. *Maryland Gazette*, 21 April 1780, 1. See also Blassingame, *The Slave Community*, 162; and Wood, *Black Majority*, 140–41.

108. *Maryland Gazette*, 21 April 1780, 1. It should be noted that while religious differences were symptomatic, they were not the only point of cultural conflict. As Sobel points out, the values of the politically active leaders of the colonies clashed with African values regarding such matters as time orientation, work schedules, dress, and language. As time went on, however, the two value systems interpenetrated, at least in the South. See Sobel, *The World They Made Together*, 15–30, 154–64; Wood, *Black Majority*, 179.

109. Farrand, *Records*, 1:579 and 2:3–8.

110. Rossiter, *Seedtime of the Republic*, 93–95. In the South, the family structure was the most pressing form of government, since most people lived outside of the cities and beyond the reach of effective regulation. Moreover, Southern patriarchs tended to represent their families in larger governmental forms. In the North, bloodlines and family were particularly important in determining governance in New England. See Bernard Bailyn, *The Ordeal of Thomas Hutchinson* (Cambridge, MA: Belknap; Harvard University Press, 1974); and *The New England Merchants in the Seventeenth Century* (Cambridge, MA: Harvard University Press, 1955). Cf. Patricia U. Bonomi, *A Factious People: Politics and Society in Colonial New York* (New York: Columbia University Press, 1971).

111. Farrand, *Records*, 2:236.

112. *New England Magazine* 2 April 1832, 274.

113. Hemphill (December 1820), *The Negro in the Congressional Record*, 10 vols., comp. Peter M. Bergman and Jean McCarroll (New York: Bergman Publications, 1970), 7:662.

114. *Annals of Congress*, 16th Cong., 2d sess., 550; (December 1820), 550; *The Negro in the Congressional Record*, 641. Note also Smythe of Virginia who posed the question: "Who, then are citizens of the United States? I would answer, 1st, those subjects of Great Britain, who, being entitled to all the rights and privileges of British subjects, became American citizens by the Revolution." He notes second that those naturalized are citizens, but naturalization bills expressly prohibited the naturalization of blacks. See Smythe, *The Negro in the Congressional Record*, 7:645.

115. *Annals of Congress*, 16th Cong., 2d sess., 1134. With some exceptions, the passport office refused to grant blacks petition for passports on the grounds that they were not citizens. Several states even moved to pass laws that explicitly excluded free blacks from rights in the government (and in some cases from the right to inhabit the state) for the same reason.

116. 19 Howard 393 (1857). The sections of the text separated by ellipses are not in the same order as in the original.

117. Farrand, *Records*, 2:3–6.

118. The corporal metaphor was pervasive, and since its linkage with brethren and bloodlines was literal, it was in all probability not coincidental. See, e.g., Elliot, *Debates*, 2:458; and Wood, *Creation of the American Republic*, 335, 362, 366.

119. *The Negro Population in the United States 1790–1915* (New York: Arno Press, 1965), 53. In Virginia, the state with the most conflicting emotions on emancipation, the population mushroomed from 3,000 in 1782 to 13,000 in 1790 and 37,000 in 1820. See MacLeod, *Slavery, Race, and the American Revolution*, 227n.5. As Robinson notes in *Slavery in the Structure of American Politics*, this is a major cause for the apparent shift in the attitudes of Virginians (and others) on the issue of emancipation. They increasingly refused to emancipate because that would require living with a black population that constituted nearly 50 percent of the total state population in Virginia. By 1820, there would be 250,000 free blacks. See P. J. Staudenraus, *The African Colonization Movement 1816–1865* (New York: Columbia University Press, 1961), 15.

120. See Litwack, *North of Slavery*, 153–86; John Hope Franklin, *The Free Negro in North Carolina, 1790–1860* (Chapel Hill: University of North Carolina Press, 1943), 157–59.

121. American Colonization Society (hereafter ACS), *Ninth Annual Report of the American Society for Colonizing the Free People of Colour of the United States* (Washington City: Way and Gideon, 1826), 6.

122. Alice Dana Adams, *The Neglected Period of Anti-Slavery in America (1808–1831)* (Boston: Ginn, 1908).

123. The varying fortunes of the Society itself are not completely indicative of the popularity of its ideology, but they are a rough and useful sign. The Society's ebb and flow is charted in Staudenraus, *The African Colonization Movement*, 135, 148, 168, 187, 241, 242–46.

124. E.g., *Southern Review* 1 (1828): 219; *New England Magazine* 2 (1832): 13.

125. Thomas Jefferson, *Notes on the State of Virginia* (Chapel Hill: University of North Carolina Press, 1955), 138.

126. Early Lee Fox, *The American Colonization Society 1817–1840* (Baltimore: Johns Hopkins University Press, 1919), 39. See also *North American Review* 41 (1835): 170–93.

127. Reprinted from 14 January in the *Maryland Gazette* of 30 January 1817, 2.

128. *Annals of Congress,* 14th Cong., 2d sess., 939–41.

129. Fox, *The American Colonization Society,* 15.

130. The *Maryland Gazette* appeared to be an antislavery paper. E.g., on 10 September 1807 it printed a piece that presented blacks as arguing for equal rights, and it promoted dry-field rice cultivation on the grounds that "none but blacks are able, it is said, to cultivate inland rice; and the circumstance has been a prime reason for slavery. This will be altogether changed [unreadable] in case a sufficient quantity of rice can be [unreadable] profitably from dry than overflowed ground." It also printed a "debate" on slavery, in which both sides agreed with the need for abolition but disagreed on the feasibility and means of effecting it. See *Maryland Gazette,* 11 November 1790 through 30 December 1790, inclusive. The *Gazette* gave extensive and favorable coverage to the Colonization Society. See also Franklin, *The Free Negro in North Carolina,* 203.

131. See Fox, *The American Colonization Society* and any of the ACS annual reports. See also "Colonization and Emancipation" and "Union of Colonizationists and Abolitionists," both in *The Spirit of the Pilgrims* 6 (1833): 322–29, 396–402; *Niles's Weekly Register,* 4 October 1817, 13 and 82.

132. Franklin, *From Slavery to Freedom,* 161; MacLeod, *Slavery, Race, and the American Revolution,* 105. See also William Lloyd Garrison's, *The Liberator.* A contemporary account of the reasons for opposition to the society by abolitionists is provided in "Union of Colonizationists and Abolitionists" by "William Penn" and submitted by Arthur Tappan to *The Spirit of the Pilgrims,* 6 (1833): 569–78. See also William Jay, "Inquiry into the Character and Tendency of the American Colonization, and American Anti-Slavery Societies," *Miscellaneous Writings on Slavery* (New York: Negro Universities Press, 1968), 7–206.

133. ACS, *Third Annual Report* (1820), 29.

134. ACS, *Memorial of the President and Board of Managers of the American Colonization Society* (Washington: Gales and Seaton, 1820), 6.

135. Henry Clay, "On African Colonization," in Daniel Mallory, ed., *The Life and Speeches of the Honorable Henry Clay* (Hartford, CT: Silas Andrus, 1855), 581.

136. ACS, *Seventh Annual Report* (1824), 105. As time went by and abolitionism gained strength in the North, the rhetoric of the ACS became more sympathetic to slavery. Later annual reports reflect this shift.

137. "Memorial to Congress" in *Maryland Gazette*, 30 January 1817, 2.

138. ACS, *Seventh Annual Report*, 105.

139. *North American Review* 35 (1832): 146.

140. Clay, "On African Colonization," 574.

141. "Memorial to Congress," 2. See also the various annual reports. The missionizing impulse was a strong and consistent, if perplexing, vein of argument. It viewed blacks as fully capable of transmitting Anglo-American civilization to Africa, even as it portrayed them as separate from that civilization.

142. ACS, *Ninth Annual Report* (1826), 6.

143. *North American Review* 18 (1824): 59. Emphasis added. See also Philip C. Wander, "Salvation through Separation: The Image of the Negro in the American Colonization Society," *QJS* 57 (1971): 57–67.

144. ACS, *Third Annual Report* (1820), 101.

145. *North American Review* 35 (1832): 156–57. See also the large number of letters written to the Society that testified to the industry and intelligence of blacks (e.g., *Second Annual Report* [1819], 23; *Third Annual Report* [1820], 125, 126). This does not deny that the majority in Congress interpreted racial difference as inferiority. What we wish to establish is that such difference was enough in itself to support the separatist impulse.

146. ACS, *Third Annual Report* (1820), 132.

147. Clay, "On African Colonization," 575–76. Emphasis added.

148. Ibid., 581.

149. *North American Review* 18 (1824): 62.

150. Committee on the African Slave Trade, *Annals of Congress*, 14th Cong., 2d sess., 939.

151. Clay, "On African Colonization," 575. See also "Memorial to Congress," 2; and the Massachusett's Colonization Society's concern about numbers in *Nile's Weekly Register*, 21 September 1822, 39; and 4 October 1817, 82.

152. *African Repository* 15, 50–64, as cited in Fox, *The American Colonization Society*, 29.

153. *North American Review* 18 (1824): 59.

154. The Society protested that it wished only to remove the annual increase of the black population in the United States—about 50,000 per year—rather than to remove all blacks. However, even this more modest goal generated cost estimates ranging from the society's own $250,000 per year to a more reasonable $1,780,000 per year, and to the opposition's estimates of $4,797,000 per year. See *New England Magazine* 2 (January 1832): 19; *Niles's Weekly Register*, 8 November 1817, 166; and 4 October 1817, 82. Thomas Jefferson's estimate of $10 million a year for thirty years

for total removal of all freed blacks was more than the federal budget. See Robinson, *Slavery in the Structure of American Politics,* 50.

155. Anglo-Americans refused to adopt a commercial colony because they wanted to repudiate the British imperialist model that had been so recently inflicted upon them. Committee on African Slave Trade, *Annals of Congress,* 14th Cong., 2d sess., 940. See also *Niles's Weekly Register,* 8 November 1817, 164. The white "managers" of the colony were more favorably oriented to trade, but they were also ultimately unsuccessful.

CHAPTER FOUR

1. *Frederick Douglass' Paper,* 29 September 1854.

2. See the "First Annual Report of the New York Commission of Vigilance for the Year 1837," in *Afro-American History Series,* 10 vols. (Wilmington, DE: Scholarly Resources, 1989) (hereafter *AAHS*), vol. 3; *The North Star,* 13 June 1850; *Frederick Douglass' Paper,* 21 July 1854; *Genius of Universal Emancipation,* October 1829; *Colored American,* 9 January 1841. See also Larry Gara, *The Liberty Line: The Legend of the Underground Railroad* (Lexington: University of Kentucky Press, 1961), 18, 100–114.

3. See Armstead L. Robinson, "In the Shadow of Old John Brown: Insurrection Anxiety and Confederate Mobilization, 1861–1863," *Journal of Negro History* 65 (1980): 279–97. References in the *Congressional Globe* are frequent. See, e.g., *The Negro in the Congressional Record,* 10 vols., comp. Peter M. Bergman and Jean McCarroll (New York: Bergman Pub., 1969), 2:177, from the *Annals of Congress,* 5th Cong., 2d sess., 23 March 1798, 1307–8. The *Weekly Anglo-African* in 1859 (e.g., 12 November) frequently indicated that free Negroes in the South led the effort to organize insurrections, attempting to create the impression that slave owners should be worried about the increased likelihood and effectiveness of insurrection. There is little doubt that the Harper's Ferry incident enraged the South and increased the general feeling that it would have to use the military to protect its interests. Goldston argues that there were over 400 "uprisings" of various sizes between 1750 and 1850. See Robert Goldston, *The Negro Revolution* (New York: Macmillan, 1968), 77; and Herbert Aptheker, *American Negro Slave Revolts* (New York: International Publishers, 1970 [1943]).

4. See *The Negro in the Congressional Record,* 2:166, 178. See also *The Emancipator* for October and November 1835, and *The North Star,* 17 March 1848.

5. Most abolitionist speakers believed that slavery could not survive free speech. We cannot be certain of that outcome, for the forces that cut off open discussion demonstrated their power as being greater in the South than in the North by their very ability to shut off discussion. However, the impact of discussion in the upper slave states might have been a balancing factor.

6. *The North Star,* 13 June 1850.

7. *Liberator,* 4 March 1831, in John Hope Franklin, *From Slavery to Freedom: A History of Negro Americans,* 5th ed. (New York: Alfred A. Knopf, 1988 [1947]), 93 ff. Slaves also developed other communicative strategies that allowed them to re-

sist the oppression of their owners. See Cal M. Logue, "Transcending Coercion: The Communicative Strategies of Black Slaves on Antebellum Plantations," *QJS* 67 (1981): 31–46.

8. Franklin notes that the majority of early supporters of Garrison's *Liberator* and of other white abolitionist causes were blacks. See Franklin, *From Slavery to Freedom,* 164. Martin R. Delany makes even clearer the lead of the black rhetors over the whites in *The Condition, Elevation, Emigration, and Destiny of the Colored People of the United States* (New York: Arno Press, 1968 [1852]), 15–25. See also the early support in the August and November 1821 issues of *Genius of Universal Emancipation;* and Benjamin Quarles, *Black Abolitionists* (New York: Oxford University Press, 1969), 19, 53. Quarles, Franklin, and Aptheker may overstate the case by emphasizing Garrison's organizational leadership of the black abolitionists. As Adams points out, whites too had over twenty-four antislavery conventions between 1794 and 1829. A contemporary version of the argument is expressed by the delegates at the National Convention of 1853, in Howard Holman Bell, *Minutes of the Proceedings of the National Negro Conventions, 1830–1864* (New York: Arno Press, 1969), 57.

9. A few blacks cooperated and others supported black-led efforts at emigration, something they had done since the time of Paul Cuffee. The majority nonetheless opposed white-induced expatriation.

10. See, e.g., the increasing abstraction and scope in the *Herald of Freedom.* On the tendency toward the abstraction of the Anglo-American tradition, see John Phillip Reid, *The Concept of Liberty in the Age of the American Revolution* (Chicago: University of Chicago Press, 1988), 20, 23; and Quarles, *Black Abolitionists,* 53–54.

11. *Frederick Douglass' Monthly* (April 1860), 244. Notice that Douglass does not argue that the Constitution is either inherently proslavery or antislavery but rather that it is a document that provides the power to end slavery.

12. Some black rhetors opposed violence, but in general the sample of documents included here indicates that many blacks stopped just short of urging all-out violence. We attribute this largely to their concern for the potential repercussions of such advocacy, not because of any authentic lack of support for it. Some whites supported the right to self-defense employed by slaves to gain their freedom. By 1859 the threat of violence was dominant and overt in the black rhetoric. See, e.g., *Weekly Anglo-African* 1, nos. 3, 4, 8, 17, and 22; along with David Walker's 1829 "An Appeal to the Colored Peoples of the World," in *Walker's Appeal in Four Articles* (New York: Arno Press, 1969); Henry Highland Garnet's 1839 *An Address to the Slaves of the United States of America* (New York: Arno Press, 1969); New York Convention of 1850s "A letter to the American Slaves from those who have fled from American Slavery," in Philip S. Foner and George E. Walker, eds., *Proceedings of the Black National and State Conventions, 1840–1865; New York, Pennsylvania, Indiana, Michigan, Ohio* (Philadelphia: Temple University Press, 1979), 1:44–47; Charles Lenox Remond's 1854 "Speech before the New England Anti-Slavery Convention," in Ernest G. Bormann, ed., *Forerunners of Black Power* (Englewood Cliffs, NJ: Prentice-Hall, 1971), 166–73. Many more whites supported the use of violence after John Brown's raid on Harper's Ferry.

13. See, e.g., "The Life of Olaudah Equiano or Gustavus Vassa, the African, as Written by Himself," in Arna Bontemps, ed., *Great Slave Narratives* (Boston: Beacon Press, 1969), esp. 26. See also *Weekly Anglo-African,* 13 August 1859.

14. Several scholars have documented the existence of cultural similarities among these African groups, but such similarities do not guarantee a political identity. See Mechal Sobel, *The World They Made Together: Black and White Values in Eighteenth Century Virginia* (Princeton: Princeton University Press, 1987); Roger Bastide, *African Civilisations in the New World,* trans. Peter Green (New York: Harper and Row, 1971); Sterling Stuckey, *Slave Culture: Nationalist Theory and the Foundations of Black America* (New York: Oxford University Press, 1987); John W. Blassingame, *The Slave Community: Plantation Life in the Antebellum South* (New York: Oxford University Press, 1979); Lawrence W. Levine, *Black Culture and Black Consciousness: Afro-American Folk Thought from Slavery to Freedom* (New York: Oxford University Press, 1977); Molefi K. Asante, *The Afrocentric Idea* (Philadelphia: Temple University Press, 1987).

15. This process is traced out in Leon F. Litwack, *North of Slavery: The Negro in the Free States, 1790–1860* (Chicago: University of Chicago Press, 1961); Quarles, *Black Abolitionists;* Franklin, *From Freedom to Slavery;* Herbert Aptheker, ed., *One Continual Cry: David Walker's Appeal to the Colored Citizens of the World, 1829–1830* (New York: Humanities Press, 1965). The first petition to claim a direct right to freedom was also the first in which the petitioners identified themselves directly as a people, i.e., "a freeborn Pepel [sic]." See "Petition to Massachusetts House of Representatives," 25 May 1775, in Herbert Aptheker, ed., *A Documentary History of the Negro People in the United States* (New York: Citadel Press, 1951), 1:9–12. Later they identified themselves as "black people" and by 1808 as "colored people."

16. See the "Petition to Massachusetts House of Representatives," 25 May 1775, in Aptheker, *Documentary History,* 1:9–12. A history of the free colored people offered by "Communipaw" cites James Forten as the turning point in the switch from "African" to "colored people" in *Frederick Douglass' Paper,* 16 February 1855, 3. The term "African" usurped the rights and identity of people living on the African continent.

17. Throughout we alternate using all of these labels, for they have been legitimized by their history, and the diversity of terms breaks down rigid two-valued thinking. There is one problematic case. It seems relatively clear that the term "negro" was assigned by Europeans to Africans and for some black persons it still carries negative loadings. We have read so many documents by authors who use even this label with pride that it has lost its negative loadings for us. Fortunately, we seem to be arriving at a time when the proper names ascribed to the race do not per se offer negative connotations. Only derivative terms (e.g., "nigger") definitely signify their hostility to the race.

18. Both conservative and leftist radical blacks have tried to make it exclusively one or the other throughout the history of their people. It is crucial to notice that elements of Afro-American culture may actually bear little or no resemblance to either African or Anglo-American culture. It is in this sense that we argue that Afrocentrism and Pan-Africanism must be distinguished from African-

Americanism. See Quarles, *Black Abolitionists,* 8; Howard H. Bell, "Negro Nationalism: A Factor in Emigration Projects, 1858–1861," *Journal of Negro History* 47 (1962): 50.

19. In Aptheker, *Documentary History,* 1:366.

20. "The 'Extinguisher' Extinguished," (New York, 1834), in *AAHS,* 6:17.

21. Aptheker, *Documentary History,* 1:367, 365. The most popular proposals for colonization among the blacks were those that chose a site in North America rather than in Africa or the islands. By the 1850s proemigration appeals became a frequent response to the sense of despair generated by the fugitive slave law, the decision in *Dred Scott* v. *Sandford,* and other failures to achieve progress. They occurred with the support of the concept of a "Negro Nationality." See Delany, *The Condition.*

22. In Foner and Walker, *Proceedings of the Black State Conventions,* 2:131.

23. Henry Highland Garnet, in Earl Ofari, *Let Your Motto Be Resistance: The Life and Thought of Henry Highland Garnet* (Boston: Beacon Press, 1972), 179.

24. Ibid., 179–81.

25. Samuel R. Ward, "Speech on the Fugitive Slave Bill," in Carter G. Woodson, ed., *Negro Orators and Their Orations* (New York: Russell and Russell, 1969 [1925]), 195.

26. The importance of the argument for assimilation in this time period should not be underestimated. Twentieth-century black academics tend to be Africanists, which places them in direct contrast to the African-Americanists who have dominated black leadership in the American political arena. As a consequence, many academic sources tend to deprecate the assimilationist position. However, in the nineteenth century conditions were significantly different. Today the majority of Americans, whether harboring some degree of racial prejudice or not, operate on the assumption that color is less significant as a difference separating people than shared humanity is a similarity that unites them. Resting safely on the presumption of shared humanity we have the luxury of arguing about the relative importance of difference and assimilation. In the eighteenth and nineteenth centuries, however, there was no basis for such discussion; the very existence of difference served as the logical warrant for denying shared humanity. As Frederick Douglass pointed out, any argument for difference provided a justification for slavery (*Frederick Douglass' Paper,* 21 July 1854). The only safe political argument available to those living within the Anglo-American worldview, which treated heterogeneity as a cause for expatriation and enslavement, was that there should be one, not two, American people. Most black leaders thus concurred with the request of the State Convention of Ohio Negroes in 1849 "that we may be one people, bound together by one common tie and sheltered by the same impartial law." In Aptheker, *Documentary History,* 1:287. See also New York Convention, 1841, in Foner and Walker, *Proceedings of the Black State Conventions,* 1:27–28.

27. *The North Star,* 19 January 1849. This was not due to Anglo superiority but rather to the greater military destructiveness and numbers of Europeans.

28. Franklin, *From Slavery to Freedom,* 93.

29. Hosea Easton, "A Treatise" (1837), in *AAHS,* 3:41. The original reads

"care you off." See also Wilson Jeremiah Moses, *Alexander Crummell: A Study of Civilization and Discontent* (New York: Oxford Press, 1989), 17.

30. Prince Hall in Benjamin Brawley, *Early American Negro Writers* (Plainview, NY: Books for Libraries Press, 1976 [1935]), 97; *Douglass' Monthly* (April 1860). See also "Memorial of Philadelphians," in *AAHS*, 6:1–2. The issue of violence cannot be underestimated. See John M. Werner, *Reaping the Bloody Harvest: Race Riots in the United States during the Age of Jackson 1824–1849* (New York: Garland Publishing, 1986), 66; *Frederick Douglass' Paper*, 23 November 1855.

31. Violence against the slave population of course took many forms, ranging from specific acts of cruelty to the generally brutal conditions of black life on the plantation. See George P. Rawick, *From Sundown to Sunup: The Making of the Black Community* (Westport, CT: Greenwood Press, 1972), 150–60; Kenneth M. Stampp, *The Peculiar Institution* (New York: Vintage Books, 1956), 111–14, 177–91, and 209–11; Robert W. Fogel, *Without Consent or Contract: The Rise and Fall of American Slavery* (New York: W. W. Norton and Co., 1989), 17–59.

32. In Aptheker, *Documentary History*, 1:59–66.

33. Ibid., 1:29–31.

34. Walker, *Walker's Appeal*, 20; Marilyn Richardson, ed., *Maria W. Stewart: America's First Black Woman Political Writer* (Bloomington: Indiana University Press, 1987), 7; Aptheker, *Documentary History*, 1:27.

35. *Colored American*, 2 May 1840, 3.

36. In Aptheker, *Documentary History*, 1:91.

37. The Anglo-American nationality had sovereignty, and African-Americans did not. However, they were both rhetorically constituted peoples on a national scale.

38. *Freedom's Journal*, 7 February 1829, 354; also "An Address from Stark County Abolition Society," in ibid., 353.

39. *Freedom's Journal*, 16 March 1827.

40. Ibid.

41. A. D. Shadd in the *Colored American*, 22 August 1840, 1.

42. Some, such as Kinshasha and Ofari, contend that black leaders were an "elite," fully out of touch with their "masses." This ignores the facts of the case. Frederick Douglass provides the classic case of a man who had experienced both slavery and black working-class life. Like him, many black leaders were fugitives or former slaves, and none of them were exempt from the almost daily stigma, abuse, and violence of being black in nineteenth-century America. It is surely the case that they often had trouble convincing others to accept their "leadership," for this is the nature of leadership. The white Marxist model is simply inapplicable to nineteenth-century black experience. More distressing is the fact that such an application denies the possibility of intellectual or cultural leadership of any form by assuming that the representatives of a race who are simple mirrors of mass opinion are preferable to leaders who create new possibilities for their people. This conflates an economically advantaged class with the holding and distribution of superior intellectual or artistic products.

43. On slave culture see Blassingame, *The Slave Community;* Stuckey, *Slave Culture;* Sobel, *The World They Made;* Asante, *The Afrocentric Idea;* and Bastide, *African Civilization in the New World.* It remains unclear how much of what is identified as African or slave culture is a product of heritage and how much of situation and circumstance. Clearly, however, there are elements of each, and, equally clearly, scholars have spent so much time arguing about which is the greater source of the culture that they have failed to describe adequately the interaction of the two.

44. Walker, *Walker's Appeal,* 14; Frederick Douglass, *Narrative of the Life of Frederick Douglass* (New York: Penguin Books, 1982 [1845]), 78–89; Prince Saunders, "An Address Delivered at Bethel Church" (1818), in *AAHS,* 10:4–8.

This does not assume the ethnocentric claim that the Anglo-American culture of the period was, on the whole, superior to that of African culture. In the first place, fugitive slaves were rarely familiar with a fully native African culture. Further, as creative and active as the slave communities were in forming healthy and productive cultures, we cannot expect that a relatively young, locally confined, and rigidly oppressed culture should be better at empowering its people than a free culture, regardless of the race or gender of its members. We need not, however, rest our observations on abstract speculation about the abilities of different cultures in toto to empower their members. The fact that ex-slaves found certain aspects of Anglo-American culture attractive is hardly a blanket claim for overall cultural superiority. The most ethnocentric cultures find some elements of other cultures attractive and compelling. The elements of the culture to which free blacks were most attracted included writing, reading, and home economics, and they chose to mix those elements with their own religious, artistic, and relational traditions. Cultures change through time and as the result of a variety of factors. The contact of cultures that is one source of such change is repugnant only on a conservative view that sees all change as inherently bad.

45. See Martin R. Delany in *Weekly Anglo-African,* 1 October 1859.

46. For a review of black participation in national life in the revolutionary era, see Sidney Kaplan and Emma Nogrady Kaplan, *The Black Presence in the Era of the American Revolution,* rev. ed. (Amherst: University of Massachusetts Press, 1989). On self-purchase see Quarles, *Black Abolitionists,* 59.

47. Quarles maintains that membership in mutual aid societies was as high as half of the local population. *Black Abolitionists,* 101.

48. Franklin, *From Slavery to Freedom,* 93.

49. On African-American newspapers, see Martin E. Dann, ed., *The Black Press, 1827–1890* (New York: Putnam's, 1971); Penelope L. Bullock, *The Afro-American Periodical Press, 1838–1909* (Baton Rouge: Louisiana State University Press, 1981).

50. *Freedom's Journal,* 16 March 1827.

51. Some advocates of "negro" nationality in this period did not simply attempt to import Anglo-American or African-American culture to Africa, but many others did. Those who did not seemed to promote a negro nationality primarily as a mechanism to demonstrate the worth of the black race, e.g., *Weekly Anglo-African,* 10 September 1859. Bell claims "Delany's one great ambition was

to place the Negro in a position where he could prove himself in the eyes of the world." See Bell, "Negro Nationalism," 44. The concept of true Pan-Africanism does not develop in this period, although its precursors—African identity, international orientation, and race pride—do.

52. The rhetorical response to Colonization has been stated imprecisely. It is inaccurate to say that the free colored people were opposed to emigration per se. Before and after the Colonization Society's proposals, black people left America seeking new homes in Canada, Haiti, Jamaica, and Africa. More to the point, anti-Colonizationists such as Bishop Richard Allen supported plans of voluntary emigration, including a planned and organized colony in Upper Canada. See *Freedom's Journal,* 2 November 1827. Others, such as Henry Highland Garnet and Martin R. Delany, vocally supported both colonization and the right to remain in America. Even Frederick Douglass supported private voluntary emigration of individuals and eventually investigated the possibility of colonizing Haiti. America's free colored people did not oppose colonization or emigration; they opposed the ideological framework of the Colonization Society. The twentieth-century split between separatists/integrationists and egalitarians/culturalists did not exist then as it does now. Those attempting to trace the roots of Black Nationalism have mistakenly portrayed the lines of contest between those such as Douglass and Delany by imposing late modern lines of demarcation upon these earlier disagreements. Clearly, some issues were so contested, but the organization of the constellation of issues was quite different. As just one example, consider that Douglass, the supposed moderate, was far harsher on Christianity than was Garnet, the supposed radical. In general, such differences operated in the context of a field of similarities.

53. See Peter Williams, "Slavery and Colonization," in Woodson, *Negro Orators,* 80, as well as later radicals such as Garnet, Remond, and Delany. The African-American community faced expulsion laws in Ohio that produced heavy support of a resettlement effort in Canada; they did this easily and distinguished the effort from that of the ACS. See the National Convention reports of 1832 in Bell, *Minutes of the Proceedings of the National Negro Conventions.* The attitude remained dominant at least until the 1850s when despair promoted a resurgence of emigrationist spirit.

54. In Bell, *Minutes of the Proceedings of the National Negro Conventions* (1833), 26–27.

55. The phrase "Liberty and Property" had virtually dropped out of the American vocabulary, but even without the slogan, the issue of slavery highlighted the fact that Property remained one of the nation's supreme values. The slogan "Liberty and Equality," though common, was never as abundant in either black or white abolitionist discourse as "Liberty and Property" had been in Anglo-American discourse. This was due in part to the way in which the egalitarian forces were scattered, thus producing multiple slogans ("Liberty and Equal Rights"; "Freedom and Equality"; "Liberty, Justice, and Equality," and "Liberty-Equality-Fraternity"). Liberty and Freedom appeared more frequently than Equality, but Equality (as equality, equal, or equally) appeared in about three-quarters of the documents we surveyed, usually multiple times (it is rarest in the sermons of the period up to 1817). Where the concerns of slavery displaced the concerns of free

people of color, Liberty and Freedom typically occurred without the term Equality.

56. 4 March 1845, in *Inaugural Addresses of the Presidents of the United States,* (Washington, D.C.: Government Printing Office, 1989), 55–56.

57. For additional examples of the Southern rejection of equality see James A. Sloan, *The Great Question Answered or Is Slavery a Sin in Itself* (Memphis: Hutton, Galloway and Co., 1857), 48; Albert Taylor Bledsoe, *An Essay on Liberty and Slavery* (Philadelphia: J. B. Lippincott, 1856), 288, 54. See also the presidential inaugurals of the period up through Lincoln's first inaugural.

58. Emphasis added. "National Convention" (1848), in Bell, *Minutes of the Proceedings of the National Negro Conventions,* 12. See also "National Convention" (1835), 25; and *Frederick Douglass' Paper,* 16 February 1855.

59. In Aptheker, *Documentary History,* 1:60.

60. *Colored American,* 30 May 1840, 3.

61. "Memorial of Philadelphians" (1834), in *AAHS,* 6:4. The memorial is quoting the Abolition Act of Pennsylvania of 1780.

62. *The North Star,* 29 September 1848. Emphasis added.

63. Douglass, in the *Liberator,* from Aptheker, *Documentary History,* 1:226.

64. Douglass, *Narrative,* 113.

65. *Frederick Douglass' Paper,* 21 July 1854, 2. He also characterized America as evolving, noting that "we have, in this country, no adequate idea of humanity, yet." *The North Star,* 2 June 1848.

66. "Ohio Convention" (1856), in Foner and Walker, *Proceedings of the Black State Conventions,* 1:310.

67. Ibid. The address borrows from European culture in employing a passage frequently alluded to by blacks that was spoken by Shakespeare's Shylock. See also Douglass, *The North Star,* 13 June 1850; as well as his justly famed Fourth of July Address, which derives from a whole genre of satiric, "Anti-Fourth of July" orations. In John W. Blassingame, ed., *The Frederick Douglass Papers, Series One: Speeches, Debates, and Interviews* (New Haven: Yale University Press, 1982).

68. John C. Calhoun, "Speech on the Oregon Bill," in *The Works of John C. Calhoun* (New York: D. Appleton and Co., 1857), 4:511.

69. Prince Saunders, "Haytian Papers," in *AAHS,* 10:154. Hosea Easton presented the most extensive development of the argument.

70. "Memorial of Philadelphians" (1834), in *AAHS,* 6:6. The memorial goes on to give comparative statistics to establish the claim.

71. 1856, in Foner and Walker, *Proceedings of the Black State Conventions,* 1:310.

72. The breadth, depth, and reach of the demand is impressive. A reading of the state conventions conveys with power this moving and active force at work in the nation. See Foner and Walker, *Proceedings of the Black State Conventions.*

73. In Foner and Walker, *Proceedings of the Black State Conventions,* 1:21–22.

74. See Frederick Douglass, *The North Star,* 13 June 1850.

75. *Frederick Douglass' Paper,* 12 May 1854. The original says "see" instead of "use," but this is in all likelihood a typesetting error.

76. This notion has been previously attributed to the British Enlightenment.

However, that version does not attribute universal human development as the grounds for humanity. Rather, it argues that Liberty provides the basis for the abilities of the few to so evolve. Such Enlightenment thinking was integrated easily with capitalism and social Darwinism. Such elitism is evident even in Mill, who uses universal development as a premise, but then discounts the developmental potential of most humans, arguing that the social payoff appears through the productions of the best and the brightest. The African-American usage rested on the potential of human development and applied, therefore, to everyone. It did not rest on the actual achievements of the brilliant few. See John Stuart Mill, chap. 8, "Of the Extension of the Suffrage," *Considerations on Representative Government*, reprinted in H. B. Acton, ed., *Utilitarianism, Liberty, Representative Government*, (London: J. M. Dent & Sons, 1972), 276–92.

77. Very few black advocates of the period were antipropertarian. In fact, most of the free black leaders joined *The North Star* in urging free blacks to greater acquisitions of property: "We advise therefore, in order to anything like equality—get money in thy purse." *The North Star*, 14 April 1848, 2. See also *Weekly Anglo-African*, 13 August 1859.

78. *Frederick Douglass' Paper*, 23 December 1853, 2.

79. Douglass borrows the latter phrase from Lord Brougham and uses it repeatedly in the next years. *The North Star*, 16 June 1848, 2.

80. In Bell, *Minutes of the Proceedings of the National Negro Conventions* (1855), 31.

81. The case is clearest with regard to the attitudes toward women as expressed in *Freedom's Journal*, a pre-Garrisonian paper, as opposed to those in Frederick Douglass's various post-Garrison papers. It shows up in other ways, however, as a basically imperialist and collectively self-centered rhetoric of the nationalists. *Freedom's Journal* also uses Equality and Equal Rights much less frequently, occasionally even calling the latter into question. Orators such as A. Ford Douglass seem to have held this position as well, and Charles Lenox Remond claimed he "held the pale faces in utter contempt." See *Weekly Anglo-African*, 6 August 1859. The pure black separatist African position was destined to be rare, since such advocates followed their beliefs and left the country. We note, however, that this Afrocentric rhetoric was never as vicious as that of the slaveholders, although the original African rhetoric was itself clearly a slaveholding rhetoric.

82. See esp. Garrison's *Herald of Freedom*, but also the *Genius of Universal Emancipation*. Kraditor makes a strong case for the long-term pragmatism of Garrison's absolutist principle, but this does not negate the excessive idealism of his positions on Union and nonresistance. See Aileen S. Kraditor, *Means and Ends in American Abolitionism* (New York: Pantheon Books, 1969).

83. Theodore S. Wright, "The Progress of the Antislavery Cause," in Woodson, *Negro Orators*, 88. Walker insisted that "this country is as much ours as it is the whites." See Walker, *Walker's Appeal*, 66.

84. Aptheker, *Documentary History*, 1:364. See also the wonderfully detailed argument by Hosea Easton, "A Treatise" (1837), in *AAHS*, vol. 3. The ultimate materialist, Easton argued that once one eats and breathes in America, one's blood is no longer African but composed of American substance.

85. "The Country Our Only Home," *Colored American,* 9 May 1840.

86. Williams, in Woodson, *Negro Orators,* 80.

87. This concept had been previously used by Anglo-American lower classes seeking to overturn property qualifications for suffrage but only on the state level. It was not a nationally developed argument.

88. "Memorial of Philadelphians" (1834), in *AAHS,* 6:3.

89. Walker, *Walker's Appeal,* 76.

90. In Bell, *Minutes of the Proceedings of the National Negro Conventions,* 16.

91. *Freedom's Journal,* 20 July 1827.

92. In Bell, *Minutes of the Proceedings of the National Negro Conventions* (1853), 8.

93. Philip F. Detweiler, "The Changing Reputation of the Declaration of Independence: The First Fifty Years," *William and Mary Quarterly* 19 (1962): 557–58.

94. In Aptheker, *Documentary History,* 1:8–10.

95. Reference to the Declaration of Independence is a dominant feature of black abolitionist discourse as well as much white abolitionist discourse. In the sample of documents used for the period 1828–38, almost one-third of the documents had direct references to the Declaration, and several more used the language of the Declaration without directly citing it.

96. Rep. Louis McClane, *Annals of Congress,* February 1820, House of Representatives, 16th Cong., 1st sess., 1154–55.

97. Rep. Benjamin Hardin, *Annals of Congress,* February 1820, House of Representatives, 16th Cong., 1st sess., 1071.

98. John C. Calhoun, "Speech on the Oregon Bill," 27 June 1848, in *Works,* 507–11.

99. Rep. John Tyler, 17 February 1820, *Annals of Congress,* 16th Cong., 1st sess., 1384.

100. In Bell, *Minutes of the Proceedings of the National Negro Conventions* (1853), 8. The unusual punctuation and emphasis is in the original.

101. Wright, in Woodson, *Negro Orators,* 86.

102. *Weekly Anglo-African,* 17 December 1859, 2.

103. *Frederick Douglass' Paper,* 12 May 1854, 1.

104. In Aptheker, *Documentary History,* 1:137–38.

105. In ibid., 1:62.

106. In Bell, *Minutes of the Proceedings of the National Negro Conventions,* 12.

107. *The North Star,* 2 June 1848, 3.

108. In Ofari, *Let Your Motto Be Resistance,* 143. See also "Address of S. R. Ward," in *The North Star,* 1 September 1848. Garnet goes on to say, "Not this man here, and that man there, but *'all men.'*" Black rhetors would later extend the same argument to the U.S. Constitution, arguing that it should be interpreted "as it *reads*" rather than as slaveholders claimed it was "meant." See *Frederick Douglass' Paper,* 6 July 1855.

109. Usages of Equal Rights had already been proposed and incorporated into Anglo-American discourse during the Jacksonian era. A great deal more precise study of these usages is needed, but see Merrill D. Peterson, ed., *Democracy, Liberty, and Property: The State Constitutional Conventions of the 1820's* (Indianapolis:

Bobbs-Merrill Co., 1966); J. R. Pole, *The Pursuit of Equality in American History* (Berkeley: University of California Press, 1978); Charles Redenius, *The American Ideal of Equality: From Jefferson's Declaration to the Burger Court* (Port Washington, NY: Kennikat Press, 1981).

110. *Freedom's Journal*, 5 October 1827, 118. See also, Aptheker, *Documentary History*, 1:27. In its full form this quotation contains enough ambiguity about the relationship between equal rights and equal conditions to suggest that it may represent a phase in the development of the concept of Equal Rights rather than repudiation of Equal Rights.

111. *Frederick Douglass' Paper*, 21 July 1854.

112. "National Convention" (1848), in Bell, *Minutes of the Proceedings of the National Negro Conventions*, 17.

113. *The North Star*, 2 November 1849, 3.

114. *Freedom's Journal*, 5 October 1827.

115. *Colored American*, 9 January 1841.

116. Ibid., 4 April 1840.

117. On "same advantages" see Prince Saunders, "Haytian Papers" in *AAHS*, 10:154; or Maria W. Stewart, in Richardson, *Maria W. Stewart*, 61–63; on the general philosophy, see *The North Star*, 14 July 1848, 3; on the "race" of life, see "National Convention" (1853), in Bell, *Minutes of the Proceedings of the Negro National Convention,"* 22; see also *Colored American*, 28 March 1840. Aptheker overstates the case in claiming that blacks routinely espoused racial superiority. He is correct, however, in arguing that the emphasis on black self-deprecation is misplaced. Black leaders routinely chastised their people in order to motivate their greater exertion, but this implied that they thought their people fully capable of greatness. The leaders had neither an inferiority nor a superiority complex, but like all rhetorically effective leaders they had delicately balanced the potential of their people against their accomplishments. See Herbert Aptheker in Rhoda L. Goldstein, ed., *Black Life and Culture in the United States* (New York: Thomas W. Crowell, 1971), 165–79.

118. *The North Star*, 23 March 1849.

119. "Petition of Massachusetts Blackes," in Aptheker, *Documentary History*, 1:9.

120. See the "Address of the California Convention" (1855), in Foner and Walker, *Proceedings of the Black State Conventions*, 2:129, where it notes, "We are engaged in a great work; it is this, we aim to render ourselves equal with the most favored, not simply nominally equal, but truly and practically, in knowledge, energy, practical skill and enterprise." There were a few exceptional rhetors who focused on economic outcomes without indicating that such equality would have to be "earned."

121. Even when the "equal footing" metaphor was not used, the image of equality was as a "place," e.g., "to be *upon* an equality," "*raised* to an equality," "*placed* on an equality," and "*elevation* to an equality," etc. (our emphasis). See *Freedom's Journal*, 5 October 1827, and 25 July 1828; Minutes of the State Convention of Pennsylvania (1848), in *AAHS*, 5:20; Ruggles (1834), in *AAHS*, 6:13.

122. Delany, *The Condition*, 41–42. Rhetors uniformly assume that ability and its products are transcultural.

123. "Minutes of the State Convention of the Colored Citizens of Pennsylvania" (1848), in *AAHS*, 5:15. See also *The North Star*, 21 January 1848.

124. *The North Star*, 3 December 1847.

125. Frederick Douglass, in Leslie H. Fishel, Jr., and Benjamin Quarles, *The Negro American* (Glenview, IL: Scott, Foresman and Co., 1967), 144.

126. This occurs in various forms, including "equal chance" and "equal advantages." See Maria W. Stewart in Richardson, *Maria W. Stewart; The North Star*, 2 June 1848, 23 March 1849, and 29 September 1848; Cuffe et al., "Taxation without Representation" (1780), in Aptheker, *Documentary History*, 1:15.

127. Andrew Jackson, "Veto of The Bank Bill, July 10 1832," in James D. Richardson, ed. *A Compilation of the Messages and Papers of the Presidents* (New York: Bureau of National Literature, 1897), 579–91.

128. "Convention of 1853," in Bell, *Minutes of the Proceedings of the National Negro Conventions*, 8.

129. David Ruggles, in *AAHS*, 6:13.

130. Hosea Easton, *AAHS*, 3:22–26.

131. Frederick Douglass "The Claims of the Negro Ethnologically Considered," 12 July 1854, in Philip S. Foner, ed., *The Life and Writings of Frederick Douglass* (New York: International Pub., 1975), 305.

132. "Minutes of the State Convention, PA" (1848), in *AAHS*, 5:14–15; and *Colored American*, 13 June 1840.

133. In *AAHS*, 3:52.

134. *Weekly Anglo-African*, 21 January 1860. See also Sojourner Truth, "Ain't I a Woman," in Patricia Schileppi Kennedy and Gloria Harmann O'Shields, eds., *We Shall Be Heard: Women Speakers in America* (Dubuque: Kendall/Hunt Publishing, 1983), 92–94.

135. *Frederick Douglass' Paper*, 16 February 1855.

136. *Colored American*, 30 May 1840, 3. In keeping with the emphasis on territorial relations between people and government, another concern was to avoid distinctions based on "origin." See, e.g., Delany, *The Condition*, 17–18.

137. *The North Star*, 2 November 1849.

138. Ibid., 5 April 1850.

139. See George T. Downing, in Aptheker, *Documentary History*, 1:325; Russel Parrott, "An Address on the Abolition of the Slave Trade" (1816), in *AAHS*, 1:12; *Frederick Douglass' Paper*, 23 December 1853; the Conventions of 1843 and 1853, in Bell, *Minutes of the Proceedings of the National Negro Conventions: Weekly Anglo-African*, 7 July 1860.

140. *The North Star*, 1 February 1850 (delivered 4 December 1849), 1.

141. Ibid., 2 November 1849; the Convention of 1853, in Bell, *Minutes of the Proceedings of the National Negro Conventions;* Ohio Convention, 1856, in Aptheker, *Documentary History*, 1:387; *Freedom's Journal*, 5 October 1827; *The North Star*, 29 September 1848.

142. *Douglass' Monthly* (May 1859): 68.

143. See Ibid. (May 1859): 68; and the minutes of the Albany Convention, in *Colored American*, 2 January 1841.

144. *The North Star*, 13 June 1850, 2.

145. "Convention of 1853," in Bell, *Minutes of the Proceedings of the National Negro Conventions*, 40.

146. "Address of the American Society to the Free People of Colour," in *AAHS*, 6:10. See also Hosea Easton, who proclaimed colored people "Americans by birth, genius, habits, language &c.," in *AAHS*, 3:21.

147. See "Address of the American Society to the Free People of Colour," 46; *Douglass' Monthly* (August 1859): 117. *The North Star*, 11 May 1849, notes, "Many of the slaves at the South are nearly or quite as white as their masters."

148. Ohio Convention, 1849, in Aptheker, *Documentary History*, 1:283.

149. Given that Douglass was the most forceful craftsperson of the vision of common humanity, and given that he exemplified the mixing of the races in his own parentage, it is not surprising that he accommodated comfortably this vision of homogeneity, but the latter vision is not a necessary consequent of the former.

150. Blacks did express the value of a separate racial identity. This argument may have implied strictures against racial interbreeding, but as far as we can determine, it did not imply strictures on interracial social interaction. See E. P. Walker, of Toledo, cited in *Douglass' Monthly* (January 1859): 4.

151. This included a strong endorsement of the Protestant work ethic and an accommodation to capitalism. See the Convention of 1853, in Bell, *Minutes of the Proceedings of the National Negro Conventions*, 39.

152. *Weekly Anglo-African*, 12 November 1859. Race pride is not the same as a demand for racial superiority, although a failure to recognize this leads some speakers to mix the two.

153. *The North Star*, 18 May 1849. In response to a query by Brodhead, Horace Mann answered this in the affirmative. This does not mean that they were unaware of the potential problems of social interaction. They argued that it did little good to be admitted to a seminary if the other students were prejudiced against you. See, e.g., *Frederick Douglass' Paper*, 16 February 1855.

154. "The Convention of 1841," in Foner and Walker, *Proceedings of the Black State Conventions*, 1:29. See also the *Colored American*, 25 April 1840, which refers to a "heterogeneous—(but *homo*-geneous) community."

155. "The Suffrage Question," in Aptheker, *Documentary History*, 1:45. See also *Colored American*, 13 June 1840. The suffrage question was the major issue of many state conventions.

156. "The Convention of 1855," in Bell, *Minutes of the Proceedings of the National Negro Conventions*, esp. 16. See also *The North Star*, 2 November 1849.

157. Charles Sumner explored the need for education as a fundamental of life in human society, while African-American orators usually argued for an equal need with the whites. Nevertheless, their extensive emphasis upon the essential importance of education has been widely noted and becomes especially significant in the postreconstruction era.

158. On the need to transcend narrative to develop a constitutional case see

Celeste Michelle Condit, "Democracy and Civil Rights: The Universalizing Influence of Public Argumentation," *Communication Monographs* 54 (1987): 1–18. As an example, see *Douglass' Monthly* (April 1859).

159. See Maria W. Stewart, "Lecture Delivered at the Franklin Hall, Boston, 21 September 1832," in Richardson, *Maria W. Stewart,* 45–46; and Delany, *The Condition,* 24–30.

160. *Frederick Douglass' Paper,* 21 July 1854, 2.

161. *Colored American,* 9 May 1840.

CHAPTER FIVE

1. "Cui Bono? The Negro Vote," *De Bow's Review* (October 1867): 292.

2. The majority of those with what we call "republican" sentiments were of the Republican party, but the two are not identical, hence we use an upper case "R" to designate the political party and a lower case "r" to indicate those who believed in an egalitarianism that extended at least to formal political equality for all men.

3. Lyman Trumbull, *Congressional Globe,* 38th Cong., 1st sess., 28 March 1864, 1313. Trumbull is arguing that the South does not live up to this minimal maxim.

4. Alexis de Tocqueville noted that "equality of condition" was the central explanatory fact in American life. His observation was focused on economic life and daily practices, not on the public vocabulary. See *Democracy in America,* trans. George Lawrence (Garden City, NY: Anchor Books, 1969 [1838]), 9. See also Arthur Schlesinger, Jr., *The Age of Jackson* (Boston: Little Brown and Company, 1945); Jack R. Pole, *The Pursuit of Equality in American History* (Berkeley: University of California Press, 1978), 146; Charles Redenius, *The American Ideal of Equality: From Jefferson's Declaration to the Burger Court* (Port Washington, NY: Kennikat Press, 1981), 38–51.

5. John Quincy Adams used the phrase "equal protection" in his inaugural address, but he applied it to the "great interests of the nation" rather than to individuals. Statements about government protection of "all the rights of each individual" were a commonplace with all the presidents after Jefferson (and "equal law" or "equal justice" were used occasionally), as the usage of Equal Rights of individuals (in the sense of personal rights) came to dominate national discourse. The concept of protecting the rights of citizens from each other or from foreign governments differed from Jackson's interest in what the government could and could not do *for* its citizens as an issue of Equality. See President Andrew Jackson, "Veto of the Bank Bill, July 10, 1832," in James D. Richardson, ed., *A Compilation of the Messages and Papers of the Presidents* (New York: Bureau of Literature, 1897): 576 ff.

6. During our research, we divided our recording of data into decades. Social change does not happen in such discrete units. Consequently, our demarcations should be taken as approximations rather than rigid boundaries.

7. Traditionally, the positions are divided along North-South lines, and the Southern position is further divided into three camps, consisting of paternalists,

liberals, and fire-eaters, while Northeners are divided into radicals, copperheads, and moderates. See C. Vann Woodward, *The Strange Career of Jim Crow*, 3d rev. ed. (New York: Oxford University Press, 1955).

8. The post–Civil War period was an age of nation building, and it featured the rise of a national press. More specifically, it witnessed the emergence of national magazines, a mass medium that played a pivotal role in crystallizing the new nationalism; see Michael Warner, *The Letters of the Republic: Publication and the Public Sphere in Eighteenth-Century America* (Cambridge, MA: Harvard University Press, 1990). We have checked our findings from the national magazines against newspapers, public speeches, and the *Congressional Record*. We concluded that the national magazines were reasonably representative of the public voices in the country, although they tend to underrepresent the most extreme positions and overrepresent moderates and the Northeast. These distortions are, however, accurate indications of the differential influence these voices held in the national arena. We draw our illustrative quotations from a wide range of sources rather than simply from our magazine sample.

9. Cf., e.g., Ira Berlin et al., " 'To Canvass the Nation': The War for Union Becomes a War for Freedom," *Prologue* 20 (1988): 227–47, with William Ghormley Cochrane, *Freedom without Equality: A Study of Northern Opinion and the Negro Issue, 1861–1870* (Ph.D. diss., University of Minnesota, 1957). See also John Hope Franklin, *Reconstruction after the Civil War* (Chicago: University of Chicago Press, 1961). Eric Foner's *Reconstruction: America's Unfinished Revolution, 1863–1877* (New York: Harper and Row, 1988) provides an excellent description of this change in attitude, although he overstates the degree to which the nation accepted the "national centralized state" and conflates different usages of Equality in the immediate postwar era.

10. We diverge from Larry E. Tise, *Pro-Slavery: A History of the Defense of Slavery in America: 1701–1840* (Athens: University of Georgia Press, 1987), where he classifies those whose technical opposition to slavery amounts to pragmatic support of it within the proslavery camp.

11. See the petitions cited in Berlin et al., "To Canvas the Nation," 243–46.

12. For a variety of rhetorical interpretations of Lincoln's Second Inaugural Address, see David Zarefsky, ed., "Special Focus: Lincoln's Second Inaugural Address," *Communication Reports* 1 (1988): 9–37, including James Arnt Aune, "Lincoln and the American Sublime," 14–19; Ronald H. Carpenter, "In-Not-So-Trivial Pursuit of Rhetorical Wedgies: An Historical Approach to Lincoln's Second Inaugural Address," 20–25; Michael Leff, "Dimensions of Temporality in Lincoln's Second Inaugural Address," 26–31; and Martha Solomon, " 'With firmness in the right': The Creation of Moral Hegemony in Lincoln's Second Inaugural," 32–37.

13. "What's to Be Done with the Negroes?" *De Bow's Review* (June 1866): 579, 578.

14. See Dan T. Carter, *When the War Was Over: The Failure of Self-Reconstruction in the South 1865–1867* (Baton Rouge: Louisiana State University Press, 1985), where he argues that the patriarchal supremacists at first outweighed the fire-eaters. See Foner, *Reconstruction*, 209.

15. Cal M. Logue, "Rhetorical Ridicule of Reconstruction Blacks," *QJS* 62 (December 1976): 400–409.

16. *Atlanta Constitution,* 17 June 1868, 4.

17. "Not Our 'Brother,'" *Atlanta Constitution,* 23 June 1868, 2. See also John L. Dawson, 31 January 1866, *Congressional Globe,* 39th Cong., 1st sess., 541.

18. "Cui Bono?" 290.

19. S. A. Cartwright, "Negro Freedom an Impossibility under Nature's Laws," *De Bow's Review* (May/June 1861): 650.

20. William Sumner Jenkins, *Proslavery Thought in the Old South* (Gloucester, MA: Peter Smith, 1960).

21. Kenneth M. Stampp, *The Era of Reconstruction, 1865–1877* (New York: Alfred A. Knopf, 1972 [1965]), 167–69.

22. "Cui Bono?" 291. Foner emphasizes that while these fears were ultimately inaccurate, to whites in the period the repeated calls for land confiscation made the fears credible, *Reconstruction,* 291–92, 304, 316.

23. "Cui Bono?" 290.

24. 8 April 1864, *Congressional Globe,* 38th Cong., 1st sess., 1457.

25. "What's to Be Done with the Negroes?" 580.

26. "Capabilities of the African Race: A Lesson for History," *Monthly Religious Review* (November 1862): 285, 291.

27. E. L. Godkin, "What Shall We Do with the Negro?" *Nation,* 12 November 1868, 387.

28. Jackson, "Veto Message," 534. The difference may have been conditioned by the fact that the North was imbued with the Jacksonian vocabulary, which had done away with the assumption that inferiority of attainment among whites worked political disqualification, whereas the South had not moved so far in this direction before the war.

29. "What Shall We Do with the Negro?" 387.

30. Edward A. Pollard, "The Negro in the South," 387.

31. "Capabilities of the African Race: A Lesson for History," *Monthly Religious Review* (November 1862): 285, 291.

32. Godkin, "What Shall We Do with the Negro?" *Lippincott's Monthly Magazine* (April 1870): 387.

33. See Philip S. Foner and George E. Walker, eds., *Proceedings of the Black National and State Conventions, 1865–1900* (Philadelphia: Temple University Press, 1986), passim. See also *New Orleans Tribune,* 21 July 1864.

34. William Nesbit, at the National Equal Rights League, 1865, in Foner and Walker, *Proceedings,* 66. See also *La Tribune de la Nouvelle-Orleans,* 8 Janvier 1865, 1.

35. E.g., Iowa State Colored Convention, 1868, in Foner and Walker, *Proceedings,* 333; Rev. E. J. Adams, Charleston, 19 March 1867, and Oscar J. Dunn, 31 July 1868, in Philip S. Foner, ed., *The Voice of Black America: Major Speeches by Negroes in the United States 1797–1971,* 2 vols. (New York: Simon and Schuster, 1972), 1:342–44, 355–57.

36. In Foner and Walker, *Proceedings,* 232.

37. "State Convention of the Colored Men of Tennessee" (1865), in Foner and Walker, *Proceedings*, 124.

38. To the extent that it was anarchistic it worked against governmental protection. See Lewis Perry, *Radical Abolitionism: Anarchy and the Government of God in AntiSlavery Thought* (Ithaca: Cornell University Press, 1973), esp. 56–57. It also could posit abstract nonearthly equality in the direct face of earthly inequality. See John R. McKivigan, *The War against Proslavery Religion* (Ithaca: Cornell University Press, 1984); William Hosmer, *Slavery and the Church* (New York: Negro Universities Press, 1969 [1853]). A few white radical abolitionists such as Wendell Phillips had more concrete visions.

39. See, e.g., Thomas Holt, *Black over White: Negro Political Leadership in South Carolina during Reconstruction* (Urbana: University of Illinois Press, 1977); Foner and Walker, introduction to the *Proceedings*, xv–xx; Howard N. Rabinowitz, ed., *Southern Black Leaders of the Reconstruction Era* (Urbana: University of Illinois Press, 1982). Many signs suggest that this was less true among church leadership and perhaps among other forms of social leadership as well. For many years some articles in the black press condemned ignorant preachers and other lower-class leaders (e.g., *Colored Citizen*, 26 July 1879, 2). There are signs of such leadership in other places. For example, white supremacists occasionally referred to black radical leaders in the South. Page claimed that Lewis Lindsay had declared in a speech to a black partisan meeting his desire to "wade in White blood up to his knees." This sentiment was not heard in the mainstream black discourse. See Thomas Nelson Page, "The Negro: The Southerner's Problem," *McClure's* (April 1904): 626. However, as with any orally based culture, few signs of such leadership remain today.

40. Pennsylvania Convention, 1865, Foner and Walker, *Proceedings*, 159. See also San Francisco *Elevator*, 5 May 1865, 3.

41. August Meier, *Negro Thought in America, 1880–1915: Racial Ideologies in the Age of Booker T. Washington* (Ann Arbor: University of Michigan, 1963), 11; Holt joins him in the general perspective emphasizing the different interests of blacks of different classes. See Holt, *Blacks over White*, 3.

42. See the convention oratory and issues of the *New Orleans Tribune*, San Francisco *Elevator*, and New Jersey *Sentinel*, all stable black newspapers in this era.

43. "State Convention of the Colored Men of Tennessee" (1865), in Foner and Walker, *Proceedings*, 125. See also San Francisco *Elevator*, 21 June 1867, 1; *La Tribune de la Nouvelle-Orleans*, 28 February 1869; *New Era*, 9 February 1871, 2.

44. Until the turn of the century, the term "equal opportunity" was used less frequently by black rhetors than before the war.

45. "State Convention of the Colored People of Georgia" (1866), in Foner and Walker, *Proceedings*, 235. The point was accentuated in the call for a National Convention in 1866 which concluded, "All we desire is equal right, equal punishment, equal protection, equal chance, no more." See J. W. M., in Foner and Walker, *Proceedings*, 222.

46. "National Convention of the Colored Men of America" (1869), in Foner and Walker, *Proceedings,* 358.

47. See Harold M. Hyman, *A More Perfect Union: The Impact of the Civil War and Reconstruction on the Constitution* (New York: Alfred A. Knopf, 1973).

48. Reverdy Johnson, 5 April 1866, *Congressional Globe,* 39th Cong., 1st sess., 1778. See also *De Bow's Review* (May 1866): 555.

49. See Hyman, *A More Perfect Union,* 465-70.

50. James A. Garfield, in "Ought the Negro to Be Disfranchised?" *North American Review* (March 1879): 245.

51. "National Convention of Colored Soldiers and Sailors" (1867), in Foner and Walker, *Proceedings,* 290. See also "Equal Suffrage: Address from the Colored Citizens of Norfolk, Va.," 5 June 1865; "Illinois State Convention of Colored Men" (1866), in Foner and Walker, *Proceedings,* 85, 254.

52. "Proceedings of the Annual Meeting of the Pennsylvania State Equal Rights' League" (1865) and "State Convention of the Colored People of Georgia" (1866), in Foner and Walker, *Proceedings,* 145, 157, 234.

53. Epideictic address plays an especially important role in effecting a consensus in the value formation process; see Chaim Perelman and L. Olbrechts-Tyteca, *The New Rhetoric: A Treatise on Argumentation,* trans. John Wilkinson and Purcell Weaver (Notre Dame, IN: University of Notre Dame Press, 1969), 48-51.

54. A particularly insightful analysis of Lincoln's rhetoric on slavery is David Zarefsky's *Lincoln, Douglas, and Slavery: In the Crucible of Public Debate* (Chicago: University of Chicago Press, 1990). See also Ernest Bormann, *The Force of Fantasy: Restoring the American Dream* (Carbondale: Southern Illinois University Press, 1985), 196-222; Michael C. Leff and G. P. Mohrmann, "Lincoln at Cooper Union: A Rhetorical Analysis of the Text," *QJS* 60 (1974): 346-58.

55. Kenneth M. Stampp argues that Lincoln never abandoned his hope for Colonization. See Stampp's *The Era of Reconstruction 1865-1877* (New York: Alfred A. Knopf, 1965), 47.

56. President Andrew Johnson, "First Annual Message," 4 December 1865, in Richardson, *A Compilation of the Messages and Papers of the Presidents,* 3556, 3553.

57. Ibid., 3558.

58. Ibid., 3558-59. On the tendency of whites to forecast the extermination of blacks see Franklin, *Reconstruction,* 6.

59. Johnson did not really account for the African-American position. He routinely referred to blacks as an alien "they," and, in stark contrast to Lincoln, he rudely refused to listen to the delegation of blacks he admitted to an audience. "Interview with a Colored Delegation," 7 February 1866, in Edward MacPherson, *The Political History of the United States of America during the Period of Reconstruction* (Washington, D.C.: Solomons and Chapman, 1875), 52-56.

60. President Andrew Johnson, "Third Annual Message," 3 December 1867, in Richardson, *Compilation of the Messages and Papers of the Presidents,* 3760-61. He made a similar suggestion in the first State of the Union Address.

61. Johnson, "Third Annual Message," 3 December 1867, in Richardson, *Compilation of the Messages and Papers of the Presidents,* 3762.

62. Ibid., 3762–63.

63. Ibid., 3764.

64. Ibid.

65. Both versions had existed in the South from the beginning, but they had not clearly been demarcated in the national arena.

66. *Atlanta Constitution*, 13 March 1877. See also "The Effects of Negro Suffrage," *North American Review* (April 1881): 247. This would be a continual refrain. See, e.g., Walter Guild, "A Plea from the South," *Arena* (November 1900): 483–85.

67. Walter B. Hill, "Uncle Tom without a Cabin," *Century* (April 1884): 863. See also, Henry Watterson, "The 'Solid South,'" *North American Review* (January 1879): 47–58.

68. See W. E. B. Du Bois, *The Souls of Black Folk* (Millwood, NY: Kraus-Thomson Organization Limited, 1973 [1903]), 110–62.

69. Montgomery Blair, "Ought the Negro to Be Disfranchised?" *North American Review* (March 1879): 263, 266. See also Watterson, "The 'Solid South,'" 47.

70. Cincinnatus Lamar, "Ought the Negro to Be Disfranchised?" *North American Review* (March 1879): 232.

71. Ibid., 233. Later, see Alfred H. Colquitt, *Forum* (November 1887): 268–70.

72. Lamar, "Ought the Negro to Be Disfranchised?," 233–34. See also *Atlanta Constitution*, 8 October 1872, 2.

73. *Atlanta Constitution*, 22 December 1874, 2.

74. Lamar, "Ought the Negro to Be Disfranchised?," 237.

75. Wade Hampton, "Ought the Negro to Be Disfranchised?" *North American Review* (March 1879): 240.

76. J. H. Sloss discounting the Congressional Hearings; Appendix to 20 May 1872, *Congressional Globe*, 42d Cong., 2d sess., 571. They also cast aspersions on the credibility of witnesses, who were "too ignorant to understand the nature of an oath, or totally and notoriously deficient in character for veracity" (572). See also Rep. Charles A. Eldridge, 4 February 1875, *Congressional Globe*, 43d Cong., 2d sess., 985. Even the *Nation* accepted this argument, disparaging the "'waving the bloody shirt'—that is, collecting stories of disorders and outrages at the South, and presenting them in exaggerated and inflammatory language." "The Federal Government and the Colored Voters," *Nation*, 13 February 1879, 113. See also William Ghormley Cochrane, "Freedom without Equality: A Study of Northern Opinion and the Negro Issue, 1861–1870" (Ph.D. diss., University of Minnesota, 1957), 397–99.

77. Lamar, "Ought the Negro to Be Disfranchised?," 236.

78. See, e.g., 3 February 1875, *Congressional Record*, 43d Cong., 2d sess., 953–57.

79. Alexander H. Stephens, "Ought the Negro to Be Disfranchised?" *North American Review* (March 1879): 251, 256–57.

80. *Atlanta Constitution*, 13 March 1877, 1. We will explain below the extent to which the white Southerner's sense of "liberty" was narrower than that of the Northerner. This produced systematic misunderstanding.

81. E.g., 3 February 1875, *Congressional Record,* 43d Cong., 2d sess., 953–57.

82. D. H. Chamberlain, "Reconstruction and the Negro," *North American Review* (February 1879): 169.

83. A. P. Peabody, "The Co-Education of the White and Colored Races," *Unitarian Review and Religious Magazine* (June 1875): 601.

84. "The Federal Government and the Colored Voters," *Nation,* 13 February 1879, 113–14. See also John B. Storm, 3 February 1875, *Congressional Record,* 43d Cong., 2d sess., 951.

85. Senator John R. Lynch, 3 February 1875, *Congressional Record,* 43d Cong., 2d sess., 945–47. See also the heartrending documents, "Petition for Kentucky Negroes" and "Memorial for Alabama Negroes," in Herbert Aptheker, ed., *A Documentary History of the Negro People in the United States: to 1910* (New York: Citadel Press, 1951), 1:594–604.

86. *The Colored Citizen,* 25 October 1879; 19 April 1878, 4. See also *New York Freeman,* "When necessary, bullet must be returned for bullet, and if every ballot cost a bullet, then let the ballot be cast," 3 April 1886, 2. For the response to lynching for rape see *Colored Citizen,* 27 September 1878, 4; "The Application of Force" (1889), in Peter Gilbert, ed., *The Selected Writings of John Edward Bruce: Militant Black Journalist* (New York: Arno Press, 1971) 29–32. On Northern migration see Nell Irvin Painter, *Exodusters: Black Migration to Kansas after Reconstruction* (New York: Alfred A. Knopf, 1977).

87. San Francisco *Elevator,* 1 July 1870, 2.

88. New Jersey *Sentinel* (April 1881), 20 May 1882, and 16 September 1882; *Virginia Star,* 11 May 1878, 2. See also Blanche K. Bruce, 7 April 1880, in Foner, *Voice,* 1:476; Daniel Payne, *Bishop Daniel A. Payne: Sermons and Addresses 1853–1891,* ed. Charles Killian (New York: Arno Press, 1972).

89. The alternate valuation is based on the equally imperialist assumption that black leaders should have run a white-style, Marxist campaign to revise completely the government in which they found themselves. The only nonculturally imperialist perspective would be to suggest that black leaders should have slipped back into the popular mass, which was organizing itself along local, tribalist lines derived from the African model. The problem with that position is illustrated by the case of the "American Indians" who followed such a local, tribalist model. Black bourgeois leaders really had only a choice between gradual extinction or productive assimilation and evolutionary modification of the nation in which they lived. Their success in producing wealth and creativity in their people, in the face of the vicious prejudice and alien culture and political system in which they lived, ought to be praised, we think, not deprecated.

90. Whites had several kinds of power including a developed communication network, organizational experience over extended territories, better armaments and military experience, and nominal control of the means of production.

91. *Colored Citizen,* 2 August 1878, 4; *New York Globe,* 29 March 1884.

92. *Colored Citizen,* 24 May 1878, 4. See also *New Era,* 9 February 1871, 4. A further understanding of this cultural adoption can be gained by exploring the San Francisco *Elevator*'s treatment of the Chinese issue. San Francisco blacks refused to

admit Chinese children to their segregated schools, and they justified this by saying that they were not opposed to the Chinese on racial grounds but on cultural ones, specifically their unwillingness to learn and adopt the American culture. See San Francisco *Elevator,* 21 June 1867, 2–3; 30 August 1867; 29 December 1871, 4.

93. *Colored Citizen,* 28 December 1878, 1; *New Era,* 13 January 1870, 3. The papers also taught lessons through moral stories, e.g., *Savannah Tribune,* 23 October 1886, 1.

94. *Colored Citizen,* 4 October 1878; *National Baptist World,* 31 August 1894, 2; San Francisco *Elevator,* 29 October 1869.

95. Whether one traces these values to Africa, to slave culture, or to the experience of prejudice, most observers of the time, black and white, agreed that the popular culture differed from puritan and capitalist culture. These values can be seen as positive ones, elements lacking from the Caucasian culture of the time (and, we might note, increasingly present in late twentieth-century culture, as African influences have become a powerful element of this culture). The status of other values, e.g., attachment to family, were much less agreed upon by contemporary observers.

96. E.g., *Virginia Star,* 27 August 1881; Bishop Daniel A. Payne, *Sermons and Addresses, 1853–1891.* There are notable exceptions. See, e.g., the *Washington Bee,* which was distinctly friendly to parades and the use of alcohol in its early years. See also *National Baptist World,* 7 September 1894, 2.

97. *Colored Citizen,* 2 August 1878, 4.

98. Ibid., 14 June 1878. See also Indianapolis *Freeman,* 26 January 1907, 4; *Colored Citizen,* 31 May 1878, 1; *National Baptist World,* 7 September 1894, 4; New Jersey *Sentinel,* 22 January 1881, 2; San Francisco *Elevator,* 13 October 1865, 3. There were, however, dissenting voices. Francis Ellen Watkins Harper urged elites not to separate themselves from the poor, 14 April 1875, in Foner, *Voices,* 1:430–34.

99. There was also growth in the rhetoric of black pride. See, e.g., *Virginia Star,* 11 May 1878, 2; *New Era,* 13 January 1870, 3; New Jersey *Sentinel,* 1 January 1881, 3.

100. The *Colored Citizen,* 13 September 1879, featured strong negative characterizations of black people on the front page and strong positive characterizations on p. 2. See also *Virginia Star,* 30 April 1881, 4; *New National Era,* 7 May 1874, 2. In some areas a refined class existed early and could be used as a wedge to characterize substantive equality. See esp. *La Tribune de la Nouvelle-Orleans,* 21 July 1864, 1.

101. August Meier, *Negro Thought in America, 1880–1915: Racial Ideologies in the Age of Booker T. Washington* (Ann Arbor: University of Michigan, 1963), 85.

102. 3 February 1875, *Congressional Record,* 43d Cong., 2d sess., 951.

103. A gradual erosion of the demand for commonly shared schools in favor of separate schools occurred throughout this era, but the shift was not based on principle. To some extent, it represented the self-interested battle of black bureaucrats who lost their positions when schools underwent integration. Others expressed a strong concern that black children be taught by teachers who were not prejudiced against them. The *Washington Bee* provides a close glimpse at the perpetual political

battles involved in local school issues. See also San Francisco *Elevator,* 2 December 1870, 2. Cf. 17 January 1868, 2. Cf. Foner's presentist interpretation in *Reconstruction,* 367.

104. The advantages and disadvantages were reported in the San Francisco *Elevator* on 29 December 1871; 27 April 1872, 2 and 3. Also, the *New York Age,* 23 August 1890, 1. See also the San Francisco *Elevator,* 23 August 1873. Recognizing the way in which forced segregation implied inferiority, the *New York Age* referred to "these outrageous laws that stamp us an inferior people," 19 September 1891, 1.

105. Theodore Crumswell, "Declaration of Sentiments," reported in the *Elevator,* 5 April 1873, 2.

106. Rep. James T. Rapier, 9 June 1874, *Congressional Record,* 43d Cong., 1st sess., 4784.

107. *Colored Citizen,* 19 April 1878, 4.

108. Rep. Thomas Whitehead, 3 February 1875, *Congressional Globe,* 43d Cong., 2d sess., 953.

109. Rep. John Lynch, 3 February 1875, *Congressional Record,* 43d Cong., 2d sess., 944–47. See also Rep. Joseph H. Rainey, 3 February 1875, 960; and Rep. James T. Rapier, 4 February 1875, *Congressional Record,* 43d Cong., 2d sess., 1001. See also *Colored Citizen,* 14 June 1878, 4; 6 September 1878, 1.

110. *Colored Citizen,* 31 May 1878, 4.

111. "Our Political Parties," Saratoga, NY, 1 April 1876, in *Freedom and Citizenship: Selected Lectures and Addresses of Honorable John Mercer Langston* (Miami: Mnemosyne Publishing Co., 1969 [1883]), 202. Blacks also applied the issue to the support of public education. See, e.g., Langston, "Pacific Reconstruction," Jersey City, NJ, 17 April 1877, in *Freedom and Citizenship,* 222.

112. *Colored Citizen,* 26 July 1878, 4. See also *The People's Friend,* 31 May 1894, 3.

113. *Colored Citizen,* 24 May 1878, 1. See also the *Washington Bee,* "[T]hey simply ask for justice and equality in the matter of Federal patronage," 15 June 1889, 2; the San Francisco *Elevator,* 11 September 1886; New Jersey *Sentinel,* 4 March 1882, 2.

114. President Rutherford B. Hayes, "Inaugural Address, 5 March 1877," in *The Inaugural Addresses of the Presidents of the United States 1789–1985* (Atlantic City, NJ: American Inheritance Press, 1985), 83.

115. President Ulysses S. Grant, "Fourth Annual Message," 2 December 1872, in Richardson, *Compilation of the Messages and Papers of the Presidents,* 4153.

116. Hayes, *Inaugural Addresses,* 82. Foner sees greater commitment to government action in the years 1870–72, but our reading of the documents indicates that such actions were reluctant at best. See Foner, *Reconstruction,* 551–55, 562–63, 582, 587.

117. President Ulysses S. Grant, "Second Inaugural Address, 4 March 1873," in *Inaugural Addresses,* 80.

118. Hayes, *Inaugural Addresses,* 83.

119. Grant, "Second Inaugural," *Inaugural Addresses,* 80.

120. Hayes, "Inaugural Address, 5 March 1877," in *Inaugural Addresses,* 83.

121. President Ulysses S. Grant, "Sixth State of the Union Address," 7 December 1874, in Richardson, *Compilation of the Messages and Papers of the Presidents,* 4252.

122. Hayes, "Inaugural Address, 5 March 1877," in *Inaugural Addresses,* 83.

123. Ibid., 82, 83.

124. Our division by decades weakens at this point. The racist rhetoric of the next few years is best divided along the lines 1880–93 and 1893–1915, whereas republican and black rhetorics are best divided along the lines 1880–98 and 1899–1915. Our chapters and headings are able to provide only rough guidelines for the dates at which the public debate shifts.

125. Andrew C. McLaughlin, "Mississippi and the Negro Question," *Atlantic Monthly* (December 1892): 828.

126. Woodward's thesis in the *Strange Career of Jim Crow* has been challenged on the grounds that segregation was widespread in the South from the beginning of the postwar period. This is true, but relationships between blacks and whites were uneven, varied, and unsettled. Moreover, when segregation was legitimated and codified in law something different of importance occurred. The relational patterns became less flexible and power relationships became more uneven. Whites no longer had to calculate what level of oppression was "safe" to practice on a particular human being. They could simply assume that the legally sanctioned oppression was "right." Thus, once protected by national law, segregation took on an obdurate tone, becoming both more rigidified and extensive. See Howard N. Rabinowitz, "More Than the Woodward Thesis: Assessing *The Strange Career of Jim Crow,*" *Journal of American History* 75 (1988): 842–56; C. Vann Woodward, "*Strange Career* Critics: Long May They Persevere," *Journal of American History* 75 (1988): 857–68.

127. Henry W. Grady, "In Plain Black and White," *Century* (April 1885): 909–17; Wade Hampton, "What Negro Superiority Means," *Forum* (May 1888): 383–95; Walter B. Hill, "Uncle Tom without a Cabin," *Century* (April 1884): 862. See also Foner, *Reconstruction,* 330.

128. Hill, "Uncle Tom," 862.

129. "The Effects of Negro Suffrage," *North American Review* (April 1881): 239–40.

130. "The Race Question," *Arena* (June 1890): 43.

131. Senator Wade Hampton, "The Race Problem," *Arena* (July 1890): 138.

132. William C. P. Breckinridge, "The Race Question," *Arena* (June 1890): 42. According to Breckinridge, "We claim, with a confidence that smacks sometimes of arrogance, that our particular race is the dominating race of the world, and its remarkable progress towards universal power during the last two centuries gives color to this claim." It may seem difficult to believe, but rather than denying this arrogance he affirms it.

133. "A Negro Emigration from America," *Spectator,* 24 January 1891, 113.

134. "The Effects of Negro Suffrage," 240.

135. "The Negro Problem," *Review of Reviews* (November 1895): 587.

136. Hill, "Uncle Tom," 863.

137. Chalmers, "The Effects of Negro Suffrage," 239.

138. "Will the Negro Relapse into Barbarism?" *De Bow's Review* (February 1867): 179. Breckinridge, "The Race Question," 47; T. U. Dudley, "How Should We Help the Negro?" *Century* (November 1885): 278.

139. See W. E. B. Du Bois, *The Souls of Black Folk,* esp. 110–62. Also, Michael Perman, *Emancipation and Reconstruction, 1862–1879* (Arlington Heights, IL: Harlan Davidson, 1987), 81. If descriptions of black (slave or African) culture as presentist, cyclical, and agricultural are correct, it should not be surprising that it was viewed as "primitive" or "barbaric" by those professing cultural commitments to a future-oriented progressivism and the accumulation of material wealth.

140. While the white supremacist perspective was unreasonably intolerant of other behaviors, comments by whites indicated clearly the real difficulty, discomfort, or pain the whites experienced when cultural change inspired by black culture was undertaken. See, e.g., the description of market behavior by whites in La Wanda Cox and John H. Cox, *Reconstruction, the Negro and the New South* (Columbia: University of South Carolina Press, 1973), 258–63; or *Congressional Globe,* 39th Cong., 1st sess., 3 February 1866, 635. As *Harper's Weekly* put it, "They will preserve their civilization and maintain social order for themselves and their descendants," 15 August 1903, 1323; also see Page, "The Negro," 620.

141. See, e.g., Mechal Sobel, *The World They Made Together: Black and White Values in Eighteenth-Century Virginia* (Princeton: Princeton University Press, 1987).

142. We do not deny that this way of speaking might have been interpreted by the white North purely in the metaphoric terms that called up "African barbarism" rather than the unique nonwhite culture of the South. The Northern whites had no direct access to the African-American culture in the South. The Northern sympathy with the fear of black cultural norms is expressed in the *Nation,* 23 January 1890, 64.

143. Senator James K. Vardaman looked back on the historical period and said that "we saw the civilization" of our fathers "vanishing from the earth," 6 February 1914, *Congressional Record,* 63d Cong., 2d sess., 3037; John T. Morgan, "Race Question in the United States," *Arena* (September 1890): 386; Wade Hampton, "The Race Problem," *Arena* (June 1890): 133.

144. Hampton, "The Race Problem," 132.

145. Ibid., 138.

146. Morgan, "Race Question," 385–98.

147. Breckinridge, "The Race Question," 49; Hampton, "The Race Problem," 138; N. S. Shaler, "The Negro Problem," *Atlantic Monthly* (November 1884): 705.

148. Henry W. Grady, "In Plain Black and White," 911.

149. Ultimately, they saw the refusal of Social Equality as a refusal of merit to African-Americans as a culture, not solely as individuals. It was, therefore, of the racial groups as a whole that Rep. Andrew Jackson Rogers spoke when he declared in Congress they would never admit "that there is a social equality between the black race and the white." 10 May 1866, *Congressional Globe,* 39th Cong., 1st sess.,

2538. See also Rep. Peter Van Winkle, 30 January 1866, *Congressional Globe,* 39th Cong., 1st sess., 498.

150. Grady, "In Plain Black and White," 911.

151. Ibid., 912.

152. Breckinridge, "The Race Question," 47.

153. E.g., Morgan, "Race Question," 385; Breckenridge, "The Race Question," 52. Even the extremely liberal George W. Cable said that "the greatest social problem before the American people to-day is, as it has been for a hundred years, the presence among us of the negro." Herein he identifies the American people as "us" (white people) and the Negro as an external "them." George W. Cable, "The Freedman's Case in Equity," *Century* (January 1885): 409.

154. Some contemporaries used "segregation" to mean a policy of territorial separateness, and "separation" to mean a policy of shared territory with different accommodations. We use the modern inversion of these terms to avoid confusing the reader.

155. Some white supremacists dreamed of exterminating the black race, and perhaps acted it out on a small scale in their violent attacks on the blacks. See the *Birmingham Alabama News,* quoted in the San Francisco *Elevator,* 24 October 1874, 2; "What's to be Done with the Negro?" *De Bow's Review,* June 1866, 580; "Relations of the Negro Race to Civilization," *De Bow's Review* (June 1860): 647; John L. Dawson, *Congressional Record,* 39th Cong., 1st sess., 31 January 1866. See also testimony at the "Report of the Joint Committee on Reconstruction" (1866), 542, 112, 117, in Walter L. Fleming, *Documentary History of Reconstruction* (Cleveland: Arthur Clark Co., 1906), 81, 542.

156. Grady, "In Plain Black and White," 912, 914–17.

157. E.g., L. A. Dutto, "The Negroes in Mississippi," *Catholic World* (February 1888): 578–79. This was an early concern. See the 5 April 1866, *Congressional Globe,* 39th Cong., 1st sess., 1783.

158. See, e.g., Page, "The Negro," 624. C. H. Smith complained that "they have ceased to show proper respect to the white people," in "Have American Negroes Too Much Liberty?" *Forum* (October 1893): 179.

159. 3 February 1866, *Congressional Globe,* 39th Cong., 1st sess., 627–37; 8 April 1864, *Congressional Globe,* 38th Cong., 1st sess., 1483.

160. *The Nation,* e.g., ranted against the "extraordinary nature of the measures devised by the friends of the negro for his elevation to an equality with the white man," in "The Negro Problem," *Nation,* 23 January 1890, 64. See also Rev. S. D. McConnell, "Are Our Hands Clean?" *Outlook,* 28 January 1899, 218; Rep. Charles Eldridge, 4 February 1875, *Congressional Globe,* 43d Cong., 2d sess., 984.

161. The *Atlanta Constitution,* 15 November 1873, 2, illustrates the presumption that men should defend themselves in its report on the whipping given by a white man to his white opponent in a protracted legal procedure. The newspaper endorsed the whipping, arguing, ". . . say what we will of the law, there is a feeling in every man's bosom that will leap responsive to this summary and violent ebulition that will honor the manhood that perpetrated it. . . . there is a stroke of nature in the occurrence that manly men will appreciate."

162. As Senator Morgan argued, "Something was needed, beyond any native virtues or powers of the negro, to lift him up to the full enjoyment of his liberty." He also described "their natural inability to preserve their freedom." See Morgan, "Race Question," 385.

163. William C. P. Breckinridge, "The Race Question," 55. The reaction against "special privilege" also repudiated the African-American request for proportional representation on the ground that blacks, being less meritorious, deserved less representation. Grady, "In Plain Black and White," 915.

164. One of the most flagrant cases is "The Negro Problem," *American Review of Reviews* (November 1895): 585–87. See also Julian Ralph, "The Plantation Negro," *Harper's Weekly,* 14 January 1893, 38.

165. Susan Showers, "A Weddin' and a Buryin' in the Black Belt," *New England Magazine* (June 1898): 478–83; "Certain Beliefs and Superstitions of the Negro," *Atlantic Monthly* (August 1891): 286–88; H. K. Carroll, "Religious Progress of the Negro," *Forum* (September 1892): 75–84; Rebecca Harding Davis, "Some Testimony in the Case," *Atlantic Monthly* (November 1885): 608.

166. "The Negro Intellect," *North American Review* (July 1889): 98.

167. "The Negro Problem," *American Review of Reviews* (November 1895): 587.

168. "The Plantation Negro," *Harper's Weekly,* 14 January 1893, 39.

169. "The Future of the Negro," *North American Review* (July 1884): 85.

170. "The Case of the Negro," *Atlantic Monthly* (November 1899): 578.

171. We are indebted to J. Robert Cox for demonstrating how gradualism might function as a central rhetoric. See "The Fulfillment of Time: King's 'I Have a Dream' Speech," in Michael C. Leff and Fred J. Kauffeld, eds., *Texts in Context: Critical Dialogues on Significant Episodes in American Political Rhetoric* (Davis, CA: Hermagoras Press, 1989), 181–204.

172. T. Thomas Fortune, "The Afro-American," *Arena* (December 1890): 115.

173. W. S. Scarborough, "The Negro Question from the Negro's Point of View," *Arena* (July 1891): 219–22; and "The Race Problem," *Arena* (October 1890): 560–67.

174. J. C. Price, "Does the Negro Seek Social Equality?" *Forum* (January 1891): 558; Fortune, "The Afro-American," 117.

175. Price, "Does the Negro Seek Social Equality?" 561. Price employs but neither explicitly endorses nor denies the concept of "race instinct." See also Grady, "In Plain Black and White," 911–12.

176. Price, "Does the Negro Seek Social Equality?" 562–63.

177. Grady, "In Plain Black and White," 915.

178. New Jersey *Sentinel,* 13 November 1880, 2; T. Thomas Fortune, 20 April 1886, in Foner, *Voices,* 1:506–10. See also John Edward Bruce, 5 October 1889, in Foner, *Voices,* 1:538.

179. Booker T. Washington, "The Case of the Negro," *Atlantic Monthly* (November 1899): 579–80; Rev. D. A. Graham, 4 June 1899, in Foner, *Voices,* 1:615.

180. E.g., Robert Browne Elliott, 6 January 1874, in Foner, *Voices,* 1:384–98, esp. 392.

181. *Washington Bee,* 25 June 1887, 1; D. W. Culp, "The Past and the Future of the American Negro," *Arena* (April 1897): 790.

182. New York *Freeman,* 3 April 1886, 2.

183. See, e.g., *Weekly Pelican,* 27 August 1887, 2. Note the difference from twentieth-century culturalism, which characterizes "culture" as possessed by and primarily of interest to the subgroup that generates it.

184. Lofgren's definitive study on Plessy is more highly nuanced. See Charles A. Lofgren, *The Plessy Case: A Legal-Historical Interpretation* (New York: Oxford University Press, 1987).

185. *Plessy* v. *Ferguson,* 163 U.S. 537, 543.

186. Ibid., 542.

187. Ibid., 544.

188. Ibid.

189. Ibid., 549.

190. Ibid., 548.

191. Ibid., 550.

192. Ibid., 551.

193. Ibid., 551–52.

194. President James T. Garfield, "Inaugural Address, 4 March 1881," in *Inaugural Addresses,* 86–87.

195. President Grover Cleveland, "First Inaugural Addresses, 4 March, 1885," *Inaugural Adresses,* 93.

196. Reported in the *Washington Bee,* 2 July 1887, 1. The black press was also happy with Cleveland for his relatively liberal patronage of blacks and for his opposition to the lynching of blacks. Nonetheless, Cleveland campaigned for a bill to prevent the lynching of foreigners but not of blacks.

197. *Washington Bee,* 2 July 1887.

198. President Benjamin Harrison, "Inaugural Address, 4 March 1889," in *Inaugural Addresses,* 95.

199. President Benjamin Harrison, "First Annual Message," 3 December 1889, in Richardson, *Compilation of the Messages and Papers of the Presidents,* 5490. Note that Harrison continued to identify the "us" of the United States with whites, while blacks remained the "other."

200. Ibid., 5490–91. On ballot fraud, see Harrison, "Third Annual Message," 9 December 1891, in Richardson, *Compilation of the Messages and Papers of the Presidents,* 5645.

201. President Grover Cleveland, "Second Inaugural Address, 4 March 1893," in *Inaugural Addresses,* 101.

CHAPTER SIX

1. To emphasize the generational shift, we recall John Hope Franklin's estimate that, in 1870, 81 percent of Negroes were illiterate whereas by 1930 the amount was only 16 percent. See *From Slavery to Freedom: A History of Negro Americans* (New York: Knopf, 1967), 405, 550.

2. This force is evidenced in porter strikes, boycotts of local businesses, employment efforts by the Urban League, interracial commissions in the South, and the impressive legal campaign of the NAACP.

3. This shift is often characterized in terms of the differences between Booker T. Washington and W. E. B. Du Bois, but they were only the most prominent spokespersons for the concepts of their times, and the differences in their views are often overstated. See Booker T. Washington, "My View of Segregation Laws," in Herbert Aptheker, *A Documentary History of the Negro People in the United States 1910–1932* (Secaucus, NJ: Citadel Press, 1973), 117–20 (hereafter referred to as *1910–1932*); W. E. B. Du Bois, *The Souls of Black Folk* (New York: American Library, 1969 [1903]). See also the William Levi Bull Lectures for the Year 1907 reprinted in Booker T. Washington and W. E. B. Du Bois, *The Negro in the South* (New York: Citadel Press, 1970).

4. In Aptheker, *1910–1932*, 81.

5. *New York Age*, 14 March 1907. "African-American" in this time period often signified mulattos. See also *American Eagle*, 17 December 1905.

6. *Colored Citizen*, 2 September 1897.

7. *The Appeal*, 25 October 1913.

8. Booker T. Washington, *The Appeal*, 2 November 1901. But note that he asked for "social rights" rather than the older formulation of "public rights." See also Pauline E. Hopkins, "Famous Women of the Negro Race," *Colored American Magazine* (May 1902): 41–46; Marcus Garvey, in Aptheker, *1910–1932*, 401, 404–7.

9. Based on our sample. See Appendix. We note that our sample is heavily influenced by *The Crisis* and that this magazine was ahead of most black publications during this period. Hence, our sample may overrepresent the frequency of the term. The term "equality," unmodified, is the second most frequent usage and provides the most likely alternative, but even this represented a dramatic increase and a significant shift away from modified usages such as "equal rights," "equality before the law," and "equal protection." Unmodified, it gradually replaced "social equality" after the 1930s. A surprisingly detailed and extensive survey of opinions on social equality is in *The Messenger* (January 1927): 4–30.

10. Mary Church Terrell, "Lynching from a Negro's Point of View," *North American Review* (June 1904): 853–68.

11. W. E. B. Du Bois, "The Social Equality of Whites and Blacks," *The Crisis* (November 1920): 16. The article goes on to suggest that individuals have a right to racial intermarriage, but that it is not desirable to do so because of the social (not biological) differences between the races.

12. W. E. B. Du Bois, "Social Equality," *The Crisis* (May 1922): 8. For another personal portrayal of the issue (which does not, however, employ the term "social equality") see Jessie Fauset, in Aptheker, *1910–1932*, 354–58.

13. See, e.g., Petition to the U.S. Congress by the National Liberty Congress (1918), in Aptheker, *1910–1932*, 215–18. We recognize that the continual use of the term "manhood" by the predominantly male national black leaders reflected a deep sexism and a desire to imitate white patriarchal versions of manhood. Detailed ex-

ploration of that issue is outside the limits of this study. We do note, however, that a widespread paternalistic approach to women pervaded the national mind-set during this time period. See *Pittsburgh Courier*, 1 November 1912, and 14 July 1956. See also *The Crisis* (January 1918): 124. This sexism is also reflected in the "cheesecake" covers and pull-out photographs in many of the articles of *Jet* and *Ebony* in the first decades of their publication. The demeaning or limiting portraits of black women by black men were not incompatible with black male support for black female voting rights or equal pay for equal work. On African-Americans and sexism see James Cone, *Martin and Malcolm and America: A Dream or a Nightmare* (Maryknoll, NY: Orbis Books, 1991), 273–80. For brilliant statements by black women on the role of black women see Aptheker, *1910–1932*, 103–16; Gerda Lerner, ed., *Black Women in White America: A Documentary History* (New York: Vintage Press, 1973 [1972]); Ann Allen Shockley, ed., *Afro-American Women Writers 1746–1933* (New York: Meridian Books, 1988).

14. *Washington Bee*, 23 November 1912.

15. *The Appeal*, 21 September 1889. *Opportunity* quoted the chief justice of the Ohio Supreme Court calling this "assimilation rather than amalgamation" (February 1928).

16. William Monroe Trotter (November 1914), in Philip S. Foner, ed., *The Voice of Black America: Major Speeches by Negroes in the United States 1797–1971*, 2 vols. (New York: Simon and Schuster, 1972), 2:706. *The Colored Citizen*, 8 July 1897, declared: "[W]e will not quietly submit [ourselves] to be branded as social lepers."

17. See W. E. B. Du Bois, *The Souls of Black Folk* (Millwood, NY: Kraus-Thomson, 1973 [1903]), 180. T. Thomas Fortune, c. 25 June 1890, in Foner, *Voice*, 1:560.

18 *The Appeal*, 11 March 1905. See also *The Appeal*, 22 November 1913; *New York Age*, 23 April 1908, 8 February 1906. For a brilliant and relatively detailed examination of the economics involved in segregation see William Pickens (1915), in Aptheker, *1910–1932*, 80–82; "A Memorial to the Atlanta Board of Education, 1917," in Aptheker, *1910–1932*, 172–73.

19. "Address of the Negro Bishops, 1908," in Herbert Aptheker, ed., *A Documentary History of the Negro People in the United States: From the Reconstruction Era to 1910* (New York: Citadel Press, 1951), 896 (hereafter referred to as *To 1910*). See also John Edward Bruce, "Practical" (1917), in Peter Gilbert, ed., *The Selected Writings of John Edward Bruce: Militant Black Journalist* (New York: Arno Press, 1971), 134; George Edwin Taylor, "A Negro Presidential Candidate's Address, 1904," in Aptheker, *To 1910*, 853; *Voice of the Negro* (January 1904): 26, 32.

20. *Colored Citizen*, 26 July 1879. See also ibid., 19 April 1878.

21. *Pittsburgh Courier*, 5 August 1911.

22. There had been an earlier appeal for whites to "open their workshops" to blacks, and even the suggestion of economic boycotts against those who refused to hire blacks, but these appeals only gradually reached the constitutive level. See *New Jersey Sentinel*, 23 October 1880; and *Opportunity* (January 1923): 4, 6, 8, 10.

23. *Colored Citizen,* 26 August 1897; *Washington Bee,* 17 June 1905. See also *Colored American Magazine* (June 1902): 112.

24. E.g., *Washington Bee,* 25 June 1904, 4. As an overview of the issue, see Benjamin Quarles, *Black Mosaic: Essays in Afro-American History and Historiography* (Amherst: University of Massachusetts Press, 1988), 145–47. For a range of views see Aptheker, *1910–1932,* 700–715, 856. Even during the Depression, the dominant cry was for "work" not government relief. By and large, the black leadership became friendly to Socialist approaches during the 1930s, but most never accepted Marxism, for they generally preferred a mixed economy. However, the combination of socialism and a mixed economy was enough to legitimate the widespread charge of "communism" leveled against them by the white supremacists after about 1924. Some contemporary historians argue that local grass roots leaders were different from the major national leadership and were something at least akin to a Marxian "proletarian leadership." They are able to find examples of such leadership because some such leaders existed. There is no evidence, however, to support the claim that the majority of blacks held these opinions, and the largest number of local black leaders were in fact church officials and bureaucrats who were even more conservative than the national leadership. See also Mark V. Tushnet, *The NAACP's Legal Strategy against Segregated Education, 1925–1950* (Chapel Hill: University of North Carolina Press, 1987), 151–58. We believe that the dominance of Marxism among post-Vietnam era white leftists has resulted in a somewhat distorted projection of Marxism onto the consciousness of the black masses. See, e.g., Nell Irvin Painter, *The Exodusters: Black Migration to Kansas after Reconstruction* (New York: Alfred A. Knopf, 1976). However, it is the case that in the 1920s some important black thinkers, influenced by the white left, adopted Marxism, or at least a modified version of socialism. See, e.g., W. E. B. Du Bois in *The Crisis* (November 1926): 8. On the appropriation process, see Wilson J. Moses, "The Lost World of the Negro, 1895–1919: Black Literary and Intellectual Life before the 'Renaissance,'" *Black American Literature Forum* 21 (1987): 61–84; Rena Fraden, "Feels Good, Can't Hurt: Black Representation on the Federal Arts Projects," *Journal of American Culture* 10 (1987): 21–29.

25. For an example of *The Messenger's* mixed message, contrast its attack on capitalism with its encouraging appeal to a chance for advancement within a matter of several pages. Its most vivid display of Marxist rhetoric appears in its attack on "Big Negro Leaders," who it claimed "are ready to sell you out." *The Messenger* (November 1917): 1, 7, 9, 11, 15. The message likewise was mixed on the collectivization for economic gains. Leaders were harshly critical of unions until they began to admit blacks in substantial numbers. Nevertheless, they urged black people to buy from black businesses and organized boycotts of businesses that did not hire blacks. See *Colored Citizen,* 9 September 1897; *Washington Bee,* 26 August 1899, 4; E. F. Roberts, among others, in Philip S. Foner and Ronald L. Lewis, eds., *Black Workers: A Documentary History from Colonial Times to the Present* (Philadelphia: Temple University Press, 1989), 405–8; *New York Age,* 10 October 1912.

26. See *Colored Citizen,* 17 June 1897.

27. At the "National Negro Conference, 1909," in Aptheker, *To 1910*, 922. He added, "and if I don't get equality, then I want superiority."

28. In Aptheker, *To 1910*, 758. See also *Voice of the Negro* (January 1904): 35.

29. *Washington Bee*, 5 October 1907, 4; 29 November 1902; 25 January 1889; *The Appeal*, 25 October 1890; Rev. D. P. Brown (August 1899), in Foner, *Voice*, 1:619; *Opportunity* (January 1923).

30. *Washington Bee*, 16 July 1910.

31. Booker T. Washington, "What the Negro Is Doing for the Negro in America," *Missionary Review* (November 1904): 833–35.

32. *New York Age*, 14 March 1907. Not all agreed. Robert Russa Moton complained that "the Negro in Africa sits listlessly in the sunshine of barbarous idleness" (May 1912), in Foner, *Voice*, 1:697.

33. *The Crisis* (May 1925): 26; (August 1924): 177–78.

34. *Washington Bee*, 23 November 1912, 8.

35. *New York Age*, 7 September 1911; *Colored Citizen*, 8 July 1897, 1. See also the *Colored American Magazine* (November 1909): 375–79.

36. E.g., *The Appeal*, 26 December 1914, 3. See also *Colored American*, 5 March 1904, 8; "[Lynching] Its Causes: A Low State of Civilization and Race Hatred," delivered 4 June 1899, in Francis James Grimké, *The Works of Francis J. Grimké*, 4 vols., ed. Carter G. Woodson (Washington, D.C.: Associated Publishers, 1942), 1:291–302 which provides a penetrating analysis of how stereotyping produces different characterizations for similar acts when done by whites and by blacks.

37. *The Appeal*, 6 August 1910.

38. Bruce, "To the Parents" (*c.* 1900), in *The Selected Writings of John Edward Bruce*, 63. See also W. S. Scarborough, "Lawlessness vs. Lawlessness," *Arena* (November 1900): 481: "There are thousands of negroes the equal of the best of white men in body, mind, and soul, and the superior of tens of thousands who can boast nothing in a mental or moral way—yes, or in a physical way either, except that they are 'white.'"

39. *Washington Bee*, 12 April 1913, 4. See also Mary Church Terrell for a depiction of women's achievements in "The Progress of Colored Women," *Voice of the Negro* (July 1904): 291–94.

40. *New York Age*, 14 March 1907, 3. See also the *Washington Bee*, 27 June 1896, 14 November 1896, and 21 August 1897; the *Pittsburgh Courier*, 12 July 1912. In the later period, the self-criticism diminished, but it did not fully disappear.

41. *The Appeal* quoting Joseph H. Choate, 4 May 1907. See also the *Washington Bee*, 26 August 1899; and *Colored Citizen*, 8 July 1897. W. S. Scarborough suggested that America was the gathering place of the nations of the world. See *Arena* (October 1890): 567.

42. The *American Eagle* argued that the people ought to be made "homo genius," 17 December 1905, 2.

43. *The Appeal*, 9 September 1911.

44. Booker T. Washington, "On an All-Negro Town, 1908," in Aptheker, *To 1910*, 873.

45. "The American Negro Academy, 1897," in Aptheker, *To 1910,* 772.

46. *Washington Bee,* 16 October 1886, 3. Also *Voice of the Negro* (February 1905): 127. W. E. B. Du Bois argued that blacks had given three special gifts to America: story and song, sweat and brawn, and the gift of the Spirit, in *Souls of Black Folk,* 275–76.

47. *The Crisis* (May 1925): 23.

48. Ibid. (November 1926): 32.

49. *Pittsburgh Courier,* 2 January 1926; *The Crisis* (November 1923): 32, (February 1929): 48, (August 1924): 182.

50. Few speakers even had developed a coherent view of their own, as is evident in the UNIA's "Declaration of Rights," which employed Anglo-American phrases from the Declaration of Independence and elsewhere as universal warrants to oppose white culture and demand protection for black culture. In John Henrik Clarke and Amy Jaques Garvey, eds., *Marcus Garvey and the Vision of Africa* (New York: Random House, 1974), Appendix 443–51. There is also a chronological progression from individualism toward more acceptance of the role of culture. Cf. *Opportunity* (January 1923): 26, where it adamantly denied a "Negro type," to *Opportunity* (April 1933): 107, where it touted "The Negro's Contribution to American Culture." For one of the most coherent statements on the issue see "Manifesto of the Second Pan-African Congress," in Aptheker, *1910–1932,* 337.

51. *The Crisis* (September 1916): 216–17.

52. Steven Graham, quoted in *The Crisis* (November 1920): 28. With regards to the Liberia movement, see *The Crisis* (May 1922): 33.

53. See ibid. (November 1926): 21; *Opportunity* (February 1928): 60 ("assimilation rather than amalgamation"); *The Messenger* (November 1917): 6 ("Human nature is uniform . . . Negro troops are just human"); *Norfolk Journal and Guide,* 12 November 1921, 4.

54. Advocates of the day recognized the difficulty. *The Messenger* asked a group of black leaders, "Is the development of Negro racial consciousness (a definite group psychology, stressing and laudation of things Negro) compatible with the ideal of Americanism (Nationalism) as expressed in the struggle of the Afroamericans for social and industrial equality with all other citizens?" and "Can a minority group like the Afroamericans maintain separate identity and group consciousness, obtain industrial and social equality with the citizens of the majority group and mingle freely with them." *The Messenger* (January 1927): 11.

55. The growth of the Women's Club Movement provided one important source of such support. See Paula Giddings, *When and Where I Enter: The Impact of Black Women on Race and Sex in America* (New York: Morrow Books, 1988 [1984]), 95–118. The NAACP had a specific set of short-term and long-term goals, ranging from federal antilynch laws, the desegregation of Washington, D.C., and interstate commerce in the short run to the repeal of all statutory recognition of race in the long run. These goals shifted throughout the years. See, e.g., *The Crisis* (September 1916): 235; (August 1921): 164; (May 1925): 8.

56. E.g., Aptheker, *1910–1932,* 254–56.

57. This is the title of a racist tract that took an internationalist perspective, by

Lothrop Stoddard, *The Rising Tide of Color against White World Supremacy* (New York: Charles Scribner's Sons, 1920).

58. E.g., Senator Thomas J. Heflin, 10 April 1928, *Congressional Record,* 70th Cong., 1st sess., 6175: "[T]he white race is the superior race, the king race, the climax and crowning glory of the four races of black, yellow, red and white. The South's doctrine of white supremacy is right and it is fast becoming the doctrine of the American Republic."

59. See, e.g., James H. Dormon, "Shaping the Popular Image of Post-Reconstruction American Blacks: The 'Coon Song' Phenomenon of the Gilded Age," *American Quarterly* 40 (December 1988): 450-71; Cal M. Logue, "Rhetorical Ridicule of Reconstruction Blacks," *Q JS* 62 (1976): 400-409.

60. M. L. Perry, "Insanity and the Negro," *Current Literature* (October 1902): 468.

61. A. J. McKelway, "The Convict Lease System of Georgia," *Outlook,* 12 September 1908, 67-72.

62. Walter H. Page, "The Last Hold of the Southern Bully," *Forum* (November 1893): 303-14; Thomas Nelson Page, "The Negro: The Southerner's Problem," *McClures* (March 1904): 549; "The Negro at the North," *Harper's Weekly,* 31 March 1906, 436.

63. Leslie H. Fishel and Benjamin Quarles, *The Negro American* (Glenview, IL: Scott, Foresman and Co., 1967), 427. They say "Between 1890 and 1920, more men were lynched than were executed by all the courts in the land." The misuse of the nongeneric "he," common at the time of publication of that book, makes it unclear whether they intended to include women in this count or not.

64. Walter L. Hawley, "Passing of the Race Problem," *Arena* (November 1900): 475. In Congress, Rep. Edward Pou, 19 December 1921, *Congressional Record,* 67th Cong., 2d sess., 549. The debate in Congress rested heavily and increasingly on issues of constitutionality and the impact of federal enforcement of police issues as well as upon the likely effectiveness of the bill.

65. See Walter Guild, "A Plea from the South," *Arena* (November 1900): 485-86; "Mr. Washington and the Negro Problem," *Harper's Weekly,* 15 August 1903, 1324-25. See also Elizabeth L. Banks, "American Negro and His Place," *19th Century* (September 1899); esp. 460-61. In Congress see, e.g., Rep. John T. Watkins, 31 May 1920, *Congressional Record,* 66th Cong., 2d sess., 8030; Rep. James Buchanan, 17 December 1921, *Congressional Record,* 67th Cong., 1st sess., 467.

66. See, e.g., George Gladden, quoting the *New Orleans Times-Democrat,* in *Current Literature* (May 1904): 491: "The higher education of the negro unfits him for the work that it is intended that he shall do." See also the inaugural address of Governor Vardaman of Mississippi, in *Current Literature* (March 1904): 271; Hoke Smith, *Message of the Governor of Georgia to the General Assembly, June 24, 1908* (Atlanta: Franklin-Turner Co.), 29.

67. William Dorsey Jelks, "The Acuteness of the Negro Question," *North American Review* 15 (February 1907): 389-95.

68. Ibid., 394. Also Chas. H. Smith, "Have American Negroes Too Much Liberty?" *Forum* (October 1893): 179.

69. Thomas Gibson, "Anti-Negro Riots in Atlanta," *Harper's Weekly,* 13 October 1906, 1459.

70. See George Gladden, *Current Literature,* for a variety of perspectives. A common line of argument was that although blacks were making intellectual progress, they were not capable of moral progress or of higher intellectual achievements.

71. A. V. Dicey, "Mr. Bryce on the Relation between Whites and Blacks," *Nation,* 10 July 1902, 27.

72. Thomas Nelson Page, "The Negro: The Southerner's Problem," 620.

73. "Passing of the Race Problem," 473.

74. J. C. Hemphill, "The President, the South, and the Negro," *Harper's Weekly,* 9 January 1909, 10. Elements of these arguments had, of course, been employed in earlier periods, but their resurrection, reorganization, and intensification violated the Separate But Equal compromise.

75. "The Disfranchisement Amendment," *Outlook* 11 (August 1900): 842.

76. By reducing the number of black voters, it made it much easier to control those potential voters through threats of violence and economic pressure.

77. The consistent argument against these appointments was that they were predicated on racial discrimination. This was a clear precursor to the "reverse discrimination" argument that would develop against Affirmative Action in the 1970s. So, e.g., President Roosevelt's motives were characterized as racist when he persisted in renominating William Crum, a black man, to the customs office on multiple occasions, despite the fact that Congress consistently rejected the nomination. See J. C. Hemphill, "The President, the South, and the Negro," 10.

78. Samuel Douglas McEnery, "The Race Problem in the South," *Independent* 19 (February 1903): 426.

79. Ibid.

80. See, e.g., Jacquelyn Dowd Hall, *Revolt against Chivalry: Jessie Daniel Ames and the Women's Campaign against Lynching* (New York: Columbia University Press, 1979).

81. In Congress see, e.g., the debate over funding Howard University, 12 February 1915, *Congressional Record,* 63d Cong., 3d sess., 4192, esp. Rep. Hardwick; Jelks, "Acuteness of the Negro Question," 392–94.

82. Thomas Gibson, "The Anti-Negro Riots in Atlanta," *Harper's Weekly,* 13 October 1906, 1459.

83. Jelks, "The Acuteness of the Negro Question," 390.

84. Jelks, "The Acuteness of the Negro Question," 390. In Congress, the hyperinflated rhetoric against the federal lynch laws routinely portrayed life for white women in the South as horrible because of the conditions existing between the races. See Rep. Finnis J. Garrett: "[M]any of you gentlemen do not know what it is to live in a section in which your wife dare not travel alone for a distance of a mile through wood or field," 19 December 1921, *Congressional Record,* 67th Cong., 2d sess., 548. However, in general, white congressional representatives spoke of the race issues as "a problem" reflecting their discomfort, and there were specific mentions of "the serious obstacles" faced in the on-going efforts to work out the race

relations, e.g., Rep. Ross A. Collins, 12 January 1922, *Congressional Record*, 67th Cong., 2d sess., 1134–38, 1339–1140.

85. Rep. John T. Watkins, 31 May 1920, *Congressional Record*, 66th Cong., 2d sess., 8030; Rep. Thomas U. Sisson, 12 February 1915, *Congressional Record*, 63d Cong., 3d sess., 3691.

86. The Commission on Interracial Cooperation and the Association of Southern Women for the Prevention of Lynching got their start at the end of this period. See Jessie Daniel Ames and Bertha Payne Newell, *"Repairers of the Breach: A Story of Interracial Cooperation between Southern Women, 1935–1940"* (Atlanta: Commission Interracial Cooperation, 1940); Jessie Daniel Ames, "Southern Women and Lynching 1932," and "Women Follow Ideals" (1933), available in the Robert W. Woodruff Library.

87. "Recent Discussions of the Negro Problem," *Harper's Weekly*, 2 February 1907, 151; "Task of the Southern Leader," *Review of Reviews* (March 1907): 353–54; Edwin A. Alderman, "The Growing South," *World's Work* (June 1908): 10376–79.

88. C. H. Smith, "Have American Negroes Too Much Liberty?" *Forum* (October 1893): 182.

89. L. Percy, "Southern View of Negro Education," *Outlook*, 3 August 1907, 733; Jelks, "The Acuteness of the Negro Question," 393–94; Samuel Douglas McEnery, "The Race Problem in the South," 426. More liberal voices responded with the call for the establishment of black police forces to hold the black community responsible for its own criminals. See "A Problem of Administration, Not Race," *Nation*, 19 April 1906, 316–17; A. B. Hart, "Outcome of the Southern Race Question," *North American Review* (July 1908): 50–61.

90. Albert B. Hart, "The Outcome of the Southern Race Question," 50–61. See also N. S. Shaler, "The Negro Problem," *Atlantic Monthly* (November 1884): 708.

91. Rep. James B. Aswell, 19 December 1921, *Congressional Record*, 67th Cong., 2d sess., 546; Jelks, "The Acuteness of the Negro Question," 390.

92. Rep. Charles F. Reavis, 17 January 1922, *Congressional Record*, 67th Cong., 2d sess., 1286.

93. "The Educational Solution of the Negro Problem," *Outlook*, 11 July 1903, 633, quoting Charles A. Gardener.

94. This article uses the example of a black girl who greatly agitated racists by defeating white students to win a spelling bee. Quincy Ewing, "The Heart of the Race Problem," *Atlantic* (March 1909): 395.

95. W. E. B. Du Bois, "Of the Training of Black Men," *Atlantic Monthly* (September 1902): 294; William E. Hutchison, "Industrial Training in Negro Education," *Independent*, 12 January 1905, 94.

96. Ida M. Wells-Barnett, "1909 National Negro Conference," in Foner, *Voices*, 2:687; Alfreda M. Duster, ed., *Crusade for Justice: The Autobiography of Ida B. Wells* (Chicago: University of Chicago Press, 1970).

97. By the second decade of the new century, congressional egalitarians routinely denied that rape was the cause of lynchings, despite the continual allegations of white supremacists.

98. Rev. Mr. Vance quoted in Booker T. Washington, "The Case of the Negro," *Atlantic Monthly* (November 1899): 586.

99. "Atlanta Outdone," *Independent,* 20 August 1908, 442.

100. "Race Purity and Social Equality," *Independent,* 19 February 1903, 453.

101. Rep. Theodore E. Burton, 17 January 1922, *Congressional Record,* 67th Cong., 2d sess., 1277.

102. Rep. Leonidas C. Dyer, 7 May 1918, *Congressional Record,* 65th Cong., 2d sess., 6177. Rep. Theodore E. Burton even argued: "State boundaries are becoming vanishing traces on the map," and the federal government would have to assume greater responsibilities, 17 January 1922, 1277. By contrast, some white supremacists claimed that the sole option the federal government had was to declare that the state government was not "republican" and end it. See Rep. James Buchanan, 17 December 1921, *Congressional Record,* 67th Cong., 2d sess., 465.

103. "Secretary Taft as a Conciliator," *Independent,* 26 March 1908, 696.

104. "Disfranchisement in North Carolina"; "Mr. Washington and the Negro Problem," *Harper's Weekly,* 15 August 1903, 1324–25; "Disfranchising the Negro," *Nation,* 23 November 1899, 384.

105. "Colored Statistics," *Nation,* 19 November 1903, 400–401; and "Race Purity and Social Equality," 455.

106. Du Bois, "Training of Black Men," 296.

107. Ewing, "Heart of the Race Problem," 393.

108. See e.g., "The Progress of the Negro in One County in the South," *Outlook,* 9 December 1905, 874–75; "Negro Self-Help," *Independent,* 23 November 1905, 1207–8; "The Story of the Negro," *Outlook,* 4 September 1909, 19–26; "Race Purity and Social Equality," *Independent,* 19 February 1903, 455.

109. This is most true of the *Nation,* which, by 1940, would make a direct appeal to subordinate race traditions to class unity. See "Toward Negro Unity," *Nation,* 11 March 1936, 302. At times, some black leaders recognized this imposition by white leftists and resisted it. See, e.g., *The Crisis* (August 1921): 151.

110. *Nation,* 10 July 1902, 26–28; "The President and the Negro: A Step in Advance," *Outlook,* 18 February 1905, 416–17.

111. As Walter Hawley noted, this legislation was important to the maintenance of supremacy because the use of violence and custom was too wearing: "The white men of the South were not slow to realize that they could not go on forever nullifying the votes of negroes by the methods employed in 1876." Walter L. Hawley, "Passing of the Race Problem," *Arena* (November 1900): 470.

112. 238 U.S. 347, 365. Similarly, in *Giles* v. *Harris,* 189 U.S. 475, the Court ruled out an obvious attempt to disfranchise blacks.

113. 103 U.S. 370, (1881). Like *Williams,* the case turned on characterizations, but the Delaware case claimed *no* blacks had the requisite positive characterizations, whereas the Williams case claimed only that *few* blacks had those characteristics. Similarly, in *Moore* v. *Dempsey,* 261 U.S. 86 (1923), the Court also defined a minimal level of equal justice extending beyond dodges based on the avoidance of the use of the term "equality."

114. 235 U.S. 151 (1914). The *Buchanan* v. *Warley* (245 U.S. 60, 1917) restric-

tive covenant case is not indicative, since it turned on the rights of whites to sell their property at will rather than on the rights of blacks per se. However, the Court did cite the equality provisions, and it was legally important in building a bridge to black rights.

115. 170 U.S. 213 (1898).

116. *Yick Wo* v. *Hopkins,* 118 U.S. 356 (1886).

117. Harding stirred up some controversy on the race issue with a speech entitled "The Rights of Black Citizens," given in Birmingham, AL, 26 October 1921, in Janet Podell and Steven Anzovin, eds., *Speeches of the American Presidents* (New York: H. W. Wilson Co., 1988), 420–23. The speech argued for voting rights for blacks, shared culture, and equal opportunity, a brave stance given the audience. However, Harding was careful to advocate a "separate path" for matters both social and racial. The black press was mildly supportive of the speech.

118. President William McKinley, "First Inaugural, 4 March 1897," in *Inaugural Addresses of the Presidents of the United States* (Washington, D.C.: Government Printing Office, 1989), 105.

119. Theodore Roosevelt, "Sixth Message to Congress, 3 December 1906," in Fred L. Israel, ed. *The State of the Union Messages of the Presidents, 1790–1966* (New York: Chelsea House, 1966), 2200–2202.

120. Ibid., 2203–4.

121. Ibid., 2201–2.

122. Ibid., "Seventh Message to Congress, 3 December 1907," 2244.

123. Ibid., "Fourth Annual Message, 6 December 1904," 2109. We do not believe that it is a historical accident that the fortunes of equal protection for blacks and for corporations were tied together. Rather, there seems to be ample discursive evidence to conclude that both originally concerned relations of free labor which served to link them together ideologically.

124. Roosevelt, "Eighth Annual Message, 8 December 1908," in *State of the Union Messages,* 2300.

125. President William Howard Taft, "Inaugural Address, 4 March 1909," in *Inaugural Addresses,* 116.

126. Taft argued that "while the fifteenth amendment has not been generally observed in the past, it ought to be observed, and the tendency of Southern legislation today is toward the enactment of electoral qualifications which shall square with that amendment. Of course, the mere adoption of a constitutional law is only one step in the right direction. It must be fairly and justly enforced as well. In time both will come. Hence it is clear to all that the domination of an ignorant, irresponsible element can be prevented by constitutional laws which shall exclude from voting both negroes and whites not having education or other qualifications thought to be necessary for a proper electorate. The danger of the control of an ignorant electorate has therefore passed." Taft, "Inaugural Address," in *Inaugural Addresses,* 120. Taft here deftly transmuted the flurry over "ignorant black voters" to deny racism any standing in national law, but he did so at the cost of rolling back the egalitarian concept of universal suffrage that the Jacksonian era had produced.

127. Taft, "Inaugural Address," in *Inaugural Addresses,* 120.

128. Ibid., 121. This became a standard claim of racists in later years and so was eventually discredited. That does not deny its significance in this circumstance.

129. Ronald H. Carpenter, "On American History Textbooks and Integration in the South: Woodrow Wilson and the Rhetoric of Division and Reunion 1829–1889," *Southern Speech Communication Journal* 51 (1985), 1–23.

130. President Warren G. Harding, "First Annual Message, 6 December 1921," in *State of the Union Messages,* 2624.

131. President Calvin Coolidge, "Third Annual Message, 8 December 1925," in *State of the Union Messages,* 2688–89.

132. Ibid.

133. Attention to police brutality extended back to the middle of the nineteenth century, but it was more sustained in this period. See *Pittsburgh Courier,* 27 April 1946, 4; (Chicago) *Defender,* 27 April 1946, 10; (Philadelphia) *Afro-American,* 27 April 1946, 2, 18; and 4 January 1936, 4, 20.

134. E.g., *The Bronzeman* (June 1931): 9–10. One important sign of that support was Myrdal's famous report on "the American dilemma" and its reception. See E. Culpepper Clark and Raymie E. McKerrow, "The Historiographical Dilemma in Myrdal's American Creed: Rhetoric's Role in Rescuing a Historical Moment," *QJS* 73 (1987): 303–16.

135. In *Color* (August 1944): 11 (Charleston, W.VA), a boxed ad stated, "WE HAVE DIFFERENT FAITHS, different cultures, different colored skins. WE HAVE THE SAME way of work, way of life. We know the same sorrows, joys, and hopes. WE ALL SHARE THE AMERICAN DREAM OF EQUALITY" (punctuation added, capitalization in original).

136. *The Crisis,* (April 1940): 99, said about the Beautiful Child Contest: "Colored children are conceded to be among the most beautiful in the world by unbiased observers. Here in the United States, where most colored children are of African, Caucasian, and Ameri-Indian descent in varying degree, they present a veritable flower garden of beauty, a preview of the human race of the future." See also *The Crisis* (February 1944): 58. *Ebony* and *Jet* gave extensive attention to the beauty of colored women. See, e.g., *Ebony* (February 1956): 30–34. Later the complaint that the models featured were not black enough would surface. See *Ebony,* April 1966, 14, 18–19.

137. *The Crisis* (August 1948): 236.

138. We make this point because each new generation of blacks tends to label itself "militant" and the previous generation as a group of "Uncle Toms," proclaiming prior methods and styles as "accommodationist" or "toadying." This has happened to virtually every black leader who has accomplished the greatest deeds for the race, including Frederick Douglass, Booker T. Washington, W. E. B. Du Bois, Thurgood Marshall, and, most recently, Martin Luther King, Jr. It occurs when people judge the rhetoric of the past in terms of its sufficiency as a principle for living in the present, an error in judgment brought on by the failure to recognize that circumstances change, and that different circumstances require different rhetorics. It also occurs because Marxists seek to stigmatize all efforts short of revolution as a bargain with the devil. The tendency to disparage the adequacy of pre-

vious leaders seems to contrast with the tendency in European-derived culture to deify earlier leaders, while shifting what it is they are taken to "stand for."

139. Elmer W. Henderson, "Negroes in Government Employment," *Opportunity* (July 1943): 98, 115, 143.

140. *The Crisis* (April 1931): 135; and (July 1936): 214. See also the *Norfolk Journal and Guide*, 3 January 1931, 10.

141. As a congressional representative, Adam Clayton Powell had some national voice, and he represented a largely impoverished urban community. He was also more stylistically militant than other black leaders. However, he did not generate a mass national following. There was conflict between Powell and the other leaders but they often incorporated his positions while distancing themselves from his flamboyance. See *Pittsburgh Courier*, 27 April 1946, 6. See also the inclusion of his attack on gradualism in the integration of D.C. schools in *Norfolk Journal and Guide*, 20 April 1946, 1. Cf. 27 April 1946, 11.

142. *Pittsburgh Courier*, 27 April 1946, 6. See also George S. Shuyler, "Do we Really Want Equality?" *The Crisis* (April 1937): 102–3, where he attacked "a little clique of Negroes gunning for teachers' jobs for their daughters at the expense of the group as a whole." Then as now, black members of the educational establishment tended to see separation as desirable, in part perhaps because it gave them increased personal wealth and power. On the role of teachers in fighting segregation, see also *The Crisis* (January 1938): 17. On the more general issue of education, see *The Crisis* (July 1939): 210. In opposition to the complacency of the middle class who willingly accepted mere "patronage" rather than broad benefits for all blacks, see *Color* (August 1944): 15.

143. There was a great deal of concern for the poor manifested by the middle class. See, e.g., Thyra J. Edwards's plea on behalf of women and the poverty-stricken, carried and supported in *Opportunity*, a middle-class publication, in Herbert Aptheker, ed., *A Documentary History of the Negro People in the United States, 1933–1945* (New York: Citadel Press, 1990 [1974]), 245–48 (hereafter referred to as *1933–1945*).

144. *The Crisis* (January 1941): 7; *Opportunity* (July 1943): 118. But see the complex debate on the issue led by Du Bois, reprinted in Aptheker, *1933–1945*, 63–84.

145. *The Crisis* (January 1938): 17.

146. They were, however, able to use "local custom" as an effective de facto method of preventing the federal government from distributing its largess equitably. E.g., *The Crisis* (October 1938): 334.

147. *The Crisis* (October 1935): 315; *Opportunity* (July 1943): 111; *Pittsburgh Courier*, 15 February 1936.

148. *The Crisis* (October 1935): 294; T. Arnold Hill in Aptheker, *1933–1945*, 278. For a similar argument with New Deal programs see *Opportunity* (July 1943): 112–13. Another application appears in the *Pittsburgh Courier*, 15 February 1936.

149. *The Crisis* (October 1935): 294–95.

150. The other part of the problem was that white supremacists consistently employed arguments from proportion to limit black opportunities. Wherever

blacks congregated in employment, they argued that blacks were getting an excessive share of resources. See, e.g., Rep. William F. Stevenson, 2 February 1928, *Congressional Record,* 70th Cong., 1st sess., 1928; Rep. John S. Gibson, 14 April 1944, 78th Cong., 2d sess., A1786; Rep. John Rankin, 18 March 1948, *Congressional Record,* 80th Cong., 2d sess., 3071. For other objections, see Rep. Tom Picket, 2 August 1948, *Congressional Record,* 80th Cong., 2d sess., 9641.

151. During the war years, black leaders backed away from the school issue, both for patriotic reasons and because of the greater potential for progress on employment and other issues during the war.

152. See Aptheker, *1933–1945,* 373; *The Crisis* (August 1939): 209; also 231, 234; also (June 1931): 208.

153. E.g., *The Crisis* (April 1934): 112; (July 1939): 215; (January 1941): 16; *Pittsburgh Courier,* 27 April 1946, 11; Robert C. Weaver, in Aptheker, *1933–1945,* 179. The proportion argument, however, predated federal involvement. It had been used both in local Northern communities with regard to public facilities and in "Buy Where You Can Work" campaigns. See *The Crisis* (April 1934): 103.

154. See, e.g., Senator Theodore Bilbo, 19 November 1942, *Congressional Record,* 77th Cong., 2d sess., 8967. Bilbo indirectly concedes the correctness of obtaining "manpower for the war effort and a fair share of jobs for the Negro," in making his stand against "social equality."

155. See A. Philip Randolph, "Keynote Address to the Policy Conference on the March on Washington," in August Meier, Elliott M. Rudwick, and Francis L. Broderick, eds., *Black Protest Thought in the Twentieth Century* (Indianapolis: Bobbs-Merrill, 1971 [1965]), 224–33.

156. E.g., *The Crisis* (November 1947): 340; *Pittsburgh Courier,* 22 March 1941, 22.

157. *Opportunity* (April 1933): 126. *Opportunity* was a business-oriented magazine, but the same argument was made by labor leaders. See George Weaver's incisive analysis, which anticipates all of the later problems that were to arise with Affirmative Action efforts, in Aptheker, *1933–1945,* 467, 471–73. The increasing availability of colored persons of the first rank was evidenced by the increased hiring of black lawyers by the NAACP. See August Meier and Elliott Rudwick, "Attorneys Black and White," in *Along the Color Line: Explorations in the Black Experience* (Urbana: University of Illinois Press, 1976), 128–73.

158. *The Crisis* (November 1947): 343.

159. Earl Brown, "American Negroes and the War," *Harper's* (April 1942): 545; Dorothy W. Baruch, "Sleep Comes Hard," *Nation,* 27 January 1945, 95–96; "RACIAL: Caucasians Only," *Newsweek,* 25 March 1946, 33.

160. Robert C. Weaver, "With the Negro's Help," *Atlantic Monthly* (June 1942): 697, 705–6; "Employment of Negroes by Federal Government," *Monthly Labor Review* (May 1943): 891; James W. Lane, "The Negro and American Democracy," *Catholic World* (November 1942): 173.

161. Jarmila Marton, Letter to the Editor, *Nation,* 17 March 1945, 315. Compare this to the downside of this issue, i.e., the forced labor for black women, most directly illustrated in WWI. See Walter F. White, in Aptheker, *1910–1932,* 237–41.

162. "Round Table on a Train," *Catholic World* (June 1946): 259; R. M. Cunningham, Jr., "Borderline Breakfast," *New Republic* (17 December 1945): 836; James W. Lane, "The American Negro and Democracy," *Catholic World* (November 1942): 172–77. This does not mean that there were no more negative statements about blacks. Emphasis on crime rate and educational lag would continue, especially in *U.S. News and World Report* (hereafter *USNWR*), but even in these cases the statistical deficiencies were not presented as the "normal" state of the descendants of Africans, and they were shorn of highly emotional language.

163. "Dark Islam," *Nation*, 1 June 1942, 29–30. Some articles took up the issue of multiculturalism. William H. Johnson argued that African cultural studies were being integrated into the Chicago school curriculum in "The Place of the Negro in the Social Studies, Chicago Public Schools," *School and Society*, 9 October 1943, 283–85. Others addressed the assimilation of black and white culture. See Herman G. Canady, "The Methodology and Interpretation of Negro-White Mental Testing," *School and Society*, 23 May 1942, 569–75; or "Our Conflicting Racial Policies," *Harper's* (January 1945): 172–79.

164. However, the characterizations of blacks and whites as essentially similar led to that conclusion. Only essential dissimilarity would lead to inequality if equal opportunity were available.

165. Rep. Oscar DePriest, 3 May 1933, *Congressional Record*, 73d Cong., 1st sess., 2823.

166. Senator Thomas F. Ford, 16 June 1941, *Congressional Record*, 77th Cong., 1st sess., 5195; Senator John Bankhead, 7 February 1944, *Congressional Record*, 78th Cong., 2d sess., A1262.

167. Rep. John Bell Williams, 12 February 1948, *Congressional Record*, 80th Cong., 2d sess., 1295.

168. Senator James O. Eastland, 9 February 1948, *Congressional Record*, 80th Cong., 2d sess., 1194.

169. Rep. Malcolm C. Tarver quoting a railroad official, 26 May 1944, *Congressional Record*, 78th Cong., 2d sess., 5027. See also same date, Rep. Jamie Whitten, 5031.

170. 294 U.S. 587, 598, 597, 599.

171. 273 U.S. 536, 541.

172. *Nixon* v. *Condon*, 286 U.S. 73 (1932); *Grovey* v. *Townsend*, 295 U.S. 45 (1936).

173. The Court after this period became about as consistent in its acceleration of support for more egalitarian positions as one could expect any human body to be. We reiterate a caution we state in Chap. 4. Our interpretation of these cases is based on a rhetorical, not a legal, focus. This leads to a different emphasis than legal interpretors might offer. E.g., Tushnet criticizes the Gaines decision as "illogical" because the Court's legal justification was not in line with either previous or later precedent. However, the Court's "logic" was based on a new public vocabulary rather than the by-then-discredited legal precedents. Tushnet, *The NAACP's Legal Strategy against Segregated Education, 1925–1950*, 70–81, 151–54. On the general relationship between legal and political discourse, especially as it affects judicial decisions, see John Brigham, *Constitutional Language: An Interpretation of Judicial*

Decision (Westport, CT: Greenwood Press, 1978), esp. 92–136, 159–64; and *The Cult of the Court* (Philadelphia: Temple University Press, 1987), 167–217; Ira L. Strauber, "Transforming Political Rights into Legal Ones," *Polity* 16 (1983): 72–95; and "The Rhetorical Structure of Freedom of Speech," *Polity* 19 (1987): 507–28.

174. 305 U.S. 337, 349, 236, 238. The alternative available to the court was presented vividly in the dissent of Justices McReynolds and Butler, who said "to break down the settled practice concerning separate schools and thereby, as indicated by experience, damnify both races . . . The State should not be unduly hampered through theorization inadequately restrained by experience." See 305 U.S. 337, 355.

175. 321 U.S. 649, 664.

176. 334 U.S. 1, 22.

177. See the condemnation of Herbert Hoover by W. E. B. Du Bois in *The Crisis*, 39 (1932): 362–63.

178. His wife served as an effective goodwill ambassador to the colored people, he gave in to pressure by A. Phillip Randolph to ban employment discrimination in federal projects, and he forwarded the rhetorical linkage of democracy and equality of opportunity in opposition to Hitler's racism. See the warm eulogy by the *Chicago Defender*, 21 April 1945.

179. President Harry S. Truman, "Civil Rights Message," 2 February 1948, and "Fair Deal for the Negro," 16 June 1952, in David Horton, ed., *Freedom and Equality: Addresses by Harry S. Truman* (Columbia: University of Missouri Press, 1960), 10–11, 19–26; "The Struggle for Civil Rights," 11 October 1952, in Janet Podell and Steven Anzovin, *Speeches of the American Presidents,* (New York: H. W. Wilson, 1988), 553–55. Truman's activity on race issues extended back at least as far as 1940. See also "The New Deal for the Negro," delivered at the Convention of the National Colored Democrats Association, 14 June 1940, in Horton, *Freedom and Equality*, 1–7.

180. President Harry S. Truman, "Second Annual Message, 6 January 1947," in *State of the Union Messages*, 2946–47.

181. Ibid., "Third Annual Message, 7 January 1948," 2952.

182. Ibid., 2952–53.

183. Ibid., "Second Annual Message," 2947.

184. President's Committee on Civil Rights, *To Secure These Rights* (New York: Simon and Schuster, 1947), 3.

185. Ibid., 4.

186. Ibid., 13.

187. Ibid., 82.

188. Ibid., 87.

189. After providing the argument for the constitutionality of federal action, the report urged that "the time for action is now" on dozens of proposals, including the use of the FBI in civil rights investigations, the enactment of antilynching codes, antipeonage codes, the end of the poll tax, federal protection of voting rights, the elimination of discrimination in the armed services, and "The elimina-

tion of segregation, based on race, color, creed, or national origin, from American life"—including schools, the military, housing, health services, and other public services. *To Secure These Rights,* 166.

190. Harry S. Truman, "Eighth Annual Message, 7 January 1953," in *State of the Union Messages,* 2997.

191. President Dwight D. Eisenhower, "Address on the Situation in Little Rock, Arkansas, 24 September 1957"; and the press conferences of 3 October and 30 October 1957 in *Public Papers of the Presidents of the United States: Dwight D. Eisenhower, 1957* (Washington, D.C.: Government Printing Office, 1958), 689–94, 704–15, 774–87.

192. *Terry* v. *Adams,* 345 U.S. 461 (1953). The decision denied a subparty level whites-only organization. Also *Cooper* v. *Aaron,* 358 U.S. 1 (1958) required state and local governments to provide active guarantees of the constitutional provisions.

193. 347 U.S. 483, 494 (1954). The Court carefully limited its finding in this case to education, where it could construct a narrow set of precedents, but the finding was quickly generalized to all other areas on the same grounds.

194. 347 U.S. 483, 494 (1954).

195. See *Gaines,* discussed above, also *Sipuel* v. *Oklahoma State Regents,* 332 U.S. 631 (1948); *Sweatt* v. *Painter,* 339 U.S. 629 (1950); *McLaurin* v. *Oklahoma State Regents for Higher Education,* 339 U.S. 637 (1950). For a detailed history of the strategies leading up to the *Brown* decision see Richard Kluger's monumental *Simple Justice: The History of* Brown v. Bd. of Education *and Black America's Struggle for Equality* (New York: Alfred A. Knopf, 1975); Tushnet, *The NAACP's Legal Strategy against Segregated Education, 1925–1950.*

196. *Brown* v. *Board of Education* (II) 349 U.S. 294, 301 (1955).

197. *USNWR* provided the major exception, and its objections came in the form of insinuations about the negative consequences of mixed schools rather than as a frontal attack.

198. Arna Bontemps, "The Bud Blooms," *Saturday Review,* 20 September 1952, 29; Howard Snyder, "Around the USA: Forty Years in the Black Belt," *Nation,* 21 March 1953, 236.

199. George S. Schuyler, "The Negro Voter Comes of Age," *American Mercury* (March 1957): 99.

200. David Lawrence quoted by Cary McWilliams in "The Heart of the Matter," *The Nation,* 31 March 1956, 249.

201. McWilliams, "The Heart of the Matter," 250. See also editorial, "White House Conference on Integration," *America,* 12 May 1956, 155.

202. Stephen P. Ryan, "After Jesuit Bend," *America,* 4 February 1956, 504. Occasionally, actions even matched these words, as in Tucson, Arizona, where school integration proceeded within this understanding of time. A school official reported, "We could have waited another five years I suppose. . . . But we'd have had the same squawks five years from now, so why not do it now?" "Arizona Progress," *New Republic,* 13 August 1951, 7.

203. Rep. Cooley, for instance, said, "I am not aware of the fact that a single

man or woman in my congressional district is being oppressed, nor am I aware of the fact that any of them are being denied the protection of the law . . . I have not received a single communication [from his constituents]." Rep. Harry D. Cooley, 19 July 1956, *Congressional Record,* 84th Cong., 2d sess., 13549–50.

204. Senator James O. Eastland, 23 July 1954, *Congressional Record,* 83d Cong., 2d sess., 11522: "[T]he salvation of Americanism lies in returning to the people in the communities of the country the control of their local affairs."

205. R. Carter Pittman, "Equality vs. Liberty: The Eternal Conflict," *American Bar Association Journal* (August 1960), reprinted in 19 August 1960, *Congressional Record,* 86th Cong., 2d sess., 16755. See also Rep. Clare Hoffman, 23 April 1952, *Congressional Record,* 82d Cong., 2d sess., 4320; Rep. Elijah L. Forrester, 18 May 1954, *Congressional Record,* 83d Cong., 2d sess., 6777.

206. See, e.g., Senator James O. Eastland, 23 July 1954, *Congressional Record,* 83d Cong., 2d sess., 11522; Senator Joseph Bryson, 12 April 1948, *Congressional Record,* 80th Cong., 2d sess., 4362. This extended the earlier use of the private property argument with regard to restrictive covenants and residential integration. Also Rep. Thomas A. Pickett, 2 August 1948, *Congressional Record,* 80th Cong., 2d sess., 9640–41.

207. Rep. John E. Rankin, 19 April 1950, *Congressional Record,* 81st Cong., 2d sess., 5391.

208. Rep. John Bell Williams, 12 February 1948, *Congressional Record,* 80th Cong., 2d sess., 1295; Senator E. L. (Tic) Forrester, 17 February 1958, *Congressional Record,* 85th Cong., 2d sess., 2292. This was an interesting move given that it was only the recent migration that made whites a definitive majority in the states of the South. Some congressional advocates also claimed that the white South was a "minority" group.

209. Rep. John Rankin went on to claim that this had crippled defense and degenerated government service, 19 April 1950, *Congressional Record,* 81st Cong., 2d sess., 5391.

210. Senator James O. Eastland, 23 July 1954, *Congressional Record,* 83d Cong., 2d sess., 11525.

211. Senator John Bell Williams, 27 March 1956, *Congressional Record,* 84th Cong., 2d sess., 5691–92.

212. Senator John Bell Williams, 27 March 1956, *Congressional Record,* 84th Cong., 2d sess., 5694. Similarly, Sen. Price Daniels claimed that "I know of no one who has ever defended the doctrine of separate and equal schools because of prejudice or a desire to discriminate . . . or a feeling of superiority." 18 May 1954, *Congressional Record,* 83d Cong., 2d sess., 6743.

213. Rep. Williams, 12 February 1948, *Congressional Record,* 80th Cong., 2d sess., 1296. The claim that both blacks and whites wanted segregation was a mainstay argument, which did not wane until demonstrations swept the South, shocking most white supremacists into realizing the depth of the discontent. See, e.g., Senator John Stennis, 4 March 1948, *Congressional Record,* 80th Cong., 2d sess., 2105.

214. Rep. Joseph R. Bryson, 12 April 1948, *Congressional Record,* 80th Cong.,

2d sess., 4361. Also, Reps. John Rankin and John Bell Williams, 12 February 1948, *Congressional Record,* 80th Cong., 2d sess., 1295–96; Rankin, 18 March 1948, *Congressional Record,* 80th Cong., 2d sess., 3070.

215. Rep. Joseph R. Bryson, 12 April 1948, *Congressional Record,* 80th Cong., 2d sess., 4361. See also Rep. Ed Gossett, 6 June 1950, *Congressional Record,* 81st Cong., 2d sess., 8173. They also accompanied this with extended attacks on the Supreme Court for its failure to follow legal precedent.

216. Senator John Stennis, 4 March 1948, *Congressional Record,* 80th Cong., 2d sess., 2105.

217. Rep. Elijah L. Forrester, 19 July 1954, *Congressional Record,* 83d Cong., 2d sess., 10981.

218. Rep. James C. Davis, 23 July 1956, *Congressional Record,* 84th Cong., 2d sess., 14154.

219. Rep. William T. Granahan, 19 August 1954, *Congressional Record,* 83d Cong., 2d sess., 15333; Rep. John D. Dingell, 23 August 1958, *Congressional Record,* 85th Cong., 2d sess., 19846.

220. Rep. Emmanuel Celler, 16 July 1956, *Congressional Record,* 84th Cong., 2d sess., 12923.

221. Senator Wayne Morse, 12 March 1956, *Congressional Record,* 84th Cong., 2d sess., 4462.

222. *The Crisis* itself reported "the race's growing impatience with words instead of deeds," and noted, "Gradualism finds easy acceptance when it is someone else's freedom that is to come later" (June–July 1957): 377. See *Ebony* (February 1956): 18–20; *Los Angeles Sentinel,* 5 July 1956, 9; *Jet,* 1 November 1951, 56.

223. *The Crisis* (February 1950): 74; (December 1955): 611.

224. Ibid., (June–July 1957): 379. Also *Jet,* 6 December 1956, 4.

225. *Ebony* (December 1951): 50, (February 1956): 6–7, 18–19; *Jet,* 6 December 1956, 15. *The Crisis* (November 1950): 616–19, (December 1955): 611.

226. *The Crisis* (March 1959): 185.

227. Abdou Anta Ka, ibid. (April 1958): 205, 207. The model of interbraiding white and black culture was also exemplified by the *Pittsburgh Courier*'s suggestion that the schools need to teach world history that included Africa and Asia. Nat D. Williams, "Down on Beale," 29 September 1951, 10.

228. *Pittsburgh Courier,* 14 July 1956.

229. *The Crisis* (January 1955): 7; but see *Ebony* (February 1956): 7, for a letter to the editor articulating the opposite position.

CHAPTER SEVEN

1. Discrimination ranges from repeated racial insults to police neglect and brutality. See Shelby Steele, *Content of Our Character: A New Vision of Race in America* (New York: St. Martin's Press, 1990), 169; and the Dahmer case in Milwaukee, *Atlanta Journal,* 5 August 1991, A11. Black women are particularly likely to live in poverty. With the genders combined, blacks lag whites substantially in median and mean income, but they lead Hispanics and Native Americans. Black males have

higher mean and median incomes than do either white females or females as a whole, but black males lag white males more than black females lag white females. See U.S. Bureau of the Census, *Statistical Abstract of the United States, 1990,* 110th ed. (Washington, D.C. 1990), 453–54.

2. See, e.g., August Meier and Elliott Rudwick, *From Plantation to Ghetto,* 3d ed. (New York: Hill and Wang, 1978), 272, 285, 296; John Hope Franklin, *From Slavery to Freedom: A History of Negro Americans,* 5th ed. (New York: Alfred Knopf, 1980 [1947]), 470; Donald Nieman, *Promises to Keep: African-Americans and the Constitutional Order, 1776 to the Present* (New York: Oxford University Press, 1991), 181.

3. The sequence here is not tidy, for Malcolm X was assassinated four years earlier than King. The mythic identity of each captures only a part of his respective programs, and these programs moved from different directions toward similar points. See Herbert W. Simons, "Patterns of Persuasion in the Civil Rights Struggle," *Communication Quarterly* 15 (1967): 25–27; Karlyn Kohrs Campbell, "The Rhetoric of Radical Black Nationalism: A Case Study in Self-Conscious Criticism," *Central States Speech Journal* 22 (1971): 151–60.

4. Note, however, that compliance within the federal appellate court system was in many places not achieved. See Nieman, *Promises to Keep,* 157–58.

5. See, e.g., "Brooklyn Area Sees Fear Grow," *Atlanta Constitution,* 5 August 1991, A4. On the moral impetus thereby engaged, see Parke G. Burgess, "The Rhetoric of Black Power: A Moral Demand?" *QJS* 54 (1968): 122–33.

6. "Negroes Are Not Moving Too Fast" (1964), in James M. Washington, ed., *A Testament of Hope: The Essential Writings of Martin Luther King, Jr.* (San Francisco: Harper and Row, 1986), 177.

7. Bayard Rustin, "From Protest to Politics," 1965, in August Meier, Elliott Rudwick, and Francis L. Broderick, eds. *Black Protest Thought in the Twentieth Century* (Indianapolis, IN: Bobbs-Merrill, 1971), 453; or Adam Clayton Powell, Jr., "Can There Any Good Thing Come Out of Nazareth?" in Philip S. Foner, ed., *The Voice of Black America,* 2 vols. (New York: Simon and Schuster, 1972), 2:1027–33.

8. John Hope Franklin, "The Emancipation Proclamation, 1863–1963," in *The Crisis* (March 1963): 137.

9. Quoting Lyndon Johnson, *The Crisis* (March 1966): 143.

10. "Showdown for Nonviolence," in Washington, *Testament of Hope,* 67.

11. Both marxissants (white and black) and opponents of racial equality portrayed "economic equality" as equivalent to state ownership of the means of production, and they tried to insinuate that this was what black militants meant. Moreover, Marxist commitments were probably more popular among the fringe groups of black activists than at any other moment in history. See, e.g., Angela Y. Davis, *Women, Race, and Class* (New York: Random House, 1981); and *Angela Davis: An Autobiography* (New York: International Publishers, 1988 [1974]).

12. *The Crisis* (August–September 1961): 401.

13. King explains this well in responding to a questioner on "Face to Face," television interview, 28 July 1967, in Washington, *Testament of Hope,* 409–10.

14. Jesse L. Jackson, *Straight from the Heart* (Philadelphia: Fortress Press, 1987), 89, 277.

15. Bayard Rustin (1965), in Meier, Rudwick, and Broderick, *Black Protest Thought,* 448. See also "Freedom Budget," in Philip S. Foner and Ronald L. Lewis, eds. *Black Workers: A Documentary History from Colonial Times to the Present* (Philadelphia: Temple University Press, 1989), 571–80.

16. See, e.g., Julian Bond, "A New Movement and a New Method," in Foner, *Voice,* 2:1161–66. Several of the speeches in this collection repeat these themes.

17. King endorsed "preferential treatment," but for all disadvantaged groups, not on the basis of race. See the *Playboy* interview (1965), in Washington, *Testament of Hope,* 367; Jesse L. Jackson, "Excellence in the Press," 3 June 1978, *Straight from the Heart,* 322. The assumption of the correctness of active government economic programs pervades the speeches in the last half of the 1960s in Foner, *Voices,* vol. 2. See also Loren Miller, "Farewell to Liberals" (1962), in Meier, Rudwick, and Broderick, *Black Protest Thought,* 379; Helen Howard, Dorothy Height, and Ruby Doss, in Gerda Lerner, ed., *Black Women in White America: A Documentary History* (New York: Vintage Books, 1973), 512–24.

18. James Farmer, "Develop Group Pride" (1966), in Meier, Rudwick, and Broderick, *Black Protest Thought,* 567.

19. See the speeches by Malcolm X in *When the Word Is Given,* ed. Louis E. Lomax (Westport, CT: Greenwood Press, 1963). For an elaboration of the impact of these doctrines see Eldrige Cleaver, *Soul on Ice* (New York: McGraw-Hill, 1968).

20. Martin Luther King, Jr., "I Have a Dream," 28 August 1963, in Washington, *Testament of Hope,* 218. For a more thorough treatment of the rhetoric of equality employed by King and Malcolm X see John Louis Lucaites and Celeste Michelle Condit, "Reconstructing ⟨Equality⟩: Culturetypal and Counter-Cultural Rhetorics in the Martyred Black Vision," *Communication Monographs* 57 (March 1990): 5–24.

21. King, "I Have A Dream," 219.

22. See Kenneth L. Smith in Ira G. Zepp, *Search for the Beloved Community* (Valley Forge, PA: Judson, 1974); and Anthony E. Cook, "Beyond Critical Legal Studies: The Reconstructive Theology of Dr. Martin Luther King, Jr.," *Harvard Law Review* 103 (1990): 985–1044; Carolyn Calloway-Thomas and John Louis Lucaites, eds., *Martin Luther King, Jr. and the Sermonic Power of Public Discourse* (University: University of Alabama Press, 1993).

23. Martin Luther King, Jr., "The Ethical Demands for Integration," Nashville, TN, 27 December 1962, in Washington, *Testament of Hope,* 118.

24. In the "Letter from Birmingham Jail," King characterized the failure to achieve total integration as a literal "sin." In Martin Luther King, Jr., *Why We Can't Wait* (New York: New American Library, 1964), 82–83.

25. Malcolm X and Alex Haley, *The Autobiography of Malcolm X* (New York: Grove Press, 1966), 272.

26. Malcolm X and Haley, *Autobiography,* 275; our emphasis after the ellipses.

27. Malcolm X, "To Mississippi Youth," 31 December 1964, in George Breitman, ed., *Malcolm X Speaks* (New York: Grove Press, 1966), 139.

28. Malcolm X, "Debate with James Farmer," in Haig Bosmajian and Hamida Bosmajian, comp., *Rhetoric of the Civil Rights Movement* (New York: Random House, 1969), 59–88. For examples of those who adopted the separatist position see Dara Abubakari, in Lerner, *Black Women in White America,* 555–58; Robert S. Browne, "A Case for Separation," in Foner, *Voice,* 2:1121–31.

29. "Manifesto to the White Christian Churches and the Jewish Synagogues in the United States and All Other Racist Institutions" (1969), in Meier, Rudwick, and Broderick, *Black Protest Thought,* 540–41.

30. The adoption of this vision of "cultural nationalism" is most vivid in the transformation of the position of James Farmer. See "Develop Group Pride," in Meier, Rudwick, and Broderick, *Black Protest Thought,* 567–83.

31. John O. Killens, "We Refuse to Look at Ourselves through the Eyes of White America" (1964), in Meier, Rudwick, and Broderick, *Black Protest Thought,* 426. In *The Crisis* this manifested itself as a move to recognize difference but to treat persons in a similar fashion regardless of difference (January 1964): 9. See James Baldwin, "The American Dream Is at the Expense of the American Negro," in Foner, *Voice,* 2:1012–17.

32. "A Case for Separatism" (1968), in Meier, Rudwick, and Broderick, *Black Protest Thought,* 525–26. See also Stokely Carmichael and Charles V. Hamilton, *Black Power: The Politics of Liberation in America* (New York: Random House, 1967), 40. For a general treatment of Carmichael's rhetoric see Wayne E. Brockriede and Robert L. Scott, "Stokely Carmichael: Two Speeches on Black Power," *Central States Speech Journal* 19 (1968): 3–13.

33. At the time, many of the older leaders agreed with whites in portraying it as "black supremacy," e.g., Kenneth Clark, interview with James Baldwin, in Leslie H. Fishel and Benjamin Quarles, *The Negro American* (Glenview, IL: Scott, Foresman and Co., 1967), 527.

34. The *Chicago Defender,* 7 October 1968, interpreted the growth of voting as a form of "black power."

35. A fairly extensive treatment of "institutional racism" is woven throughout Carmichael and Hamilton, *Black Power.* The phrase "institutional racism" emerged in the 1960s as part of the collectivization process, functioning in black power discourse in particular as a blanket label for white American social practices. See, e.g., "San Francisco State College," in Meier, Rudwick, and Broderick, *Black Protest Thought,* 529. By 1980, the identification of institutional racism had become full-fledged, paired with the concept of "subtle forms of discrimination," as in Jesse Jackson's characterization of "the impersonal violations and indirect acts of institutionalized racism." See Jackson, *Straight from the Heart,* 296, 40. Vernon Jordan, *Ebony* (December 1980): 36.

36. James Farmer, "Develop Group Pride," 582; Robert Dudnick, "Black Workers in Revolt," in Foner and Lewis, *Black Workers,* 632.

37. "Manifesto," in Meier, Rudwick, and Broderick, *Black Protest Thought,* 542. The tendency was difficult to resist. Eldridge Cleaver, e.g., would in some

places admit the possibility of including whites in antiracist work but would nonetheless often talk of whites in the collective sense as racists. See *Soul on Ice,* 56–57 vs. 156.

38. The strongest version of this was the strident attack on "Uncle Toms" or "house Negroes" in favor of "field Negroes" by Malcolm X. See "Twenty Million Black People in a Political, Economic, and Mental Prison," in Bruce Perry, ed., *Malcolm X, the Last Speeches* (New York: Pathfinder Press, 1989), 28–31; Carmichael and Hamilton, *Black Power,* 41; Louis Lomax, in Fishel and Quarles, *The Negro American,* 502–7; Robert S. Browne, "A Case for Separation," in Foner, *Voices,* 2:1121–31. For the other side, see Meier, Rudwick, and Broderick, *Black Protest Thought,* 408.

39. Chicago Office of SNCC: "We Must Fill Ourselves with Hate for All White Things" (1967), in Meier, Rudwick, and Broderick, *Black Protest Thought,* 486. This definition of equality was close to what many marxissant advocates supplied in the same period, but it was not precisely that of Marx himself.

40. This is most evident if we compare the phrasing of the SNCC proposal, with its constant hostile statements against the "bourgeoisie," to the closely related way in which the earlier merit-tolerant version of equality was stated by a letter writer in *The Crisis* (March 1963): 190: "[T]here is *no* justification for discrimination, for unequal class treatment, whether Negroes are inferior, *or* superior. Negroes are humans, and all humans are to fall within the equal treatment of the laws." Martin Luther King, Jr., attacked the issue in a similar way. As the *Norfolk Journal and Guide* reported it, "He said that there are inferior and superior individuals but not inferior and superior races," 8 July 1961, 2.

41. Bayard Rustin (1965), in Meier, Rudwick, and Broderick, *Black Protest Thought,* 445. See also "Needed: A Black Cross," in *Ebony* (March 1961): 86; *Norfolk Journal and Guide,* 8 July 1961, 12.

42. *Ebony* (April 1966): 118; John Henrik Clarke, "The Meaning of Black History," in Foner, *Voice,* 2:1138–45.

43. For an ample discussion of the range of issues see Derrick A. Bell, *Race, Racism and American Law* (Boston: Little Brown and Co., 1980 [1973]). Bell emphasizes the shortcomings in these court decisions from the perspective of one who desires that absolute protection be guaranteed to black persons in all arenas.

44. President John F. Kennedy, "Second Annual Message," 11 January 1962, in Fred L. Israel, ed., *The State of the Union Messages of the Presidents, 1790–1966* (New York: Chelsea House, 1966), 3137.

45. President John F. Kennedy, "Radio and Television Address to the American People on Civil Rights," June 11, 1963, in *Public Papers of the President of the United States, John Fitzgerald Kennedy, January 1–November 22, 1963* (Washington, D.C.: Government Printing Office, 1964): 468–71. See Steven R. Goldzwig and George N. Dionisopoulos, "John F. Kennedy's Civil Rights Discourse: The Evolution from 'Principled Bystander' to Public Advocate," *Communication Monographs* 56 (1989): 179–98.

46. President John F. Kennedy, "Second Annual Message," in *State of the Union Messages,* 3137.

47. Ibid., "Third Annual Message," 14 January 1963, 3148.

48. Kennedy, "Radio and Television Address," *Public Papers,* 471.

49. President Lyndon B. Johnson, "First Annual Message," 8 January 1964, in *State of the Union Messages,* 3156–61.

50. Ibid., 3160.

51. Ibid., "Second Annual Message," 4 January 1965, 3168.

52. In the late 1980s and early 1990s news magazines and newspapers ran issues pointing out that shortly after the millennium the nation would no longer be a "white" majority, persons of Hispanic origin having become included in the category "colored." See *Time,* 27 May 1991, 74; *USA Today,* 11 March 1991, A5:1.

53. David Zarefsky, *President Johnson's War on Poverty: Rhetoric and History* (University: University of Alabama Press, 1986).

54. Senator Jack R. Miller, 10 April 1964, *Congressional Record,* 88th Cong., 2d sess., 7508.

55. Ibid.; citing *US News and World Report,* 17 February 1964, 7510 (hereafter USNWR).

56. Rep. John M. Ashbrook, 8 June 1966, *Congressional Record,* 88th Cong., 2d sess., 12604. These were accompanied by attacks on the demonstrations which portrayed them as "hurting their cause" or "poorly timed." See, e.g., Senator Spressard L. Holland, 1 March 1960, *Congressional Record,* 86th Cong., 2d sess., 3918.

57. William M. Colmer, 3 October 1962, *Congressional Record,* 87th Cong., 2d sess., 22109; Senator Herman Talmadge, 28 March 1960, *Congressional Record,* 86th Cong., 2d sess., 6722.

58. Senator Kenneth Keating, 24 April 1962, *Congressional Record,* 87th Cong., 2d sess., 7136; Rep. William Pettis Ryan, 14 May 1962, *Congressional Record,* 87th Cong., 2d sess., 8283.

59. For a condensed statement of this perspective which displays most of its rhetorical facets see Senator Herman E. Talmadge, debate on the issue from *Reader's Digest* (July 1960), reprinted in *Congressional Record,* 22 June 1960, 86th Cong., 2d sess., 13714–16. In the earlier period, some white supremacists in Congress had conceded Equality before the Law, but now it became the centerpiece of their defense, and the argument about the supremacy of whites vanished, while even resistance to biological interbreeding became only a rarely mentioned fringe argument.

60. R. Carter Pittman, cited in 19 August 1960, *Congressional Record,* 86th Cong., 2d sess., 16757.

61. Senator Herman Talmadge, 22 June 1960, ibid., 13714; Glenn Andrews, 6 October 1966, *Congressional Record,* 89th Cong., 2d sess., 25530.

62. Rep. John D. Waggonner, 20 July 1966, *Congressional Record,* 89th Cong., 2d sess., 16306; Rep. Thomas C. Abernathy, 4 February 1964, *Congressional Record,* 88th Cong., 2d sess., 1935.

63. Rep. John M. Ashbrook, 16 March 1964, *Congressional Record,* 88th Cong., 2d sess., 5311 and 9 March 1964, *Congressional Record,* 88th Cong., 2d sess., 4736.

64. Senator Robert C. Byrd, 21 February 1968, *Congressional Record,* 90th Cong., 2d sess., 3755.

65. From the *Times-Picayune,* August 1970, in *Congressional Record,* 24 September 1970, 91st Cong., 2d sess., 33536.

66. Rep. Teno Roncalio, 8 August 1966, *Congressional Record,* 89th Cong., 2d sess., 18631.

67. Senator Strom Thurmond, 17 May 1968, *Congressional Record,* 90th Cong., 2d sess., 13840.

68. Actually, this left-wing position was only implicit in the stands of a few congressional representatives at this point. It would not be worked out in full until much later, and even then it would be the view of a small minority. For examples of representatives thinking about the durability of poverty, see Senator Jacob Javits, 21 April 1966, *Congressional Record,* 89th Cong., 2d sess., 8693; Rep. James C. Corman, 12 May 1966, *Congressional Record,* 89th Cong., 2d sess., 10492.

69. Rep. Alphonzo Bell, 26 September 1968, *Congressional Record,* 90th Cong., 2d sess., 28434; Rep. Robert N. C. Nix, 5 April 1968, *Congressional Record,* 90th Cong., 2d sess., 9092.

70. See the *Wall Street Journal,* 13 May 1966, in *Congressional Record,* 18 May 1966, 89th Cong., 2d sess., 10952.

71. See Ernest R. House, *Jesse Jackson and the Politics of Charisma: The Rise and Fall of the PUSH/Excel Program* (Boulder: Westview Press, 1988).

72. For a highly critical but informative view of PUSH/Excel see Thomas H. Landess and Richard M. Quinn, *Jesse Jackson and the Politics of Race* (Ottawa, IL: Jameson Books, 1985). For a more balanced analysis see House, *Jesse Jackson and the Politics of Charisma.*

73. In 1983, there were approximately 5,200 elected black officials in the United States but that was only about 1 percent of all elected officials in the nation. Jackson, *Straight from the Heart,* 20. Many of these leaders operated in predominantly black districts and adopted a "blacks first" leadership style akin to that of Adam Clayton Powell, Jr.

74. Rep. Barbara Jordan, nationally televised speech of 25 July 1974 before the House Committee on Judiciary, *Debate on Articles of Impeachment. Hearings pursuant to H. Res. 883, July 23–30, 1974,* 93d Cong., 2d sess. (Washington, D.C.: Government Printing Office, 1974), 110–13.

75. Rep. Barbara Jordan, "Democratic Convention Keynote Address, Speech 12 July 1976," in *Vital Speeches* 42, 15 August 1976, 645.

76. Jordan, "Democratic Convention Keynote Address," 646.

77. Rep. Barbara Jordan, "Testimony," Senate Committee on the Judiciary, *Nomination of Robert H. Bork to Be Associate Justice of the Supreme Court of the U.S.,* 100th Cong., 1st sess., 1987, S. Hrg. 100–1011, pt. 1, 1004–6.

78. All metaphors are limited, and this one is also erroneous, for it fails to recognize that each individual can belong to many different groups, drawing a unique individual identity from multiple sources.

79. Senator Shirley Chisholm, "For the Equal Rights Amendment," 10

August 1970, *Congressional Record,* 91st Cong., 2d sess., 28028–29. Reprinted in Halford Ross Ryan, ed., *American Rhetoric from Roosevelt to Reagan* (Prospect Heights, IL: Waveland, 1987 [1983]), 222–31.

80. Landess and Quinn, *Jesse Jackson and the Politics of Race,* 67, 179.

81. Young's sexist language use should be considered in the context of his continuing efforts to learn feminism and to be sensitive to women. For his discussion of the "new man," see "Minority Involvement in Making Foreign Policy," 2 March 1990. For remarks on sexism, see "Speech at the Judge Edward R. Finch Law Day USA Award," 29 April 1978; and "Oglethorpe University Commencement Address," 13 May 1990. We are indebted to Cal Logue and Jean DeHart for providing advance access to these speeches, all of which will appear in their forthcoming anthology on Andrew Young's public discourse.

82. King and Malcolm X employ the dream and nightmare visions in their own discourse. See Martin Luther King, Jr., "I Have a Dream"; and Malcolm X, "The Ballot or the Bullet," *Malcolm X Speaks,* 23–44. The tension is highlighted as symptomatic of their discourse in James H. Cone, *Martin and Malcolm and America: A Dream or a Nightmare* (Maryknoll, NY: Orbis Books, 1991).

83. Andrew Young, speech at the University of Georgia, Athens, Georgia, 17 January 1991.

84. Actually, black economic conditions were on a split track: the economic standing of "middle class" two-adult families was improving, while the economic standing and quality of life of single-headed families and inner-city residents was deteriorating. See the reports of the National Urban League and the EEOC, in David M. Alpern and Diane Camper, "The Plight of Black America," *Newsweek,* 31 January 1983, 26–27; W. F. Buckley, "Grim News," *National Review,* 19 August 1983, 1037; "How Blacks Fare," *USNWR,* 30 January 1984, 8.

85. University administrators complied with these demands because it was obvious that "something was wrong" insofar as the statistics at most major private and state universities continued to reflect extremely low enrollment, retention, and graduation rates for black students. The administrators followed black leadership, both students and scholars, on the nature of the solutions to be undertaken.

86. See Cone, *Martin and Malcolm and America: A Dream or a Nightmare.*

87. See, e.g., Alphonso Pinkney, *Red, Black, and Green* (Cambridge: Cambridge University Press, 1976); Rodney Carlisle, *The Roots of Black Nationalism* (Port Washington, NY: Kennikat Press, 1975); Wilson Jeremiah Moses, *The Golden Age of Black Nationalism, 1850–1925* (New York: Oxford University Press, 1978), esp. 15–31; Bernard Makhosezwe Magubane, *The Ties That Bind: African-American Consciousness of Africa* (Trenton, NJ: Africa World Press, 1987).

88. See August Meier and Elliot Rudwick, *Black History and the Historical Profession, 1915–1980* (Urbana: University of Illinois Press, 1986).

89. See interview of Henry Louis Gates, Jr., *Time,* 22 April 1991, 16–18.

90. Molefi Kete Asante, *The Afrocentric Idea* (Philadelphia: Temple University Press, 1987). For an application of this idea see William Oliver, "Black Males and

Social Problems: Prevention through Afrocentric Socialization," *Journal of Black Studies* 20 (1989): 15–39.

91. The difference is most provocatively depicted by Professor Leonard Jeffries's theory of European "ice people" and African "sun people" as reported in Joseph Berger, "Professor's Theories on Race Stir Turmoil at City College," *New York Times,* 20 April 1990. Cf. Yvonne R. Bell, Cathy L. Bowie, and Joseph A. Baldwin, "Afrocentric Cultural Consciousness and African-American Male-Female Relationships," *Journal of Black Studies* 21 (1990): 162–89.

92. The National Association of Scholars constitutes one major organization that has worked to resist multiculturalism. See "Academics in Opposition," *Time,* 1 April 1991, 68.

93. The white supremacists had learned by this time to use "code words" in place of the rhetoric of white supremacy, so that their discourse merged almost imperceptibly with the conservative, right wing.

94. The gaps are very small, and sometimes the self-proclaimed liberal magazines seem more conservative than those that identify themselves as conservatives. See Ellis Cose, "Are Quotas Really the Problem?" *Time,* 24 June 1991; "Cheating on the Tests," *Time,* 3 June 1991; vs. "Affirmative Action," *USNWR,* 24 December 1990, 40–42; or 3 March 1986, 20–21.

95. E.g., John Leo, "A Fringe History of the World," *USNWR,* 12 November 1990, 25–26. Sometimes, the multiculturalist thrust is tainted by identifying it as being "P.C." or "Politically Correct." See "Upside Down in the Groves of Academe," *Time,* 1 April 1991, 66–67.

96. See, e.g., the special issue of the *New Republic* on "Race on Campus," 18 February 1991; Kay Sunstein Hymowitz, "Babar the Racist: PC in Nursery School," *New Republic,* 19 August 1991, 12–14. See also Arthur Schlesinger, Jr., "The Cult of Ethnicity, Good and Bad," *Time,* 8 July 1991, 21.

97. See, e.g., Charles Krauthammer, "Hail Columbus, Dead White Male," *Time,* 27 May 1991, 74; "Whose America?" *Time,* 8 July 1991, 12–17.

98. Jackson, *Straight from the Heart,* 189.

99. Ibid., 296, 104.

100. Ibid., 88, 186, 275.

101. Ibid., 111, 277.

102. Ibid., 20, 304. Jackson's rhetoric is heavily laced with statistical comparisons of blacks and whites on many subissues.

103. Jackson, *Straight from the Heart,* 128.

104. Ibid., 128, 194, 322.

105. Spike Lee's films have been consistently interpreted as statements of black power and separatism. Clearly, he positions himself as a militant, and his early films, like *Do the Right Thing,* invite such interpretations. However, more recent films, such as *Mo' Better Blues* and *Jungle Fever,* incorporate clear commitments to family and the work ethic. They also express strong antidrug messages and a potent statement about the boundaries of ethnic cultures. The same is true of John Singleton's *Boyz 'n the Hood.*

106. Jackson, *Straight from the Heart,* 18.

107. Jackson's use of "we" generally refers to the black community, although he expanded this in 1988 to include "the poor." See Jackson, "Common Ground and Common Cause."

108. Jesse Jackson, "The Rainbow Coalition," 17 July 1984, in Ryan, *American Rhetoric,* 278.

109. In a 1984 televised debate with Senators Walter Mondale and Gary Hart, Jackson pointed out that simply "having" a job was not enough to solve the problems of the members of the Rainbow Coalition, for, as he pointed out, "in slavery everybody had a job," 28 March 1984, from personal viewing. This is not to say that Jackson's rhetoric necessarily offers realistic policy options for a free enterprise system. Consider, for example, his idea of a "good wage," which includes paying ghetto trainees $12–$20 an hour as apprentice carpenters and brick masons to rebuild the inner city. See Jackson, *Straight from the Heart,* 272.

110. Jackson does this with special skill in "Common Ground and Common Sense," his 20 July 1988 Address to the Democratic National Convention, in *Vital Speeches* 54, 15 August 1988, 649–53.

111. See Jackson, "The Rainbow Coalition." Note that he could have referred to the backing of the quilt, a large, solid piece of material, as the common ground for all of the different patches. In choosing not to do that, he created a vision that foregrounded ethnic and cultural differences rather than commonalities.

112. Landess and Quinn, *Jesse Jackson and the Politics of Race,* 218, 222, 246–47.

113. This is illustrated most graphically in the growing hostilities between politically organized blacks and politically organized Hispanics. In Compton, California, e.g., Walter Tucker, the black city council chair, faced by complaints from Hispanics, argued that "we worked hard to get power and we are not going to give it up" (our paraphrase), and he associated Latinos with bringing into the community "graffiti, crime, and gangs." McNeil-Lehrer, 30 July 1991. See also "Browns vs. Blacks," *Time,* 29 July 1991, 14–16.

114. The Supreme Court has taken the lead in forwarding this definition in its vaunted "turn to the right." Both Presidents Ronald Reagan and George Bush have supported the revision. The majority of Congress remains supportive of the liberal vision of individual Equality, but they are still willing to buttress that vision with activist short-term, federal measures. Only a few leftists in government support group rights.

115. See, e.g., Sylvester Monroe, "Does Affirmative Action Help or Hurt?" *Time,* 27 May 1991, 22–23.

AFTERWORD

1. Although it represents an extreme, one of the most interesting, albeit absurd, examples of the disjunctive, us/them logic generated by such situations is the recent controversy over whether or not Egyptian culture was "black." This is clearly not a decidable issue in the terms in which it is put. Egyptian culture was Egyptian; it was neither as Negroid as Southern Africa nor as white as Caucasian Europe.

There is a real futility to the efforts of those who insist on devoting significant resources to a battle over which side of the ideological color line—black or white—a
particular culture falls. It is of course no less absurd or futile to try to determine the
racial category in which to place an individual whose genetic make up is three-
sixteenths Negroid. On the larger question concerning the African vs. European
roots of classical civilization see Martin Bernal, *Black Athena: The Afroasiatic Roots
of Classical Civilization, volume I, The Fabrication of Ancient Greece 1785–1985* (New
Brunswick: Rutgers University Press, 1987) and the controversy it has generated
in both the academy and the national media: Molly Myerowitz Levine, ed., "The
Challenge of Black Athena to Classics Today," *Arethusa* (special issue), Fall 1989;
David Gress, "The Case against Martin Bernal," *New Criterion* (December 1989):
36–43; Jasper Griffin, "Who Are These Coming to the Sacrifice?" *New York Review
of Books* 36, 15 June 1989, 25–27; J. T. Hooker, rev. of Martin Bernal, *Black Athena,*
in *Times Literary Supplement,* 14 June 1991, 29; Sharon Begley, rev. of Martin
Bernal, *Black Athena,* in *Newsweek,* 23 September 1991, 49.

2. Blacks have always engaged in some retaliation for white violence. It is difficult to decide at what point racial violence might be equally engaged by members
of both groups, especially given the different ways in which black and white violence is interpreted. It would seem, however, that more latitude is now available for
black-on-white racial violence than in the past. So, e.g., in August 1991 the *Atlanta
Constitution* reported an incident in which a group of black women in Detroit
shouted racist epithets while surrounding, assaulting, and harassing two white
women. In other areas of the country, from New York to Los Angeles, routine
tensions between blacks and whites have all too frequently resulted in groups of
blacks attacking isolated whites and vice versa. See "Brooklyn Area Sees Fear
Grow," *Atlanta Constitution,* 5 August 1991, A4.

3. It offers a conservative vision of culture, which leads people back into the
past and ties them there, rather than allowing them to move forward toward an
innovative and creative future. We recognize that such a negative evaluation of
social stasis is Eurocentric. Enshrining group rights also provides an incentive for
particular groups to try to outbreed one another, something that the frail earth cannot tolerate. Male black power advocates in the 1960s labeled abortion as a form of
"genocide" on the grounds that it cut out the population gains among the black
populace. Black female anti-abortion advocates currently emphasize the propaga-
tion of the race as a rationale for their position. Some white, anti-abortion advocates make a similar argument, maintaining that it is important to produce more of
"our kind."

4. Lawrence W. Levine, *Black Culture and Black Consciousness: Afro-American
Folk Thought from Slavery to Freedom* (New York: Oxford University Press, 1977);
Henry Louis Gates, Jr., *The Signifying Monkey: A Theory of Afro-American Literary
Criticism,* (New York: Oxford, 1988); Molefi Kete Asante, *The Afrocentric Idea*
(Philadelphia: Temple University Press, 1987).

5. And, in the end, the concept of the group would trump the identity of the
individual. Black students we have known report frustration with their friends
who have chosen black universities. Black students who choose white colleges and

universities are frequently called "Oreos" or chastised with the phrase "don't forget who you are." Individual identity is ruthlessly subordinated to group identity, just as when black children successful in school are attacked for "trying to be white."

6. Benjamin J. Broome, "Building Shared Meaning: Implications of a Relational Approach to Empathy for Teaching Intercultural Communication," *Communication Education* 40 (July 1991): 235–49.

7. We know that many cultures, including native Americans, Africans, and the ancient Chinese have prized cultural stasis enough to forbid intercultural contact, precisely because they recognize that this interaction inevitably produced change. Global conditions today are such that intercultural contact is inevitable, and hence so too is change. Those who refuse to recognize and accommodate change clearly deserve the title "reactionary." We believe that the cross-cultural nature of these dynamics indicate that they are products of identifiable universal human tendencies of particularly placed individuals rather than the sacred products of unique cultures. Hence, we do not accede to the claim of "cultural privilege" maintained for them. See, e.g., Randall Lake, "Between Myth and History: Enacting Time in Native American Protest Rhetoric," *QJS* 77 (May 1991): 123–51. This does not mean that one should adopt a disrespect for those cultures or the persons involved in them; it does mean that one should refuse to sacralize their demands for conservative reaction as privileged and unassailable. The case is different where contact has not yet occurred. Hence, we would support a "prime directive" in space travel, and a modified version of such a "hands-off" principle for those few earth tribes not yet overrun by more technologically dependent groups.

8. See Arthur M. Schlesinger, Jr.'s discussion of the relationship between "unum" and "pluribus" in the American credo in *The Disuniting of America: Reflections on a Multicultural Society* (New York: Whittle Direct Books, 1992), 70–83.

9. Marsha Houston Stanback, "Language and Black Woman's Place: Evidence from the Black Middle Class," in Paula A. Treichler, Cheris Kramarae, and Beth Stafford, eds., *For Alma Mater: Theory and Practice in Feminist Scholarship* (Urbana: University of Illinois Press, 1985), 177–93 and "Black Middle-Class Women's Communication Styles," Southern States Communication Conference, April 1990.

10. We do not believe that this justifies economic discrimination within the confines of contemporary American society. We are merely pitting the most radical version of economic equality against the most radical version of cultural difference as a means of highlighting the essentially different underlying values and economic structures implied by each. This argument does not hold for moderate positions on cultural diversity which locate and restrict difference at the level of style. In such a system cultural *and* economic equality might be possible, and if so we might support such a combination.

11. Severe problems arise from the mathematical standard, for there is no consistent agreement concerning the criteria for determining the basis from which "uniform proportionality" should be derived. A mathematical impossibility is created when one state, which has less than an average percentage of black population,

assumes proportionality of employment based on a *national proportion* of 12 percent, and another state, which has a greater than average percentage of black population, assumes proportionality of employment based on a *state or local proportion* of 40 percent. There are just not enough blacks in the country to be 12 percent of all states with less than a 12 percent black population *and* 40 percent of workers in states with a 40 percent black population. Something akin to this mathematical gridlock seems to be developing at the level of expectations, although we are still far enough from achieving these expectations that they have not yet generated any real stress in terms of demanding impossible legal performances from state bodies.

12. Terence Moore, an African-American sports reporter, recently complained because blacks constituted only 20 percent of professional baseball players. We do not know why he thought that this rate (substantially above the 12 percent of black population nationally) was too low. Perhaps he had the black nationalist vision of 50 percent participation in mind. Or, alternatively, he may have presumed higher black participation because the "local" conditions are more suitable for blacks in some way. The latter seems more likely because his comparison was to other professional sports, but that does not rule out a contributory effect from the sublimated expectation of "equality" as "50-50." "Blacks in Baseball Now Just Pitiful, Not Pathetic," *Atlanta Constitution*, 7 August 1991, E2.

13. Liberal philosophers have recognized that such need not necessarily be the case, though such arguments have been slow to make any headway in the efforts of liberal public advocates. See Steven Lukes, "Equality and Liberty: Must They Conflict?" in David Held, ed., *Political Theory Today* (Stanford: Stanford University Press, 1991), 48–66; Ronald Dworkin, "Foundations of Liberal Equality (Stanford University, May 5 and 10, 1988)," *The Tanner Lectures on Human Values* 11 (1990): 1–119.

14. We recognize that scholars speaking on behalf of cultural groups have claimed that non-European cultures do not value individuals above the collective. However, in our experience the individual members of these cultures do not always agree with such assessment. Scholars tend to amplify nuanced differences into absolute strictures that are unfaithful to lived experience. So, for example, the United States is supposed to be a radically individual culture, yet young people run off to die for their country with frequency. By the same token, individual members of supposedly collectivist cultures bitterly resent the imposition of state needs over personal needs, e.g., China's forced birth control policy.

15. See W. E. B. Du Bois's assessment of the American Negro's "double consciousness" in *The Souls of Black Folk* (Millwood, NY: Kraus-Thomson Organization Ltd., 1973 [1903]), 43–47.

RESEARCH AND BIBLIOGRAPHY ESSAY

1. For those seeking a traditional bibliographical essay that covers the general time span of this book, focusing on the relationship between blacks and whites with regard to equality in governance, we recommend the excellent essay by

Donald G. Nieman in *Promises to Keep: African-Americans and the Constitutional Order, 1776 to the Present* (New York: Oxford University Press, 1991), 241–56.

2. Bernard Bailyn, *The Ideological Origins of the American Revolution* (Cambridge, MA: Belknap, 1962); Jack P. Greene, *All Men Are Created Equal: Some Reflections on the Character of the American Revolution* (Oxford: Clarendon Press, 1976); Jennifer Nedelsky, *Private Property and the Limits of American Constitutionalism: The Madisonian Framework and Its Legacy* (Chicago: University of Chicago Press, 1990).

3. We have relied as much as possible on the secondary literature that is cited and used most frequently by historians working in the various areas, but we have supplemented this with the most recent work in each area. We have also been careful to cover the range of major perspectives where dramatically different interpretations of the historical record exist.

4. J. R. Pole, *The Pursuit of Equality in American History* (Berkeley: University of California Press, 1978); Charles Redenius, *The American Ideal of Equality: From Jefferson's Declaration to the Burger Court* (Port Washington, NY: Kennikat Press, 1981); Nieman, *Promises to Keep;* Derrick A. Bell, *Race, Racism and American Law* (Boston: Little, Brown and Co., 1973). See also Mark Tushnet, *The American Law of Slavery, 1810–1860: Considerations of Humanity and Interest* (Princeton: Princeton University Press, 1981).

5. John Hope Franklin, *From Slavery to Freedom: A History of Negro America,* 5th ed., (New York: Alfred A. Knopf, 1988 [1947]; August Meier and Elliot Rudwick, *From Plantation to Ghetto,* 3d ed. (New York: Hill and Wang, 1976).

6. Penelope L. Bullock, *The Afro-American Periodical Press: 1838–1909* (Baton Rouge: Louisiana University Press, 1981); Martin E. Dann, ed., *The Black Press 1827–1890* (New York: Capricorn Books, 1972); Henry Lewis Suggs, ed., *The Black Press in the South 1865–1979* (Westport, CT: Greenwood Press, 1983). See also Roland E. Wolseley, *The Black Press, USA* (Ames: Iowa State University Press, 1990); Theodore G. Vincent, ed., *Voices of a Black Nation: Political Journalism in the Harlem Renaissance* (Trenton, NJ: Africa World Press, 1973).

7. Winthrop P. Jordan, *White over Black: American Attitudes toward the Negro, 1550–1812* (New York: W. W. Norton and Co., 1968); David Howard-Pitney, *The Afro-American Jeremiad: Appeals for Justice in America* (Philadelphia: Temple University Press, 1990).

8. Ann Allen Shockley, ed., *Afro-American Women Writers 1746–1933: An Anthology and Critical Guide* (New York: Meridian Books, 1988); Gerda Lerner, ed., *Black Women in White America: A Documentary History* (New York: Vintage Books, 1973). For a historical narrative about black women's experience see Paula Giddings, *When and Where I Enter: The Impact of Black Women on Race and Sex in America* (New York: Bantam Books, 1984); Beverly Guy-Sheftall, "Books, Brooms, Bibles, and Ballots: Black Women and the Public Sphere," *Daughters of Sorrow: Attitudes toward Black Women, 1880–1920* (Brooklyn and New York: Carlson Publishing, 1990).

9. *Afro-American History Series,* 10 vols. (Wilmington, DE: Scholarly Resources, 1977); Herbert Aptheker, ed., *A Documentary History of the Negro People in the United States,* 4 vols. (New York: Citadel Press, 1951); Philip S. Foner, ed., *The*

Voice of Black America: Major Speeches by Negroes in the United States 1797–1971, 2 vols. (New York: Simon and Schuster, 1972).

10. Philip S. Foner and Ronald L. Lewis, eds., *Black Workers: A Documentary History from Colonial Times to the Present* (Philadelphia: Temple University Press, 1989); Carter G. Woodson, ed., *Negro Orators and Their Orations* (New York: Russell and Russell, 1969 [1925]); Leslie H. Fishel, Jr., and Benjamin Quarles, eds., *The Negro American* (Glenview, IL: Scott, Foresman and Co., 1967); Roy L. Hill, ed., *Rhetoric of Racial Revolt* (Denver: Golden Bell Press, 1964).

11. Charles Evans, *American Bibliography: A Chronological Dictionary of all Books, Pamphlets, and Periodical Publications Printed in the United States of America from the Genesis Down to and Including the Year 1820,* 14 vols. (New York: P. Smith, 1941).

12. We have since discovered that this problem is noted and described by Peter H. Wood as the mistaking of Boston for New England and New England for America, in "'I Did the Best I Could for My Day': The Study of Early Black History during the Second Reconstruction, 1960–1976," *William and Mary Quarterly* 35 (1978): 188.

13. Bernard Bailyn, ed., *Pamphlets of the American Revolution 1750–1776* (Cambridge, MA: Belknap, 1965).

14. Merrill Jensen, ed., *Tracts of the American Revolution 1763–1776* (Indianapolis: Bobbs-Merrill, 1977).

15. Henry Steele Commager and Richard B. Morris, eds., *The Spirit of 'Seventy-Six* (Indianapolis: Bobbs-Merrill, 1958).

16. Jack G. Gravlee and James R. Irvine, eds., *Pamphlets and the American Revolution* (Delmar, NY: Scholars' Fascimiles and Reprints, 1976); Samuel E. Morison, ed., *Sources and Documents Illustrating the American Revolution, 1764–1788* (Oxford: Clarendon Press, 1923).

17. David Potter and Gordon L. Thomas, eds., *The Colonial Idiom* (Carbondale: Southern Illinois University Press, 1970).

18. Bernard Bailyn, *The Ideological Origins of the American Revolution;* and *The New England Merchants in the Seventeenth Century* (Cambridge, MA: Harvard University Press, 1955); Paul K. Conkin, *Self-Evident Truths* (Bloomington: Indiana University Press, 1974); Edmund S. Morgan, *Inventing the People* (New York: W. W. Norton and Co., 1988).

19. Elisha P. Douglass, *Rebels and Democrats* (Chapel Hill: University of North Carolina Press, 1955); Carl Becker, *The Declaration of Independence: A Study in the History of Political Ideas* (New York: Alfred A. Knopf, 1951); Gary B. Nash, *Red, White and Black: The Peoples of Early North America* (Englewood Cliffs, NJ: Prentice-Hall, 1974); and *Race, Class, and Politics: Essays on American Colonial and Revolutionary Society* (Urbana: University of Illinois Press, 1986); Chilton Williamson, *American Suffrage, from Property to Democracy: 1760–1860* (Princeton: Princeton University Press, 1960).

20. Jennifer Nedelsky, *Private Property and the Limits of American Constitutionalism;* Carl Becker, J. M. Clark, and William E. Dodd, *The Spirit of '76 and Other Essays* (Washington, D.C.: Robert Brookings Graduate School, 1927).

21. John Phillip Reid, *The Concept of Liberty in the Age of the American Revolution* (Chicago: University of Chicago Press, 1988); and *The Concept of Representation in the Age of the American Revolution* (Chicago: University of Chicago Press, 1989).

22. Garry Wills, *Inventing America: Jefferson's Declaration of Independence* (New York: Vintage Books, 1978).

23. Stephen E. Lucas, *Portents of Rebellion: Rhetoric and Revolution in Philadelphia, 1765–76* (Philadelphia: Temple University Press, 1976); Kurt W. Ritter and James R. Andrews, *The American Ideology: Reflections of the Revolution in American Rhetoric* (Falls Church, VA: Speech Communication Association Bicentennial Monograph, 1978).

24. Jack P. Greene, *All Men Are Created Equal;* but see also David Brion Davis, *Revolutions: Reflections on American Equality and Foreign Liberations* (Cambridge, MA: Harvard University Press, 1990).

25. WordCruncher Ver. 4.1, "The Constitutional Papers: Bicentennial Edition 1789–1987," Book Shelf Series (Provo, UT: Electronic Text Corp., 1987).

26. Mark Olsen and Louis-Georges Harvey, "Contested Methods: Daniel T. Rodgers's *Contested Truths,*" *Journal of the History of Ideas* 49 (1988): 653–68.

27. Daniel T. Rodgers, "Keywords: A Reply," *Journal of the History of Ideas* 49 (1988): 669–76.

28. Max Farrand, ed., *The Records of the Federal Convention of 1787* (New Haven: Yale University Press, 1937); Jonathan Elliot, comp., *The Debates in the Several State Conventions on the Adoption of the Federal Constitution* (New York: Burt Franklin, 1888).

29. M. St. Claire Clarke and Peter Force, ed., *American Archives* (Washington, D.C., 1840); *Annals of America* (Chicago: Encyclopaedia Brittanica, 1968).

30. Paul Leicester Ford, ed., *Pamphlets on the Constitution of the United States, Published during Its Discussion by the People 1787–1788* (New York: Da Capo Press, 1968); Herbert J. Storing, ed., *The Complete Anti-Federalist* (Chicago: University of Chicago Press, 1981).

31. Gordon S. Wood, *The Creation of the American Republic 1776–1787* (Chapel Hill: University of North Carolina Press, 1969).

32. Forrest McDonald, *Novus Ordo Seclorum: The Intellectual Origins of the Constitution* (Lawrence: University Press of Kansas, 1985); Clinton Rossiter, *Seedtime of the Republic* (New York: Harcourt, Brace and Co., 1953); Edmund S. Morgan's *Inventing the People* (New York: W. W. Norton and Co., 1988). But see also William Peters, *A More Perfect Union: The Making of the Constitution* (New York: Crown Publishers, 1987).

33. Bailyn, *The Ideological Origins of the American Revolution.*

34. Leon F. Litwack, *North of Slavery: The Negro in the Free States, 1790–1860* (Chicago: University of Chicago Press, 1961); Donald L. Robinson, *Slavery in the Structure of American Politics, 1765–1820* (New York: Harcourt Brace, Jovanovich, 1971); David Brion Davis, *The Problem of Slavery in the Age of Revolution, 1770–1823* (Ithaca: Cornell University Press, 1975); Arthur Zilversmit, *The First Emancipation* (Chicago: University of Chicago Press, 1967); Duncan J. MacLeod,

Slavery, Race and the American Revolution (London: Cambridge University Press, 1974).

35. Sidney Kaplan and Emma Nogrady Kaplan, *The Black Presence in the Era of the American Revolution* (Amherst: University of Massachusetts Press, 1989).

36. John W. Blassingame, *The Slave Community: Plantation Life in the Antebellum South* (New York: Oxford University Press, 1979); Sylvia R. Frey, *Water from the Rock: Black Resistance in a Revolutionary Age* (Princeton: Princeton University Press, 1991); Eugene D. Genovese, *Roll, Jordan, Roll: The World the Slaves Made* (New York: Pantheon Books, 1974); Lorenzo Johnston Greene, *The Negro in Colonial New England* (New York: Atheneum, 1968); Allan Kulikoff, *Tobacco and Slaves: The Development of Southern Cultures in the Chesapeake 1680–1800* (Chapel Hill: University of North Carolina Press, 1986); Lawrence W. Levine, *Black Culture and Black Consciousness: Afro-American Folk Thought from Slavery to Freedom* (New York: Oxford University Press, 1977); Nash, *Red, White and Black;* Mechal Sobel, *The World They Made Together: Black and White Values in Eighteenth-Century Virginia* (Princeton: Princeton University Press, 1987); Sterling Stuckey, *Slave Culture: Nationalist Theory and the Foundations of Black America* (New York: Oxford University Press, 1987); Wood, "I Did the Best I Could for My Day."

37. Early Lee Fox, *The American Colonization Society, 1817–1840* (Baltimore: Johns Hopkins Press, 1919); Philip J. Staudenraus, *The African Colonization Movement, 1816–1865* (New York: Columbia University Press, 1961).

38. George M. Frederickson, *The Black Image in the The White Mind: The Debate on Afro-American Character and Destiny, 1817–1914* (New York: Harper, 1971), 1–42.

39. James D. Richardson, ed., *A Compilation of the Messages and Papers of the Presidents* (New York: Bureau of National Literature, 1897); Samuel Denny Smith, ed., *The Negro in Congress, 1870–1901* (Port Washington, NY: Kennikat Press, 1966 [1940]); *The Negro in the Congressional Record*, 10 vols., Peter M. Bergman and Jean McCarroll, comps. (New York: Bergman Publishers, 1970). For an excellent rhetorical analysis of Lincoln's position, see David Zarefsky, *Lincoln, Douglas, and Slavery: In the Crucible of Public Debate* (Chicago: University of Chicago Press, 1990).

40. *Afro-American History Series*, 10 vols.; Aptheker, *A Documentary History of the Negro People in the United States;* Ernest G. Bormann, ed., *Forerunners of Black Power* (Englewood Cliffs, NJ: Prentice-Hall, 1971); John H. Bracey, August Meier, and Elliott Rudwick, eds., *Black Nationalism in America* (Indianapolis: Bobbs-Merrill, 1970); Benjamin Brawley, *Early Negro American Writers* (Freeport, NY: Books for Libraries Press, 1976 [1935]); Leslie H. Fishel, Jr., and Benjamin Quarles, *The Negro American;* Lerner, *Black Women in White America;* Woodson, *Negro Orators and Their Orations;* Shockley, *Afro-American Women Writers 1746–1933.*

41. Howard Holman Bell, *Minutes of the Proceedings of the National Negro Conventions 1830–1864* (New York: Arno Press; and the *New York Times*, 1969); Philip S. Foner and George E. Walker, eds., *Proceedings of the Black National and State Conventions, 1865–1900* (Philadelphia: Temple University Press, 1986).

42. John W. Blassingame, *The Frederick Douglass Papers* (New Haven: Yale University Press, 1982); Philip S. Foner, *The Life and Writings of Frederick Douglass,* (New York: International Publishers, 1975).

43. Earl A. Ofari, *Let Your Motto Be Resistance: The Life and Thought of Henry Highland Garnet* (Boston: Beacon Press, 1972); Marilyn Richardson, ed., *Maria W. Stewart: America's First Black Woman Political Writer* (Bloomington: Indiana University Press, 1987).

44. But see the fine examination in Waldo E. Martin, Jr., *The Mind of Frederick Douglass* (Chapel Hill: University of North Carolina Press, 1985).

45. E.g., Kwando Kinshasa, *Emigration vs. Assimilation: The Debate in the African American Press, 1827–1861* (Jefferson, NC: McFarland and Co., 1988); Bernard Makhosezwe Magubane, *The Ties That Bind: African-American Consciousness of Africa* (Trenton, NJ: Africa World Press, 1987). Far more balanced, but still attending primarily to this single axis, is Wilson Jeremiah Moses, *The Golden Age of Black Nationalism, 1850–1925* (New York: Oxford University Press, 1978). See also Floyd J. Miller, *The Search for a Black Nationality: Black Emigration and Colonization 1787–1863* (Urbana: University of Illinois Press, 1975); Bill McAdoo, *Pre–Civil War Black Nationalism* (New York: Walker Press, 1983).

46. Benjamin Quarles, *Black Abolitionists* (New York: Oxford University Press, 1969); Litwack, *North of Slavery;* Herbert Aptheker, *American Negro Slave Revolts* (New York: International Publishers, 1969); Howard Holman Bell, *A Survey of the Negro Convention Movement, 1830–1861* (New York: Arno Press and the New York Times, 1969 [1953]). See also John Hope Franklin, *The Free Negro in North Carolina, 1790–1860* (Chapel Hill: University of North Carolina Press, 1943); Bert James Loewenberg and Ruth Bogin, *Black Women in Nineteenth-Century American Life* (University Park: Pennsylvania State University Press, 1976).

47. Gary B. Nash, *Race and Revolution* (Madison, WI: Madison House, 1990).

48. In addition to the items cited elsewhere, see John B. Boles, *Black Southerners, 1619–1869* (Lexington: University of Kentucky Press, 1983); Leon Litwack and August Meier, eds., *Black Leaders of the Nineteenth Century* (Urbana: University of Illinois Press, 1988); Joel Schor, *Henry Highland Garnet: A Voice of Black Radicalism in the Nineteenth Century* (Westport, CT: Greenwood Press, 1977); William Edward Farrison, *William Wells Brown* (Chicago: University of Chicago Press, 1969); Sheldon H. Harris, *Paul Cuffe: Black America and the African Return* (New York: Simon and Schuster, 1972); Wilson Jeremiah Moses, *Alexander Crummell: A Study of Civilization and Discontent* (New York: Oxford Press, 1989); Victor Ullman, *Martin R. Delany: The Beginnings of Black Nationalism* (Boston: Beacon Press, 1971).

49. Robert A. Goldwin and Art Kaufman, eds., *Slavery and Its Consequences: The Constitution, Equality, and Race* (Washington, D.C.: American Enterprise Institute for Public Policy Research, 1988).

50. Alice Dana Adams, *The Neglected Period of Anti-Slavery in America (1808–1831)* (Gloucester, MA: P. Smith, 1964 [1908]); Gilbert Hobbs Barnes, *The Anti-Slavery Impulse, 1830–1844* (New York: Harcourt, Brace and World, 1964); Robert W. Fogel, *Without Consent or Contract: The Rise and Fall of American Slavery* (New

York: W. W. Norton and Co., 1989); Aileen S. Kraditor, *Means and Ends in American Abolitionism: Garrison and His Critics on Strategy and Tactics, 1834–1850* (New York: Pantheon Books, 1969); James M. McPherson, *The Struggle for Equality: Abolitionists and the Negro in the Civil War and Reconstruction* (Princeton: Princeton University Press, 1964); Jane H. Pease and William H. Pease, *They Who Would Be Free* (New York: Atheneum, 1974); John M. Werner, *Reaping the Bloody Harvest: Race Riots in the United States during the Age of Jackson 1824–1849* (New York: Garland Publishing, 1986). See also Larry E. Tise, *Proslavery: A History of the Defense of Slavery in America: 1701–1840* (Athens: University of Georgia Press, 1987); William Sumner Jenkins, *Pro-Slavery Thought in the Old South* (Gloucester, MA: Peter Smith, 1985 [1960]).

51. Foner, *Voice of Black America;* Woodson, *Negro Orators and Their Orations;* Fishel and Quarles, *The Negro American;* LaWanda Cox and John H. Cox, eds., *Reconstruction, the Negro and the New South* (Columbia: University of South Carolina Press, 1973); Annjennette Sophie McFarlin, ed., *Black Congressional Reconstruction Orators and Their Orations, 1869–1879* (Metuchen, NJ: Scarecrow Press, 1976).

52. In addition to the collections listed for Chap. 4, see John Edward Bruce, *The Selected Writings of John Edward Bruce: Militant Black Journalist,* ed. Peter Gilbert (New York: Arno Press, 1971); John Mercer Langston, *Freedom and Citizenship: Selected Lectures and Addresses* (Miami, FL: Mnemosyne Publishing, 1969 [1883]); William Edward Burghardt Du Bois, *W. E. B. Du Bois Speaks: Speeches and Addresses 1890–1919,* ed. Philip S. Foner (New York: Pathfinder Press, 1970); Louis R. Harlan et al., eds., *The Booker T. Washington Papers,* 14 vols. (Urbana: University of Illinois Press, 1972–89); Daniel A. Payne, *Bishop Daniel A. Payne: Sermons and Addresses 1853–1891,* ed. Charles Killian (New York: Arno Press, 1972); Francis James Grimké, *The Works of Francis J. Grimké,* ed. Carter G. Woodson (Washington, D.C.: Associated Publishers, 1942); Alexander Crummell, *Africa and America: Addresses and Discourses by Alex Crummell* (Miami, FL: Mnemosyne Publishing Co., 1969 [1891]). See also Alfreda M. Duster, ed., *Crusade for Justice: The Autobiography of Ida B. Wells* (Chicago: University of Chicago Press, 1970).

53. August Meier, *Negro Thought in America 1880–1915: Racial Ideologies in the Age of Booker T. Washington* (Ann Arbor: University of Michigan, 1966). But see also Howard N. Rabinowitz, ed., *Southern Black Leaders of the Reconstruction Era* (Urbana: University of Illinois Press, 1982); Harold Cruse, *The Crisis of the Negro Intellectual* (New York: William Morrow, 1967).

54. Nell Irvin Painter, *Exodusters: Black Migration to Kansas after Reconstruction* (New York: Alfred A. Knopf, 1976); Moses, *The Golden Age of Black Nationalism, 1850–1925.* See also n. 45 above.

55. McFarlin, *Black Congressional Reconstruction Orators and Their Orations 1869–1879;* Cox and Cox, *Reconstruction, the Negro and the New South.*

56. Charles F. Lofgren, *The Plessy Case: A Legal-Historical Interpretation* (New York: Oxford University Press, 1987); Harold M. Hyman, *A More Perfect Union: The Impact of the Civil War and Reconstruction on the Constitution* (New York: Alfred A. Knopf, 1973).

57. William G. Cochrane, "Freedom without Equality: A Study of Northern Opinion and the Negro Issue 1861–1870" (Ph.D. diss. University of Minnesota, 1957).

58. George M. Fredrickson, *The Black Image in the White Mind: The Debate on Afro-American Character and Destiny, 1817–1914* (New York: Harper, 1971).

59. Eric Foner, *Nothing But Freedom: Emancipation and Its Legacy* (Baton Rouge: Louisiana State University Press, 1983); and *Reconstruction: America's Unfinished Revolution, 1863–1877* (New York: Harper and Row, 1928); John Hope Franklin, *Reconstruction: After the Civil War* (Chicago: University of Chicago Press, 1961); William Gillette, *Retreat from Reconstruction, 1869–1879* (Baton Rouge: Louisiana State University Press, 1979); Michael Perman, *Emancipation and Reconstruction, 1862–1879* (Arlington Heights, IL: Harlan Davidson, 1987); Howard N. Rabinowitz, *Race Relations in the Urban South, 1865–1890* (New York: Oxford University Press, 1978); George C. Rable, *But There Was No Peace: The Role of Violence in the Politics of Reconstruction* (Athens: University of Georgia Press, 1984); Roger L. Ransom and Richard Sutch, *One Kind of Freedom: The Economic Consequences of Emancipation* (Cambridge: Cambridge University Press, 1977); Kenneth M. Stampp, *The Era of Reconstruction 1865–1877* (NY: Alfred A. Knopf, 1972 [1965]); Herman Belz, "The New Orthodoxy in Reconstruction Historiography," *Reviews in American History* 1 (1973): 106–13; Joel Williamson, *The Crucible of Race: Black-White Relations in the American South since Emancipation* (New York: Oxford, 1984).

60. C. Vann Woodward, *The Strange Career of Jim Crow,* 3d rev. ed. (New York: Oxford University Press, 1974 [1955]). For the most recent debate on this volume see Howard N. Rabinowitz, "More Than the Woodward Thesis: Assessing *The Strange Career of Jim Crow,*" *Journal of American History* 75 (1988): 842–56; C. Vann Woodward, "*Strange Career* Critics: Long May They Persevere," *Journal of American History* 75 (1988): 857–68.

61. Nicholas Lemann, *The Promised Land: The Great Black Migration and How It Changed America* (New York: Alfred A. Knopf, 1991).

62. Harvard Sitkoff, *A New Deal for Blacks: The Emergence of Civil Rights as a National Issue* (New York: Oxford University Press, 1978); Robert L. Zangrando, *The NAACP Crusade against Lynching, 1909–1950* (Philadelphia: Temple University Press, 1980); Mark Naison, *Communists in Harlem during the Depression* (Urbana: University of Illinois Press, 1983).

63. Ralph J. Bunche, *The Political Status of the Negro in the Age of FDR* (Chicago: University of Chicago Press, 1973 [1940]). Gunnar Myrdal, *An American Dilemma: The Negro Problem and Modern Democracy* (New York: Harper and Row, 1962 [1944]).

64. E.g., Houston A. Baker's *Modernism and the Harlem Renaissance* (Chicago: University of Chicago Press, 1987).

65. All cited above.

66. August Meier, Elliott Rudwick, and Francis L. Broderick, eds., *Black Protest Thought in the Twentieth Century,* 2d ed. (Indianapolis: Bobbs-Merrill, 1965, 1971); Hill, *Rhetoric of Racial Revolt.*

67. Bell, *Race, Racism and American Law;* and *And We Are Not Saved: The Elusive*

Quest for Racial Justice (New York: Basic Books, 1987); Mark V. Tushnet, *The NAACP's Legal Strategy against Segregated Education, 1925–1950* (Chapel Hill: University of North Carolina Press, 1987); Morroe Berger, *Equality by Statute: Legal Controls over Group Discrimination* (New York: Columbia University Press, 1952); Richard Kluger, *Simple Justice: The History of Brown v. Board of Education and Black America's Struggle for Equality* (NY: Vintage Books, 1977).

68. Franklin, *From Slavery to Freedom;* Herbert Aptheker, *Afro-American History: The Modern Era* (New York: Citadel Press, 1971); John Hope Franklin and August Meier, eds., *Black Leaders of the Twentieth Century* (Urbana: University of Illinois Press, 1982); Nieman, *Promises to Keep.*

69. Taylor Branch, *Parting the Waters: America in the King Years, 1954–1963* (New York: Simon and Schuster, 1988); Harvard Sitkoff, *The Struggle for Black Equality, 1954–1980* (New York: Hill and Wang, 1981).

70. Robert Frederick Burk, *The Eisenhower Administration and Black Civil Rights* (Knoxville: University of Tennessee Press, 1984), esp. 267–77.

71. Lehmann, *The Promised Land.*

72. Mark V. Tushnet, "The Politics of Equality in Constitutional Law: The Equal Protection Clause, Dr. Du Bois, and Charles Hamilton Houston," *Journal of American History,* 74 (1987): 884–903.

73. Gunnar Myrdal, *An American Dilemma: The Negro Problem and Modern Democracy;* David W. Southern, *Gunnar Myrdal and Black-White Relations: The Use and Abuse of an American Dilemma, 1944–1969* (Baton Rouge: Louisiana State University Press, 1987).

74. Harold Cruse, *Plural But Equal: A Critical Study of Blacks and Minorities and America's Plural Society* (New York: William Morrow, 1987); James H. Cone, *Martin and Malcolm and America: A Dream or a Nightmare* (Maryknoll, NY: Orbis Books, 1991); E. Culpepper Clark and Raymie E. McKerrow, "The Historiographical Dilemma in Myrdal's American Creed: Rhetoric's Role in Rescuing a Historical Moment," *QJS* 73 (1987): 303–16.

75. Stokely Carmichael and Charles V. Hamilton, *Black Power: The Politics of Liberation in America* (New York: Random House, 1967); Eldridge Cleaver, *Soul on Ice* (New York: McGraw-Hill, 1968); Angela Y. Davis, *Women, Race, and Class* (New York: Random House, 1981, 1983); Molefi Kete Asante, *The Afrocentric Idea* (Philadelphia: Temple University Press, 1987).

76. Haig A. Bosmajian and Hamida Bosmajian, eds., *The Rhetoric of the Civil Rights Movement* (New York: Random House, 1969).

77. Martin Luther King, Jr., *A Testament of Hope: The Essential Writings of Martin Luther King, Jr.,* ed. James M. Washington (San Francisco: Harper and Row, 1986); *Jesse Jackson, Straight from the Heart,* ed. Roger D. Hatch and Frank E. Watkins (Philadelphia: Fortress Press, 1987).

78. Cal Logue and Jean DeHart, eds., forthcoming.

79. Malcolm X, *Malcolm X Speaks: Selected Speeches and Statements,* ed. George Breitman (New York: Grove Press, 1966); *Two Speeches by Malcolm X* (New York: Merit Publishers, 1969); *By Any Means Necessary: Speeches, Interviews, and a Letter by Malcolm X,* ed. George Breitman (New York: Pathfinder Press, 1970); *Malcolm*

X Talks to Young People: Speeches in the U.S., Britain, and Africa (New York: Pathfinder Press, 1991 [1965]); *Malcolm X: The Last Speeches,* ed. Bruce Perry (New York: Pathfinder Press, 1989).

80. Louis Lomax, *When the Word Is Given* (Cleveland: World Publishing, 1963); and *To Kill a Black Man* (Los Angeles: Holloway House, 1968).

81. Barbara Jordan and Shelby Hearon, *Barbara Jordan: A Self Portrait* (Garden City, NY: Doubleday, 1979).

82. Manning Marable, *Black American Politics: From the Washington Marches to Jesse Jackson* (London: Verso, 1985); and *Race, Reform and Rebellion: The Second Reconstruction in Black America, 1945–1982* (Jackson: University Press of Mississippi, 1984).

83. Thomas H. Landess and Richard M. Quinn, *Jesse Jackson and the Politics of Race* (Ottowa, IL: Jameson Books, 1985); Ernest P. House, *Jesse Jackson and the Politics of Charisma: The Rise and Fall of the PUSH/Excel Program* (Boulder: Westview Press, 1988).

84. Adolph L. Reed, Jr., *The Jesse Jackson Phenomenon* (New Haven: Yale University Press, 1986).

85. See the very useful bibliography by Timothy V. Johnson, *Malcolm X: A Comprehensive Annotated Bibliography* (New York: Garland Publishing, 1986); Bruce Perry, *Malcolm: The Life of a Man Who Changed Black America* (Barrytown, NY: Station Hill, 1991); George Breitman, *The Last Year of Malcolm X: The Evolution of a Revolutionary* (New York: Merit, 1967); Peter L. Goldman, *The Death and Life of Malcolm X* (New York: Harper, 1973). See also the collection of essays, John Henrik Clarke, ed., *Malcolm X: The Man and His Times* (New York: The Macmillan Co., 1969).

86. David J. Garrow, *Bearing the Cross: Martin Luther King, Jr., and the Southern Christian Leadership Conference* (New York: Vintage Books, 1988); Stephen B. Oates, *Let the Trumpet Sound: The Life of Martin Luther King, Jr.* (NY: Harper, 1982); David L. Lewis, *King: A Biography,* 2d ed. (Urbana: University of Illinois Press, 1978).

87. Carolyn Calloway-Thomas and John Louis Lucaites, eds., *Martin Luther King, Jr. and the Sermonic Power of Public Discourse* (University: University of Alabama Press, 1993).

INDEX

Abolitionists, white, 7, 79; role in ending slavery, 37, 41, 58, 69–72; and African colonization, 63, 78

Abortion, 333n.3

Adams, John, 19, 27, 28, 263n.58

Adams, John Quincy, 292n.5

Adams, Samuel, 19, 23, 28, 30, 33

Affirmative action, 13–14; in redemption period, 125; in 1950s, 185; in 1960s, 191, 199–200; in 1970s and beyond, 207, 210, 212; white backlash against, 221. *See also* Quotas, racial

"AFRI," 93

Africa, 168, 206, 231; as land of slavery, 27; culture of, 153, 185, 192–95, 209. *See also* African colonization

African-American rhetoric of equality: importance of, 1–3; in postrevolutionary period, 6–7, 69–98, 240–42; in reconstruction period, 9, 107–15; in redemption period, 9, 120–29; in polarization period, 10, 148–55; in separation period, 10, 139–46; in 1930s and 1940s, 11–12, 167–71; in 1950s, 12, 184–87; in 1960s, 12–13, 189–97; in 1970s and beyond, 13–15, 202–16. *See also* Afrocentrism; Black nationalism/separatism; Black power movement

African colonization, 5, 41; and Lincoln, 63, 113; rationale for, 63–68; failure of,

67; black opposition to, 71, 77–78, 84–85. *See also* Colonization

African Methodist Episcopal Church, 74

Afrocentricity. *See* Afrocentrism

Afrocentrism, 14, 206, 215, 231; on elevation of black community, 76; on African curriculum, 209, 229; critique of, 209–11, 220–21; media on, 210–11

Allen, Richard, 74

Alleyn, C. C., 153

American Anti-Slavery Society, 69

American Colonization Society, 5, 97, 132; history of, 63–67; black opposition to, 71, 77–78

American Revolution: rhetoric of, versus prerevolutionary rhetoric, 19–21; conventional view of, 40–41, 57. *See also* Anglo-American revolutionary rhetoric, equality in

"Americanus," 32

Anglo-American revolutionary rhetoric, equality in, 4–6, 40–68, 219, 239–40; and natural rights doctrine, 42–46; use of term, 46–58; and freed blacks, problem of, 58–68; response of black orators to, 69

Anne-Arundel County, 24, 26, 30

Anti-Federalists, 54

Appeal to the Coloured Citizens of the World (Walker), 77

Aptheker, Herbert, 289n.117

345

Aristocracy: hereditary, 31, 49–51; of
    wealth, 53–56; of color, 184
Arthur, Chester A., 143
Asante, Molefi, 215, 222
Ashbrook, John M., 199–200
Asian-Americans, 163, 174, 226
Atlanta, Ga., 205–6
Atlanta Constitution, 104, 117–18, 303n.161
Atlantic Monthly, 137
Autobiography (Malcolm X), 193

Backus, Rev. Isaac, 45
Bailyn, Bernard, 36
Barnett, Ida B. Wells. *See* Wells-Barnett,
    Ida B.
Beecher, Henry Ward, 69
Bigamy, 60
Bilbo, Theodore, 173, 232
Bill of Rights, 48, 55, 75
Birth of a Nation, The (film), 154
Black Codes, 9, 104
Black middle class: in reconstruction pe-
    riod, 108–9; in polarization period,
    148; in 1930s and 1940s, 168–69, 186;
    and black separatism, 195; and Jack-
    son, 212; and culture of poverty, 224
Black Muslims, 172, 185–86, 191–92, 214
Black nationalism/separatism: in 19th cen-
    tury, 73–75, 83, 95; in integrated
    equality period, 150, 161, 172, 179,
    185–86; in 1960s, 191–96, 198–200; in
    1970s and beyond, 206, 215–16; on
    poverty, 223
Black power movement, 206, 220, 222;
    rise of, 189, 194–95; and Jackson, 212;
    and economic equality, 225
Black studies, 207
Blair, Montgomery, 117
Bland, Richard, 21, 31
Bork, Robert, 205
Boston, 21, 25, 30, 34, 42
"Boston Colored Men," 150
Boston Gazette, 22
Boston Massacre, 28; Orations, 21, 22,
    33, 59
Boston Post-Boy, 21
Boston Tea Party, 28
Bowdoin, James, 49
Breckinridge, William, 134, 301n.132

British American, 30, 31
British rhetoric of revolt, equality in, 3–4,
    19–39, 236–39; use of term, 20–21,
    33, 39; as mathematical equivalency,
    29–30; radical concepts of, 30–34; hu-
    man rights rhetoric versus, 33–34; and
    abhorrence of political slavery, 34–38
Brotherhood of Sleeping Car Porters, 148,
    170
Browne, Robert S., 194
Brownsville affair, 166–67
*Brown v. Board of Education of Topeka, Kan-
    sas,* 12, 140, 150, 179–80, 184, 188
Bryson, Joseph R., 183
Buchanan v. Warley, 314n.114
Burton, Thomas E., 160
Busing, 201
Butler, Pierce, 52, 53

Cable, George Washington, 133, 136,
    303n.153
Calhoun, John, 82, 86–87
California Negro Convention, 73
Capitalism, 230
Carey, A. J., 149
Carmichael, Stokely, 198
"Cato," 29
Celler, Emmanuel, 184
Chalmers, H. H., 130–31
Chamberlain, D. H., 119
Chinese launderers, 163
Chisholm, Shirley, 14, 203, 205
Christian Century, 210
Christianity: religious liberty in, 44–45;
    and Anglo-American social compact,
    60; equality in, 81, 108, 196; human
    dignity in, 227
Church, Benjamin, 22, 31, 37
Cinema, 154
Citizenship: of freed blacks, 58–59; *Dred
    Scott* decision on, 61–62; equal, 79,
    84–89, 98; and 14th Amendment, 110–
    12
Civil equality, 94
Civilian Conservation Corps, 170
Civil Rights Act: of 1874, 116; of 1957,
    179, 184
Civil Rights Cases (1883), 163
Civil Rights Committee, 177–79

Civil rights movement: in 1950s, 179,
    184–85; in 1960s, 189, 196, 198, 201;
    in 1970s and beyond, 202
Civil War, U.S., 1, 7, 63, 186; conse-
    quences for equality, 101, 103, 145
Clark, Kenneth, 188
Clay, Henry, 63–66, 218
Cleveland, Grover, 143–44
Cold War, 172
Colonization, 141, 199; and Andrew John-
    son, 114; in separation period, 132,
    144; Bilbo's scheme, 173. See also Afri-
    can colonization
Colored American, 75, 76, 80, 84
Colored Citizen, 121–25, 151
Common Sense (Paine), 42, 60
Communism, 183, 308n.24
Congo, 152
Congress, U.S., 72; and African coloniza-
    tion, 64, 66; in reconstruction period,
    105, 111, 115; in redemption period,
    116, 119; in separation period, 143; in
    polarization period, 154–55, 160, 164;
    in 1930s and 1940s, 167, 173–75; in
    1950s, 181–84; in 1960s, 199–201; Wa-
    tergate hearings, 203–4
Congressional Record, 199
Connecticut Courant, 21, 22, 37
Constitution, British, 4, 23–25, 30, 41–42
Constitution, U.S., 8, 9, 45, 79, 101, 160,
    231; ratification debates, 46–58; and
    freed blacks, problem of, 58–62, 67–
    68; black orators' role in interpreting,
    69, 71, 83, 88, 97, 185, 191; Declara-
    tion of Independence versus, 87; 13th
    Amendment, 110–11, 113, 141; 14th
    Amendment, 110–12, 141, 175–76;
    15th Amendment, 110–12, 130, 162–
    63; and popular government, 158; Jor-
    dan on, 203–4. See also Bill of Rights
Constitutional Courant, 23, 36
Continental Congress, 34, 41
Contracts, 75, 178
Coolidge, Calvin, 163, 166
Cornish, Samuel E., 77
Cowan, Edgar, 101
Crime, 154–56, 182, 202, 207
Crisis, The, 149–50, 153, 168, 185, 188–
    90, 217

Crummell, Alexander, 153
Cultural equality: in 1960s, 190–91; and
    economic equality, conflict between,
    213–14, 223–26; and liberty, 227;
    meaning of, 228–29
Culture: rhetorical, xii–xv; protection of
    white, 132–34, 187; African, 153, 185,
    192–95, 209; and interbraiding, 161;
    and heterogeneity, 220–23. See also
    Cultural equality

Davis, David Brion, 41
De Bow's Review, 105
Declaration of Independence, xv, 30, 33,
    70, 78, 160; black rhetors' use of, 6–7,
    79, 85–86, 98; and slavery, 40; and nat-
    ural rights, 42; and equality, 46, 47, 52
Delany, Martin R., 90, 109, 218, 285n.52
Democracy, 53, 171–72, 183, 223
Democratic party, 116, 125, 175–76; Na-
    tional Convention of 1976, 204;
    National Convention of 1984, 213
Depression, Great, 147, 167, 169, 177
DePriest, Oscar, 173–74
Detweiler, Philip, 85
Diachronic structures, xiii–xiv
Dickinson, John, 19, 22–23, 36–37, 53,
    263n.64
Dominant ideology, xiv
Douglass, Frederick, 2, 70, 106, 191, 218;
    influence of, 71; on disunion, 72; on
    separatism, 74; and elevation of black
    community, 76; on equality, 80–81,
    94; on slavery, 80–81, 92, 282n.26; on
    need for black achievement, 91; mar-
    riages of, 95, 108; gradualist rhetoric
    of, 136; as leader, 283n.42; and coloni-
    zation, 285n.52
Douglass, H. Ford, 73
Dred Scott v. Sandford, 61–62
Du Bois, W. E. B., 2, 159, 161, 306n.3;
    on equality, 149–50; on "rainbow of
    humanity," 152–53, 211
Dulany, Daniel, 21, 32

Eastland, James O., 174
Easton, Hosea, 92
Ebony, 185, 206

Economic equality: in 1960s, 190–91, 200–201; and cultural equality, conflict between, 213–14, 223–26; meaning of, 230. *See also* Poverty

Education, 114, 144; demand for universal public, 96–97; white supremacist view of, 156, 159; curriculum debate, 207, 225, 229–30; and black academy, 207–10

Education, integration in: in redemption period, 122, 124; in separation period, 142; in polarization period, 150–51; in 1930s and 1940s, 170, 173, 176; in 1950s, 170, 179–80, 183; in 1960s, 190, 198; in 1970s and beyond, 207, 214

Egalitarian rhetoric, 86, 101, 146; in reconstruction period, 103, 105–7, 110–15, 123–29; in redemption period, 103, 119–20, 125–29; in separation period, 103, 135–39, 141–46; in polarization period, 147–48, 154, 159–67; in 1950s, 180–81, 184, 186, 187; of new black leaders, 203

Egyptian culture, 332n.1

Eisenhower, Dwight D., 179

Eliot, Andrew, 25

Emancipation Proclamation, 101, 181

Employment, integration in: in polarization period, 157; in 1930s and 1940s, 169–71, 173; in 1950s, 187; in 1960s, 198; in 1970s and beyond, 202, 214. *See also* Patronage

Enforcement Acts, 128

Enlightenment, 19

Equal ability, 90–91

Equal citizenship, 79, 84–89, 98

Equality: rhetoric of, ix, xv–xviii, 217–19; and liberty, conflict between, 83, 98, 164–65, 177–78, 182, 199, 226–30; and heterogeneity-homogeneity conflict, 220–23; and culture-economics conflict, 223–26. *See also* African-American rhetoric of equality; Anglo-American revolutionary rhetoric, equality in; British rhetoric of revolt, equality in; White supremacist rhetoric

Equality, cultural. *See* Cultural equality

Equality, economic. *See* Economic equality

Equality, political. *See* Political equality

Equality, social. *See* Social equality

Equality before the law, 7, 14; in African-American postrevolutionary rhetoric, 90, 93–94, 98; in reconstruction period, 107–9, 112; in redemption period, 117, 126, 128; in separation period, 134–35; in polarization period, 151, 161, 166; in 1960s, 199, 214; in 1990s, 215; and definition of equality, 228

Equal justice, 170–71

Equal liberty, 6; in Anglo-American revolutionary rhetoric, 46–48, 52, 58–59, 64; in African-American postrevolutionary rhetoric, 71–72, 78–84, 88–89; Polk on, 78–79; and Grant, 127; and Hayes, 127. *See also* Equal rights

Equal opportunity, 7, 15, 222; in African-American postrevolutionary rhetoric, 90–93, 98; legal equality contrasted with, 94; economic, 97, 230; in reconstruction period, 108–9; in redemption period, 122; in polarization period, 151, 161, 166; in 1930s and 1940s, 167, 173, 179; in 1950s, 184, 187; in 1960s, 189–91, 196, 197, 201, 214; in 1970s and beyond, 210

Equal protection: Jacksonian, 7, 91, 102–3, 109, 139, 151; in reconstruction period, 109, 111, 112; in separation period, 135, 139; and definition of equality, 228

Equal representation, 39; in Anglo-American revolutionary rhetoric, 5, 46, 49–53, 58–59, 68. *See also* Voting rights

Equal rights, 7, 39; in African-American postrevolutionary rhetoric, 71–72, 78, 89–90; in reconstruction period, 107–15; in separation period, 139; in polarization period, 151. *See also* Equal liberty

Equal Rights Amendment, 205

Equal school rights, 96–97

"Etiocles," 44

Fair Employment Practices Commission (FEPC), 170, 175, 183

Farmer, James, 195
Farrakhan, Louis, 214
Federalist Papers, 53, 56–57
Ford, Gerald, 204
Forman, James, 193
Forten, James, 75, 79, 88
Fortune, T. Thomas, 137
Fox, Early Lee, 63–64
Fraud: black property, 75; election, 116, 117, 131
Frederick Douglass' Paper, 87
Freedman's Bureau, 106, 110–11, 135
Freedom. *See* Liberty
Freedom of speech, 48
Freedom's Journal, 76, 77, 89–90
Freed slaves: problem of, 5, 58–62, 68; and equal liberty concept, 48; growth in numbers, 57, 58, 62; and colonization, 63–67
Freemen, rights of, 42–46, 50

Garfield, James, 143
Garnet, Henry Highland, 73, 88, 218, 285n.52
Garrison, William Lloyd, 2, 7, 69, 71, 72, 197
Garvey, Marcus, 161, 168, 186
Gates, Henry Louis, Jr., 215, 222
Georgia Gazette, 21
Gerry, Elbridge, 53
Godkin, E. L., 106–7
Government, role of: for postrevolutionary black rhetors, 90–94, 97; in reconstruction period, 109, 110; in redemption period, 124, 126, 128; in polarization period, 151, 160, 165; in 1930s and 1940s, 167, 169, 177; in 1950s, 179–80; in 1960s, 190, 196–97, 199–200; in 1970s and beyond, 207, 213. *See also* Affirmative action; Congress, U.S.; Presidency; Supreme Court, U.S.
Government employment of blacks, 157–59
Grady, Henry W., 130, 133–34, 138
Gramsci, Antonio, 255n.22
Grant, Ulysses S., 115, 116, 126–29
Great Britain, 64, 226; Constitution of, 4, 23–25, 30; natural rights of citizens of, 24–27. *See also* British rhetoric of revolt, equality in

Great Society, 202
Griffith, D. W., 154
Grigg, Charles, 217
Group rights, 221–22
Guinn and Beal v. *US,* 162

Hamilton, Alexander, 56–57, 203
Hamilton, Charles Houston, 180
Hamilton, William, 69
Hampton, Wade, 117, 118, 130, 132
Hancock, John, 19, 22, 23, 28
Happiness, pursuit of, 47–48
Hardin, Benjamin, 86
Harding, Warren G., 163, 166, 315n.117
Harlem Renaissance, 11, 153
Harper, Robert G., 65, 67
Harper's, 172
Harper's Weekly, 157
Harrison, Benjamin, 143, 144
Hawley, Walter L., 157
Hayes, Rutherford B., 115, 116, 118, 126–29
Head Start, 200
"Heart of the Matter, The" (McWilliams), 181
Heflin, Thomas J., 311n.58
Hegemony, 255n.22
Hemmenway, Moses, 44–46, 50
Hemphill, J. C., 157
Hendricks, Thomas A., 105
Henry, Patrick, 40, 56
Heterogeneity, and equality, 220–23
Hill, Walter B., 130
Hispanic-Americans, 174, 219, 222, 225–26
History, and rhetoric, 252n.5
Hitchcock, Gad, 33
Hitler, Adolf, 171, 177
Homogeneity, and equality, 220–23
hooks, belle, 215
Hoover, Herbert, 177
Hope, John, 151
Hopkins, Stephen, 24, 30
Housing: in integrated equality period, 170, 171, 173, 187; in 1960s, 197, 198; in 1970s and beyond, 202, 214
Hughes, Langston, 168
Human equality, 94
Humanities, 209
Hyman, Harold, 119

Ideographs, xii–xiv
Ideology, and rhetoric, xiv
Immigration, 198, 220
Institutional racism, 195, 212, 326n.35
Integrated equality, 11–13, 147–87, 244–46;
    African-American rhetoric of, 148–55,
    167–71, 184–86; mainstream ideas on,
    154–55, 171–73, 180–81; white suprem-
    acists on, 155–59; and Supreme Court
    decisions, 161–63, 175–77, 179–80; and
    presidential actions, 163–67, 177–79;
    and Congress, 173–75, 181–84; eco-
    nomic equality versus, 191; King on,
    192; black separatist rejection of, 195,
    207; Jackson on, 212. See also Education,
    integration in; Employment, integration
    in; Housing; Public accommodations,
    access to
Intelligence, and race, 82, 152
Interbraiding, 14, 161, 205, 207
Interracial marriage, 174, 231–32; black
    rhetors on, 73–74, 95, 185; opposition
    to, 106–8, 123, 138, 199, 214
Isocrates, x–xii

Jackson, Andrew, 91, 102–3
Jackson, Jesse, 14–15, 190, 215; career and
    influence, 211–14
Jackson, Michael, 222
Jay, John, 56
Jefferson, Thomas, xv, xvi, 1, 2, 38, 218;
    sincerity of, questioned, 19; radicalism
    of, 21; natural rights doctrine, 42, 47–
    48; equality concept, 47–48; and slav-
    ery, 56; and colonization, 63. See also
    Declaration of Independence
Jet, 185
Johnson, Andrew, 113–15
Johnson, Lyndon B., 198
Jones, Absalom, 2, 74, 218
Jones, Colonel, 60
Jones, John Coffin, 54
Jordan, Barbara, 2, 14, 203–5, 211
Jury service, 97, 110, 162, 175
Justice, 29, 54, 56, 97, 216, 228; equal, 170–
    71

Kennedy, John F., 197–98
Killens, John O., 194

Killian, Lewis, 217
King, Martin Luther, Jr., 2, 13; style of,
    185; on equality, 189, 190, 192; influence
    of, 189, 196, 198; Young contrasted
    with, 206
King, Rufus, 52
Ku Klux Klan, 120

Lamar, Cincinnatus, 117, 118
Land ownership, 109
Langston, John Mercer, 124
Lathrop, John, 33, 34
Law, and rhetoric, xv
Lee, Spike, 212, 331n.105
Legal equality. See Equality before the law
Le Guin, Ursula K., 232
Liberty, 4–5, 7, 16; in prerevolutionary
    rhetoric, 20–27, 34–39; as property, 22–
    24, 38–39; as English, 24–27, 39; and
    natural rights, 33; slavery as loss of, 34–
    39; in Anglo-American revolutionary
    rhetoric, 40, 46–52, 57; religious, 44–
    45, 48; aliens as threat to, 59–60; in
    African-American postrevolutionary
    rhetoric, 69, 78, 83, 88, 98; and equality,
    conflict between, 83, 98, 164–65, 177–
    78, 182, 199, 226–30; and states' rights,
    114; in separation period, 131, 143;
    meaning of term, 218. See also Equal
    liberty
Life, right to, 47–48
Lincoln, Abraham, 2, 8, 218; and African
    colonization, 63, 113; Second Inaugural
    Address, 103–4, 113
Little Rock, Ark., 184
Litwack, Leon F., 41
Lloyd, David, 22–23
Local control, 182
Locke, John, 6, 25, 26, 39, 41, 83
Logos, xi
Los Angeles riots, 219
Lovell, James, 24
Lynch, John R., 120, 123–24
Lynching, 199, 219; in 19th century, 139,
    144; in polarization period, 154–56,
    159–60, 164, 166; in 1930s and 1940s,
    167, 175

McCabe v. Atchison, Topeka and Santa Fe R.
    Co., 162

McClane, Louis, 86
McDonald, Forrest, 270n.32, 271n.52
McEnery, Samuel, 157
McKinley, William, 163–64
McLaurin v. *Oklahoma,* 180
McWilliams, Carey, 181
Madison, James, 27, 53, 55, 57
Malcolm X, xvi, 2, 13, 188, 199, 220; influence of, 189, 196, 208, 212; on equality, 192–93; Young contrasted with, 206
"Man's A Man For A' That, A" (song), 96
Marshall, Thurgood, 168, 180, 203
Marxism, 76, 151, 190, 207, 308n.24
Maryland, 25, 43, 44, 60
Maryland Gazette, 21, 22, 27, 29, 32, 43, 277n.130
Mason, George, 53, 55, 61
Mason, Jonathan, 45
Massachusetts Spy, 21, 22, 27, 31, 36
Mass media, 161, 180–81, 191, 210–11
Mather, Cotton, 33
Mather, Increase, 33
Mathews, William, 136
Meier, August, 109, 122
Merchants, 28
Messenger, The, 151, 308n.25
Middle-class blacks. *See* Black middle class
Military, blacks in, 154, 166, 170, 172, 174
Mill, John Stuart, 287n.76
Miller, George Frazier, 151
Miller, Jack, 199
Minorities, 174, 225–26
Miscegenation. *See* Interracial marriage
Missouri ex rel Gaines v. *Canada,* 176
Montgomery Bus Boycott, 184
Monthly Religious Review, 106
Moore, Terence, 335n.12
Moore v. *Dempsey,* 314n.113
Morgan, John T., 137
Morris, Gouverneur, 51, 53, 55–56
Muhammad, Elijah, 191–93
Mulattoes, 108–9. *See also* Interracial marriage
Multiculturalism, 14, 209–11, 215

NAACP. *See* National Association for the Advancement of Colored People (NAACP)
Nash, Gary B., 20

Nation, 106–7, 119
National Association for the Advancement of Colored People (NAACP), 148, 149, 154, 168, 185, 189
National Negro Conventions, 77, 78, 82–85, 88
National Review, 210
Native Americans, 226, 229
Natural rights: in prerevolutionary rhetoric, 5, 24–25, 30, 33–34, 39; in Anglo-American revolutionary rhetoric, 41–48, 51–52, 56, 58; African-American rhetors on, 82–83, 89. *See also* Liberty
Neal v. *Delaware,* 162, 175
New Deal, 190, 196
New Republic, 210
New York Age, 149, 152
New York Convention of Colored Citizens, 96
Nicocles or the Cyprians (Isocrates), xi
Nixon, Richard, 198, 203–4
Nixon v. *Herndon,* 175–76
Norris v. *Alabama,* 175
North Star, The, 74, 88
Northwest Ordinance, 57

Okoye, Mwabueze F., 267n.114
Olympic Games, 206
Operation Breadbasket, 190, 202
Opportunity (journal), 171
Opportunity, equality of. *See* Equal opportunity
Orwell, George, 1
Osborne, Peter, 88
Otis, James, 22–23, 25, 28, 263n.58

Paine, Thomas, 42, 50, 60
Parity, 190
Paterson, William, 53
Patronage, 9, 125, 139
Payson, Phillip, 60
Pendleton, Edmund, 59
Pennsylvania Declaration of Rights, 43
Pennsylvania Journal, 26–27
Perry, M. L., 155
Philadelphia, 21, 22, 25, 29–30, 34, 35
Philadelphia Chronicle, 21, 22
Phillips, Wendell, 69
Philosophy, and rhetoric, x–xii

Pickens, William, 148
Pinckney, Charles Cotesworth, 53, 56, 61
Pittsburgh Courier, 147
Plato, x–xi
Plessy v. *Ferguson,* 139–44, 147, 179, 197
Police brutality, 167
Political equality, 11–15, 219, 228; in African-American postrevolutionary rhetoric, 94; in reconstruction period, 105–7, 110–13; in redemption period, 117; in separation period, 129, 134; in polarization period, 158, 159; in 1930s and 1940s, 167; in 1950s, 181–82, 186; in 1960s, 199, 201, 214. *See also* Voting rights
Polk, James Knox, 78–79
Poverty, 222; of freed blacks, 62; in 1960s, 189, 198; and black identity, 195, 223–24; Jackson on, 212–13
Powell, Adam Clayton, Jr., 190, 203, 317n.141
Power, and equality, 192–93, 196
Presbyterian Church, General Assembly of the, 66
Presidency: in reconstruction period, 113–15; in redemption period, 126–29; in separation period, 143–45; in polarization period, 163–67; in 1930s and 1940s, 167, 177–79; in 1950s, 186; in 1960s, 197–98; Jesse Jackson's bids for, 212–13; in 1990s, 215
Price, J. C., 138
Property, 4, 7, 16; in British prerevolutionary rhetoric, 20–27, 29, 31–34, 38–39; liberty as, 22–24, 38–39; slaves as, 36, 52, 56–58, 70; in Anglo-American revolutionary rhetoric, 41, 42, 46, 48, 52–58, 67, 68; in African-American postrevolutionary rhetoric, 69, 78, 83, 88, 98; of blacks, 75, 109; as voting qualification, 96, 160; in separation period, 131; integration vs. right of, 182; use of term, 218
Public accommodations, access to, 97, 228; in reconstruction period, 106, 107, 110; in redemption period, 118, 124, 126, 127; in separation period, 132–34, 137–38, 140–42, 146; in polarization period, 150–51, 162; in 1930s and 1940s, 167, 173, 174; in 1950s, 187; in 1960s, 197, 198
Public argumentation, xii–xv, 218–19
Pufendorf, Samuel, 25
Puritans, 43
PUSH/Excel, 190, 202

Quakers, 69
Quintus, Lucius, 117
Quotas, racial, 125, 191, 199–200, 207, 210, 212

Race: and natural rights, 26, 45; and colonization, 65–67; in Declaration of Independence, 88; homogeneity of, 95, 97, 228; white supremacists on, 105–6, 117, 155–57, 182–83; in *Williams* v. *Mississippi* decision, 162–63; black separatists on, 195; as product of culture, 224
Race riots. *See* Riots
Racism: of colonization advocates, 65; of Nazism, 171, 174, 177; negative view of, in postwar period, 172; institutional, 195, 212, 326n.35. *See also* White supremacist rhetoric
Randolph, A. Philip, 2, 170
Randolph, Edmund, 53
Rankin, John, 182
Rape, 156, 159, 164
Rapier, James T., 122–23
Reagan, Ronald, 190
Reavis, Charles R., 158–59
Reconstruction, 103–15, 135, 141, 145, 148; white supremacist views, 104–5, 119; egalitarian views, 105–7; African-American views, 107–15; Griffith on, 154
Reid, John Phillip, 48, 260n.19, 267n.114
Religion: freedom of, 44–45, 48; African, 60, 95; segregation of churches, 74. *See also* Christianity
Remond, Charles, 2
"Report on African Colonization," 78
Representation: English right to, 23, 35; in U.S. Constitution, 52–53. *See also* Equal representation

Republican party, 9, 69, 116, 125, 139, 204
Reverse discrimination, 200, 212, 312n.77
Rhetoric: of equality, ix, xv–xviii, 217–19;
    revival of, ix–x; Isocrates on, x–xii; vs.
    philosophy, x–xi
Rhetorical culture, xii–xv
Rhetorical history, xvii
Rights of man. *See* Equal rights; Natural
    rights
Riots, 160, 166, 189, 201, 219
Robinson, Donald, 41, 56
Roosevelt, Franklin Delano, 12, 170, 177
Roosevelt, Theodore, 163–67
Ruggles, David, 73, 92
Russwurm, John B., 77
"Rusticus," 45
Rutledge, John, 52, 53

San Francisco Elevator, 120
"Sarcasticus," 32
Saunders, Prince, 82
Scarborough, W. S., 101, 137
Schools. *See* Education
Segregation. *See* Integrated equality; Sepa-
    rate but equal doctrine
Self sovereignty, 47, 51
Senate, U.S., 55. *See also* Congress, U.S.
Separate but equal doctrine, 2, 8–10, 101–
    46, 102, 146, 228, 242–44; and race
    identity rhetoric, 140; and *Plessy* v. *Fer-
    guson,* 140–44; decline of, 147–87; and
    Brown v. *Board of Education,* 179–80; and
    black militants in 1960s, 191. *See also*
    Black nationalism/separatism; Inte-
    grated equality
Seward, Henry, 69
Sexism, 306n.13
Shakespeare, William, 208
Shelly v. *Kramer,* 176
Shutes, Daniel, 32
Sierra Leone, 64
Singletary, Amos, 54
Singleton, John, 212
Slavery, 1, 4–6, 9, 159, 226, 228; in pre-
    revolutionary rhetoric, 4, 25–27, 34–39;
    in Anglo-American revolutionary rhet-
    oric, 40–41, 50–52, 56–58; abolition in
    North, 51; Constitutional compromise
    on, 56–58; colonization as alternative to,
    63, 64; degrading effects of, 67, 92–93;
    black orators' role in ending, 70–71; and
    equal liberty, 78–83, 98; Douglass on his
    victory over, 80–81; and equal citizen-
    ship, 86; abolition in South, 103, 110,
    113; attempt at de facto restoration in
    South, 104, 117; and Grant, 127; and
    Hayes, 127; and *Plessy* v. *Ferguson,* 141;
    as equality, 199; Malcolm X on, 220
Slaves: as property, 36, 52, 56–58; fugitive,
    56, 70, 77, 81; insurrections by, 66, 70–
    71, 279n.3; death rates for, 262n.55. *See
    also* Freed slaves
Smith, Gerrit, 69, 87
Smith, M., 54
Smith v. *Allwright,* 176
Smythe, John H., 140, 276n.114
Social compact, 145; in prerevolutionary
    rhetoric, 5, 6, 33; in Anglo-American
    revolutionary rhetoric, 43–47, 51, 59–
    60; African-American rhetors on, 80, 85
Social equality, 7, 11; in African-American
    postrevolutionary rhetoric, 94–96; in re-
    construction period, 106–8, 110; in
    redemption period, 122–28, 146; in sep-
    aration period, 133, 137–38, 143; in
    polarization period, 149–50, 154, 158; in
    1930s and 1940s, 172, 174–75; in 1950s,
    186, 187; and definition of equality, 228
Society of Friends, 69
Socrates, x
Sons of Liberty, 22
South, 10–13, 221, 227; prerevolutionary,
    38; in revolutionary period, 43, 45, 50–
    51; and ex-slaves, problem of, 58–59;
    and fugitive slave laws, 70; fear of slave
    revolts in, 70–71; black collective iden-
    tity formation in, 77; on Declaration of
    Independence and equality, 86–87; Civil
    War consequences for, 101; in recon-
    struction period, 104–5, 110, 112–14; in
    redemption period, 116–17, 122–23; in
    separation period, 129–35; in polariza-
    tion period, 152, 155, 157–66; in 1930s
    and 1940s, 168, 173–74; in 1950s, 180–
    85. *See also* White supremacist rhetoric
South Africa, 227
Southern Christian Leadership Conference,
    185

Speaking of Equality (Westen), 256n.23
Speech, freedom of, 48
State Convention of Colored People of
    Georgia, 107–8
State of nature, 145; in prerevolutionary
    rhetoric, 33, 39; in Anglo-American
    revolutionary rhetoric, 45–47; African-
    American rhetors on, 80, 83; Calhoun
    on, 86
State of the Right of the Colonists (Adams), 33
States' rights, 10, 70, 114, 115, 128, 182
Steele, Shelby, 215
Stephens, Alexander H., 117
Stewart, Maria Miller, 2, 218
Storm, John, 124
Student Nonviolent Coordinating Com-
    mittee (SNCC), 195–96
Suffrage. *See* Voting rights
Sumner, Charles, 93
Supplement to Maryland Gazette, 24
Supreme Court, of Mississippi, 162–63
Supreme Court, U.S., 10, 12; *Dred Scott* v.
    Sandford, 61–62; *Plessy* v. *Ferguson,* 138–
    42, 147, 179, 197; in polarization period,
    161–63; in 1930s and 1940s, 167, 175–
    77, 319n.173; in 1950s, 179–80, 182,
    186; in 1960s, 189, 197; Bork nomina-
    tion to, 205; Thomas appointment to,
    215. See also *Brown* v. *Board of Education
    of Topeka, Kansas*
Sweatt v. *Painter,* 180
Sydney, Algernon, 25, 39
Synchronic structures, xiii–xiv

Taft, William Howard, 163–65, 315n.126
Taney, Roger B., 62
Taxation, 75; British, 22–23, 25, 46; in
    South, 131
Tennessee Valley Authority (TVA), 169
Terrell, Mary Church, 2
Texas, University of, 180
Thacher, Peter, 45
Thomas, Clarence, 215
Thomas's Boston Journal, 22
Time, 210
Tocqueville, Alexis de, 1, 292n.4
To Secure These Rights (report), 177–79
Truman, Harry S., 12, 177–78
Truth, Sojourner, 218

Tucker, John, 32, 35
Tudor, William, 59
Turkey, 36
Turner, Charles, 35
Tyler, John, 87

Underground Railroad, 70
US News and World Report, 199, 210

Vietnam War, 201
*Vindication of the Government of New England
    Churches, A* (Wise), 21
Violence: in American colonies, 28; of
    American Revolution, 40; against ex-
    slaves, 59, 74–75; white versus black ab-
    olitionists in use of, 72; white
    supremacist fears of, 105; in redemption
    period, 116, 120, 126; in separation pe-
    riod, 129, 139; in polarization period,
    154, 159–60; in 1950s, 183–85; and
    black power, 194; and oppositional het-
    erogeneity, 221, 222, 333n.2. *See also*
    Lynching; Riots
Virginia, 23, 25, 34–36, 38, 276n.119
Virginia Declaration of Rights, 47
Virginia Gazette, 22
Virginia Resolutions, 36
Voting rights: in Anglo-American revolu-
    tionary rhetoric, 43; in Constitutional
    debates, 52, 55; pre–Civil War, 96; ex-
    pansion of, 102; in reconstruction
    period, 110, 112–13; in redemption pe-
    riod, 118, 127; in separation period, 139;
    in polarization period, 157–60, 162–63;
    in 1930s and 1940s, 176; in 1950s, 181–
    82; in 1960s, 197, 199. *See also* Fraud

Walker, David, 77
Wallace, George, 13
Ward, Samuel, 73–74
War of 1812, 86
War on Poverty, 198
Warren, Joseph, 30–31, 33, 36
Washington, Booker T., 2, 11, 122, 306n.3;
    on South, 136–37; on elevation of black
    community, 152, 153
Washington, George, 36, 38, 203
Washington Bee, 140, 152, 153

Watergate scandal, 203–4
Watterson, Henry, 117
Webster, Daniel, 218
Weekly Anglo-American, 76
Weekly Anglo-African, 87
Wells-Barnett, Ida B., 139, 159
West, Cornell, 215
West, Samuel, 32
West, U.S., 55–56, 61, 62
Westen, Peter, 256n.23
Western Appeal, 150–51
West Indies, 72
Whigs, 20, 21, 27, 29, 39
Whitehead, Thomas, 123
White supremacist rhetoric, 8–13, 71, 101,
    103, 145–46; in reconstruction period,
    103–5, 108, 110–15; egalitarian republi-
    can rhetoric compared with, 106; in
    redemption period, 116–18, 120; in sep-
    aration period, 129–35, 137–46; in
    polarization period, 147–48, 155–61; in
    1930s and 1940s, 169, 173–75; in 1950s,
    180–84, 187; decline of, 186, 197–99,
    201, 210; in 1960s, 189, 191, 194; on
    black poverty, 223
Wilder, Douglas, 14, 215
Wilkins, Roy, 217
Williams, John Bell, 183
Williams, Peter, 84
Williams v. Mississippi, 162–63
Wills, Garry, 47, 268n.7
Wilson, James, 47, 49, 53
Wilson, Woodrow, 163, 165–66
Wise, John, 21
Women: rights of, 80, 112, 205; white,
    blacks as threat to, 156, 158, 312n.84;
    and paternalism of black leaders,
    306n.13
Woodward, C. Vann, 301n.126
World War I, 154, 170, 171
World War II, 167, 170–74
Wright, Theodore S., 84, 87

Yick Wo v. Hopkins, 163
Young, Andrew, 14, 203, 205–6, 211
Young, Robert Alexander, 75

1. "craft" metaphor (Plato) — and constitutive effect

2. substantive point — collision between egalitarianism and commitment to property (pg 58)

3. interested in uncovering discourse that stretches limits of Constitution, but they don't deal w/ radical interpretation of Courts (pg 71)

④ allegiance / protective move (84)
   obedience

5. radical appropriation of Dof I 87—
   └ key .. links to conceptual struggle / hermeneutic rhetoric - gloss note p 85